Methods of Instruction in

Social Studies

Education

Third Edition

James L. Barth

Social studies is the Interdisciplinary Integration of social science and humanities concepts for the purpose of practicing citizenship skills on critical social issues.

UNIVERSITY
PRESS OF
AMERICA

Lanham • New York • London

Copyright © 1984, 1990 by

University Press of America®, Inc.
4720 Boston Way
Lanham, Maryland 20706

3 Henrietta Street
London WC2E 8LU England

Third edition published in 1990 by
University Press of America

Library of Congress Cataloging-in-Publication Data

Barth, James L., 1931-
Methods of instruction in social studies education / James L.
Barth.—3rd ed.
p.   cm.
Includes bibliographical references.
1. Social sciences—Study and teaching (Elementary)   2. Social
sciences—Study and teaching (Secondary)   I. Title.
H62.B343   1990   300'.71'073—dc20   90–39617 CIP

ISBN 0–8191–7866–7 (pbk. : alk. paper)

The paper used in this publication meets the minimum requirements of
American National Standard for Information Sciences—Permanence
of Paper for Printed Library Materials, ANSI Z39.48–1984.

Now, rewritten for the 1990's.

PREFACE

The field of social studies, like all other fields, is evolving and changing. Changes in the schools, in students, and in consequence teaching, require a constant revision of the method books that prepare teachers. This third edition is quite different from its predecessors and hopefully reflects what social studies teachers at all levels of instruction will need to know during the decade of the 90s.

From Being a Student to Becoming a Teacher

There is a message, some might call it a point of view, expressed in this text. That message is, as a school teacher you teach students not content. Perhaps the whole purpose of a teacher education program is to convince you that your first priority is students. Without their attention, there will be no learning, thus, the statement, "from being a student to becoming a teacher." The transition from student to teacher is, for many college students, most difficult, for what made for success in college was the consumption, retention, and accurate recall of great quantities of information. Yet those qualities are of secondary importance when teaching students. The college professor model where success is driven by scholarship, in most cases, proves ineffective in a school setting because, simply, the school is not a miniature college. It's the difference between someone who voluntarily accepts college responsibility in contrast to those who are in school not by choice and view the school as an adversary. No one believes the adversarial relationship ideal, but it is real and affects entirely the character of the teacher-student relationship.

Any methods text that pretends to cope with the real school must suggest how teachers might best perform in the school environment. This text was written with the real school in mind, and the first chapter is about real students and teachers discussing their relationship. That discussion sets the tone for the remainder of the text. The chapter on the meaning of social studies makes the point that the field is dedicated to citizenship education with emphasis on the real problems and issues that students bring to school. The remaining chapters place emphasis on teaching students. Methods, reading, discipline, working with exceptional as well as disadvantaged students, and planning are all special functions of effective teaching practices.

This text, from its very inception in the mid 70s, was intended to be different from most other social studies methods texts. Most methods texts that the author has known, tend to talk about skills, attitudes, and requirements. In short, they tend to want to persuade one to practice teaching in a particular way. Of course, a methods book is intended to persuade, but after readers have been persuaded, there is little or no opportunity to practice the knowledge, skills, or attitudes suggested. This book intends to persuade as well as provide the practice necessary to perform the skill or acquire the attitude. In brief, this text should be a classroom guide and function much as a teacher's resource book to remain as a permanent part of a teacher's library of professional books. A companion to this methods book is a curriculum series by the author: Elementary and Junior High/Middle School Social Studies Curriculum, Activities and Materials, and Secondary Social Studies Curriculum, Activities and Materials. This series develops at each grade level, kindergarten through twelfth grade, a social studies curriculum that follows a scope and sequence consistent with social studies programs in most school districts throughout the nation. One other related professional book by the author et al. is The Nature of the Social Studies which is an in-depth examination of teaching social studies from three different points of view. This third edition methods book, the curriculum series, and The Nature . . . are a basic foundation to understanding the meaning of social studies, why it was created, how it is developing as a field, and your role as a social studies teacher in the classroom.

About 70% of this third edition is new or revised. The process of revision has included many people all of whom contributed in different ways. The illustrations are unique; some by an American and some by a Southern African from Botswana. The American artist, Ann Timberman, former Indiana State Arts Consultant, produced many of the sketches for the 1978 Indiana Social Studies: A Guide for Curriculum Development, a publication of the Indiana State Department of Public Instruction. Mr. Langenbacher, the Botswana artist, rendered his sketches for a 1989 USAID project trial social studies text. James Spencer, the 1989-90 Purdue Master Teacher-in-Residence, critically reviewed the manuscript several times and added immeasurably to the authenticity by offering a classroom teacher's perspective. Some chapters of the book retain the style evolved in the second edition by that edition's co-author, S. Samuel Shermis. As always there is one person who edits the manuscript and keeps the language and style consistent throughout the book, Bonnie Nowakowski performed that task magnificently. Finally, Barbara Barth, as in the two previous editions, has provided the main support and has been the manager that brought this edition to publication.

James L. Barth   1990
Professor of Social Studies Education

ii

TABLE OF CONTENTS

CHAPTER VI - QUESTIONING: A FUNCTION OF EFFECTIVE TEACHING PRACTICES

CHAPTER VII - TECHNOLOGY AND INSTRUCTIONAL RESOURCES: A FUNCTION OF EFFECTIVE TEACHING PRACTICES

CHAPTER VIII - READING COMPREHENSION: A FUNCTION OF EFFECTIVE TEACHING PRACTICES........................155

CHAPTER IX - DISCIPLINE: A FUNCTION OF EFFECTIVE TEACHING PRACTICES..................................169

CHAPTER X - SOCIAL STUDIES FOR SPECIAL STUDENTS: A FUNCTION OF EFFECTIVE TEACHING PRACTICES............205

CHAPTER XV - PRACTICE TEACHING: MICROPEER-TEACHING, FIELD EXPERIENCE, AND STUDENT TEACHING.................323

Learning what we can, serving
where we're able, preserving what
we should, and changing what we
must.
                            Richard Wood

"Think you can, think
you can't, either way
you're right."
Henry Ford

x

CHAPTER I
SOCIAL STUDIES ACCORDING TO TEACHERS AND STUDENTS

OBJECTIVE: Given the responses of students and teachers in this chapter, identify why social studies has consistently earned a negative reputation among students and imagine what changes need to occur for social studies to achieve a positive reputation.

"Most people believe they see the world as it is. However, we really see the world as we are."

Unknown

BEING A STUDENT TO BECOMING A TEACHER
you have to face the critics

How do we rate?

Has the social studies field justifiably earned a negative reputation from students? Can social studies achieve a positive reputation? If so, how? Those who created social studies never intended a boring, disjointed series of courses which appeared, apparently to most students, to be irrelevant. The mystery is why a curriculum designed essentially to examine students' relationships to the social, political, and economic world of which they are a part would be considered boring and irrelevant. We are told by psychologists that students in their development from early childhood to adolescence are essentially interested in themselves, and in their teenage years are frantically interested in themselves and others. How is it possible then, that a series of courses designed to explore personal/social relationships becomes boring and irrelevant? Perhaps one way to understand how people view social studies and to identify problems that arise in teaching social studies is to listen to what they are saying.

The following responses from students and teachers about their schooling, and in particular social studies, will help identify why social studies may be viewed unfavorably and why teachers may have difficulty teaching students. Teachers and students speak for themselves. Your task will be to summarize their responses and from those responses identify if there are problems and, if so, what are they?

I. Students Speak for Themselves About School [1]

Interviewer: "I'm glad for the chance to meet with you middle school and senior high students, and appreciate your willingness to talk about your school and in particular social studies. First, I'd like to ask you, what are your concerns about school? Mike, what are your concerns?"

Mike: "We have a respectable school mostly, but it may not stay that way. Students rebel only because they aren't getting what they want and to a reasonable degree, should have. For instance, the boys' haircuts. They would wear them at a reasonable length if they weren't being called down about it. Some of our teachers are absolutely boring. They teach like they've memorized this stuff and it is a tape recording playing. Students should have more of a weight on decisions made. Teachers have feelings too and if students don't respect them,

then they should throw them out. These little things going on behind their backs aren't hurting the teacher any but it shows students how childish some of our classmates are."

Interviewer: "Tim, did you want to add something to that?"

Tim: "Another thing is the inconsistency in the discipline. Some get in trouble because of hair and clothes' styles, yet there are a few who are just as extreme in their styles as the next person and they don't get bothered. A problem that exists that no one can help is the 'pet.' It makes me want to get up and walk out when there are favorites in a class. Another thing I hate about school is that classes you do have to take usually have the most boring teachers possible."

Interviewer: "Nancy?"

Nancy: "I know I should be glad to be in school. So many schools turn you away if you're married. I dropped out of school my junior year, just with five weeks left in the year and lost part of the year. I want to go to work, but I didn't even start to find a job. I knew I would have to come back first. I always hated school before, but really I have found this year to be different. I have all new friends and really it helps."

Interviewer: "Matt, what's your feeling?"

Matt: "I know I hated school for I felt teachers were only teachers, but one took interest in me while I was having school difficulty and home problems. She went to the dean, and you know I found they cared and really wished to help. And I tried harder and now I enjoy school 99% more than I did and I try harder and grades are higher. If this does this for one and changes the life of one, it surely could help more. I dislike teachers who dish out work but never discuss it or try to explain it. A subject should have a teacher who is greatly interested in it; and not one who accepts it as just a job. I get more out of a subject when I can tell and feel his interest."

Interviewer: "Robin, what did you want to say?"

Robin: "This year I find school one fat bore! It is so uninteresting I sometimes feel as if I don't care at all. Why can't teachers at least try to make their classes worthwhile instead of wasting a whole year? The little things that some teachers feel are so important are just a waste of time. We should have subjects that we know would help us in the near future with our jobs, etc., because some of us aren't going to college so why on earth do they teach dumb stuff that is so useless to us? Also, classes should have more discussions. I mean problems of today, what we are faced with, etc. Why must the teacher do all the talking? I would think that he or she would get almost as bored as the student. We shouldn't always

4

have to stick to the boredom of the subject of the class. We should have more rights and free speech in the schools. The students should make the rules. I know that school is supposed to be a place to learn, but how on earth can a person learn if it is so boring that even the teachers don't act as if they care or not? I can almost say I hate school. That is terrible to say during my senior year, but that is the way it seems to me."

Interviewer: "Do you want to add anything to that, Jeffrey?"

Jeffrey: "Teachers (not all are like this) need to make us feel that they are human by getting to know some of the shyer or backward students better. These students need more challenges in class, and question and answer sessions (even on paper if not oral) more often. Many hold back questions as well as feelings on topics discussed because of other students gaining all the attention. The most encouraging sign a teacher can give a student is by a general acknowledgement out of class by just saying 'hello' or 'how are you this morning?' etc."

Interviewer: "Jim, what's on your mind?"

Jim: "I think school is uninteresting. Many classes are very boring because the teachers don't teach anything new, different or important. Some teachers know their subjects but they don't know how to teach it so they might as well be dumb. They also pass out so much homework, and they go wild when it comes to tests and themes. For this entire year (at least so far) I feel as though I could drop out or just stay at home and know as much as I would if I went to school every day and listened. Even when I sit in class I find it very difficult to listen because the topics are boring, and the teachers don't even try to make their subjects interesting. If I wasn't going to college next year, I don't think I would even try to learn anything. Generally you can just read the book and forget about what the teachers say because everything seems so trivial."

Interviewer: "Jim, do you have something else to add?"

Jim: "I also dislike the favoritism shown by some teachers toward a few select students. This seems as unfair to the favored student as well as to the entire class, even if he is the best and most likeable student, the others should be dealt with equal consideration as this seems only fair. I also think that classes have become boring. The teachers all seem to do the same thing--lecture. There are few who take the time to prepare a lesson that will not only be educational, but interesting, perhaps exciting. It would be nice to actually look forward to a class."

Interviewer: "Barbara?"

Barbara: "One of my dislikes about school is the attitude of teachers in general. Sure some teachers are nice, have a good attitude towards their career, and really care about their students' success in their course. But there are the other ones who don't care and seem to be old gripes day after day. They seem to be in it for the money and nothing else. If the teacher doesn't enjoy what he is doing, then the student won't accomplish anything and will end up hating that class and the teachers. These teachers could change and students would like school better."

Interviewer: "How about the rest of you? What would you like to say? Just say what's on your mind."

Student: "A need for greater freedom in high school is really evident. College is a shock to most students because of the freedom from rules and early curfews. They simply go joy-happy and thus their studies aren't done on time. They don't know how to handle their time because they've always had it done for them. Of course, there are a few who must always violate rules and this would be no exception. But I wish they'd listen to our side for once instead of always trying to suppress us."

Student: "The subjects aren't interesting. If they were related to our present-day situations, they would be more meaningful. An example would be current history. Couldn't the present event be related to things that have happened in the past and their solutions?"

Student: "School is a nice place to be when there is nothing else to do, or no place to go. When you are bored stiff at home or wherever you may be, school would be a great joy to be in. One good thing about going to school is seeing and talking to your friends and many different types of people, each with unlike personalities."

Student: "Being around people is a need that I don't care to have. There are too many things happening in high school that are not worth knowing. Teachers make everything seem so important when it really isn't. When there are so many things to do and learn, we're here in high school taking up time and knowledge that could be put to use for a more important reason. High school cannot help me meet my needs. It only makes me realize I have them."

Student: "I feel that our teachers up at this middle school are ignorant when it comes to the students. Some teachers think that all they have to do is lecture all period and others are constantly on our backs about something that doesn't really amount to much."

6

Student: "There should be something done about classes, too. Many students just go because they have to and the teachers usually feel and act the same way. The teachers use all stuff that they learned from their prof in college. If they could use modern examples, more students would be interested."

Student: "Some teachers couldn't care less about their students. As long as they get paid, they're happy. They don't really care if their students learn anything or not. This type of teacher can't seem to find time to stay after school to help students either."

Student: "If a teacher does not put pressure on a student frequently, the student will naturally not do as much work as he otherwise would, thus learning less. I realize that the student must also want to learn, but the teacher must first provide the subject in an interesting and meaningful manner."

Student: "I like teachers who are interested and enthusiastic about their subject; but I dislike it when they forget about all other subjects, considering theirs the best and only important subject. I like teachers who tell jokes occasionally but not for half the period every day."

Instructions: Having read through the students' responses, summarize in your own words what you consider five (5) of their chief complaints to be.

```
SUMMARIZE STUDENTS' RESPONSES ABOUT SCHOOL

1._____

2._____

3._____

4._____

5._____
```

II. Students Speak for Themselves About Social Studies Teachers

Interviewer: "From our opening discussion I take it that many of you feel that your school has not come up to your expectations. Perhaps we ought to talk about social studies teachers and the way they teach. What are your concerns? Bob?"

Bob: "Students want to give a teacher a chance and there's really no need to be nervous. This is because the student is waiting to see what the teacher will provide, what the social studies teacher has to offer."

Interviewer: "Phyllis?"

Phyllis: "I haven't had the problem of teachers not knowing enough about their topic, but I have met teachers who know a little bit too much. They try and teach you everything they know when you don't know anything in the first place. It's too much all at one time and you feel like an idiot and you don't learn."

Interviewer: "Jake?"

Jake: "But the only time a teacher isn't very successful is when he gives up. Some days the students are acting up, you know, everybody has their bad days. But sometimes the teacher makes the students act that way because, well, we know teachers have bad days and we accept that; but some teachers don't seem to understand."

Interviewer: "Ben, what would you like to say?"

Ben: "I have one thing to say. The teaching system in most schools now is based on negativeness. I think if I was telling social studies teachers how best to teach students, I would tell them that they should go into the classroom and praise students for what they do right instead of continually telling them what they do wrong. But in a lot of classes teachers keep saying, 'You're not doing it right,' or 'That's a bad way to do it,' and they should always tell you how to do it right or praise you when you do things right."

Interviewer: "Other thoughts?"

Ben: "The teacher motivates the student by being interested himself. When you see a teacher and you realize that he really wants you to learn about this certain social studies topic, then you want to go deeper into that topic to find out what there is about it that this particular teacher wants to bring out. We had a different teacher last year and he just thought we knew certain things. Actually, we may not have learned as much last year as we should, but he just takes it for granted that you know this and he goes on when he should explain a little more. And I also don't like a teacher who just takes it for granted that you don't know anything. I like teachers who can adjust to the different students, who realize that some students work at

different paces and there is something for every student, not just a standard for everybody that everybody can't work up to."

Interviewer: "Mary, do you want to get in on this?"

Mary: "I don't think the social studies teacher has taught the students anything unless they can apply it to what they do every day. Because there's no use going and learning something unless you can use it in some way or another. That's the only way I'll ever learn anything--using it--and that's the only way a teacher can say, 'I've taught the students something.'"

Interviewer: "Barbara, what do you think?"

Barbara: "I like the one who realizes that sometimes you just can't get it."

Interviewer: "Any other thoughts?"

Student: "I think it helps a lot if you apply what you're teaching to something that the students do in their own life or at home. Things that they do in life away from school. That's one way to get them interested. And then when you have tried whatever it is, then let the student try so that he can get some enjoyment out of accomplishing something."

Student: "Some of the teachers here are really dumb. They think they're better than anybody else. It makes me so mad for teachers to have their pets. In class the teacher calls on the same students each day. They should treat kids the same with no exceptions."

Student: "Some social studies teachers think all they have to do is give tests constantly until pretty soon there will be one every day of the school week."

Student: "I want someone who goes home and does their homework like we do ours, who will plan something for the student, come back and have something definite in mind, something profitable. This to me is very important. I want a teacher who will go out and get extra things for the student."

Student: "I think I have an understanding social studies teacher. When we have an assignment, some of the boys on the football team stay out late and then come in and don't have their homework. My teacher, I think, is understanding. He said to them 'I understand how it is. You had to stay out later last night; you couldn't get all your homework in. But you're still going to have to get it in sometime.' Whereas there are other teachers, when they come in they say, 'Oh, that's an F,' and write it right down in the book. You just don't have a chance."

Student: "For a couple of times the teachers say, 'You'll have to get it in.' Well, then they never bring it in and at this point they start to take advantage of the teacher. So the teacher, you know, has to start to be strict, and this is when they'll just have to give them an F or else they'll just take advantage of them. Most of the athletes, they disrespect all the teachers."

Interviewer: "Mike, what are your thoughts?"

Mike: "I was just going to say that I have a social studies teacher who is dynamic, who comes in with something new once in a while. I have teachers who have you do the same thing every day. You can't expect the students to be interested in that subject. Pretty soon you'll hear a lot of the students saying, 'Well, I can't stand that subject, we do the same thing every day.' Once in a while, have a little change. Sometimes we might not even discuss math in math class, we may talk about life."

Interviewer: "Do you want to add to that, Tim?"

Tim: "For instance, in social studies I remember that we would go over different types of countries, their customs. We wouldn't just learn how high their mountains are and how deep their rivers are. We learned about the people. I think you can develop a lot better interest by going deeper into the subject and discussing it and making projects."

Interviewer: "Bonnie, you get the last word."

Bonnie: "When I first started junior high I didn't like social studies too much. And then in high school when I was a freshman, the social studies teacher I had, she really understood, you know. She was talking about it to explain it to me so I could understand it. When I finished social studies that year, I decided I might major in it because she was really interesting and made me understand. She would take the time to help you to understand and demonstrate how you do it."

Instructions: Having read through the students' responses, summarize in your own words what you consider five (5) of their chief complaints to be.

```
┌─────────────────────────────────────────────────────────────────┐
│          SUMMARIZE STUDENTS' RESPONSES ABOUT TEACHERS             │
│                                                                   │
│      1._____   │
│                                                                   │
│      2._____   │
│                                                                   │
│      3._____   │
│                                                                   │
│      4._____   │
│                                                                   │
│      5._____   │
│                                                                   │
└─────────────────────────────────────────────────────────────────┘
```

III. Social Studies Teachers Speak for Themselves

Interviewer: "I particularly appreciate your taking the time to meet with me in the teachers' lounge after school. I know how busy social studies teachers are, but I hope our discussion will help others to understand how teachers feel about school and teaching social studies. Mrs. Kane, would you give me your thoughts?"

Mrs. Kane: "Most of the teachers follow a set pattern. Even the younger members of the faculty express the opinion that they have so many chapters to cover in the textbook, and only a certain period or time slot to cover these chapters in; so deviation from the textbook is not desirable or permissible. This method, however, leaves little time to work with those who are slower in learning, and no time to spend an extra few days on an interesting subject."

Interviewer: "How do you see it, Mr. Herron?"

Mr. Herron: "Perhaps the most frustrating experience teaching is the constant feeling of unsureness. What I mean is that in all the other jobs I've held, I could tell when I was finished whether or not I had done it correctly. My problem comes from the fact that I am dealing with people, and with people things are seldom so black or white, so to speak. What works for one person is not necessarily right for someone else. I may be able to reach the majority of my class, but what about the minority? How can I reach them all?"

Interviewer: "Mrs. Franklin, you look as though you want to add something to that?"

Mrs. Franklin: "The most frustrating thing that I find while teaching cannot be described as an incident but as an attitude which is held by the majority of the students. This attitude is that the teacher should force them to learn. They have absolutely no desire to learn for themselves. They misbehave in class. They fail to do their reading assignments and their extra credit problems. To illustrate this attitude of the students, I would like to use some examples. This first example happened in my fourth period world history class. There were two students who sit in the back of the room and talk to each other creating such a disturbance that no one else in the class could study or listen to the discussion. When I discipline them, they swear that they had done nothing wrong and had not been talking. It was frustrating when I made an assignment to have only half the class complete it. This happened in my first period class. I had made an assignment which was due the following day, but when it was time to collect the papers only six or seven of the twenty-seven had finished the assignment. This attitude was not limited to any classes, but from what I could learn during my talks with other teachers, they too resented the idea of having to spend most of their time as policemen and prodders. I feel this attitude of the students is not only a hindrance to the teacher, but also a detriment to our society because many capable students fail to realize their complete potential because they fall in with a crowd where this poor attitude is prevalent. The only way I see to overcome this problem is for the teachers to continue acting as policemen while trying to make their classes as interesting as possible. Hopefully this will stimulate a few students and therefore overcome the problem of students not liking school."

Interviewer: "Mr. Tuttle?"

Mr. Tuttle: "On the other hand, I notice that many of the teachers never seem to do any school work outside of the classroom teaching situation. I found out, as we all know, that these teachers were using the same units, texts, and tests year after year. One teacher told me that she could run off all her handouts and tests in two days and thus have the rest of the year free."

Interviewer: "What, Mr. Greenlee?"

Mr. Greenlee: "Well, actually, students quickly become bored, and their attention turns to other things. This is what is frustrating because as a social studies teacher, one can see the students wandering away. To prevent this the teacher has to be armed with different techniques that can hold the students' attention. I was not well prepared, nor was I fully aware, of how short a high school student's attention span really is."

Interviewer: "At this point I'd like to have a free-for-all. Just throw in what's on your mind."

Teacher: "No teacher has to be 'boring.' Most teachers that I know are, simply because it is easier to get into a rut than it is to try to stay out of one. There are ways of keeping one's vitality and enthusiasm, but, of course, they all require effort on the teacher's part. A teacher must be dedicated and hardworking and must truly want to make his job a profession. Otherwise, he will become just one more tired and uninteresting educator and these we have too many of already."

Teacher: "Get to know individual students better. To see one's class as a group of individuals with special needs and goals and to attempt to help each student on a personal basis is a nearly impossible feat. But it is usually only on an individual basis that teachers receive the rewards and the hope they need to continue teaching."

Teacher: "I realize that if the student makes no effort to learn, whether this effort is motivated from within or without, he will not profit from any class or course. Although it is satisfying whenever any of the students display an interest in learning, it is most rewarding when some of the so-called slow students do so."

Teacher: "I am apprehensive when I encounter an unfamiliar situation. It bothers me that for a given situation or problem there is no definite response. I am told that I will learn or that with experience I will know what to do. I realize this and agree but while I'm acquiring this experience and knowledge, am I doing right? Before, if I made a mistake, the mistake was rectified by replacement or repair, etc., but how does one repair or replace the results of a poor teacher? Could I somehow be responsible for the future failure in life of one of my students?"

Teacher: "Doctors, merchants, farmers, and yes even teachers often find themselves, after a few years in their profession or occupation, in a routine. They will follow the same routine day after day, and sometimes year after year. They are unable to bring a fresh perspective to their work. In the classroom a teacher should keep in mind all the various aspects of his subject material. For example, social studies includes economics, political science, history, sociology, geography. The information available concerning these subjects is endless; the different ways to combine and present these materials before the class should also be 'almost' endless. No day, month, or year need be like the previous one."

Interviewer: "Mrs. Kane, you get the last word."

Mrs. Kane: "To be a good teacher one must have a good sense of humor and not be afraid to show it in front of the students. A lot of students think that teachers are not human. Their reasoning is that students don't think of us as humans so why should we take time to prepare new and different classes."

Instructions: Having read through the teachers' responses, summarize in your own words what you consider five (5) of their concerns to be.

```
┌─────────────────────────────────────────────────────────────────────┐
│                   SUMMARIZE TEACHERS' RESPONSES                       │
│       1._____    │
│                                                                       │
│       2._____    │
│                                                                       │
│       3._____    │
│                                                                       │
│       4._____    │
│                                                                       │
│       5._____    │
│                                                                       │
└─────────────────────────────────────────────────────────────────────┘
```

IV. A Master Social Studies Teacher Speaks for Himself

Interviewer: "Jim, I am pleased that you would spend the time with me for this in-depth interview. You are well-known as a master teacher, greatly respected by administrators, parents, and students in your community. Your almost thirty years of teaching both junior high/middle school and senior high social studies would be considered successful by any measure. And so, your thoughts are particularly important because they carry the weight of an accomplished educator. Any insights on preparing college students to become teachers? What are your concerns about teaching social studies?" Any insights on preparing college students to become teachers?

Jim: "Maybe it's old age, or maybe you can just fill out so many meaningless forms, but I often feel as if we are more concerned about the movement of students from room to room than what happens inside the room. Lists of goals and objectives, climate audits, North Central self-evaluations, requests for assignments, midterm failure notices, weekly learning disabled reports, gifted and talented check lists, endless piles of make-up work and lunch tickets which have to be color-coded,

distributed, collected and counted daily all seem to have very little impact on what happens in my classroom."

Interviewer: "What should college students know about teaching social studies? What's happening in social studies classrooms?"

Jim: "It is difficult to maintain any self-respect when you know you are not doing that which you are supposed to be doing. I feel there is very little real accountability in public schools. Whether teachers knock themselves out or just slide by has no consequence, and it really seems to make little difference whether a student passes or fails a class. By seventh grade students have learned to work the system well. They do literally hundreds of assignments without reading a single page and process thousands of pieces of information without thinking. Trying to be a teacher without students who want to learn is a lot like a long-distance marriage--you may have the title but you are missing the best part."

Interviewer: "Tell me about your students?"

Jim: "Hour after hour, day after day, week after week, I can force them to be quiet, but I can't force them to listen. That is a totally frustrating experience to anyone who has ever experienced the incredible magic of teaching. I'm not even able to get them to listen to each other in small groups or any other classroom configurations that I try, and believe me, I try them all. Today's students will look at the image, but they will not listen to the word. The problem is that we think with words, not images."

Interviewer: "I have heard you refer to yourself as an activity director, yet you are recognized as a master classroom teacher. What do you mean by activity director?"

Jim: "I see myself as an activity director rather than a teacher. My job is to come up with one hundred and eighty activities, duplicate them, pass them out, collect them and grade them and then pass them back out. It looks good, the principal is impressed. The students think they are doing 'school work' as this is what they do in most of their classes. Best of all parents have lots of papers to hang on their refrigerators and know I am a good teacher because I really give my students lots to do. The only problem is I know it is phony."

Interviewer: "Why phony? What do you see as the problem?"

Jim: "It seems as if I spend a lot of time apologizing to students for asking them to do rather obvious things like reading, writing, homework, etc. The majority of students seem to have little respect for

education as such but see school only as a place where a great
deal of socialization takes place. That is not a new phenomenon,
and I could live with puberty and all its accompanying craziness.
The difference is in the last few years we seem to have been
forced into an implicit trade-off in which the students have
agreed to not quite go to the brink in their behavior if we agree
to pull back from making any serious academic demands. What used
to go on in the hallways now continues almost unabated in the
classroom as well. We don't seem to deal very seriously with
disruptive students. I see the same students in the office day
after day."

Interviewer: "What is the school doing about these problems?"

Jim: "There is very little, if any, peer support for me as a
teacher. Although I make a diligent and conscious effort to
maintain a positive attitude and to encourage other teachers,
most of them are so discouraged it is contagious. I seldom feel
that school administrators have any commitment to me as a person.
As long as I show up, keep my students under control and take
tickets a couple of times a year, everyone seems to be happy."

Interviewer: "I know that you have made a difference to many of
your students. You have affected many lives. Your students are
first, then content. What do you see in the future?"

Jim: "One of the great dilemmas of public schools is that we do
not know what to do with our old teachers. It is one
of those professions where you are supposed to do
the same things after thirty years that you did
the first year. There is no advancement for
classroom teachers, no lessening of loads
or anything to look forward to short of
retirement. I still love to teach.
There is nothing more exciting. I am
still a strong supporter of education
for I know full well the cost of
the alternative. I am looking
forward to the future and
whatever adventures lie ahead.
Who knows, there still may be a
few lessons to teach--provided
I can find a few students who
really want to learn."

16

Instructions: Having read Jim's responses, summarize in your own words what you consider to be the concerns of this master teacher.

```
+-----------------------------------------------------------+
|             SUMMARIZE THE IN-DEPTH INTERVIEW              |
|                                                           |
|   _____       |
|   _____       |
|   _____       |
|   _____       |
|   _____       |
|                                                           |
+-----------------------------------------------------------+
```

WHAT DO THESE OPINIONS AND OBSERVATIONS MEAN?

Now having read the responses of teachers and students, what do these opinions and observations mean? Buried within the various opinions and observations are perhaps some problems with teaching social studies that ought to be addressed by any professional teacher. One way to think about the responses is as raw data. What problems do you see emerging from this raw data? (a) Using the raw data of the student/teacher responses, refer back to the four summary boxes and identify at least five problems and rank them from most to least important on the work sheet provided on the following page.

question: which ones are worth the trouble?

Further Instructions: Two additional sections are provided on the work sheet with the hope that your instructor will give you an opportunity to (b) meet in small groups to identify by consensus problems the group ranks as important, and (c) meet as a class to identify by consensus the problems the class ranks as important. I want to assure you this is an important task, for your personal ranking of problems and the class consensus problems will provide a basis for the remainder of this text. In short, the effective teaching of social studies starts with college students becoming teachers who are able to identify the problems that prevent the subject field from accomplishing its goal and purposes.

A. Rank order at least five problems that you identified.

    1. (most important)

    2.

    3.

    4.

    5. (least important)

B. Rank order at least five problems that your group identified.

    1. (most important)

    2.

    3.

    4.

    5. (least important)

C. Rank order at least five problems that were identified through class consensus.

    1. (most important)

    2.

    3.

    4.

    5. (least important)

V. Postscript

If you have participated by identifying the concerns of students and social studies teachers and further if you have rank ordered what you and perhaps your methods class believe are the most important problems, then you may be on the way to understanding how social studies can achieve a positive reputation and some notion of how to do it. We challenged you at the beginning of the chapter: "Can social studies achieve a positive reputation? If so, how?" Can you begin to imagine what you personally will need to know about teaching social studies to overcome the problems that were mentioned by the students and teachers?

Being a Student to Becoming a Teacher

The Preface warned that there is a message in this book, a message that you just possibly might not have wanted to hear, but you have heard the message from the students and teachers who have spoken loudly and clearly in this chapter: **as a school teacher you teach students not content.** Almost none of the students' and teachers' responses spoke about content. In fact, they talked about interpersonal relations, motivation, interest, empathy, boredom, misunderstanding, and discipline, but almost never about content. It is difficult to hear this message because your college preparation has not emphasized interpersonal relations, but instead the successful mastery of content. Now, as you are about to enter the school classroom, all of a sudden you are informed about a difference between being a successful college student and becoming a successful teacher. Given the adversarial relationship between students and teachers in many schools, as so often mentioned in the responses of students in this chapter, your ability to win, convince, cajole, and motivate students to accept your instruction comes first.

The remainder of this social studies methods text is dedicated to finding answers to the problems you and the class have rank ordered. Working on these problems will help your **conversion from being a student to becoming a teacher.** The remaining fourteen chapters are a response to one or more of the problems, for I believe that the field of social studies can gain a positive reputation by achieving the goal and objectives of the field; however, to do so, teachers and students will have to change. But, you say, "How can I or any teacher change if we don't know what the social studies field is, what it was created for, what the goal and objectives are?" The next chapter, "The Meaning of Social Studies," should help to answer these questions. It is at this moment that you are beginning the conversion from being a student to becoming a teacher.

How're you going to do it?

change

THINK

NOTES

The American Experience

CHAPTER II

THE MEANING OF SOCIAL STUDIES

OBJECTIVE: Having read this chapter you will be able to identify the origins of social studies as a reform movement, the common agreement on goal and objectives, how social studies ought to be taught according to guidelines of the National Council for the Social Studies, and the Three Traditions interpretation of teaching social studies.

> With Aristotle we declare that the ultimate test of understanding rests on the ability to transform one's knowledge into teaching. Those who can do. Those who understand, teach.
>
> Lee S. Shulman

Rationale
Social Studies

Chapter I focused on student and teacher concerns about school and teaching social studies. Those concerns are the basis for this chapter. The teachers and students were at times angry and confused about social studies: "Why," the students asked, "is it so boring and irrelevant as a subject?" What was the subject intended to do for students? Teachers wondered if it was to be taught in a particular way. And if there is a goal and objectives, why don't they know what it is? This chapter is written with the belief that a clear idea of the goal and objectives, in short, the meaning of social studies, would add measurably to a clear idea as to what ought to happen in the classroom.

What is social studies? The field is a mystery to most people and particularly perplexing to college students who are elementary education, liberal arts, or social science majors. Having majored in elementary education or history, political science, economics, sociology, psychology, philosophy, or American studies, without ever hearing about social studies is perplexing. College students must at sometime have wondered why a preparation in elementary education or social science and humanities would end with certification to teach social studies? Our immediate concern is to clear up the mystery. What is social studies? Why social studies?

What Is Social Studies? Four Basic Beliefs
NEW DIRECTIONS

The field of social studies was conceived a bit after the turn of the twentieth century as a school curriculum from kindergarten to the twelfth grade that would deal primarily with

citizenship education. Those who consider themselves social
studies teachers might believe the following: (1) social studies
is preparation for citizenship, (2) the content to be studied
should be concepts and themes that reflect on social/personal
issues, (3) the content should be interdisciplinary and
integrated throughout the social studies curriculum, and (4)
practicing the process of decision making is the guide to
classroom instruction. How did social studies teachers arrive at
these four beliefs? Imagine the period in American history at
the end of the 1800s and beginning of the twentieth century. The
country had just passed through a metamorphosis--everything was
changing and the country was no longer the rural, agrarian
society of the founding fathers of the eighteenth century.

Why Social Studies?

change

Change is what social studies is all about, how to control
change. Why this emphasis on change? What is the problem? If
anthropology and history tell us anything, they tell us we are
constantly in a state of social change. If change happens slowly
as in the stone age when man spent half a million years learning
to make stone tools, humans adjust slowly to the change. If
change happens very rapidly as in a highly developed technological society, then change can be dislocating. Rapid change is
unsettling, leading to unhappiness, fractured families, identity
crises, unemployment, drug abuse, crime, world wars, economic
depression, crises and chaos.

Change Is Chaos, and Chaos Is Change

When the United States was emerging as a technological
society, those who would look into the future asked the question,
"How do we teach citizens to control the chaos
brought on by rapid change?" In short, "How
can democracy work if there is chaotic
change?" The more rapid the change, the
greater the chaos. "How do we in a technological society empower the American citizens to make effective, critical decisions?
How do American citizens learn to control
their lives when they are in a constant
state of change?" The social studies
curriculum was to be the school subject
that focused on change with the aim of
practicing citizenship skills to control
one's life by making effective decisions.

Social studies, a reform proposed as
part of the twentieth century Progressive Movement, was a powerful new idea at
the beginning of the century. That idea
was rather simple: citizens could learn
to control their own lives (think for them-

selves) by practicing the skills of gathering knowledge, reasoning, valuing, and participating. The practice of skills was not new, but that the skills of citizenship would be formally practiced in a school curriculum was a new idea. In the beginning social studies was created as a reform move-ment in response to a changing society where persist-ent social, political, and economic problems were caus-ing instability and chaos. Immigration of what was then considered undesirables and also World War I con-tributed to the chaos helping to create an envi-ronment for educational reform. Social studies was simply a suggested change in the school's approach to citizenship education. Traditionally, citizenship education was taught by example in rural, Jeffersonian, small-town America, where in the one-room schoolhouse of the 1880s the subjects of history, civics, and geography were taught separately for the purpose of citizenship indoctrination. There was no intent to practice citizenship skills in an integrated curriculum. Practicing citizenship skills was the responsibility of the family and the community. The intent was to Americanize all citizens through the melting pot called the public school. The social studies reform emphasized the importance of educating students to the office of citizen, but also required the study of social/personal issues, the interdisciplinary integration of the social sciences and humanities facts, concepts, and generalizations, and the practice of the skill of decision making. Turn with me to a brief explanation of the circumstances which led to the social studies reform.

American*Experience*

Jeffersonian, Rural America Became Urban, Technological America

Those who proposed reform citizenship education knew that before the industrial revolution the country was essentially rural. Citizens drew water from their own wells, graded their own roads, at times administered their own justice, built their own one-room schoolhouses, supplied most of their own food, and harvested their own crops, all with the aid of an independent large family. That family did the planting, pitching, hauling, and gathering. With industrialization and technological sophistication, America became an urban society. People moved from rural isolation to urban cities in multilevel apartments and tract homes, and the independent behavior that characterized the farm family became, in the city and suburbs, interdependent cooperation. The quality of water, condition of streets, generation of electrical power, collection of garbage, disposal of waste, and safety of the community depended upon interdependent,

The way it was

24

cooperative problem-solving and community decision making with neighbors who were not only strangers, but racially and ethnically different. The independent American society, by 1900, had become an interdependent society which called for a different kind of citizenship education, and thus a demand for reform.

Education to Control Change and Manage Crisis: The Foundations of Social Studies

In the early twentieth century social scientists, educators, and social workers envisioned reform, a citizenship curriculum that would educate all the children about how to control their urban interdependence; in short, how to live effectively in an ever more complex, difficult, chaotic world. They reasoned social problems should not be left to chance, nor should learning the process of making decisions in a democratic society be left to the precinct and ward politicians. Citizens had to learn about social issues and participation. The school curriculum was to deal with questions of the quality of one's life. The practice of decision making skills determined one's quality of life. In other words, living an effective life meant making effective decisions. In summary, social studies was an educational reform founded on a vision of a rapidly changing, interdependent, democratic, and problem-laden crisis society that required some systematic, rational thought process that would provide general training in the skill of citizenship education.

Challenges to Social Studies

Opposition to Reform

The social studies reform was not universally accepted. In fact, it could be argued that the reforms have never been successfully applied throughout the American school system. There has been a century of continuous strong opposition to the suggested reforms, first by those who felt that citizenship was best served by continuing nineteenth century citizenship education featuring history, geography, and government as separate courses with the aim of indoctrinating Americanism: in short, melding all citizens to the same values and beliefs. Other opponents to reform felt that the study of contemporary social issues would lack substance. They believed social studies would degenerate into a study of popular culture, and if there was decision making, those decisions would also lack substance. The proper issues to study, according to the social scientists and historians, were those from the past or those issues that have persisted in each of the social sciences. Also, some believed in identifying a basic structure in a social science discipline. That structure yields concepts that should be the center of any study. Content, then, should be a study of basic social science concepts. Thus, a substantive issue emphasizes "hard" basic concepts that are best applied in discrete social science disciplines. Interdisciplinary integration would confuse the issue and weaken the application of concepts.

Alternatives

Strong opposition has always been voiced by professional organizations that support the social sciences and humanities. The interdisciplinary integration of their facts, concepts and generalizations would, from their point of view, diminish the importance of their fields. Such an integration of content might turn disciplined social science and history content into soft, undisciplined, disjointed generalizations that would allow students to remain ignorant of the meaning of history and social sciences as fields of thought. Separate subjects that draw their content from the separate social sciences and history, as found in most colleges, was to be preferred. Historians have always declared their primacy, meaning that history should be the core of all citizenship instruction with emphasis on linear, chronological organization of content. Other fields, economics, political science, sociology/anthropology, psychology, and recently geography, rely on structure function as a guide to organizing content. Each has declared its ownership of first place among other social science fields in preparation of citizens. In short, none of the social sciences and humanities found the reform of citizenship education based on the study of issues, practicing the process of decision making, and an interdisciplinary integration approach appealing, and in the end would essentially reject either part or all of the reform suggesting that social studies be replaced by the "hard" social sciences and humanities undiluted by the unrealistic and unworkable social studies reform.

Where we stand now

Where do we stand now? About every fifteen to twenty years attempts are made to reconcile the social sciences and humanities disciplinary approach with the social studies reform approach. National commissions, studies by independent professional organizations, and federal government funding of national projects are all ways to find compromise between the approaches. However, fundamental differences continue to arouse fierce debate on which approach best educates citizens.

Linear Chronology and Structure Function vs. Social Issues, Integration, and Decision Making

For some the opposition to social studies as a reform has been simplified to linear chronology and structure function versus social issues, integration, and decision making. Admittedly such a simplification is over generalized and tends to be, in part, inaccurate. But there is sufficient accuracy to at least identify the opposing views on an approach to citizenship education. Linear chronology is an approach to organizing content generally favored by historians. For example, school history textbooks tend to be linear, meaning a progression of events that are written in a cause and effect straight line. The chronology is the events sequenced according to time. The structure function refers to how systems work. This approach to organizing content tends to be favored by the social sciences. Textbooks based upon structure function discuss: the structure of the government; how a bill becomes a law; how the economic system works to deliver goods and services; how the social system works; how the ecosystem works. A recent alternative to structure function has been the behavioral social science approach which favors examining systems as they actually function rather than emphasizing an idealized and often mythical structure function.

School reform

Reformers believe structure function is dysfunctional. They would argue that teaching how the system works should be done as a study of an issue which involves making a decision. Investigating an issue and making decisions would require participation in a political, social, or economic system, and one would learn how the system works by, in fact, working through that system. In short, reading about how the system works is not sufficient training for the office of citizen in a democracy. Actual participation in the community is the training required. Keep in mind, the question is how best to prepare students for the office of citizen. Is it best done in separate, discrete social science and history subjects as is the model in college, or by integrating the subjects around a core of social issues and problems that students will be called upon to make decisions about as they assume full citizenship as adults in the future?

The argument over opposing approaches is admittedly complex, more complex than suggested here, but allow this introduction to stand as one view of opposing approaches to citizenship education. Clearly the linear chronology, structure function approach is practiced in secondary schools and colleges and universities where the emphasis is on learning content. Just as clearly the interdisciplinary integration approach is followed in elementary schools where teachers tend toward a student-centered approach. The practice of decision making on social/personal issues through a twelve-year social studies curriculum has yet to be realized in most schools. One might conclude that the beliefs of social studies teachers, though often discussed, in fact, are rarely practiced. The reform approach is occasionally applied in experimental settings but has yet to be accepted in most schools as the best answer to educating citizens.

LAST LOOK

In Summary

Do you get the picture? The community, the family, traditional values and beliefs were coming apart. The twentieth century inherited urbanization, technology, social disintegration, instability, and chaos. In other words, the system was changing. Suppose you want some stability rather than continuous disintegration and chaos. Well, what in the twentieth century was to help bring order out of chaos and preserve traditional values? What would substitute for the lost traditional community and family where children learned beliefs and values?

Clearly the twentieth century response was to try to educate all the children in a public school system. The school would become the surrogate parent and provide the supervision for the social and special interest activities that had once been centered in the traditional community, i.e., home, church. American society was suffering through the stress of change. If the schools were, in fact, to be both the surrogate parent and community, then what curriculum in the school was intended to specifically deal with citizenship education? As you have read, social studies reform calling for interdisciplinary integration of content around social issues for the purpose of decision making was one of the answers. But then how best does a school as surrogate prepare citizens for a democratic, interdependent, technological, diversified, multicultural society? Opponents to the reform provided other answers. The other answers on how best to provide surrogate citizenship training centered around the separate, discrete social science and history disciplines content approach.

So what are important points to summarize? First, citizenship was taught during the 1800s, but that citizenship, by 1900, was considered inadequate because it was remote from contemporary experience and did not seem to prepare citizens for the twentieth century. Second, social studies was to reform the earlier "irrelevant" citizenship. Third, many classroom teachers and professional social science and history organizations rejected the social studies approach. Fourth, as you will learn, considerable disagreement arose within the field of social studies among those who accepted the reform as to its goal, objectives, and practices in the classroom. Fifth and finally, after eighty years of experience within the field some agreement appears to have emerged, but yet serious disagreement continues on practices in the classroom. So, the argument continues (1) within the field of social studies, and (2) between those who accept the reform and those who reject all or part of it.

The right choice

The question, how best to prepare students for the office of citizen, continues to be studied, argued over, and pronounced upon, but surely the question has not been settled. Of course, the issue of how to prepare citizens is quite complex, in fact, more complex than suggested above. How complex might be gathered by noting (1) the definition of social studies as a field, (2) how the social studies reform proposed to develop curriculum materials based on interdisciplinary integration of content and themes at each grade level, and (3) the three different traditions that interpret how social studies should be taught. The following should help to clear up how a social studies school program could be aimed at developing citizenship.

YOUR DECISION

How Do You Define Social Studies?

As you might assume given the history of social studies as a reform and the opposition to that reform, defining the field accurately has been difficult. To define a field of study one has to know what makes up that study. How was the field conceived? You know that social studies was proposed as a subject field to prepare citizens. The social sciences and humanities are the source of most of the content at each grade level. Interdisciplinary social sciences and humanities are integrated according to themes and issues in a social studies scope and sequence. Assuming that all the above is basic to social studies, a definition might be:

Social Studies

Social studies is the interdisciplinary integration of social science and humanities concepts for the purpose of practicing citizenship skills on critical social issues.

"Citizenship" is emphasized because, despite all the differences in meaning and application of social studies, the goal which most teachers accept is that students should be prepared to become functioning citizens in a democracy. In short, the goal of social studies instruction is citizenship. "Integration" is emphasized because social studies is the only school subject which deliberately attempts to integrate data and concepts from social science, history, and humanities disciplines as far apart as history, psychology, literature, geography, folklore, and philosophy. Are there other reasons for integrating content? Yes.

Every American Citizen

We all start formal education integrated. When children enter school for the first time, they come to that experience with an integrated understanding of their world. Integrated means that the children make sense of their world by understanding how things, objects, events, and people fit together. The school experience begins by breaking that integrated sense of the world into exact words, facts, definitions, descriptions, concepts and generalizations. The formal school experience continues through the grades and into higher education to separate knowledge into fields or disciplines called English, history, math, science, art or music. The trend in modern education is to fragment knowledge into ever smaller bites, and from bites into mini-bites. There are almost no subjects that integrate knowledge, almost none with the exception of social studies. Citizenship requires the skill to integrate (mix, combine, incorporate) knowledge. Citizens face the problems of life not as sociologists, historians, economists, or anthropologists, but rather as people who take into consideration all of the knowledge that they have so that they might live more effective lives. Citizens face social issues that require an integration of life experiences. From the social studies reform point of view, the continuous education of citizens in the fragmenting of knowledge without an equal emphasis on integration is poor preparation for the office of citizen.

The child's understanding of the family

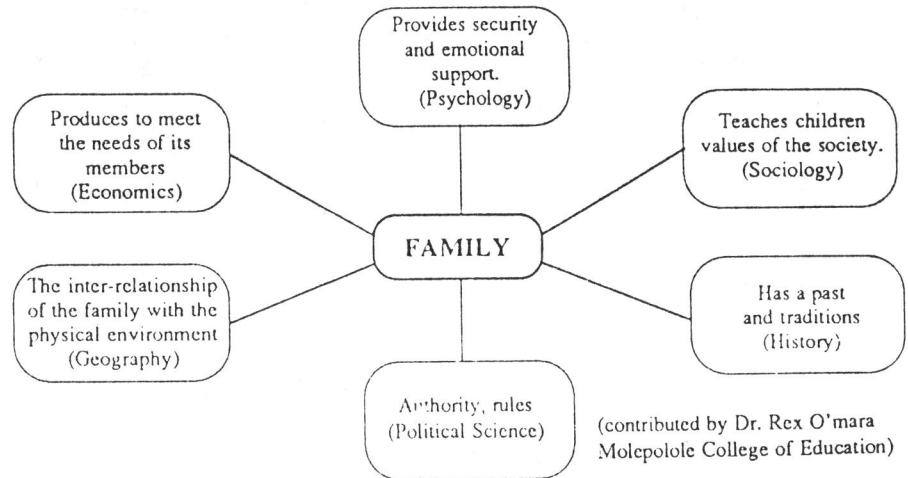

Provides security and emotional support. (Psychology)

Produces to meet the needs of its members (Economics)

Teaches children values of the society. (Sociology)

FAMILY

The inter-relationship of the family with the physical environment (Geography)

Has a past and traditions (History)

Authority, rules (Political Science)

(contributed by Dr. Rex O'mara Molepolole College of Education)

Agreement on a Goal and Skill Objectives in Social Studies

Teachers have different interpretations of how schools should promote the practice of decision making. The professional organization for social studies teachers, the National Council for the Social Studies, in an attempt to bring some consensus to the field, has suggested a set of curriculum guidelines.[1] These guidelines translate the larger goal of citizenship into four skill objectives. According to the guidelines, all social studies instruction should include practice of the four skills at each grade level. It is the practice of these skills that provides an integrated, consistent approach to citizenship education throughout a social studies curriculum. In short, the four following skills are those a citizen must use to integrate information and reasoning to make citizenship decisions. The point is made on the first page of this chapter that social studies teachers generally share four beliefs about how to prepare students for citizenship. One of the beliefs is in practicing the skill of decision making. But what are the skills and how would those skills be taught in class?

National Council for the Social Studies

1.   The skill to gain knowledge about the human condition which includes past, present and future.

2.   Acquire skills necessary to process information.

3.   Develop skills to examine values and beliefs.

4.   Apply knowledge through active participation in society.

Reflect a moment on each of the four skill objectives. What does it mean to teach students to gain knowledge? Of course, you know what this means. Most of your schooling has centered on gaining knowledge: reading textbooks, writing reports, researching, and all the things you did to pass tests. The skill of processing information is a bit more difficult. Processing is reasoning, and has to do with how knowledge is used. Some rational processing systems are called "reflective thinking," "problem-solving," "scientific method," "critical thinking," "inquiry," and "inductive" or "deductive" reasoning. All of these reasoning systems are designed to establish proof, which simply means a system to establish what is accurate and true. The third skill is the examination of values and beliefs. The assumption is that students ought to have the skill to identify what they believe and value and to examine the consequences of holding those beliefs and values. What the skill is getting at is that values drive behavior, and because citizens make choices by supporting and voting, they should be as clear as possible about what they value. In short, learn to "know thyself." The fourth skill is participation. What should be the end product of gaining knowledge, processing information, and examining values in a democratic society?--using those skills to participate in the decision-making that is basic to a democratic system. Be sure to note on the scope and sequence spiral that the four skill objectives are integrated at each grade level.

Social Studies Interdisciplinary Integration of Concepts Spiraling through a Scope and Sequence

Hopefully the mysteries of what social studies is and why it
was proposed as a school curriculum have now been answered. Of
course, you know that social studies was a school curriculum
focused on citizenship education, and it was an educational
reform of earlier citizenship training aimed at preparing
students for the office of citizen, and that is why it was
created. Much has been said about the beliefs of social studies
teachers, one of which is that the social studies curriculum
(that is what is taught at each grade level) should be interdisciplinary and integrated. However, it is not easy to imagine
what a social studies curriculum would look like if it were
interdisciplinary and integrated. Interdisciplinary refers to
how the disciplines, i.e., history, geography, sociology, etc.,
relate to each other. Integration refers to how the concepts and
generalizations, i.e., change, interdependence, family, etc., are
held in common by the social science and humanities disciplines.
In truth, social studies curriculum development is complex and
will not be fully treated here. However, Chapter III will
discuss in detail precisely how the social studies approach is
applied to the creation of curriculum materials. Of most
importance is that the social sciences and humanities are
interrelated and in many cases use the same concepts and
generalizations but from different points of view. The social
studies approach attempts to integrate those different points of
view as they relate to certain specific issues and themes.

The social studies curriculum is organized in what is called
a scope and sequence. A number of social studies scopes and
sequences have been proposed over the years. All of these are
organized to prepare citizens in a developmental (which means
progressively developing) series of facts, concepts, and
generalizations. The following scope and sequence is an
illustration of one organized social studies curriculum, K-12.
Be sure, as you examine the spiral, to note the meaning of scope
and sequence. That knowledge will be helpful when reading
Chapter III.

WHAT IS SOCIAL STUDIES SCOPE AND SEQUENCE?

THE EXPANDING HORIZONS OR EXPANDING ENVIRONMENT APPROACH TO ORGANIZING CONCEPTS

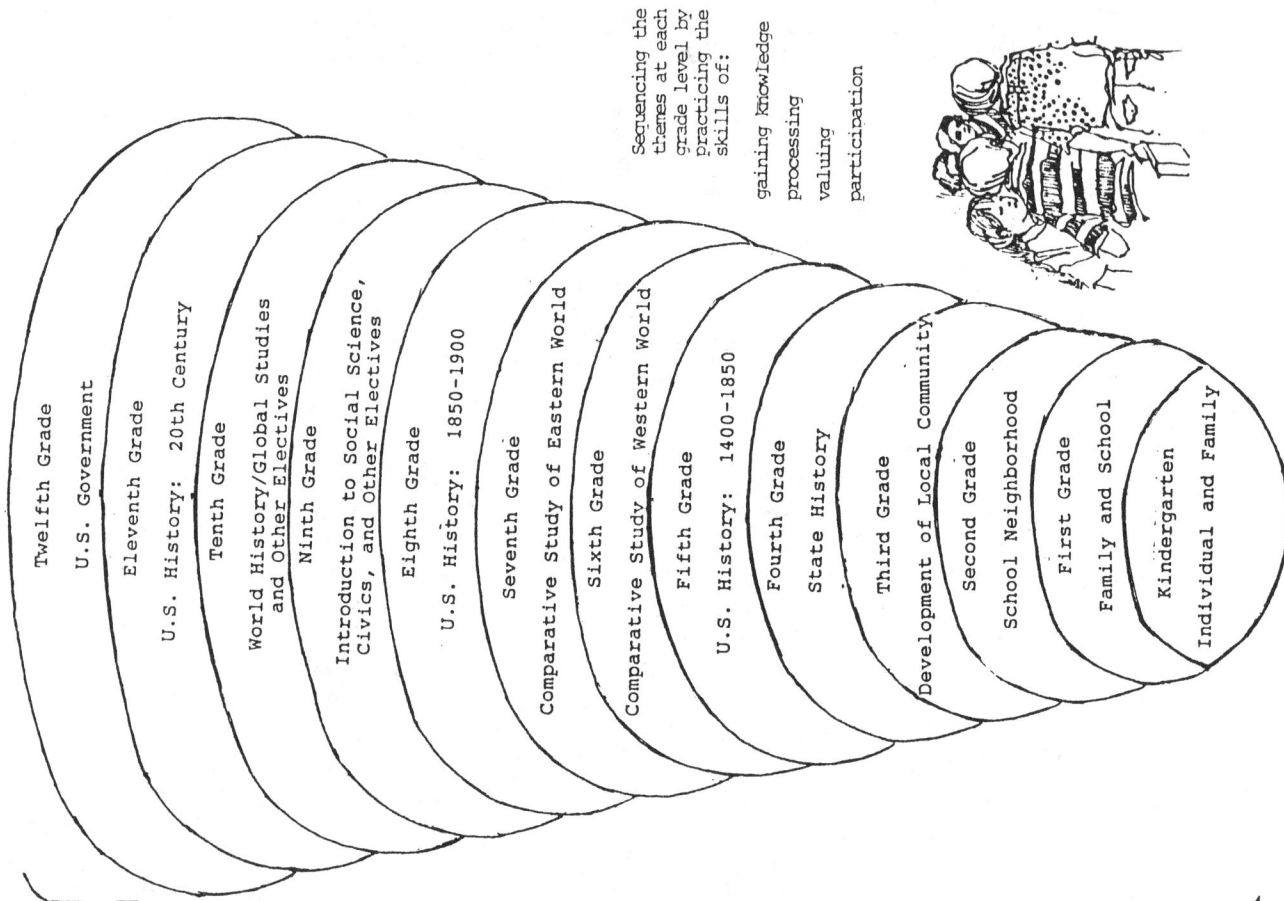

Twelfth Grade
U.S. Government

Eleventh Grade
U.S. History: 20th Century

Tenth Grade
World History/Global Studies and Other Electives

Ninth Grade
Introduction to Social Science, Civics, and Other Electives

Eighth Grade
U.S. History: 1850-1900

Seventh Grade
Comparative Study of Eastern World

Sixth Grade
Comparative Study of Western World

Fifth Grade
U.S. History: 1400-1850

Fourth Grade
State History

Third Grade
Development of Local Community

Second Grade
School Neighborhood

First Grade
Family and School

Kindergarten
Individual and Family

Sequencing the themes at each grade level by practicing the skills of:

gaining knowledge

processing

valuing

participation

Sequence is the spiral.

Scope is the depth of study at each grade level.

SEQUENCING

SEQUENCING is progressing from themes that are near at hand, concrete experiences, to those that are abstract experiences for the purpose of expanding the environment. For example, in the first grade the theme is family and school (a personal concrete experience). In second grade the theme is school neighborhood. In brief, the child's environment has expanded from family to include in second grade the school and neighborhood. This does not mean that the theme of family has been forgotten, but two additional themes have been added, and students study the relationship between family, school, and neighborhood. Sequencing is spiraling the theme from kindergarten (individual and family, concrete and personal) up to twelfth grade United States government which tends to be abstract and removed from personal experience.

SCOPE

SCOPE is the development of a theme and depth of study undertaken on each theme at a particular grade level. How deep or extensive should the study be of the family, the school, the neighborhood, or the U.S. government? See the illustration of the spiraling social studies curriculum and the expanding scope of themes at the right.

INTERDISCIPLINARY INTEGRATION

This scope and sequence is an example of an interdisciplinary integration of social science and humanities concepts that are themes.

Disagreement on the Meaning and Application of the Citizenship Goal and Skill Objectives

If teachers agree that young people can learn to function effectively as citizens by practicing the skills of gaining knowledge, processing information, analyzing values, and practicing participation, where exactly is the disagreement? The disagreement is at the level of meaning and application. That is, although it is relatively easy to talk about "citizenship," "knowledge," "values," "processing" and "participation," it is difficult to agree about what these terms mean in concrete, everyday classroom practice. One further thought, American educational theory proclaims the fundamental principles of dignity, worth and respect for the individual, recognition of differences and support for constitutional freedoms, and yet there are obvious differences on the interpretation of these principles. For example, though the school may proclaim these principles, the practice of them in the school is interpreted to mean central control where decree, not need, and command, not choice, are the actual practice. It is tempting to say that the school and teachers may say one thing and do another. If it is true that some schools have become the family in a society of fractured families, and if the school system espouses fundamental principles which are denied in the actual practice by administrators and teacher, then such contradictory behavior makes the teaching of social studies, which is supposed to proclaim those fundamental principles, difficult if not impossible.

Three Traditions Approach to Clarifying Meaning[2]

As the goal and skill objectives emerged, so did alternative views or perceptions as to the meaning of social studies. To examine these perceptions of meaning that have evolved over the past century of teaching social studies we asked three questions: (1) What was the **purpose** for teaching social studies? (2) How was social studies taught (**methods**, techniques, strategies)? (3) What should be the **content**? What emerged from the study of the history of the movement were three different dominant perceptions/interpretations of how social studies should be theoretically applied in the classroom. These dominant perceptions became known as the Three Traditions Approach to Teaching Social Studies. Each tradition has a wide spectrum representing different applications of the approach, but there remains a central core of agreed upon beliefs that all in that tradition would hold.

The right choice

OVERVIEW OF THE THREE TRADITIONS

Social Studies Taught as Citizenship Transmission

Citizenship Transmission is one view that
favors a continuing tradition of transmitting a
body of knowledge, values, and beliefs that
illustrates a proper standard of citizenship
behavior. One particular example of this
tradition, and the most commonly found in
American social studies classes, emphasizes
linear chronology used as the means to transmit traditional American values. Being
conservative or liberal does not determine
whether or not you are in this tradition,
but if the intention is to use social studies
content to shape right and proper citizenship, then one fits in this tradition. All social studies teachers who
have as their core belief the teaching
of values that should be inculcated
are in this tradition. The tradition
is called Teaching Social Studies as Citizenship Transmission.

Social Studies Taught as Social Science

Social Science tradition is a second view widely
held by teachers who specialize in teaching
history, government, economics, sociology,
psychology, and geography in secondary schools.
The social studies curriculum, according to
this view, should emulate the methods,
problems, and content of the separate social
science disciplines. They favor a social
studies that would teach scientific
social science content identified by the
scholars in each discipline. They
believe that citizens would be more
effective if they would follow the
reasoning process of social scientists.
Some believe in chronology while others
identify social issues. Some believe in
an interdisciplinary integration of
social science concepts while others argue
for separate social science courses, yet
all who follow this tradition believe all
social problems and curriculum materials
should be based on social science disciplines.
This tradition is called Teaching Social
Studies as Social Science.

Social Studies Taught as Reflective Inquiry

Reflective Inquiry tradition as a third view was based essentially on John Dewey's notion of reflective thinking. The Progressive educators who followed Dewey saw social studies as a curriculum based on the perceived needs and interests of students. Students would identify significant social/personal problems and would sat- isfy their needs and interests by practicing citizen- ship behavior through the reasoning process of reflective inquiry. The core belief rejects linear chronology in favor of social issues which students must identify, define, and hopefully solve through a rational process. The focus in this tradition is on the indi- vidual not the textbook, the values of the teacher, or the structure of a social science discipline. This tradition is called Teaching Social Studies as Reflective Inquiry.

Teaching Portraits from the Classroom

Every American Citizen

What follows is the Three Traditions chart. A careful study of the chart should reveal the differences between the traditions on the meaning of social studies.

THE THREE SOCIAL STUDIES TRADITIONS[3]

	1 Social Studies Taught as Citizenship Transmission	2 Social Studies Taught as Social Science	3 Social Studies Taught as Reflective Inquiry
PURPOSE	Citizenship is best promoted by inculcating "right" values as a framework for making decisions.	Citzenship is best promoted by decision-making based on mastery of social science concepts, processes, and problems.	Citizenship is best promoted through a process of inquiry in which knowledge derives from what citizens need to know to make decisions and solve problems.
METHOD	Transmit Transmission of concepts and values as textbook, recitation, lecture, question-answer, and problem exercises.	Discovery Each social science has its own method of gathering and verifying knowledge. Students should discover the discipline's problems through a structure that is appropriate to each social science.	Reflective Inquiry Decision-making is structured and disciplined through reflective inquiry process which aims at responding to conflicts by means means of testing insights.
CONTENT	Content is selected by an authority, interpreted by the teacher and has the function of illustrating values, attitudes, and beliefs.	Proper content is the structure, concepts, problems, and processes of both the separate and integrated social science disciplines.	Analysis of individual citizen's values yields needs and interests, which in turn form the basis for student self-selection of problems. Problems therefore constitute the content for reflection.

PURPOSE. All three traditions accept citizenship as the purpose of social studies, but there is disagreement about how to achieve citizenship as an objective. Citizenship Transmission (CT) teachers tend to believe that there are certain right beliefs and traditional values which must be indoctrinated--that is, must be held in order to perpetuate society. Social Science (SS) teachers would ask students to concentrate on mastery of social science and history content because these contain the method of knowing that is more relevant to a person's future as a citizen. Reflective Inquiry (RI) teachers focus on a process which involves active consideration of problems which are both personal and social in nature on the assumption that this is the problem-solving involved in citizenship.

METHOD. Some who read about the traditions say, "Let's be eclectic. I'll just take what I like from each of the three traditions. I'll teach students about the meaning of citizenship by covering all three traditions." Unfortunately, this approach--which is extremely common--has some built-in problems. The categories within the three traditions are mutually contradictory. For example, look back at the chart and examine the category "method." Note that CT transmits commitment to preconceived values and beliefs. Now note that RI emphasizes decision making through a reflective inquiry process that deals with value conflicts. If you still say, "I don't care. I believe in using bits and pieces from each tradition," please consider the consequences of that belief. How does one transmit commitment to beliefs and also get students to make decisions about value conflicts? How does one get students to ponder the meaning of a given piece of knowledge while also getting students to memorize "right" answers? Techniques can be the same for all three traditions, but methods not the same. For a discussion on this see Chapter V, "Social Studies Methods, Techniques, and Strategies."

For Social Science teachers method is based on discovery. What does this term mean? First, understand that social scientists talk about a "structure of knowledge." Second, they think that this structure is knowable. That is, students can come to understand this structure just as scientists or social scientists do. Third, teaching and learning consists largely of teachers posing the "right" questions or problems--the ones within the discipline--and students eventually coming up with the "right" answers. Thus, discovery consists largely of gradually coming to understand the relationship between or among social science concepts. In a SS government class, a traditional problem might concern civil disobedience. In a SS sociology class, a traditional problem is "social stratification." An SS economics teacher would identify a problem about supply and demand. Civil disobedience, social stratification, and supply and demand are basic concepts which illustrate what the social scientists call the structure of knowledge. It is this structure that a social scientist would want a citizen to know when making citizenship decisions. In an elementary class a SS problem might

be on interdependence as illustrated in the first graders' study of self, the school, and the neighborhood, and the second graders' study of community helpers. But at any grade the SS method of discovery consists first of posing a disciplinary problem generated in the subject field and then demonstrating the approved method of gathering and examining evidence and reaching a defensible conclusion.

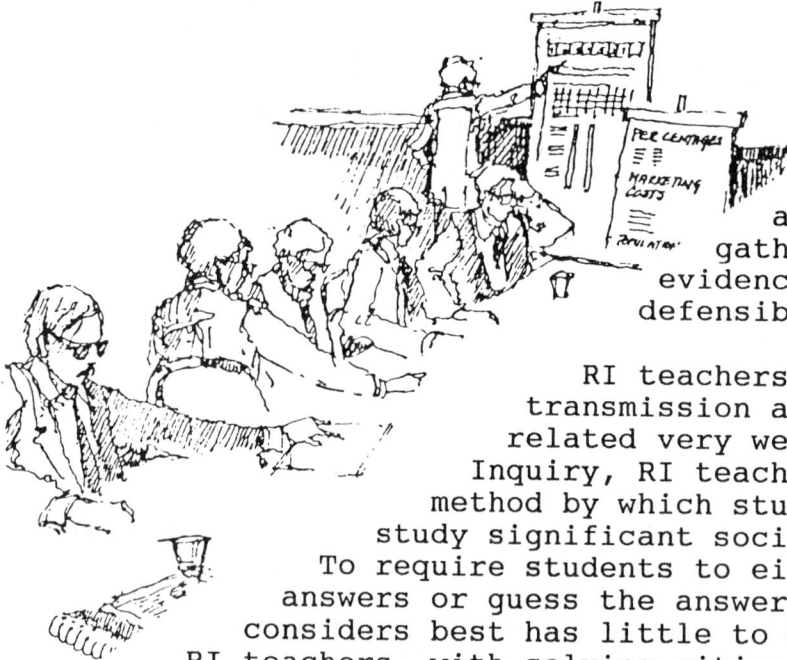

RI teachers tend to look upon both transmission and discovery as not related very well to inquiry.
Inquiry, RI teachers believe, is the method by which students best identify and study significant social/personal problems.
To require students to either memorize the right answers or guess the answer that the teacher considers best has little to do, in the opinion of RI teachers, with solving citizenship problems. Thus, for RI teachers the critical task is for the students to identify those aspects of a social problem which they perceive to be troublesome, important, meaningful, confusing--or all of these. This is the meaning of the simple but deceptive term "identifying problems based on students' own needs, interests, and values."

Try to distinguish between the use of the term "problem" in SS and RI. The difference is not at all insignificant. SS teachers want students to study those problems already iden- tified by the particular social science discipline. RI teachers insist that unless students identify--that is feel, internalize, "own"--and define a problem, it is simply not a problem for them. If it is not a problem, then students have no reason to go through a problem-solving process: hypothe- size, examine data, make predictions and projections, test meanings, examine their own value structure. But SS teachers maintain that the social sciences and history generate intrinsically interesting and powerful prob- lems, content, and research processes that are truly useful for all citizens. They also maintain that the problem-solving models within the social science disciplines pro- vide a pattern for all future citizenship activities.

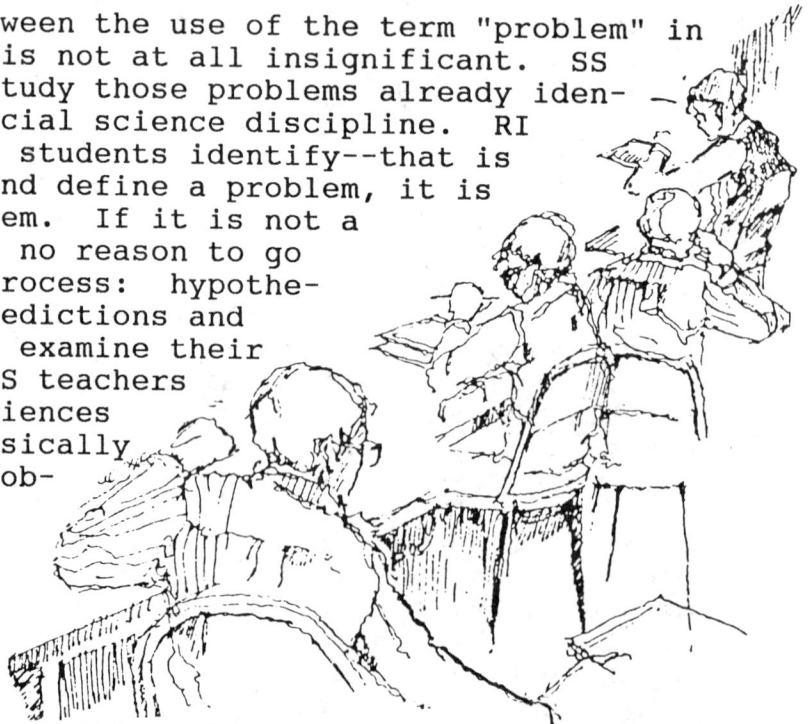

Try to understand what the problem of communication has been among social studies educators and classroom teachers. All use the term "problem" and all believe that everyone else should have the same meaning for this critical term. But research suggests very strongly that there has been no common understanding of problem--or of "democracy," "discipline," "citizenship," "knowledge," "values," or any of the other terms that are used by all those who teach or talk about teaching. It is precisely because teachers have not communicated about just those matters which are important to them that large philosophical differences exist, and therefore, often the meaning of social studies is not clear.

CONTENT. Consider how the traditions employ different content to realize their particular purposes. CT teachers select the content which illustrates and shapes values, attitudes, and beliefs they would wish students to adopt. In practice this means, for instance, that elementary teachers read stories or conduct show and tell sessions on "sharing" or "being kind to animals." It means that teachers conduct a discussion about newspaper pictures students bring in that illustrate the folly and destruction of war or the tragedies of automobile accidents. It has meant that CT teachers may use a history lesson to support a belief such as "the worth and value of all mankind." The teacher may draw on a current event to illustrate a moral lesson. CT teachers may just teach the textbook, thinking that the author, a historian, political scientist, or economist, is value free and just presents a chronology, facts, or true interpretations. Of course, this approach is CT because the author is not value free but, in fact, has a point of view that determines what chronology to follow and what facts to select. The point is that the content taught is interpreted in such a way that facts and generalizations in the form of values and beliefs are transmitted as knowledge. Some CT teachers follow such interpretations with open reflective discussion. Others will allow the interpretation to stand without critical review.

For SS teachers proper content, as you might infer from the discussion above about methods, includes those concepts, generalizations, theories, processes, and problems of the separate social science disciplines, i.e., political science, geography, sociology, anthropology, economics, and psychology. This list must also include history, but be aware that some regard history as a social science while others consider it a field in the humanities. In sum, the SS teachers want reflection within the problems and processes defined by the field. Note how this differs from the CT conception of content. SS teachers are not trying to find materials that will indoctrinate certain points of view. Rather they seek content that can be used to train knowledge-gathering skills, or as the term is often used, "modes of analysis," of the various social sciences.

An RI teacher would have grave doubts about CT and SS conceptions of content. For an RI teacher content arises out of one's values, needs, interests, and problems. But this raises an important question: Where does an RI teacher get ideas about content? Look for a moment at the world with the eye of an RI teacher. This look requires one to accept the assumption that people behave according to their value and belief systems. Out of one's perceptions of values come one's needs and interests. The best way to interpret "interest" is to place the word "self" before interest so that one is talking about what is one's self-interest. The best way to understand "needs" is to see that what one needs is ultimately decided by what is in one's best self-interest. An individual's needs are often in conflict, thereby creating problems. A reflective inquiry process is required to sort out competing claims and eventually decide which need is greatest. From an RI viewpoint, then, the way to teach people to become citizens in a democracy is to teach them to sort out and solve problems through a reflective inquiry process by resolving conflicts among values and interpretations.

YOU SHOULD KNOW

Summary on the Meaning of Social Studies

This chapter has been complex, some might even say difficult, because within a few pages the meaning of social studies as an educational reform was discussed and examined. Remember the objective for reading this chapter? Are you able to identify social studies as a reform, the Three Traditions, a definition of social studies, and the common agreement on goal and the four skill objectives, all of which make up the meaning of social studies? Perhaps a summary would be helpful.

CRUSADE

In summary, defining the reform beliefs of social studies flows from recognition that the United States is a pluralistic, self-governing society in which conflict and change are realities. The accelerating pace of change and deepening social problems, such as industrialization, urbanization, mass immigration, racial and religious animosity, led some to believe that future citizens needed formal school training in the skills of self-government and decision-making, skills that were not practiced during formal education in the 1800s. At the beginning of the twentieth century the traditional collection of courses in government, history, and geography, which were taught in a linear, chronological, structure function way to shape right values and behavior, gave way to a proposed educational reform. The reform proposed a new field of study which became social studies. That field emphasized (1) an interdisciplinary integrated approach to identifying social science and humanities concepts with the intent of (2) practicing citizenship skills including decision making on (3) contemporary social problems and issues. We noted that disagreement both about how the reform social studies was to be applied in the classroom and about the very existence of the field continues to be a hot issue.

Social Studies
curriculum development

What social studies teachers might believe is: first, the goal of social studies is preparation for citizenship and involves an integration of concepts in a spiraling scope and sequence taken largely from the humanities and the social sciences. Second, the national professional organization for social studies teachers, the National Council for the Social Studies, proposed that one way to integrate social studies in a scope and sequence was to apply the four skill objectives: (1) gaining knowledge, (2) processing information, (3) clarifying values, and (4) engaging in social participation, in every social studies classroom. In short, citizenship is not so much a definition as it is a set of the four skill objectives which, if followed, would prepare students to function as self-governing, decision-making citizens. However, though there appears to be agreement on the goal and four skill objectives, a significant disagreement continues on just how those four objectives should be applied in the classroom. One way to understand the disagreement is the Three Traditions approach which identifies essentially three ways teachers think about social studies: Citizenship Transmission, Social Science, or Reflective Inquiry.

The field of social studies is changing and emerging as are all other subject fields. The fact that there continues to be disagreement about meaning and conflict over definition should not be a source of discouragement, but rather a sign that debate on the issue of how best to prepare citizens continues. Simply, social studies was created to prepare citizens for a changing, complex, chaotic twentieth century. The social studies practiced in today's classroom is not necessarily an example of the reform beliefs envisioned as a reform at the turn of the century. Practicing the skill objectives is not yet standard practice in most social studies classes. Perhaps students and teachers interviewed in Chapter I were unhappy with social studies because the reforms have yet to reach the classroom. The students and teachers were never asked to integrate the twelve-year social studies program. Social/personal issues and a decision making process were never part of the program. What actually exists in many secondary schools is not the reform social studies but the traditional social studies of the 1800s where linear sequence and structure function continue to dominate the organization of concepts and classroom instruction. Examine the five problems selected as the most significant in teaching social studies at the end of Chapter I. What are the students and teachers protesting about--the practice of citizenship skills and decision-making on relevant personal, social problems? No, that's the reform approach. They are complaining about irrelevant, uninteresting, boring and disjointed social studies

42

classes, the very reasons that called forth a demand for reform almost a century ago.

The Social Studies

The meaning of social studies emerges through a history of the field, definition, goal, and objectives, scope and sequence, and an interpretation of the field through the Three Traditions. The meaning of social studies is complex but establishing a meaning for yourself is essential when deciding how you will teach. But then, there are other difficult decisions. For example, the next chapter, "The Social Studies Interdisciplinary Integration Approach to Curriculum Development," will discuss how content was intended to be organized for instruction in social studies classes. This topic was briefly treated in this chapter and illustrated by an example of a scope and sequence. In the next chapter we will take a close, intensive look at how social studies curriculum emerges from facts, concepts, and generalizations to become an integrated scope and sequence.

To end this chapter we return to the powerful thought: social studies is all about change. Rapid change characterizes what happened during the twentieth century. Learning to live with social/personal chaos and doing something constructive with it is the simplest expression of the goal of social studies. Our thoughts are now turning to the twenty-first century, wondering what form of citizenship education will be the most effective. Will the reform beliefs of social studies teachers finally be realized or will the new century demand a different set of beliefs about citizenship education? We conclude with a statement that summarizes what social studies was intended to be as a field.

The Social Studies
change

SOCIAL STUDIES, as all education, IS about CHANGE, but

SOCIAL STUDIES IS about the POWER to participate, which means

SOCIAL STUDIES IS THE POWER TO participate by directing CHANGE.

CHAPTER III

THE SOCIAL STUDIES INTERDISCIPLINARY INTEGRATION APPROACH TO CURRICULUM DEVELOPMENT

OBJECTIVE: Having read this chapter you should be able to identify patterns of reasoning that include facts, concepts, and generalizations, and how that reasoning is organized into content according to a social studies interdisciplinary integration approach.

"Life is the sum of all your choices."

A. Camus

Rationale

Chapter II on the meaning of social studies identified a definition, scope and sequence, goal and objectives, and a Three Tradition interpretation of how social studies has evolved over the past century. The chapter also included the four beliefs that are basic to social studies, (1) citizenship education, (2) interdisciplinary integration, (3) issue orientation, and (4) decision making, as explanations of what social studies is and why it emerged as a twentieth century school subject. In this chapter the intention is to concentrate on one of the basic beliefs, interdisciplinary integration, because this belief bears directly on how facts, concepts, and generalizations are organized and applied in a curriculum to social issues. In short, interdisciplinary integration is shorthand for a complex set of ideas about the organization of concepts in a social studies curriculum.

Curriculum

But Why Should You Be Concerned about Curriculum Development as You Progress from Being a College Student to Becoming a Teacher?

The answer is teachers decide what and how content, skills, and attitudes will be presented. Consider the following argument. As a student you were handed textbooks and other curriculum materials, and you assumed that textbooks were the proper organization of content. You literally did not have to think about how content was organized and presented by the teacher or the text. But as a teacher you are very much concerned. One of the tasks of a professional teacher is curriculum development. Curriculum development is a shorthand way of saying teachers identify and organize the materials used to teach the class. In brief, teachers make decisions on how to organize and present content. Why should the organization of content be your concern now? To this point in your formal education you have not been asked to organize curriculum materials, but as a teacher you will be asked to

perform that task. So the question you need to ask is, "How do I organize social studies curriculum materials?" This chapter will help you answer that question. The answer lies in a series of complex ideas about the nature of content. The series starts with (1) words are symbols, (2) symbols are used to think and reason, (3) symbols are categorized into facts, concepts, generalizations, and finally (4) facts, concepts, and generalizations are organized in social studies according to the interdisciplinary integration approach in a scope and sequence.

The Process of Creating Knowledge: Words Are Symbols

we have to create

It sounds complex but, in fact, you have experienced all of what is called the nature of content your whole academic life. Only now you are, perhaps for the first time, introduced to the process by which content and finally curriculum materials are created. In short, all of the hundreds of textbooks and other instructional materials you have read, and all of the knowledge you have was created and organized by the following process.

You know very well that words are symbols. We think and have thoughts using symbols. No words--no thoughts, just images. Words are easily manipulated, images are not. Suppose you imagined the concept "change" but had no word for it. If you wanted to tell someone else about the concept change but had no words only images in your mind, how would you verbally translate "change?" The mental manipulation of symbols, vocabulary (words, numbers) is what we normally refer to as thinking. Symbols can be categorized into facts, concepts, and generalizations, and it is these categorized symbols that we use to think and also to reason.

自由

Freedom

Thinking Requires Symbols: Facts, Concepts, and Generalizations

Demonstration

Examine this series of symbols that represent facts, concepts and generalizations.

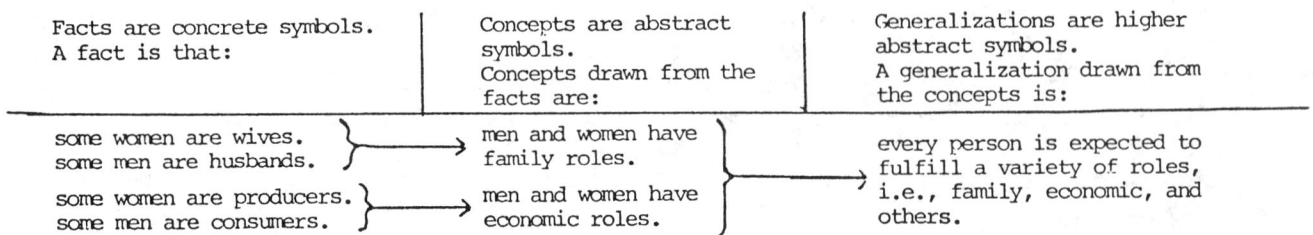

Facts are concrete symbols. A fact is that:	Concepts are abstract symbols. Concepts drawn from the facts are:	Generalizations are higher abstract symbols. A generalization drawn from the concepts is:
some women are wives. some men are husbands. → men and women have family roles. some women are producers. some men are consumers. → men and women have economic roles.		every person is expected to fulfill a variety of roles, i.e., family, economic, and others.

Of course, we know what a fact is. We have memorized, repeated, researched, and analyzed facts throughout our schooling. Something that is concrete, that has been objectively verified and known as a certainty, or at least predictable, is a fact. However, a concept is abstract and therefore a bit more difficult to imagine. Concepts are a grouping of facts that have been interpreted as a main idea or understanding. In short, a group of facts may have similarities. Those similarities, when interpreted, become a concept. For example:

FACTS: become a	CONCEPT:
(One can observe that these roles exist.)	(What are the similarities of these roles?)
Teacher Student Advisor Evaluator Supervisor Mentor Curriculum Developer Administrator	All of the roles, when interpreted, have similarities. The concept that explains these similarities is educational roles.

Examples of concepts for anthropologists and sociologists are diversity, change, culture, diffusion, social control; while for historians a concept would be time; for a political scientist, power and authority; and for a geographer, sunlight and temperature. A generalization is even more abstract and complex an idea than a concept. The conclusion drawn from a group of related concepts is known as a generalization. A generalization can be defined as an idea that identifies the relationship between concepts and has universal application. For example:

Illustration of How Social Scientists Organize Facts, Concepts, and Generalizations

Geography

A geography generalization is: A country's climate is determined by many geographic factors.[1]

Climate is determined by sunlight, temperature, humidity, precipitation, atmospheric pressure, winds, unequal rates of heating and cooling of land and water surfaces, irregular shape and distribution of land and sea, ocean currents, and mountain systems.

This generalization has imbedded within it a number of concepts that must be understood if the statement is to make

46

sense: sunlight, temperature, humidity, precipitation, atmospheric pressure, winds and so forth. Moreover, each of the concepts has many specific facts associated with it that give it meaning, as for example: sunlight--variation, intensity, composition; temperature--variation, change, effects; winds--direction, patterns, causes; humidity--degree of moisture, dampness, effect on comfort. Concepts and generalizations are transferable from one setting to another. Facts, on the other hand, have no transfer value--they are useful and applicable only in their specific settings: Columbus discovered America in 1492; The Chicago Fire took place on October 8, 1871; The Great Depression followed the stock market crash on October 1929. Conceptual approaches are intended to provide a framework or design for the building up of meanings from facts to concepts and concepts to generalization.

For example, the facts, concepts, and generalization could be expressed this way:

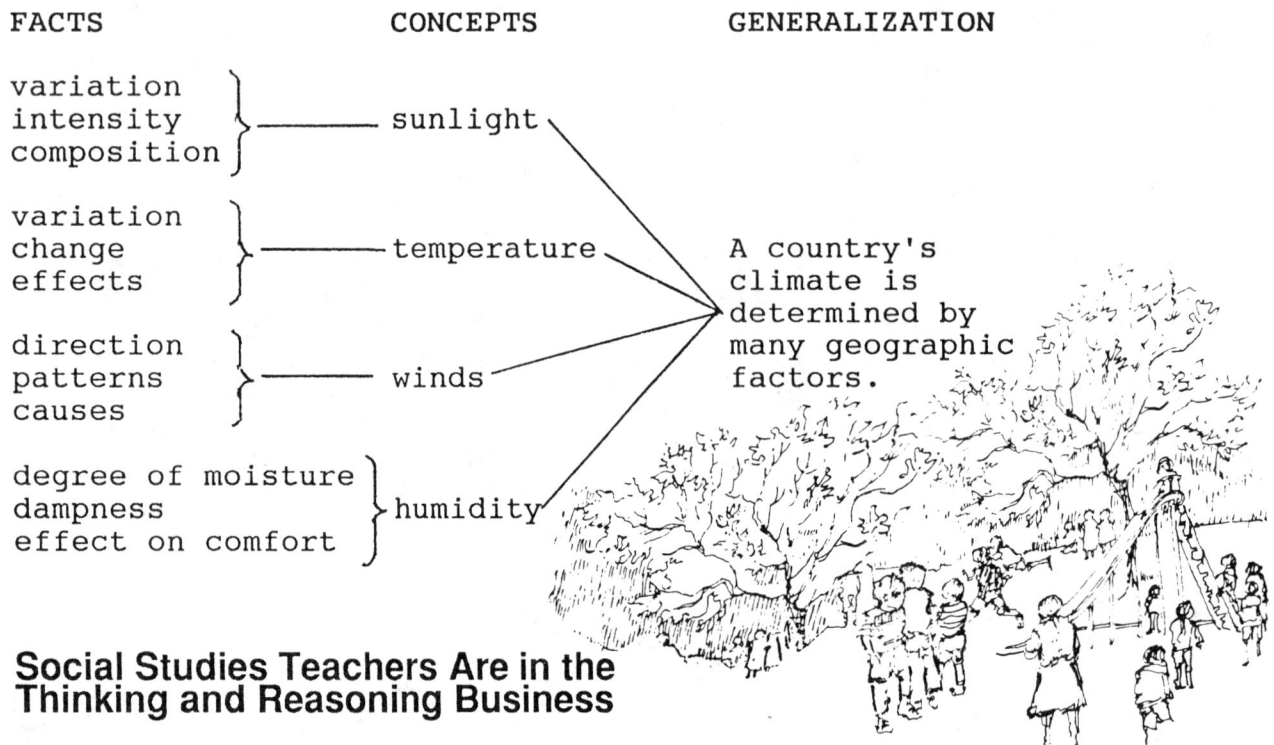

FACTS   CONCEPTS   GENERALIZATION

variation
intensity   }——————— sunlight
composition

variation
change   }——————— temperature
effects   A country's
                                               climate is
direction   determined by
patterns   }——————— winds   many geographic
causes   factors.

degree of moisture }
dampness   }— humidity
effect on comfort }

Social Studies Teachers Are in the Thinking and Reasoning Business

The point of this illustration is that we manipulate facts, concepts, and generalizations in a disciplined, organized process. Facts become concepts, and concepts become generalizations. In short, the process of going from facts to generalization is the same as from specific to general or from concrete to higher abstraction. So what does this have to do with a teacher's task? Organizing and presenting facts, concepts and generalizations is a teacher's task. Therefore, you should conclude that, as a social studies teacher, you ought to become familiar with how facts become concepts and concepts become generalizations because this is

the way knowledge is organized, whether you organize it, the textbook organizes it, or some teacher's guide organizes it. Manipulating facts, concepts and generalizations is the formal process by which we learn to think and reason. Reasoning, the way we integrate information and ideas, can be either from the particular (facts) to the general (inductive reasoning), or just the reverse--from the general to the particular (deductive reasoning). The point is no matter if reasoning is inductive or deductive, the person reasoning is manipulating facts, concepts, and generalizations for the purpose of integrating that knowledge.

We need to produce students who know how to think.

One other complicating factor--how does one know how to organize (integrate) facts, concepts, and generalizations in social studies? If you are a social studies teacher, then the answer to "How do you know?" is clear, by following an interdisciplinary integration approach to the selection and organization of curriculum materials.

The following is a concept wheel illustration of an interdisciplinary integration approach. A concept wheel visually shows the relationship between facts, concepts, and generalization. This approach can be either inductive or deductive. Note the arrows are pointing both ways which means a study on a topic could start with a generalization and proceed deductively from the general to the specific, or start with facts and proceed inductively from the specific to the general. The topic, stated as a generalization is: Emerging nations have development problems.

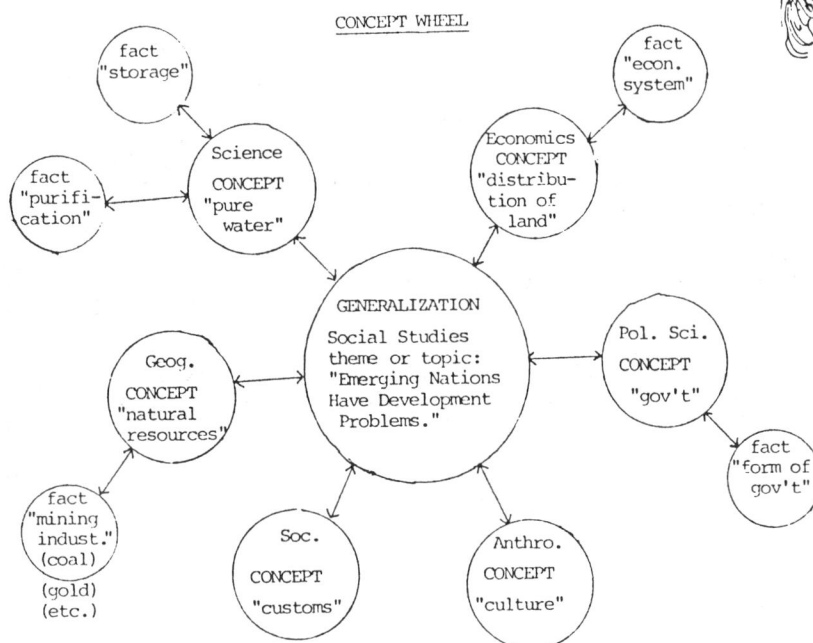

CONCEPT WHEEL

Note on the concept wheel how the facts, purification, storage, form of government, mining industries, lead to higher abstractions, concepts, such as natural resources, government, economics, which lead to a higher abstraction, a generalization-- "Emerging nations have development problems." Can you identify how this concept wheel is an illustration of an interdisciplinary integration study? Read the following to get the answer.

Organizing Social Studies by an Interdisciplinary Integration Approach

Chapter II, "The Meaning of Social Studies," introduced the interdisciplinary integration approach by defining social studies as "the interdisciplinary integration of social sciences and humanities for the purpose of citizenship education." The integration mentioned in the definition refers to the concepts, i.e., change, interdependence, that are held in common by the social science and humanities disciplines. Interdisciplinary refers to how the disciplines, i.e., history, geography, sociology, relate to each other. For example, each discipline has facts, concepts, and generalizations that contribute to a study on the topic "Change." In short, every social science field contributes facts, concepts, and generalizations to a study of the topic: the world is always in the process of change.

Do you recall the social studies scope and sequence in Chapter II? The scope and sequence integrates facts, concepts, and generalizations from all relevant disciplines into themes at each grade level demonstrating how the interdisciplinary integration approach is applied in social studies. The scope and sequence describes how the social studies curriculum develops citizenship education starting with self, family, and school, then expanding and spiraling through each succeeding year. At each grade level facts and concepts focus on the generalization. For example, at the fourth grade level a generalization (theme or topic), "I am a citizen in a state or region," consists of a deductive study of concepts from the general to the specific, i.e., government, change, interdependence, location. The facts to support the concepts are derived from questions such as: "Where is the state or region located?" (geography question); "What are the characteristics of the culture that make up the state or the region?" (economics, sociology, political science question); "How has the state or region changed?" (sociology, anthropology, history question).

Fourth Grade

The following statement illustrates how one state in a
curriculum guideline describes how teachers at the fourth grade
level should integrate social studies:

> [Theme: I live in a state, but] we can compare and
> contrast how we live in [a state with how] cultures
> exist in different parts of the world. Students
> examine how different cultures and ethnic groups
> within [the state] influence the ways in which similar
> geographic and environmental conditions are utilized.
> Students note the ways in which human and natural
> resource distribution affects lifestyles and how
> interaction among humans is related to social control
> in the midst of changing requirements and deepening
> social problems. Reading for context clues, maps
> and globe skills and social skills are emphasized.[2]

Do You Own the Curriculum or Does the Curriculum Own You?

TAKING CONTROL

Do you identify why this state's fourth grade curriculum
guideline is relevant to this chapter? Of course, you see the
point. The curriculum guidelines could not have been written if
there were no facts, concepts, and generalizations; no curriculum
materials (textbooks) could be written, and, finally, there would
have been no way to instruct fourth grade teachers on what to
teach. So conclude that if you wish to own, i.e., control, have
ownership of, the curriculum you teach, then know the process by
which (1) facts become (2) concepts become (3) generalizations,
and how all three become the curriculum you teach. A final
thought, as a teacher your task is to organize and select and
create appropriate curriculum materials, methods, techniques, and
strategies. How can you do that if you don't know the process?

INDIVIDUALIZED INSTRUCTION AND WORKING WITH GROUPS

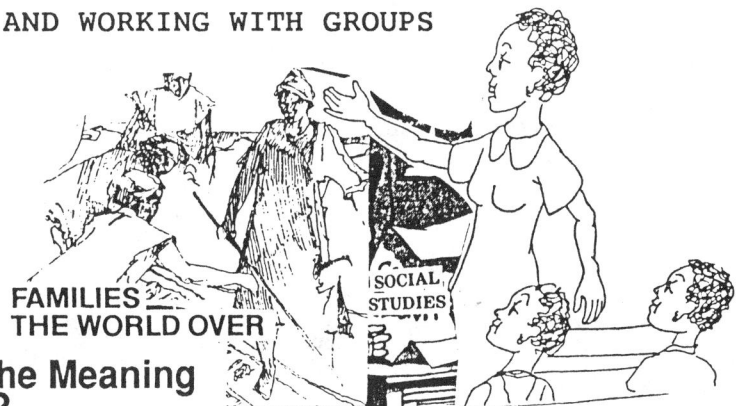

FAMILIES THE WORLD OVER

SOCIAL STUDIES

How Well Do You Understand the Meaning of Interdisciplinary Integration?

Notice how the fourth grade theme, "I am a citizen of a
state," begins with an interdisciplinary approach by requiring
facts from sociology, history, anthropology, economics,

geography, and political science. Turn back to the illustration
on geography. Why does that illustrate integration but not
interdisciplinary? Respond here: _

_____

_____

Also did you note that the fourth grade state curriculum
guidelines required deductive reasoning? What made this study
deductive? Respond here:

_____

_____

How could the fourth grade theme, state citizenship, have been
organized as an inductive reasoning lesson? Respond here:

_____

_____

(If you have difficulty answering the above question, see the
concept wheel on the following page.)

    The practice of categorizing facts, concepts, and
generalizations will not necessarily make you a perfect
curriculum materials developer. We can hope, however, that
knowing how information is formally processed will impress you to
the point where you identify that the process of thought is
related to creating and organizing curriculum materials. In
short, creating effective social studies curriculum materials
depends on how the interdisciplinary integration approach is
applied to the formal process of reasoning. This is what you
should know as you progress from being a college student to
becoming a teacher.

**Multicultural Awareness for Classroom
Teachers**

Practice on the Concept Wheel

    You know that the social studies scope and sequence
illustrated in Chapter II starts with the study of self, family,
home, in kindergarten/first grade. Assuming you were a teacher
assigned to teach those topics, how might you apply the
interdisciplinary integration approach to a concept wheel? As
you examine the wheel note how facts in the outer circles lead to
concepts which eventually lead to the generalization in the inner
circle, the point being that all facts, concepts, and
generalizations are integrated in an interdisciplinary approach.

Now

INTERDISCIPLINARY INTEGRATION APPROACH
TO TEACHING SOCIAL STUDIES
CONCEPT WHEEL

Drawing Inferences

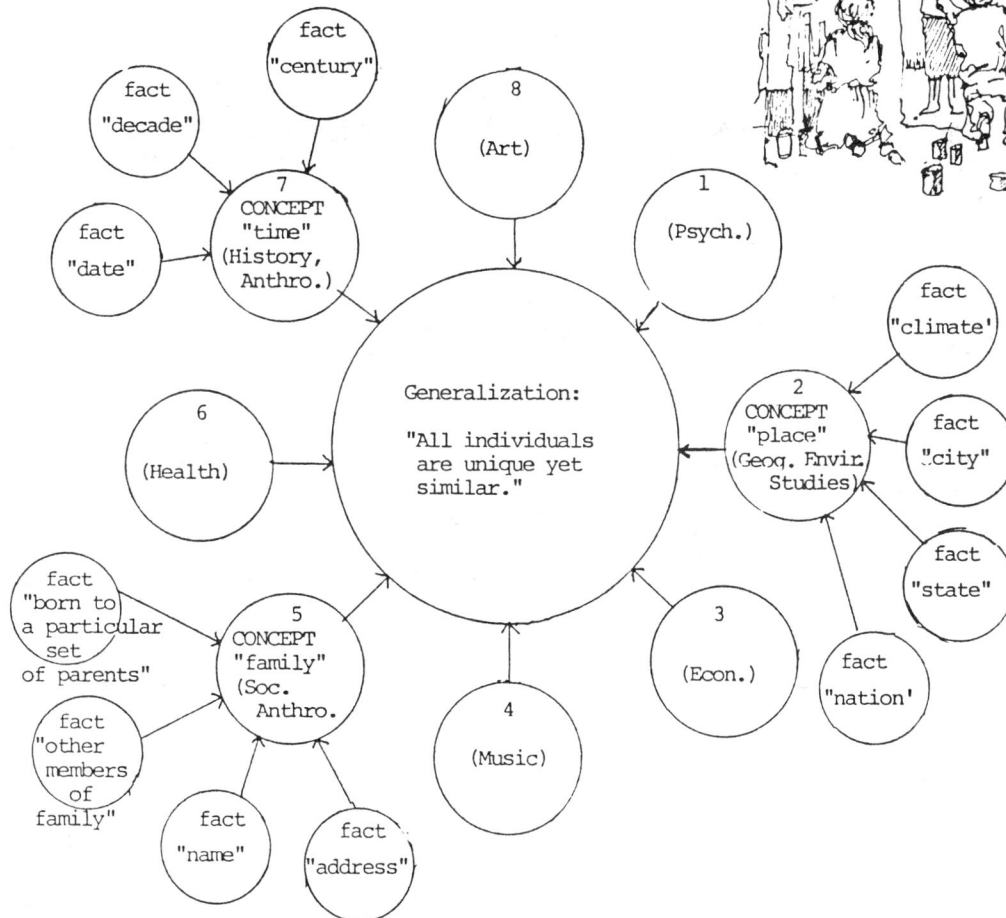

fact "century"

fact "decade"

fact "date"

7 CONCEPT "time" (History, Anthro.)

8 (Art)

1 (Psych.)

fact "climate"

2 CONCEPT "place" (Geog. Envir. Studies)

fact "city"

fact "state"

6 (Health)

Generalization: "All individuals are unique yet similar."

3 (Econ.)

fact "nation"

fact "born to a particular set of parents"

fact "other members of family"

5 CONCEPT "family" (Soc. Anthro.

4 (Music)

fact "name"

fact "address"

This concept wheel demonstrates the different levels of inductive reasoning.³ The lowest level is to know a fact. A second level is concepts which are arrived at based upon a series of related facts, and a third level is generalization which, as you can see on the wheel, is based on the relationship of eight concepts. These three different levels of reasoning are extremely important to the practice of social studies because, as you know, "Citizens face the problems of life not as philosophers, historians, or anthropologists, but rather as citizens who should know how to integrate relevant knowledge so that they might make more effective decisions about life." In short, you teach students facts, concepts, generalizations, skills, and attitudes, but you also teach them to integrate from facts to attitudes--that is, to reason either or both deductively and inductively in a rational thinking process. After all, is that not what is required of a citizen in a democracy?

Undoubtedly, practice with facts, concepts, and generalizations is important--to distinguish between them and then to be able to use them to think and reason. Try to distinguish differences in the following exercise. Mark on the line before each word F for fact or C for concept:

_____husband	_____parent	_____advisor
_____child	_____family roles	_____cook
_____wife	_____disciplinarian	_____homemaker

Did you identify husband, child, wife, parent, disciplinarian, homemaker, and cook as facts because they can be verified? Family roles is a concept because it describes how the facts are similar and includes all the roles of the family.

Now try the following exercise to distinguish between facts, concepts, and generalizations. Mark on the line before each word(s) F for fact, C for concept, or G for generalization:

_____voter	_____citizenship role
_____husband	_____homemaker
_____taxpayer	_____family role
_____child	_____disciplinarian
_____parent	_____institutional role
_____candidate	

FAMILY

Did you identify voter, husband, child, taxpayer, parent, candidate, housekeeper, and disciplinarian as facts? You know from the exercise earlier that family role is a concept drawn from the facts about families. Citizenship role is drawn from the facts of voter, candidate, taxpayer. The generalization, institutional role, is drawn from the concepts of family role and citizenship role, which are summarized to mean every person is expected to fulfill a variety of institutional roles. The following is an illustration of the inductive thinking process from facts to concepts to generalization.[4]

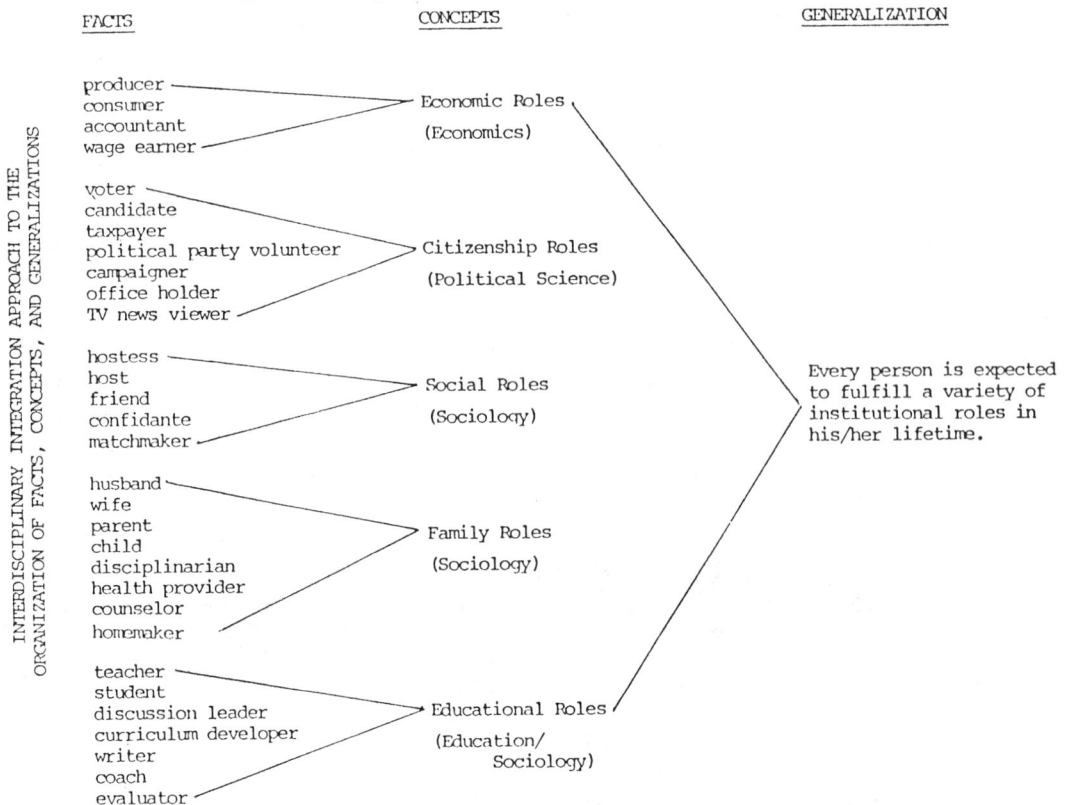

FACTS   CONCEPTS   GENERALIZATION

INTERDISCIPLINARY INTEGRATION APPROACH TO THE ORGANIZATION OF FACTS, CONCEPTS, AND GENERALIZATIONS

producer
consumer
accountant
wage earner → Economic Roles (Economics)

voter
candidate
taxpayer
political party volunteer
campaigner
office holder
TV news viewer → Citizenship Roles (Political Science)

hostess
host
friend
confidante
matchmaker → Social Roles (Sociology)

husband
wife
parent
child
disciplinarian
health provider
counselor
homemaker → Family Roles (Sociology)

teacher
student
discussion leader
curriculum developer
writer
coach
evaluator → Educational Roles (Education/Sociology)

Every person is expected to fulfill a variety of institutional roles in his/her lifetime.

Sociology

Have you noted how the facts, concepts, and generalization are integrated in an interdisciplinary way? The facts, when their similarity was interpreted became concepts. The concepts, when their similarity was interpreted, became a generalization. That is what we mean by integrating facts, concepts, and generalization. But how is this illustration an example of interdisciplinary? Respond here:

_____

_____

Of course, you know the answer. The facts and concepts are derived from the disciplines of economics, political science, sociology, and education.

You could conclude that as ideas become more generalized, they also become more abstract and for many students more difficult to understand. Facts are concrete and can be personally verified, but concepts and generalizations require higher thinking skills. They represent interpretations of facts, thus providing the social studies teachers with a special challenge. The challenge is to clearly demonstrate the process by which concepts and generalizations are drawn from facts so that students will understand how ideas are summarized and expressed.

Concepts

Test Your Ability to Turn Concepts into Generalization

The following is a list of concepts that are taught in a K-12 social studies curriculum. Can you identify a generalization from the selected concepts? Remember the criteria: a generalization represents similarities and relationships between concepts. Both concepts and generalizations are transferable from one setting to another. Generalizations apply the same everywhere. Given the list of concepts below, what generalization would you draw?

Write Your
Generalization Here

1. Goods   6. Resources (human)
2. Income   7. Service   _____
3. Industrialization   8. Specialization   _____
4. Interdependence   9. Supply   _____
5. Labor   10. Wants   _____

A Practical Application of What You Have Learned as You Are Transformed from College Student to Classroom Teacher

As a final check of your knowledge on how facts become concepts and concepts become generalizations fill out the concept wheel below using any social science or history text. Why? Because it's time you prove to yourself that the process by which a textbook is organized can be easily identified, and by knowing how the content was structured you can yourself take charge of facts, concepts and generalizations and do your own structuring, thus designing your course for your students.

Instructions: Select any chapter in a textbook, then find the concepts and generalizations in a chapter along with the supporting facts. Though not always true, normally the title of the chapter will be a generalization and major headings are usually key concepts. Facts will be in the body of the text. Your task is to identify what facts, concepts, and generalizations the author has used in a chapter. Fill out the concept wheel by reasoning from the general to the specific (deductive) or from the specific to the general (inductive).

Don't miss a thing.

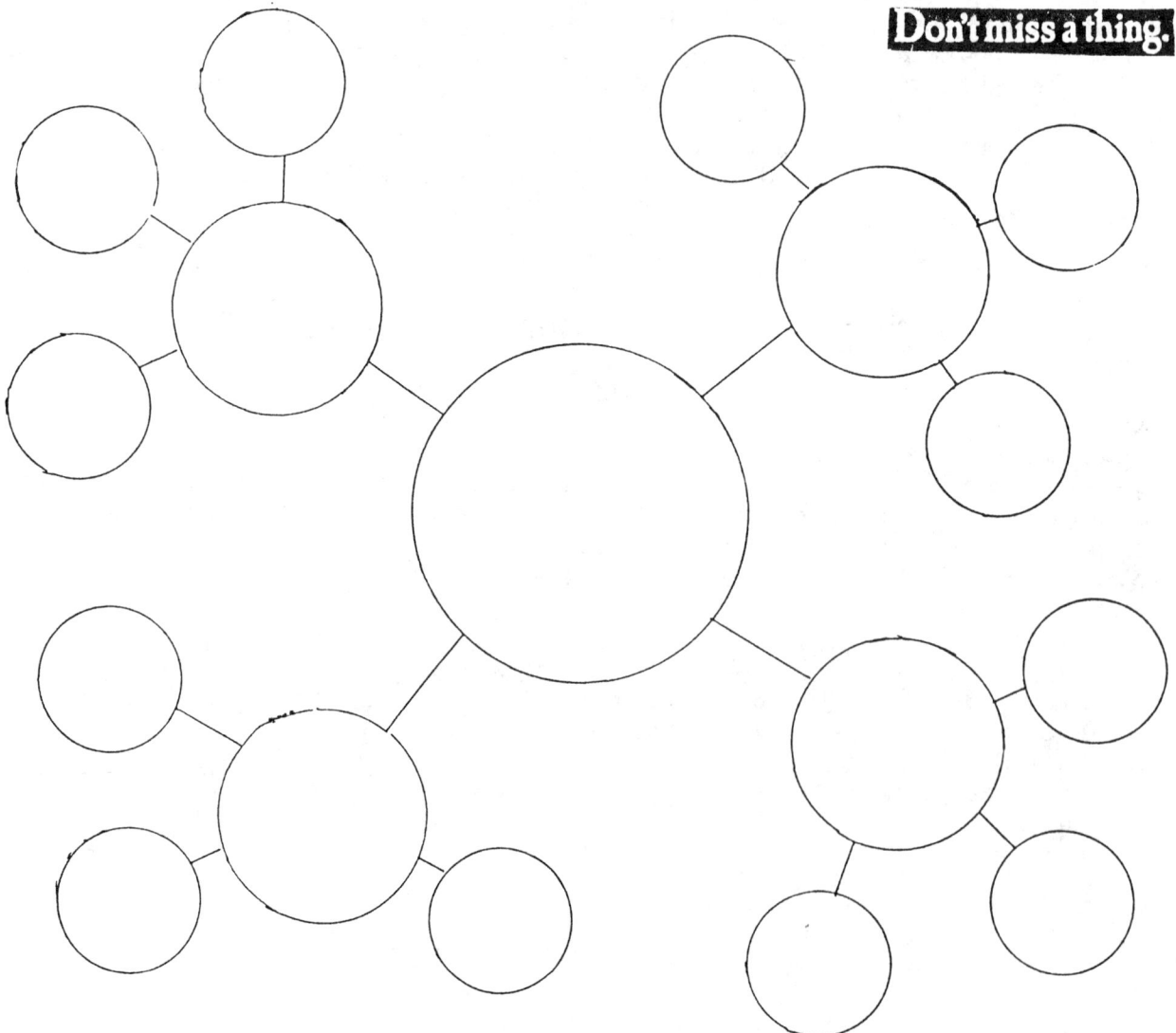

Conclusion

Review and Conclusion

This chapter has introduced a series of complex relationships, and one could be forgiven if all the relationships were not clearly understood at this point. The following review should be carefully read with the purpose of gaining a clear idea of how content is organized to support thinking and reasoning. The major point addressed to you in this chapter is that a teacher's task includes curriculum development. But how can you carry out this task if you do not know the formal process by which knowledge is organized? That is, if you are unfamiliar with the process, how can you effectively participate in curriculum development? A second argument is that students also need to know how content is processed because they should be learning content, skills and attitudes, integrating them, and using them to reason.

The discussion on thinking focused first on the capacity of humans to attach symbols to reality and then associate and manipulate those symbols. However, all symbols are not equal. Some symbols represent concrete reality (facts), whereas other symbols represent higher order abstractions (concepts and generalizations). In short, we think and reason by following a formal process that requires manipulation of facts, concepts, and generalizations. Two ways of manipulating information are inductive which is reasoning from the specific to the general, and deductive which is reasoning from the general to the specific.

Pause for a moment, ask yourself, "Why is the above of any particular importance? What have symbols, abstractions, thinking and reasoning processes to do with the task of teaching?" The answer is, teachers are in the thinking and reasoning business and all of the curriculum materials (content) that you will use to teach have been organized according to a formal process. You have just reviewed that process. If it is your task to organize and develop curriculum materials, then knowing the process by which curriculum materials are developed is important. In practical terms you will be asked to plan resource units, units and daily lessons, all of which are ways of determining what and how to teach. In short, you are developing the curriculum. Thus, most everything you do as a teacher illustrates how you think and reason using facts, concepts, and generalizations.

Now to continue the review. We have said above that thinking and reasoning follow a formal process. Every discipline applies its own unique approach to that formal process. That is the reason sociology, geography, psychology, and all social science disciplines, are distinct from each other. Social studies also applies an approach to the formal process. The name

of that approach is interdisciplinary integration.
Interdisciplinary requires the integration of facts, concepts,
and generalizations from the social sciences and humanities for
the purpose of instruction in citizenship education. The
development of citizenship education through an interdisciplinary
integration approach is demonstrated in a social studies
curriculum scope and sequence where themes, concepts, and facts
are spiraled through an expanding horizons environment at each
grade level, K through 12.

How does knowing the social studies approach to organizing
and presenting curriculum materials help a teacher? It goes
without saying that classes and individuals are different. One
set of curriculum materials, i.e., textbooks, workbooks, teaching
aids, will not be sufficient to teach all those classes and
individuals effectively. Teachers are constantly working on
curriculum development in an effort to design materials that are
appropriate for their classes. Therefore, understanding how
content is organized in a social studies approach is basic to
performing the job of a social studies teacher. In short,
successful social studies teachers need to have ownership of the
curriculum. Understanding this process allows teachers to own
the curriculum they teach.

Social Studies

This is a scope and sequence
model of a social studies
interdisciplinary integration,
K-12.

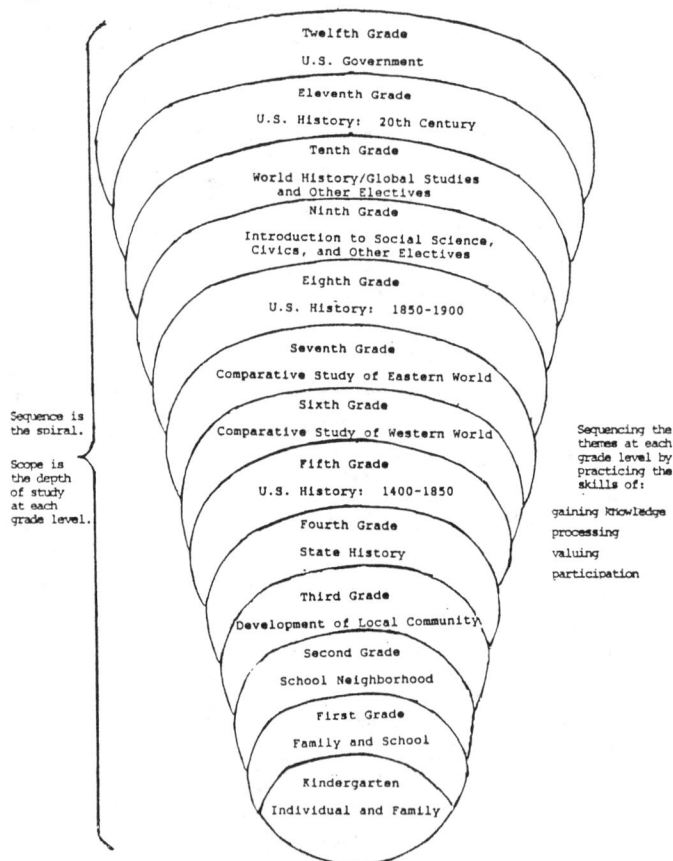

Twelfth Grade
U.S. Government

Eleventh Grade
U.S. History: 20th Century

Tenth Grade
World History/Global Studies
and Other Electives

Ninth Grade
Introduction to Social Science,
Civics, and Other Electives

Eighth Grade
U.S. History: 1850-1900

Seventh Grade
Comparative Study of Eastern World

Sixth Grade
Comparative Study of Western World

Fifth Grade
U.S. History: 1400-1850

Fourth Grade
State History

Third Grade
Development of Local Community

Second Grade
School Neighborhood

First Grade
Family and School

Kindergarten
Individual and Family

Sequence is
the spiral.

Scope is
the depth
of study
at each
grade level.

Sequencing the
themes at each
grade level by
practicing the
skills of:

gaining knowledge

processing

valuing

participation

Coming Events

In this chapter we have talked about how content is evolves
from facts, concepts, and generalizations in a social studies
interdisciplinary integration approach. We turn now to Chapter
IV where a summary of research on learning and effective teaching
offers guidance on how best to teach students.

CHAPTER IV

WHAT RESEARCH SUGGESTS ABOUT EFFECTIVE TEACHING AND LEARNING IN SOCIAL STUDIES

OBJECTIVE: Having read this chapter you should be able to compare and contrast active and passive learning and identify effective teaching practices that will focus student attention on spending quality time on task.

Being Educated

It's not what you know, it's what you want to know.
Thus, the questions you ask are the key to being educated.

Rationale

Do you remember from Chapter I several of the problems that students and teachers discussed as reasons for ineffective teaching and learning in social studies classes? Were some of the problems defined as motivational, boredom, lack of enthusiasm, irrelevance, and inadequate communication, suggesting that the school system was out of touch with students? Where can teachers turn for authoritative suggestions on specifically how to treat these problems? One authoritative source is the following summary of fifty years of research studies on effective learning. There are relatively clear answers to some of the problems raised in Chapter I. Turn now to the summary and the possible answers to those problems. The research studies relevant to the summary are listed in the References at the end of this chapter. The research findings are what you need to know when progressing from being a college student to becoming a teacher.

Research Findings

Focusing Attention as Quality Time on Task

All results from research studies on learning and effective teaching agree that students learn better--learn faster, remember more, and derive greater enjoyment--when they are actively involved in learning. It follows that passive students, that is students who are inactive, non-participating, and indifferent, quickly forget what they learn, are bored, and resist being forced to retain what is to be learned. So what should you conclude? Conclude that activities that focus and prolong attention of students on the task at hand are most effective in achieving learning and remembering. And the least effective are activities that encourage short attention span where minds tend to wander from the task at

CONCENTRATE

58

hand. In short, focusing and sustaining attention are the keys
to learning and remembering. Focusing and sustaining attention
is called spending quality time on task. Methods books such as
this begin with a sure knowledge, based upon studies, that
methods, techniques, and strategies of teaching should emphasize
quality time on task--active rather than passive learning.

Active vs. Passive Learning in Teaching Social Studies

YOU HAVE AN EXCITING TEACHING RESOURCE IN YOUR HANDS

   In brief, research on learning and effective teaching for
any school subject clearly shows that teaching is more effective
when the students in the classroom are actively involved in
learning the lesson. For example, a summary of research findings
on student learning suggests that:[1]

ask questions

1.   Students learn best when there is clarity (which means
     students know what they are supposed to do), enthusiasm, a
     positive attitude, and a specific goal to be accomplished.

2.   Students learn best when they are asked
     stimulating questions rather than being
     lectured to. This means students
     learn best when they are asked the
     different levels of questions, and
     also by inference, students who ask
     stimulating questions focus atten-
     tion and encourage feedback.

3.   Students learn best when teachers
     respond to their actions in an
     encouraging manner. This means stu-
     dents learn best when they receive
     constructive, positive feedback on
     their work and when they are
     taught as though they are expected
     to succeed.

4.   Students learn best when there is student-to-student
     interaction. This means students learn best when there is a
     discussion in which they participate in an exchange of
     ideas.

   Stop for a moment and reflect: Does the preceding four-
point summary on student learning offer a clue as to how a
teacher might avoid boredom, motivational problems, and lack of
relevance, enthusiasm, and communication? This next section,
"Students and How They Learn," ought to help with the answer.

All the questions you were afraid to ask.

Students and How They Learn

A summary of studies suggest that students learn and retain (remember what they learn) at differing rates, "all things being equal," according to the degree that students are involved in the lesson. The more students actively participate, that is cooperate and share in the lesson, the more they will learn and remember. The following approximate percentages of learning and retention (remembering) are based upon a summary of studies over the last fifty years. This summary, though approximate, indicates what teachers should know about how students learn best.

WE LEARN AND REMEMBER:
10% of what we hear
15% of what we see
20% of what we both see and hear
40% of what we discuss with others
80% of what we experience directly or practice
90% of what we attempt to teach others

Would it be accurate to generalize that the higher the percentage of learning and remembering, the more likely the student has focused attention and experienced quality time on task?

We learn and remember 10% of what we hear at any given time. This means that on the average at any given time during a lecture only 10% of the students are actually listening and mentally recording what they hear, and further, at the end of the lecture only 10% of the lesson will be remembered. For example, if a teacher is lecturing to a class of 30 students, only 3 students at any given moment are listening and mentally recording what the teacher is saying. The other 27 students' thoughts may be drifting to other things. Students "tune in and out" when they are just being lectured to, meaning they listen for a few seconds to the teacher and then their thoughts stray to something else, and then back to the teacher. They repeat this process of "tuning in and out" to what the teacher is saying all during a lecture. At the end of the lecture approximately 10% of what was said has been remembered and learned.

lecture

Also, studies on lecturing suggest what could be called "What you heard is not what I meant." The consequences of focusing on part of the lecture by tuning in and out can be summarized as:

I know you believe you understand what you think
I said, but I am not sure you realize that what you
heard, is not what I meant.

The same holds true for anything that one just hears such as
radio, audio-cassettes, or just random conversations. In short,
having students listen to a lecture is the least effective
teaching technique for getting students to remember what you as a
teacher want them to remember.

lecture  radio   listening to audio cassette

   We learn and remember 15% of what we see. Think of all the
things you see in a day. This includes the reading you do,
pictures you see, signs you read. The point is on the average
you remember 15% of what you see. Also the point is that you
learn and remember more of what you read than what you hear.
However, what is important to know is that asking students just
to read an assignment may result in only 15% learning and
remembering. Perhaps seeing is believing, but surely seeing is
not necessarily the best way to encourage learning and
remembering.

book   chalkboard   newspaper

   We learn and remember 20% of what we both see and hear. If
you both see and hear, such as watching television, seeing a
film, taking notes on a lecture, on the average you will learn
and remember 20% of what you have both seen and heard. Studies
suggest teaching that includes both seeing and hearing is
significantly more effective than merely seeing or hearing by
themselves for the simple reason that the combined senses of both
eye and ear focus attention more keenly than one sense alone.
But you already know this because it is the difference between
just listening to radio and both listening to and watching
television. Television is a more powerful means of

communication. If you doubt this, just watch children--what do they prefer to sit in front of for on the average of six hours a day, radio or television?

chalkboard lecture &   films   television
taking notes

We learn and remember 40% of what we discuss with others. Suppose you are listening to a lecture. You probably will remember 10% of what you hear. Now suppose the lecture is over and you take part in a discussion on the topic of the lecture. This improves learning and remembering to 40% if you seriously participate by listening to the other students, responding yourself, and concentrating on the teacher's remarks, in short, if you focus on the topic and integrate the ideas into your store of knowledge. A reasonable generalization could be: learning improves substantially when there is a discussion, particularly if the discussion focuses attention and calls for an exchange of ideas. In other words, the more you put into it, the more you get out of it.

small group discussion   class discussion

We learn and remember 80% of what we experience directly or practice. Suppose you went on a field trip, practiced an experiment, played in a game, participated in micropeer-teaching, studied a computer interactive multimedia lesson with hyper card stacks, CD-ROMs, and videodiscs; then you can expect that direct experience to help you learn and remember up to 80%. This explains why micropeer-teaching is effective and why sports, singing, interactive multimedia and other activities where you participate increase learning and remembering.

micropeer-teaching   making a poster

62

We learn and remember 90% of what we attempt to teach others
(teaching, student teaching, peer teaching). Suppose you really
wanted to learn your subject well, what would be the best way to
learn and remember your subject? The answer is teaching. That
is, you will learn and remember 90% of what you attempt to teach
others. Perhaps you can understand why student teaching is such
a powerful experience, because you must focus your entire
concentration and energy on organizing content and pedagogical
knowledge. Focusing that attention causes you to learn and
remember more than you would if you were just listening to a
lecture where you may be focusing attention only a small part of
the time. Also, studies suggest that peer teaching is a powerful
way to focus and reinforce what has been learned, and that
students in classrooms who tutor other students learn the most.

practice teaching

In Summary

Discussion

What should you conclude about the above approximate
percentages on learning and retention (remembering)? Lecturing
is the least effective way to help a student learn and remember.
When you lecture to students you should enhance the learning and
remembering of your students by providing experiences including
teaching aids, audio-visual materials, and instructional
resources that illustrate what you are trying to say. Further,
learning and remembering are greatly enhanced
through class and small group discussion where
most students participate, with the highest
levels of remembering occurring when students
experience directly or practice the
skills they are expected to know.
When students teach other students (peer
teaching), the student doing the teaching is most likely to learn and retain
information and understanding at the
highest level. In summary, passive and
unfocused teaching will yield the
least learning and remembering.
In contrast, active and focused
teaching will tend to prolong attention leading to learning and

'Kids Listen to Kids

remembering. In other words, the higher the percentage of learning and remembering, the more likely the student focused attention and experienced quality time on task.

EFFECTIVE TEACHING PRACTICES

Setting the standard for success

A good guess would be that you already know from personal experience what studies on learning and remembering reported: focusing attention on a task was key to learning. Reading a chapter, realizing that you do not recall a thing and having to reread and this time focus quality attention on the task to "get" something out of the chapter is a common experience.

Pause for a moment and reflect on how focusing quality attention on a task relates to effective teaching. If you have reliable information on how students learn and remember best, then how should this information be applied to teaching? To help you think about applying learning and remembering to effective teaching, focus attention on the following quality suggestions.

REINFORCEMENT

1.   Reinforcement: Effective teaching should build in powerful reinforcement of ideas by repeating the same ideas in different forms of presentation. For example, in a map location exercise the social studies teacher would have a large map in the front of the room. A student or students would be called to the map to point out locations, and each student would have at his/her desk paper on which the student would draw a map and mark the proper locations. This exercise then would repeat the locations three times, but each time in a different form of presentation.

FEEDBACK

2.   Feedback: Effective teaching provides an opportunity to practice with feedback or coaching in a real situation (peer teaching, practice teaching, student teaching, or a clinical experience); for example, when a coach works with a young football player during a practice session, or a music teacher works with a choral group, or when a classroom social studies teacher has student projects where students are expected to work on a problem and report to the class with expectation of feedback from both teacher and students.

64

CHALLENGE

3.   Challenge: Effective teaching involves a challenging experience which questions, disputes, raises doubts, or suggests a reasonable risk through:

a.   a new experience such as a field trip to an historical site or meeting new and different people.

b.   demanding or extending performance such as role-playing or simulating an historical event.

c.   unfamiliar, uncomfortable, or embarrassing situations such as giving an oral report, panel discussion, debate, role-playing, or surveying in the community.

d.   attempting a new game or skill activity without previous practice.

MODELING

4.   Modeling: Effective teaching provides models of behavior. For example, social studies teachers who use a problem-solving inquiry behavior should model open-minded attitudes, allow freedom to investigate, or practice the skills and attitudes they want their students to have, and encourage that behavior from students. In short, "Do as I say and as I do."

REWARDING

5.   Rewarding: Effective teaching is rewarding for both teachers and students. Rewarding means a satisfying, mutual experience that is shared by both. For example, a teacher who wants to encourage performance, achievement, and participation sets incentives such as rewards a class may work towards. Rewards are often a visible recognition of success.

INQUIRY AND QUESTIONING

SELF-ESTEEM

6.   Self-esteem: Effective teaching sets a climate of warmth and trust and enhances the self-esteem of both teacher and students. Classrooms that emphasize a positive attitude where social studies teachers believe students are capable and where students know they can achieve some success are likely to be effective places to learn.

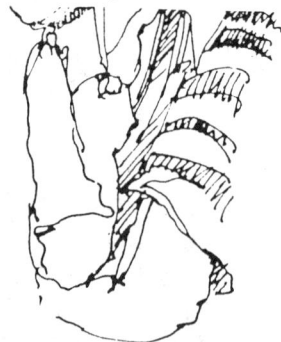

ACCOMMODATING

7. Accommodating: Effective teaching accommodates students' needs and learning styles. This is particu- larly important to remember when working with special, exceptional, disadvantaged, and multicultural students. The fact is people do have different learning styles. Just as they have differing values and beliefs, they have different preferences for learning. In short, students focus attention on different experiences: expressed in the popular wisdom as, "Different strokes for different folks."

SELF-DIRECTION

8. Self-direction: Effective teaching, in part, emphasizes self-direction. Exam- ples of self-direction would be students planning their own projects, research, small group work, simulation and gaming. Also, students encouraged to use problem-solving discovery and reflective inquiry reasoning are practicing self-direction. The assumption is that your own needs and interests provide self-direction, an intrinsic motivator.

INTEGRATES

9. Integrates: Effective teaching integrates new information and knowledge with applied practice and performance. For example, after students have been practicing map skills on the United States, then other countries are introduced and the map skills are applied to those countries. Integration at the highest thinking level of theory means knowing the content, identifying why the content is valid, why it is worth knowing, and finally how it relates to other content; in short, using a popular cliche, "Getting it together and understanding what it means."

GOAL

10. Goal: Effective teaching results from a clear idea of the goal to be accomplished. Classroom activities are selected to attain intentional outcomes. For example, if at the beginning of a daily lesson there are specific objectives which the students know, then the students are more likely to focus attention on what is to be learned. As illustrated in this text, each chapter begins with an objective which is intended to focus attention on important ideas.

11. Self-fulfilling prophecy: Effective teaching uses the principle of self-fulfilling prophecy. The accomplishments or success of students will depend on the teacher's treatment and expectations of them. If students are taught as though the teacher thinks they cannot learn, they probably will not learn. What you think you can do, you probably can do. When students know that teachers believe them to be capable, then it is easier for students to attempt new tasks and reach higher goals.

Research Application in the Classroom

In summary, research on effective teaching including learning and remembering should lead you to the reasonable conclusion that students will remember information and develop skills and positive attitudes if they focus attention and spend quality time on task. If teachers are willing to challenge students with active learning by modeling learning behavior, rewarding and reinforcing good performance, enhancing self-esteem by providing feedback, personalizing instruction, permitting some self-direction, holding positive expectations for the class, and proposing clear instructional goals, then they can expect to be very effective classroom teachers. Hopefully this has been an important chapter. Many of the concerns of the teachers and students in Chapter I could be successfully addressed if the effective teaching suggested here were actually put into practice in social studies classrooms.

You can reach more

Good practices that promote learning, remembering and effective teaching are what this methods book is all about. Methods books are written for teachers who are dedicated to developing the best if not the maximum from their students. Studies on learning over the past half century, as summarized in this chapter, point us in the right direction. It is our challenge to identify promising teaching methods, techniques and strategies that will encourage motivation, enthusiasm, relevance, and promote communication with students. The summary of research suggests where to start looking for answers. The following chapter on methods, techniques, and strategies is an application of the effective teaching practices noted in this chapter.

The following references provide the basis for the summary of the research on learning, remembering, and effective teaching.

REFERENCES

Andre, T. 1979. Does answering higher level questions while reading facilitate productive thinking? Review of Educational Research, 49, 280-318.

Armento, B.J. 1986. Research on teaching social studies. Handbook of Research on Teaching, 3rd edition, ed. M.C. Wittrock, 942-51. New York: Macmillan Publishing Co.

Atwood, V.A., ed. 1986. Elementary Social Studies: Research as a Guide to Practice, Bulletin 79. Washington, D.C.: National Council for the Social Studies.

Ausubel, D., Novak, J., & Hamesian, H. 1978. Educational Psychology: A Cognitive View, 2nd edition. New York: Holt, Rinehart & Winston.

Barnes, S. 1981, September. Synthesis of Selected Research on Teaching Findings (Report 9009). Austin, TX: Research and Development Center for Teacher Education.

Bransford, J. 1979. Human Cognition: Learning, Understanding and Remembering. Belmont CA: Wadsworth.

Brophy, J., & Good, T. 1987. Teacher behavior and student achievement. Handbook on Research on Teaching, 3rd edition, M. Wittrock, Ed. Rand McNally.

Case, R. 1975. A developmentally based theory and technology of instruction. Review of Educational Research, 45, 59-87.

Clifford, G.J. 1973. A history of the impact of research on teaching. Second Handbook of Research on Teaching. R. Travers, Ed. Chicago: Rand McNally.

DiVesta, F. 1982. Cognitive development. Encyclopedia of Educational Research, 2nd edition. H. Mitzel, Ed. New York: Macmillan. 285-296.

Duchastel, P. & Merrill, P. 1973. The effect of behavioral objectives on learning: A review of empirical studies. Review of Educational Research, 43, 53-70.

Dunkin, M. 1978. Student characteristics, classroom processes and student achievement. Journal of Educational Psychology, 70, 998-1009.

Ehman, L.H. & Hahn, C.L. 1981. Contributions of research to social studies education. The Social Studies, H. Mehlinger & O.L. Davis, Eds. Chicago: The University of Chicago Press. 60-81.

68

Frase, L. 1968. Questions as aids to reading: Some research and a theory. American Educational Research, 5, 319-322.

Gage, N.L. 1984. What do we know about teaching effectiveness? Phi Delta Kappa, 66, 87-93.

Gagne, E. 1985. The Cognitive Psychology of Social Learning. Boston: Little Brown.

Hahn, C.L. 1977. Research on the diffusion of social studies innovations. Review of Research in Social Studies Education: 1970-75. F.P. Hawkins, Ed. Washington, D.C: National Council for the Social Studies. 137-78.

Hepburn, M.A. & Dahler, A. 1985. An overview of social studes dissertations, 1977-1972. Theory and Research in Social Education, 12, 73-82.

Herman, W.L. Current Research in Elementary School Social Studies. Toronto, Canada: Collier-Macmillan Ltd., 1969.

Hunkins, F.P., ed. 1977. Review of Research in Social Studies Education: 1970-75. Washington, D.C: National Council for the Social Studies, and Boulder, CO: Eric Clearing House for Social Studies/Social Science Education and Social Science Education Consortium. ED 141, 192.

Jantz, R.K. & Klawiller, K. 1985. Early childhood/ elementary social studies: A review of research in social studies education: 1976-83. Review of Research in Social Studies Education: 1976-83. Bulletin 75. W.B. Stanley, Ed. Washington, D.C: National Council for the Social Studies. 65-121.

Leming, J.S. 1984. Curricular effectiveness in moral/ values education: A review of research. Journal of Moral Education, 10. 147-164.

Leming, J.S. 1985. Research on social studies curriculum and instruction. Interventions and outcomes in the socio-moral domain. Review of Research in Social Studies Education: 1976-83. Bulletin 75. W.B. Stanley, Ed. Washington, D.C: National Council for the Social Studies. 123-213.

Mayer, R. 1975. Information processing variables in learning to solve problems. Review of Educational Research, 45, 525-541.

Mayer, R. 1979. Twenty years of research on advance organizers: Assimilation theory still the best predictor. Instructional Science, 8, 133-167.

Massiales, B. and Smith, F. (Eds.). Current Research in Social Studies, Bulletin - Indiana University School of Education, 40, 2 (March 1964).

Medley, D. 1982. Teacher Effectiveness. Encyclopedia of Educational Research. H. Mitzel, Ed. New York: Free Press. 1894-1903.

Nelson, J.L. & Shaver, J.P. 1985. On research in social education. Review of Research in Social Studies Education. Bulletin 75. W.B. Stanley, Ed. Washington, D.C.: National Council for the Social Studies. 401-433.

Rosenshine, B.V. 1979. Content, time, and direct instruction. Research on Teaching, Concepts, Findings, and Implications. P.L. Peterson & H.J. Walberg, Eds. Berkeley: McCutcheon.

Rosenshine, B.V. & Furst. 1973. The use of direct observation to study teaching. Second Handbook of Research on Teaching. R. Travers, Ed. Chicago: Rand McNally.

Sharan, S. 1980. Cooperative learning in small groups: Recent methods and effectiveness of achievement, attitudes, and ethnic relations. Review of Educational Research, 50, 241-271.

Shaver, J.P., Davis, O.L., & Helburn, S.W. 1979. An Interpretative Report on the Status of Pre Collegiate Social Studies Education Based on Three NSF-Funded Studies. Washington, D.C: National Science Foundation.

Stanley, W.B. Ed. 1985. Review of Research in Social Studies: 1976-83. Washington, D.C: National Council for the Social Studies.

Tennyson, R. & Park, O. 1980. The teaching of concepts: A review of instructional design research literature. Review of Educational Research, 50, 55-70.

Tobias, S. 1982. When do instructional methods make a difference? Educational Researcher, 11, 4-9.

U.S. Office of Educational Research and Improvement. 1988. Youth Indicators 1988: Trends in the Well-Being of American Youth. Washington, D.C.: U.S. Department of Education.

70

Wallen, N.E. & Frankel, J.R. 1988. An analysis of social studies research over an eight year period. Theory and Research in Social Education, 16, 1-22.

Weinstein, C.E. 1978. Elaboration skills as a learning strategy. Learning Strategies. H.F. O'Neil, Jr. Ed. New York: Academic Press.

White, R. 1973. Research into learning hierarchies. Review of Educational Research, 43, 361-375.

Research Report

Getting Ready

classroom

Where Imagination Becomes Reality

Social Studies Educators

CHAPTER V

SOCIAL STUDIES METHODS, TECHNIQUES, AND STRATEGIES

OBJECTIVE: Having read this chapter you should be able to compare and contrast the differences between methods, techniques, and strategies in a class discussion, and identify in writing ten teaching techniques and the conditions under which the techniques are most likely to be successfully applied to effective teaching practices.

> Wisdom is knowing what to do next,
> virtue is doing it.
> David Jordan

What Does Research on Learning, Remembering, and Effective Teaching Practices Suggest about Methods, Techniques, and Strategies of Teaching?

AN EXCITING TEACHING RESOURCE

Do you remember from Chapter IV that most research studies support the proposition that students learn better--learn faster, remember more, and derive greater enjoyment--when they are actively involved in learning? It is for this reason that methods courses begin with the assumption that methods, techniques, and strategies should emphasize active learning with the aim of focusing and retaining students' attention through effective teaching practices.

What's in it for you

Even if the summary on research studies was unconvincing, you know from personal experiences that active involvement in what you are doing is likely to help you focus attention and remember. All students in a class are not usually actively involved with each activity because of different styles of learning. Suppose you organize the class into small groups. Out of a class of thirty, twenty might actively participate while ten may be passive, indifferent, about the grouping. As you already know, at any given moment during a lecture, only ten percent of the class is actively, thoughtfully listening. Students are skilled at taking notes, staring at you, appearing to be actively involved when, in fact, their minds are somewhere else. Students are tuning in and out of the lecture from moment to moment, thus you can never be quite sure which ten percent of the students actually heard and understood what you were trying to say.

What's in it for us

The point is teachers need to use a variety of techniques in the hope of focusing and retaining students' attention. Expect during an average class period, 55 minutes, that at least three different techniques are needed to keep active attention. One last thought: students are not equally attracted to each technique. Some respond to debate, others would dislike debate. Some enjoy and actively watch films, some sleep (are passive) through films. Five or six students might actively participate in class discussion while twenty-five sit silent and passive. Lecturing is a favorite for perhaps ten percent. Use a variety of techniques. A variety will increase chances of reaching a greater number of students and improve their quality time on task. It is for this reason that you should identify a method and a variety of techniques which you plan as a strategy to actively involve all students.

Coming Events

Before diving into the definition of method, realize that authors may have different definitions of method, technique and strategy. The fact that these definitions may differ because they reflect different fields of study should not cause you great concern. What you should focus on is the relationship between method (overall approach), techniques (activities performed in class), and strategies (the order in which the activities are carried out in class). Why discuss methods, techniques, and strategies? Because they describe how a lesson is going to be taught starting from the general method to the specific techniques as part of a strategy that is called planning. In short, method, technique, and strategy describe what the class will do and how it is going to be done.

What Is a Method? Transmission or Problem-Solving?

Point of View

Some authorities believe there are only two general methods of social studies teaching. One method centers around transmission, meaning to hand down or impart facts, concepts and generalizations; and the second is concerned with problem-solving (reasoning), meaning to examine, investigate, and explore facts, concepts, and generalizations. A teacher whose intention is to impart information directly to students is using the transmission method. Teachers who wish students to deal with problems and think deductively or inductively about solutions to those problems are employing the problem-solving method. Very simply, teachers tend to emphasize one or the other of these two methods--although, of course, teachers at times use a mixture of both. Generally speaking, teachers who lecture and have recitation and discussion most all the time tend toward the Citizenship Transmission Tradition and favor the transmission method. Those who emphasize discovery and reflective inquiry favor a problem-solving method consistent with the Social Science and Reflective Inquiry Traditions.

Method is defined as the systematic way teachers generally approach their teaching. The method is how the teacher intends to proceed with the lesson. One teacher intends to present information while another teaching the same lesson intends the

lesson to be problem-solving where the student is required to
work on a problem. One teacher might plan a lecture over the
content of the text, the other might plan projects in which the
students are required to be self-directed problem-solvers. So,
if a method is how a teacher generally intends to systematically
approach the lesson, what is a teaching technique?

What Is a Technique?

Often method and technique are thought to be the same.
However, methods and techniques are not the same. The general
approach of teachers--the way they systematically organize
themselves to teach--is what is meant by method. Teachers select
specific teaching techniques that direct how the method will be
achieved. (see Figure 1).

(Figure 1)

METHOD > TECHNIQUE

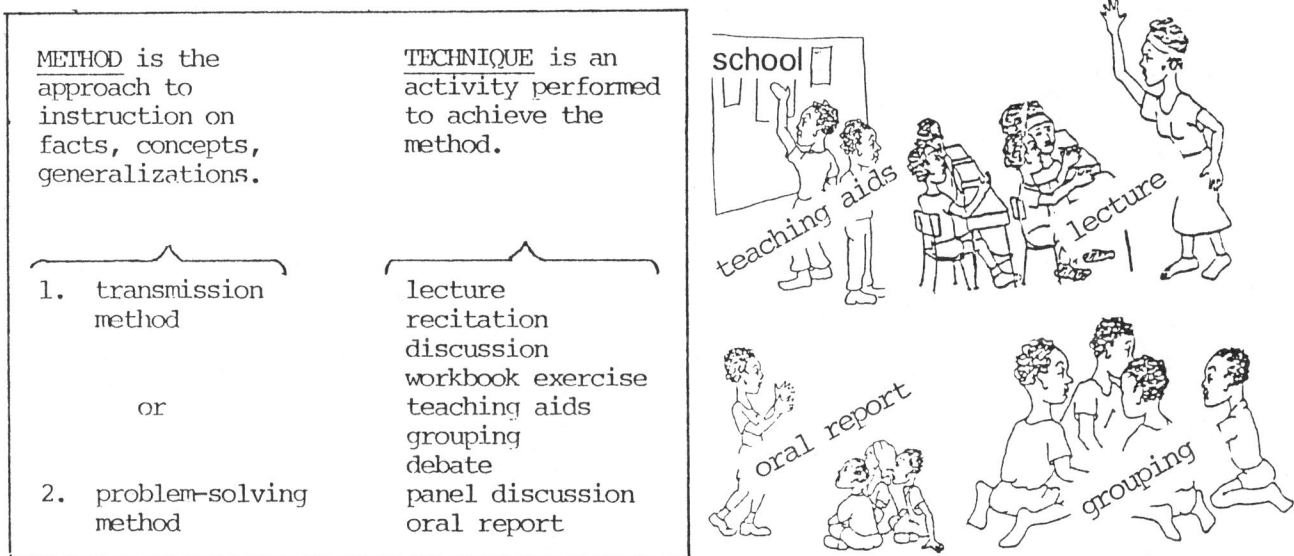

METHOD is the approach to instruction on facts, concepts, generalizations.	TECHNIQUE is an activity performed to achieve the method.
1. transmission method or 2. problem-solving method	lecture recitation discussion workbook exercise teaching aids grouping debate panel discussion oral report

Participation

For example, a method is problem-solving; techniques to
achieve the method might call for participation in projects,
grouping, role-playing, or simulation. If the method is
transmission, then the techniques might be lecturing and
recitation or workbook exercises. Another way of expressing the
relationship between method and technique is to ask the question,
"What do you want to do, what is your intent?" Answer, "I want
to cover the content in the chapter (transmission)."
"Specifically how are you going to go over the chapter?" Answer,
"By the techniques of lecture and recitation." Now, specifically
I know your method which is transmission and your teaching
techniques, lecture and recitation.

Test Your Understanding of Method

classroom

Suppose you were intending to plan a role-playing/simulation which asked students to work on social/personal problems.
What is your method? Circle either
TRANSMISSION or PROBLEM-SOLVING.
Did you circle problem-solving?
Why?_____

_____

Suppose your method was to transmit information about the war of 1812.
What techniques are you likely to use?
(Respond here.)_____

_____

Did you name techniques such as lecture, recitation, perhaps a workbook exercise?

ORAL REPORTS

In summary, method refers to the systematic approach to the lesson, and essentially there are two: transmission and problem-solving. Technique (of which there are many) is concerned with ways of achieving the method.

What Is a Strategy?

Increasingly teachers talk about strategies, a term popularized by the military which suggests the plan for winning a battle--in this case the classroom. How does strategy relate to method and technique? Very simply, strategy refers to sequencing (organizing) a given selection of techniques. (see Figure 2).

(Figure 2)

TECHNIQUE > STRATEGY

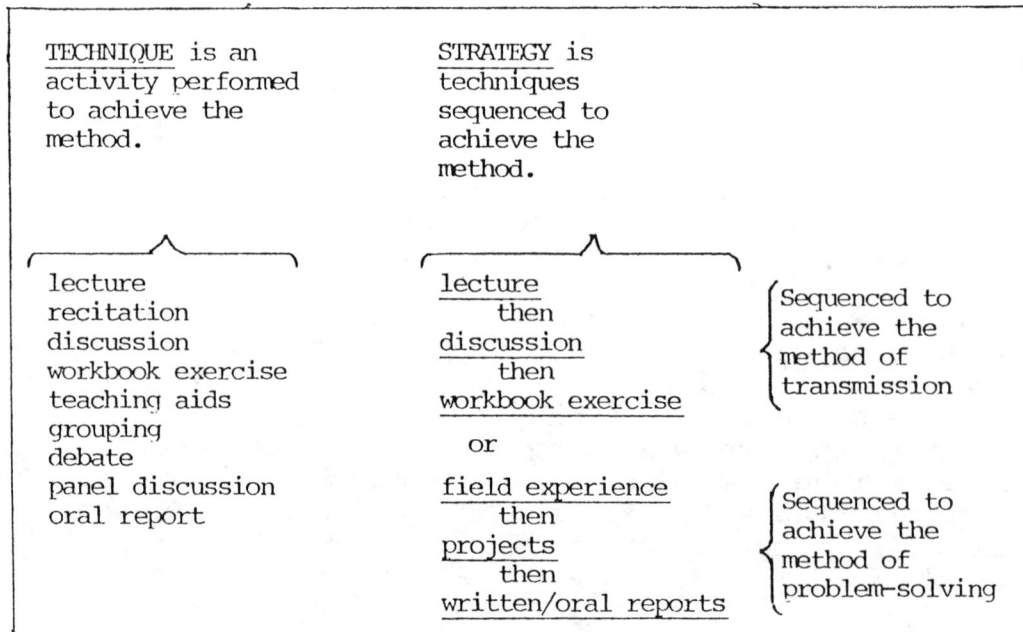

TECHNIQUE is an activity performed to achieve the method.

STRATEGY is techniques sequenced to achieve the method.

lecture
recitation
discussion
workbook exercise
teaching aids
grouping
debate
panel discussion
oral report

lecture
  then
discussion
  then
workbook exercise

or

field experience
  then
projects
  then
written/oral reports

Sequenced to achieve the method of transmission

Sequenced to achieve the method of problem-solving

For example, if one were to select such teaching techniques as introductory lecture, grouping, and panel discussion, these techniques sequenced one after the other are called a strategy. To summarize, you know what a method is--systematic approach to a lesson. The lesson would start with techniques. For example, (1) an introductory lecture is followed by, (2) small group discussion, and (3) panel discussion. What is that sequencing of techniques called? It is called a teaching strategy. Strategy is simply the way techniques are sequenced (organized) to accomplish the method. If you have read the author's curriculum series, either _Elementary and Junior High/Middle School Social Studies Curriculum, Activities and Materials_ or _Secondary Social Studies Curriculum, Activities and Materials_, then the sequenced activities in those books could be defined as strategies. Each activity may well include a number of techniques; i.e., reading, reporting, grouping, researching. You could conclude that the illustrative, sequenced activities found later in this chapter are examples of strategies. To check your understanding of how techniques and strategies are related to method, see Figure 3 below entitled "Method > Technique > Strategy."

(Figure 3)

METHOD > TECHNIQUE > STRATEGY

Point of View

METHOD is the approach to instruction on facts, concepts, generalizations.

TECHNIQUE is an activity performed to achieve the method.

STRATEGY is techniques sequenced to achieve the method.

1. transmission method

or

2. problem-solving method

lecture
recitation
discussion
workbook exercise
teaching aids
grouping
debate
panel discussion
oral report

lecture
then
discussion
then
workbook exercise

or

field experience
then
projects
then
written/oral reports

Sequenced to achieve the method of transmission

Sequenced to achieve the method of problem-solving

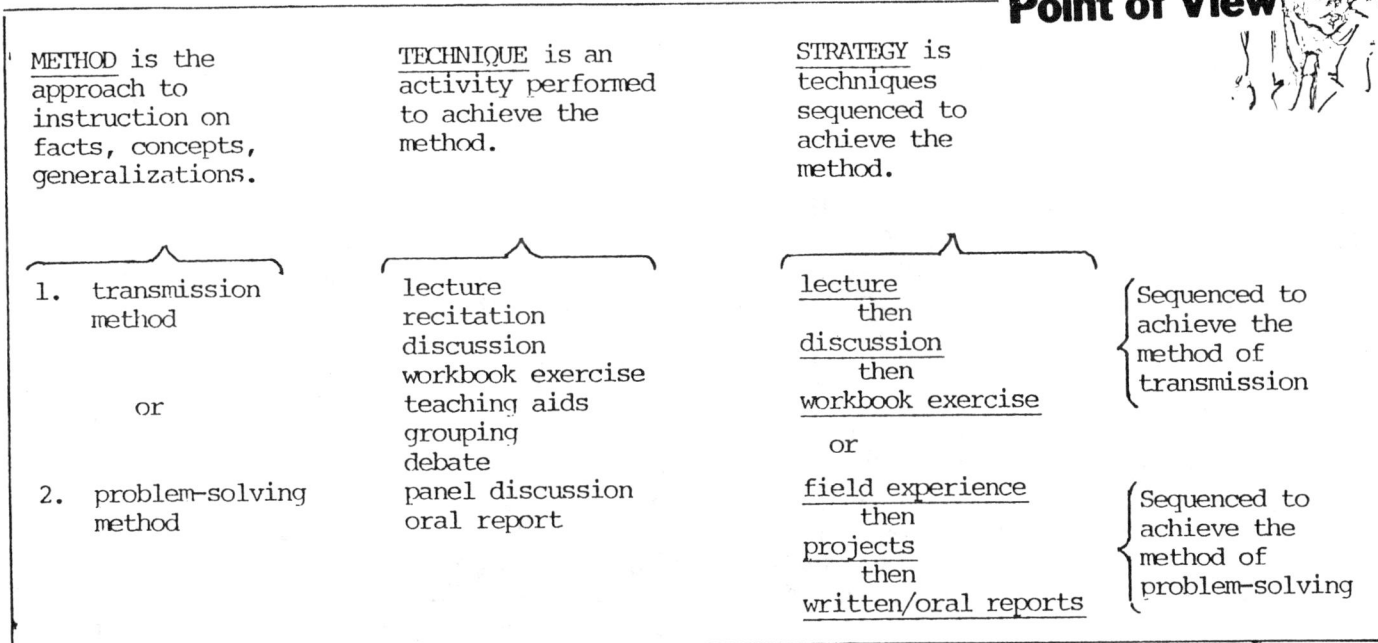

Summary and Conclusion on Definition of Method, Technique, and Strategy

It is not the case that social studies is inherently more passive than other subjects. Nevertheless, it is the case that many students complain, as you are well aware from reading Chapter I, about how uninteresting, dull, lifeless, and obscure social studies can be. If all you use is one or two techniques, be prepared to face students who are silent, passive, bored, and

uncooperative, attitudes which were problems from Chapter I. If, however, you wish to reach a greater number of students, be prepared to plan a strategy using a variety of techniques. No one can tell you what techniques you must use. But we do insist that whatever techniques you select should emphasize active participation. Please understand this: any given technique may be either passive or active. For example, lectures, grouping, oral reports, field trips, debates, panel discussions, simulations, or computer assisted instruction may be either active or passive, depending on whether students are focused and spend quality time on the lesson. In summary, methods, techniques and strategies are ways of translating (planning the use of) facts, concepts, and generalizations. Need we say as a final comment, overcoming problems of teaching social studies starts with research on effective teaching practices but ends with the practical application of the different methods, techniques and strategies. Think about it!

TEACHING TECHNIQUES:
The Building Blocks of Effective Teaching Practices

A few suggestions

Are you persuaded that students need to focus attention, and the means of focusing attention are methods, techniques, and strategies? Plan an approach (method) either transmission or problem-solving, then sequence the techniques to achieve active learning. Sounds easy enough to plan active learning, yet we know that the traditional teaching of social studies is passive. There are liter- ally hundreds of different teaching tech- niques. Teachers are told to use their own imaginations to think up interesting methods, techniques, and strategies. Many teachers, when asked to recall different techniques, find difficulty in recalling more than a few. Suf- fice it to say that social studies teachers gen- erally have a limited recall of specific techniques, even though they have read about hundreds of them, and their classrooms often remain passive environments.

Suppose you were teaching the topic "Presidential Elections" and you were asked to list at least ten different techniques that might be used to teach this topic. Could you list ten techniques? It is not unusual for social studies teachers to list no more than perhaps two or three. Elementary teachers are usually better at identifying techniques than secondary teachers simply because they are more interested in child development, whereas secondary teachers usually are interested in transmitting their content. A conclusion--that elementary and junior high/middle school teachers tend to know a greater variety of techniques than do senior high teachers--is probably true. This further suggests that there tends to be more active learning in elementary and middle school and more passive learning in senior high school. Though there are hundreds of techniques, this fact is meaningless if only a few can be recalled and fewer applied in the classroom. The students bitterly complained about social studies in Chapter I. In many cases those complaints are legitimate as can be witnessed in classrooms throughout the United States. A good place to begin to deal with those complaints is by identifying and applying different techniques.

150 Teaching Techniques

Setting the standard for success.

Following are 150 teaching techniques, listed not in any order or sequence, but just as they came to mind. This list is a demonstration that many techniques do, in fact, exist. You are not expected to remember 150 techniques, but ten basic techniques will be identified and you should be expected to recall and practice them. The following list should stand as a reference. Keep in mind that you ought to try at least three per class period and as many different techniques as possible during the school year. You are in the thinking business. Motivating thinking is your everyday objective, a difficult, frustrating, and occasionally rewarding challenge. The ten types of techniques underlined in this list will be examined in depth and illustrated at different grade levels in the final part of this chapter.

How're you going to do it?

1.   **Lecture** by teacher (and what else can you do!)
2.   **Class discussion** conducted by teacher (and what else!)

3.   **Recitation** oral questions by teacher answered orally by students (then what!)
4.   Discussion groups conducted by selected student chairpersons (yes, and what else!)
5.   Lecture-demonstration by teacher (and then what 145 other techniques!)
6.   Lecture-demonstration by another instructor(s) from a special field (guest speaker)

7.   Presentation by a panel of instructors or students
8.   Presentations by student panels from the class: class invited to participate
9.   Student reports by individuals
10. Student-group reports by committees from the class
11. **Debates** (informal) on current issues by students from class

12. Class discussions conducted by a student or student committee
13. Forums
14. Bulletin boards

15. **Small groups such as task- oriented, discussion, Socratic**
16. Choral speaking

17. Collecting
18. Textbook assignments
19. Reading assignments in journals, monographs, etc.
20. Reading assignments in supplementary books
21. Assignment to outline portions of the textbook
22. Assignment to outline certain supplementary readings
23. **Debates (formal)**

24. Crossword puzzles
25. Cooking foods of places studied
26. Construction of vocabulary lists
27. Vocabulary drills
28. Diaries
29. Dances of places or periods studied
30. Construction of summaries by students
31. Dressing dolls
32. Required term paper
33. **Panel discussion**

34. Biographical reports given by students
35. Reports on published research studies and experiments by students
36. Library research on topics or problems

37. Written book reports by students
38. Flags
39. Jigsaw puzzle maps

40. Hall of Fame by topic or era (military or political leaders, heroes)

Making History SOCIAL STUDIES

41. Flannel boards
42. Use of pretest
43. Gaming and simulation

44. Flash cards
45. Flowcharts
46. Interviews
47. Maps, transparencies, globes
48. Mobiles

49. Audio-tutorial lessons (individualized instruction)
50. Models

51. Music

52. Field trips
53. Drama, role-playing

54. Open textbook study
55. Committee projects--small groups
56. Notebook
57. Murals and montages
58. Class projects
59. Individual projects
60. Quizdown gaming

61. Modeling in various media
62. Pen pals
63. Photographs
64. Laboratory experiments performed by more than two students working together
65. Use of dramatization, skits, plays
66. Student construction of diagrams, charts, or graphs
67. Making of posters by students
68. Students drawing pictures or cartoons to vividly portray principles or facts

69. Problem-solving or case studies
70. Puppets
71. Use of chalkboard by instructor as aid in teaching

72. Use of diagrams, tables, graphs, and charts by instructor in teaching
73. Use of exhibits and displays by instructor
74. Reproductions
75. Construction of exhibits and displays by students

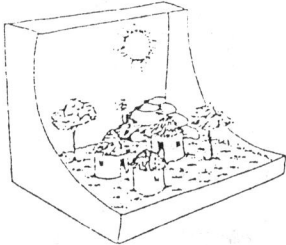

76. Use of slides
77. Use of filmstrips
78. Use of motion pictures, educational films, videotapes
79. Use of theater motion pictures
80. Use of recordings
81. Use of radio programs
82. Use of television
83. **Role-playing**

84. Sand tables

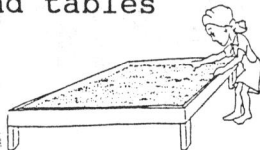

85. School affiliations
86. Verbal illustrations: use of anecdotes and parables to illustrate
87. Service projects
88. Stamps, coins, and other hobbies

89. Use of community or local resources

90. Story telling
91. Surveys
92. Tutorial: students assigned to other students for assistance, peer teaching
93. Coaching: special assistance provided for students having difficulty in the course
94. **Oral reports**

95. Word association activity
96. Workbooks
97. Using case studies reported in literature to illustrate psychological principles and facts
98. Construction of scrapbooks
99. Applying simple statistical techniques to class data
100. Time lines
101. "Group dynamics" techniques

102. Units of instruction organized by topics
103. Non-directive techniques applied to the classroom
104. Supervised study during class period

105. Use of sociometric text to make sociometric analysis of class

106. **Use of technology and instructional resources**

107. Open textbook tests, take home tests
108. Put idea into picture
109. Write a caption for chart, picture, cartoon

110. Reading aloud
111. Differentiated assignment and homework
112. Telling about a trip
113. Mock convention
114. Filling out forms (income tax, checks)
115. Prepare editorial for school paper
116. Attend council meeting, school board meeting
117. Exchanging "things"
118. Making announcements
119. Taking part (community elections)
120. Playing music from other countries or times

121. Studying local history
122. Compile list of older citizens as resource people
123. Students from abroad (exchange students)

124. Obtain free and low-cost materials
125. Collect old magazines

126. Collect colored slides
127. Visit an "ethnic" restaurant
128. Specialize in one country

129. Follow a world leader (in the media)
130. Visit an employment agency

131. Start a campaign

132. Conduct a series
133. Investigate a life
134. Assist an immigrant

135. Volunteer (tutoring, hospital)
136. Prepare an exhibit
137. Detect propaganda
138. Join an organization
139. Collect money for a cause

140. Elect a "Hall of Fame" for males

141. Elect a "Hall of Fame" for females
142. Construct a salt map
143. **Construct a drama**
144. Prepare presentation for senior citizen group
145. Invite senior citizen(s) to present local history to class including displaying artifacts (clothing, tools, objects, etc.)
146. Prepare mock newspaper on specific topic or era

147. Draw a giant map on floor of classroom
148. Research local archaeological site
149. Exchange program with schools from different parts of the state
150. In **brainstorming small group,** students identify a list of techniques and strategies that best fit their class

Use This Now

Check Your Understanding of Method, Technique, and Strategy

Instructions: Examine the following list of items. Label each item either M for method, T for technique, or S for strategy. When you have finished, check your answers below.

1. _____ Vocabulary drill
2. _____ Film followed by discussion and lecture
3. _____ Problem-solving by discovery
4. _____ Field trip
5. _____ Reading aloud
6. _____ Mock convention with grouping and oral reports

Correct answers: 1-T, 2-S, 3-M, 4-T, 5-T, 6-S

Instructions: Select from the list of 150 techniques three techniques and sequence into a strategy.
For example: FLAGS with FLANNEL BOARD with FLASH CARDS.
Explain how you would sequence the three techniques. For example, have students make FLAGS of countries studied on map exercise, put these flags on FLASH CARDS and arrange on FLANNEL BOARD. Now it is your turn:
Name the three techniques: _____
    (See list of 150.)   _____
                                   _____

Explain how you would sequence these techniques in a strategy to teach lesson:
_____

_____

_____

Ten Basic Techniques You Ought to Know

If you are a professional

From the list of 150 techniques ten have been identified that are "basic," that is, ten techniques which are most likely to offer a variety of ways to teach and can be easily sequenced into a strategy. The three most popular techniques experienced throughout your formal school and college education are lecturing, recitation and discussion. But can you distinguish recitation from discussion? There is a difference. Recitation is the oral delivery of memorized materials normally addressed to the teacher, whereas discussion is a purposeful consideration of a topic by class members addressed to other class members and the teacher. Do you identify the difference between recitation and discussion? For example, a recitation is when the teacher asks the class, "What were the three major reasons for America entering World War I?" The only way to answer that question is to have read the text and memorized the three reasons. Reciting the reasons is called recitation.

Though lecturing, recitation and discussion are not naturally passive, they are so often remembered and used by teachers that through repetition (used every day) they become passive for students, but then this is true for any technique when overused. Besides the well-known lecturing, recitation, and discussion techniques, the seven additional techniques you ought to review are grouping, drama/role-playing, oral report, debate, panel discussion, game/simulation and the application of technology and instructional resources.[1]

Alternatives

Criteria for Using Active Learning Techniques

Each of the ten techniques will require planning for their proper application. Before planning to use techniques, consider the following questions:

Of what value is this activity to your students? For example, is this activity intended to develop the ability to gain knowledge, process information, identify values and beliefs and/or participate?

What specific procedures have you developed for carrying out this activity? For example, what rules have you set up for debate? What procedures have you announced for holding an effective panel discussion? What rules have you set up for oral reports?

Can you identify common mistakes? For example, a common mistake with grouping is that groups are not sure what they are supposed to do. Another common mistake is that students are not provided time limits for oral reports, and quizdowns do not fulfill their promise if questioning is not kept at a fast pace.

What criteria have you developed for evaluating the students' performance? If you are to evaluate the students' performance you must develop a clear set of criteria that both you and the students understand. What are the ingredients of a good oral report? By what criteria are you going to evaluate a panel discussion? How will you know that a grouping is successful? How will you evaluate the quality of a drama?

> You will find examples of how to plan a lesson using the techniques mentioned in this chapter and in Chapter XIV called "Organizing to Teach: Unit and Daily Lesson Planning."

Effective Teaching Practices Require Skill Development

It seems so natural, logical, and reasonable, given (a) students' objections to social studies and (b) research on effective teaching, for teachers to use a variety of different techniques. Why is it that many teachers do not use a variety of techniques? The answer is complex, but a major reason is techniques generally require skill development. In short, research requires research skills, reading requires reading skills, writing requires writing skills, oral reports require speaking skills. If the students do not have the skills and the teacher is unwilling to develop the skills, then the technique will not work. The truth is lecture, recitation and discussion usually do not require much skill development, and that is one of the major reasons they are the most widely practiced teaching techniques. In brief, they are easy to use--user friendly.

SKILL DEVELOPMENT

What teachers discover as they try new techniques is that students do not have the skills and attitudes necessary to make the techniques work. Grouping, debates, panels, and projects do not normally work unless students have reading, research, and oral presentation skills. Elementary teachers expect to develop the students' skills, but this is not equally true for all junior high/middle school and secondary teachers who expect to apply the technique but not teach the skills necessary for its successful use. If as a teacher your interest is rooted in covering historical events, and you can find no time to develop the skills of reading comprehension, oral communication, writing, and researching, then you ought not to use active learning techniques because they will not be successful for you or your students. If on the other hand, you develop a plan throughout the school year to improve students' oral, written, and research skills, then your students will be prepared to participate in active learning techniques and activities. Realize that the successful practice of teaching techniques requires a sufficient level of student skill development. If the technique does not work it probably means the students are not sufficiently skilled. Do not abandon the technique, but develop the skills necessary to use the technique. In short, effective teaching techniques normally require skill development in reading, writing, speaking, researching, and studying. These skills will be discussed in following chapters.

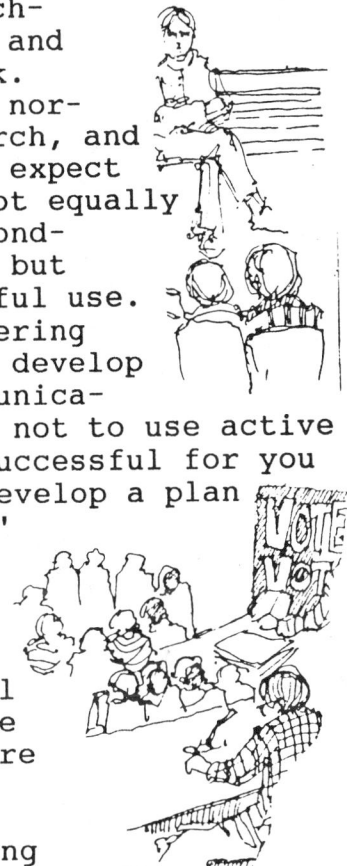

1. LECTURING

You hardly need an introduction to lecturing having experienced this technique most of your life. However, because you have experienced it often does not mean that the lectures were well-planned, and skillfully presented. We have never said that lecturing is not an important technique; it is obviously one of the most important, and actually you will use this technique often to introduce, summarize, explain, share and provide

information. Of course, we are talking about effective lecturing
that focuses attention. Do you remember the research in Chapter
IV that said "we learn and remember 10%
of what we hear?" We believe that a
well-planned and skillfully presented
lecture can be an exciting learning
experience. Lecturing should fit
effective teaching practices by focusing
students' attention. The following are
guidelines for the effective use of
lecturing.

If it's to be heard but not listened to

1.   Use lecture to focus attention: introduce a lesson,
summarize a discussion or lesson, explain an activity. When you
plan a lecture, you should prepare an introduction that will
"grab" students' attention. When you end a lecture or lesson, a
brief summarization will focus attention on the main points of
the lesson. (See Chapter XV on "Practice Teaching," the section
on "Micropeer-Teaching," for the skill of introducing a lesson
and the skill of lesson closure.)

2.   A lecture is a quick way to give information, but
not information students can get from their textbook,
reading materials, or student handouts. Use a lecture to
impart new information. As already noted in Chapter IV,
research indicates that students will learn and remember
more of what they see than what they hear. Use teaching
aids with the lecture.

3.   Keep lecturing to a minimum and combine it with
other active teaching techniques in a single class
period. Two or three different teaching techniques in a
class period will prolong students' attention and
increase quality time on task. Several short lectures
combined with other teaching techniques is an effective use of
lecture.

4.   Based on the average attention span of students, lectures
should last only 5-10 minutes for elementary students, 15 minutes
for junior high/middle school, and no more than
20 minutes for senior high. The longer you talk,
the less students will listen.

SOCIAL STUDIES

GEOGRAPHY

5.   Lecture from notes, do not read a prepared
"script." An outline of the main points of
your lecture written on the board, overhead
projector, or in a handout will help students
focus as you lecture. A lecture interspersed
with higher level, thought-provoking questions
will also encourage students to focus attention and increase learning and remembering.
(See Chapter VI on "Questioning" for the skill of asking
different levels of questions.)

2/3. **RECITATION AND DISCUSSION**   # Discussion

Recitation and discussion both engage the class but for different purposes. As in the case of lecturing, we are not talking about just any kind of discussion. We are talking about effective use of the discussion technique to improve your students' learning and remembering. Do you recall in Chapter IV the research on effective teaching which states that "we learn 40% of what we discuss with others?" Of course, that is 40% if the members of the class participate. If only two students are actively discussing with the teacher and the other members of the class are passive and indifferent, then only two students may be getting full benefit from the discussion. On the next page guidelines will be offered for the practice of discussion techniques, but first you are to reflect on your own experience by responding to the following questions.

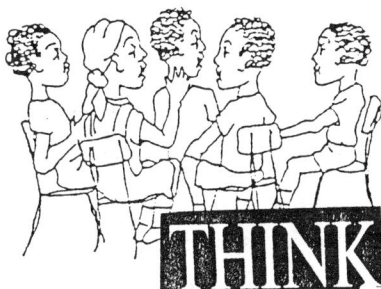

Discussion Response Questions

Write your response on the lines:
1.   What would be the reasons for holding a
      social studies discussion?

      _____
      _____

2.   What rules would you establish before
      starting the discussion?

      _____

3.   How would you arrange the student
      seating?

      _____

4.   Should participation be forced?

      _____

5.   How would you encourage participation?

      _____
      _____

6.   How would you discourage one or two
      students from dominating the discussion?

      _____
      _____
      _____

Instructions: In a class discussion go over your responses to the questions you have just written on the exercise above with other members of the class. There are no right answers, but there are some answers that are more effective than others. To help you think about some effective ways to develop successful recitation and discussion techniques we offer the following guidelines.

about Learning

The teacher should, according to the research studies in Chapter IV:

1.   Clearly identify the purposes/objectives for the discussion; in short, be sure there is a point to the discussion and students know what you want, i.e., "The lesson we are going to discuss is on the Emancipation Proclamation."

2.   Suggest and guide the development of a topic to be discussed, i.e., "First identify the conditions in the South that created a demand for the Emancipation Proclamation."

3.   Assist students in maximum participation in the discussion. Be sure to include all students in the class by the skillful use of different levels of questions. (See Chapter VI on "Questioning" for the skill of asking different levels of questions.)

4.   Accept student contributions as worthwhile no matter how limited the value may be. In fact, encourage students' questions for this is one of the best techniques to encourage focused, prolonged attention.

5.   Suggest appropriate time schedules, how long the discussion will continue, i.e., "We will discuss the reasons for the Emancipation Proclamation for five more minutes."

6.   Provide summary remarks or conclusions based on what students have discussed. (See Chapter XV on "Practice Teaching," the section on "Micropeer-Teaching," for a discussion on the skill of lesson closure.)

7.   Evaluate the discussion activity--what went well and what needs to be improved, i.e., how many students participated? Do you believe you are getting 40% learning and remembering that a discussion is intended to achieve, or does the participation suggest more like 10%? Do your discussions often become lectures? Was it actually your intention to lecture rather than have a discussion?

4.   GROUPING   Introduction to

Grouping has become popular because this technique emphasizes active student participation. Participation in small group discussion may help students' learning and remembering. It is difficult for a teacher with a large class to provide an opportunity for every student to participate during each class period. Grouping offers one technique by which students in groups participate among themselves and in so doing become actively involved in class work. Students reluctant to participate in class recitation or discussion can be encouraged to be involved in small group discussions.

The most recent development in grouping has been the identification of at least five different types of groups for instructional purposes. The following five types illustrate the different purposes and guidelines for organizing small groups. Recommendation: provide a copy of the five following types of groups to your class at the beginning of the year. The guidelines will explain what the students are expected to do in a particular type of small group. This will save you from explaining each time how the group is to function.

Grouping Purposes and Guidelines

1. **Task-Oriented** Small Group
Purpose: to bring the various members of the small group together to focus on a specific project or proposal.
Guidelines: (a) Clearly define your task so that all members understand and agree. (b) Sharply delineate roles and assignments for the individual members of the group. (c) Set a time limit such as "This task should be completed in 15 minutes."

2. **Brainstorming** Small Group
Purpose: to bring the various members of the small group together to discuss freely and uninhibitedly a topic which is problem centered or solution centered.
Guidelines: (a) The ideal number for a "brainstorming" small group is between eight and twelve. (b) The topic should be relatively simple, familiar, and talkable. (c) Criticism is ruled out; judgment of ideas is done at a later time. (d) Quantity of participation is wanted. (e) Set a time limit.

3. **Tutorial** Small Group
Purpose: to emphasize individual instruction, usually of a remedial nature, or to evaluate an independent study project.
Guidelines: (a) Remedial work should be of a type that is general enough to benefit all members of a small group. (b) The emphasis is on the teacher dealing with each member of the group in turn. (c) No attempt is made here for group dynamics and interaction between students. Useful when student needs special attention after an absence.

4.   Discussion Small Group

Purpose: to encourage free and uninhibited discussion by students of a topic which has some previous structure and relevance to material under consideration.
Guidelines: (a) Structure of topic should be presented to students prior to their coming to class.
(b) The teacher acts primarily as an interested observer--listens attentively, notices who participates, watches for student reaction. (c) Set a time limit such as, "Your group discussion should last no more than 30 minutes."

5.   Socratic Small Group

Purpose: to bring students and instructor(s) together to discuss a problem posed by the teacher for which an answer can best be determined through the open and honest exchange of informed opinion.
Guidelines: (a) Begins in stage 1 with the teacher challenging, disturbing, demanding definitions, driving discussants back into a corner to examine their prejudices, to defend their positions.
(b) During stage 2 the teacher does a lot of good hard listening, then becomes a leader and participant--probing, directing, stimulating, enticing, responding, challenging, and synthesizing--which is the purpose of a Socratic discussion.

we have to create

Successful Grouping

Grouping often fails when students do not know what to do in their groups which means the group is not focusing on the task at hand. How do you focus the students' attention to achieve quality time on task?

```
Keys to Successful Grouping

1.    How do you get students into groups?  Some
suggestions:  (a) arbitrarily assign; (b) do it by
interest groups, i.e., "All those studying World
War I meet over here."  (c) when students enter class,
hand students a piece of colored paper.  Groups are
determined by the colored paper, i.e., "All greens meet
by the window."  (d) have students count off by
number of groups desired, "All ones are in the back
corner of the room."

2.    Does the group need a leader?  Either appoint
a leader or have group select a leader if needed.

3.    Will there be a report from the group?  Who will
give a report?  Do notes need to be taken?  Who will
take notes?  Either you or the group will make these
decisions.

4.    Set a time limit if that is appropriate.  You or
the class should determine how long it will take to
accomplish the purpose of the grouping.  Groups will
fill whatever time you give them.  Suppose the task
could be done in ten minutes--if you give them no
limit, they might take the whole class period and
still not be done.  The class that takes an hour to
do what could be done in ten minutes is not
practicing quality time on task.

5.    Evaluation.  A common complaint is a few
students do most of the work.  The other group members
are passive and unfocused.  Also, not all students
work well in or enjoy grouping.  There is a need for
evaluating what is happening and what students think
about grouping.  Be sure the class knows that you
will be asking for an evaluation that identifies who
did not contribute and for students' attitudes about
grouping.  Be sure to see "Evaluation of Self and
Group" at the end of this section.

            Be sure to apply these five
            key ideas about grouping to
            the following activities that
            illustrate grouping techniques.
```

Activities/Strategies that Illustrate Grouping Techniques

To know the names of the five different types of small group organization and keys to successful grouping is not necessarily to know how to use these small groups in classroom activities.

92

The following activities illustrate types of grouping and an evaluation form used in both elementary and secondary schools.

1. Activity for Elementary
Objective: Use task-oriented small group technique to develop the processing skill of classifying and categorizing.

WHAT WE NEED

when: three class periods

what: magazines, newspapers, brochures, etc.

how: Divide the class into task-oriented small groups of four or five students each. Have each group cut out pictures of things students think are necessary in order to live. Groups should place similar things (i.e., clothing) in paper folders (first class period). Have one folder labeled "Group Problems" for pictures that do not easily fit into a category such as shelter, heat, health, food.

Have a class discussion. Each group shows its folders to the entire class. Do other groups have folders of similar categories? Put similar pictures from all the groups together and label each category, i.e., clothing, food, tools. Then have each group look at its problem pictures, such as television set, car, electrical appliances, etc. (second class period). Groups should discuss each problem picture to see if it fits a category, needs a new category, or if the item is not necessary (third class period).
Teacher should help groups as they work.

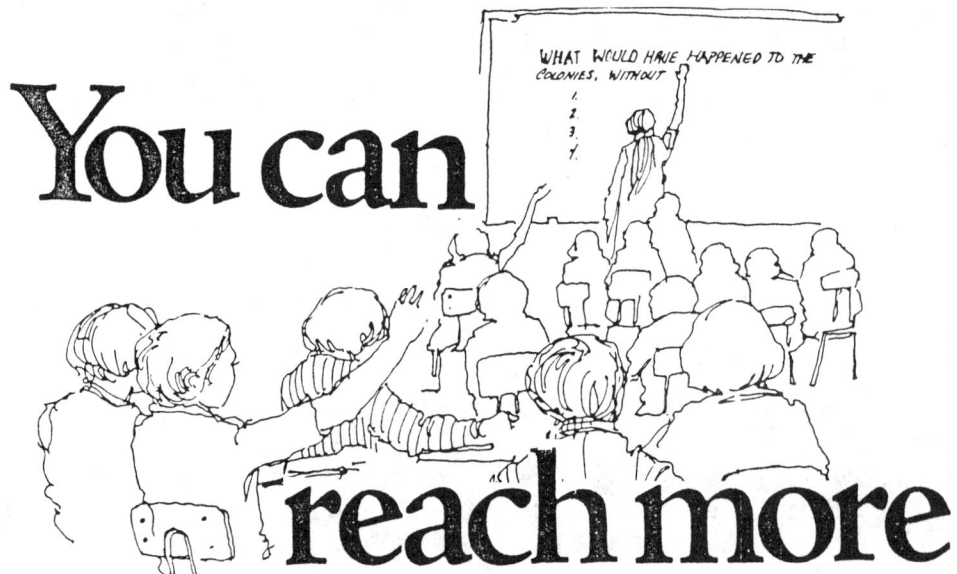

You can reach more

2. Activity for Junior High/Middle School
Objective: Use brainstorming small group technique to identify values and cultural characteristics of contemporary society, and also practice categorizing.

IN THE YEAR 2020

when: one week

what: waterproof container (time capsule)

Do-It-Yourself Time Capsule Kit

how: (1) Hold a class discussion with students about what
    people in 2020 would be interested in learning about
    our current civilization. Have students suggest every-
    day items that could tell someone in the future some-
    thing about how we live. Establish categories such
    as food, clothing, etc.
        (2) Divide students into small brainstorming groups.
    Give each group a category. Have each group discuss
    and decide on objects that fit its category that they
    would like future people to know about. Group members
    should then each bring in the objects to fit into the
    waterproof container (time capsule).
        (3) Get permission to bury the capsule somewhere on
    school grounds or in a park. Make a map of the
    location. Have a small ceremony to bury the capsule
    and preserve the map.

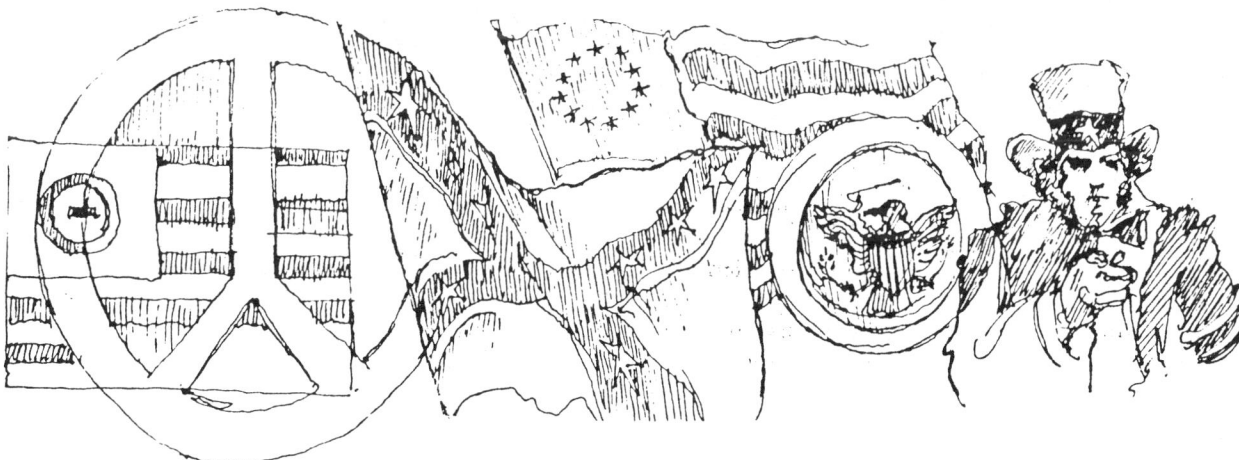

3. Activity for Secondary
Objective: Use discussion small group technique to identify the process of consensus and the skills and attitudes necessary for participation in community problem-solving.

HOW DO YOU TEACH STUDENTS TO WORK IN SMALL GROUPS?

when: one period

what: list of statements

how: (1) Divide the students in discussion small groups of
      five or six and give each group a copy of the list of
      statements. See example below.

      List of Statements
      Mark each statement with the number that represents
      your group's response to each statement.
      1 = agree strongly, 2 = agree, 3 = no opinion,
      4 = disagree, 5 = disagree strongly.

      _____1. Violence is necessary sometimes to achieve
              a citizen's rights.
      _____2. Some U.S. citizens should have more rights
              than others because they contribute more.
      _____3. U.S. citizens should be free to do absolutely
              anything they want.
      _____4. It is important to be U.S. citizens; it
              is not important to be citizens of the world.

      Teacher adds other appropriate statements.

(2) Explain to groups that they must reach a consensus
on how they feel about each statement. Make sure
students understand that consensus is not a majority.
Consensus means that every member of the group must
agree to the strength of feeling they record on their
list. Tell groups they have 15 minutes to get agreement on the list.

(3) After groups have worked only seven or eight of the
15 minutes, stop them and tell them to leave the task.
Discuss the following:
      (a) Would it help to have a group leader? If you
          had a leader how did that person get
          elected?
      (b) Is each member of the group allowed to
          express his/her opinion or are some
          members ignored?
      (c) Did your group work out a plan on how to
          respond to the statements before you began?

(4) Have the groups go back to reaching a consensus on
the statements. After seven or eight minutes again
stop the groups.

(5) Discuss how each group worked and whether they
were more efficient after they had considered their

structure and procedure. What did the class learn
about working in a group? For example, these
questions might be appropriate:
- (a) What attitudes does one need to make a
  contribution to the group? (cooperation)
- (b) What skills are important to group work?
  (leadership, recording)
- (c) Is it always possible to arrive at consensus
  in a small group?
- (d) Does consensus require compromise? Should
  you always be expected to compromise? Is
  compromise always good?

4. The following is an "Evaluation of Self and Group" form.
Students can evaluate their own participation with the group and
the group's participation as a whole. If the technique of
grouping is used often in class, then a form such as this should
be periodically administered.

AN EXCITING
TEACHING RESOURCE

EVALUATION OF SELF AND GROUP

Instruction:
Check the response that best fits your feeling about the group you have
been working with. Comments are welcome.

date_____

name_____

	most all the time	frequently	average	not often	did not do
SELF					
1. I participated by making suggestions, arguing and discussing.					
2. I cooperated by listening to others and tried to work out difficulties (compromises).					
3. I am satisfied that I did my best to accomplish the group task.					
GROUP					
4. The group made a real effort to accomplish the group task.					
5. The group worked well together by cooperating with each other.					
6. The group shared the responsibilities; no one was left out.					

5. DRAMA/ROLE-PLAYING

The technique of drama involves the students in a dramatization (role-playing) of some event or feeling. This technique encourages students to learn through dramatization, by expressing in their own words the drama of the event. Some authorities will classify drama under the heading of role-playing and, of course, most of what happens in drama is role-playing. Many teachers have begun to take role-playing seriously because this activity does force students to be actively involved in historical, political, or social events. The dramatization provides an active situation in which the student not only participates but must interpret, thus developing feelings, attitudes, and reinforcing knowledge, an exceptionally good technique to focus quality time on task. Normally drama is used in one of two ways in the classroom: extemporaneous drama or formal drama.

Many teachers use an extemporaneous form of drama. Extemporaneous, meaning without preparation, emphasizes the students responding to a situation or a set of feelings without prior preparation. The teacher might ask students to dramatize an historical situation; for example, role-playing George Washington crossing the Delaware River to attack the Hessians on Christmas Eve. We often see pictures of him standing in the boat while soldiers are rowing. Role-play by selecting students to play George Washington and the soldiers. The soldiers, pretending rowing, are asking Washington why they are crossing the river Christmas Eve in the middle of the might. George Washington explains where they are going and why. Other dramatizations are Lincoln before the Gettysburg Address walking over the battlefield, or an eyewitness reporting the bombing of Pearl Harbor on December 7, 1941.

Teachers also use a formal written drama or play to emphasize certain historical events. The play is often written by students and acted for the class. The following are two drama or role-playing activities.

AN EXCITING TEACHING RESOURCE

1. Drama/Role-Playing Activity for Elementary
Objective: To participate with others to solve and find solutions through drama technique.

```
WE'VE GOT PROBLEMS

when:  recurring

what:  puppets.  Possible problems to dramatize for puppet
    show:  health, how to earn some money, how to make
    friends.

how:  Have two or three students plan and present a puppet
    show on a problem situation or conflict.  The students
    can stop the show before the problem is resolved.
    Class discusses possible solutions.  Students
    presenting puppet show pick solution they will
    use to complete the show.
```

2.   Drama/Role-Playing Activity for Secondary
Objective: Learn to identify differences between fact and
opinion by role-playing stereotypes. (A stereotype is a commonly
held opinion or mental picture we have about something or some
people that may or may not be true.)

```
I AM PRETENDING TO BE A . . . STEREOTYPE


when:   one class period

what:   small cards with the name of an occupation or
    person that is often stereotyped; for
    example, dentist, television star, pro
    football player, garbage collector,
    policeman, politician, mailperson.

how:  Have each student draw a card with name of occupation
    or person.  Can the class guess who or what occupation
    is being role-played?  Discuss characteristics
    commonly used to stereotype each specific occupation.
    For example:
    (a) Are the characteristics true to life?
    (b) What are other characteristics common to
        this occupation?
    (c) Suppose you worked at this occupation, would
        you try to practice a different set of
        characteristics?
    (d) Are stereotypes of occupations helpful or harm-
        ful when trying to understand the world of work?
```

6. ORAL REPORT

One of the favorite techniques among experienced teachers is the oral report. Normally this technique requires a student to report to the class on a particular topic. Teachers have traditionally favored this technique because it has placed emphasis upon research and oral presentation, both of which are thought to be important citizenship skills. Oral reports can be informal such as when the students are asked to report on some personal incident of which they have knowledge, or formal as when the student is required to research a topic.

The fact that oral reporting is a favorite technique also suggests that as a technique it is often abused. The obvious intention of the teacher is to encourage the student to have something to say (through research, personal experience, or reporting results) and thus practice the skill of communicating this to the class. The oral report tends to break down when there is no criteria for a good presentation. The practice has been for teachers to concentrate on research techniques and other means of gathering information, but they have not offered equal standards for oral presentations. Keep in mind that oral reporting as a technique can be very effective if there are criteria (standards) by which the student and the teacher can judge the quality of the presentation. Simply, students cannot improve their oral presentations if the teacher cannot identify the difference between a good and bad oral report. As minimum, set limits, encourage preparation, and develop criteria by which the reports will be evaluated. Be sure to see the "Oral Report Checklist and Teacher Evaluation" and "Oral Report Evaluation Forms for Students" in the following activities. Both report forms are an important part of effective practice in oral reporting.

ORAL REPORTS   classroom

1. Oral Report Activity for Elementary
Objective: Identify historically important persons, places, or events through the use of oral report technique.

```
ORAL REPORT

when:  require reports as appropriate to the development
       of the lesson

what:  list of historical persons, places, or events for
       students to report on

how:   (1) Assign or let students select a topic to report
       on from the prepared list.  Allow some time for
       students to research topics.
       (2) Have students find or draw a picture or
       prepare a poster about the event or person or
       place they have researched.
       (3) Have students dress up as the person they
       researched if they wish to.
       (4) Have students locate on a map where the
       person they researched lived or where the event
       they researched took place.  A little flag with
       the event or person's name might be pinned to a
       map where the event took place.
       (5) Students should report orally to class, displaying
       their pictures and explaining who their person, event,
       or place is and why it is important.
```

The following activities include forms for preparing and evaluating good oral reports.

Practical Suggestions

2. Oral Report Activity for Elementary or Secondary

```
ORAL REPORT CHECKLIST AND TEACHER EVALUATION

when:  time length of report determined by teacher

what:  oral report checklist

how:   (1) Students must choose topic related to what
       class is studying.
       (2) Students must outline report and get teacher's
       approval of outline.  Students should check out
       anything they do not understand at this time with
       teacher.
       (3) Students must use more than one source to
       obtain information from more than one point of
       view.
       (4) Teacher should give copy of oral report form
       to students so they can use it as a guide.
       Teacher will use form to evaluate student while
       he /she is giving report and then will give check-
       list to student after report.
```

100

The following checklist sets criteria for evaluation. Be sure students review these criteria.

ORAL REPORT CHECKLIST			
_____ (student's name) What's in it for you	well done	satisfactory	needs attention
1. Approved outline			
2. Write subject on board			
3. Face class, speak slowly			
4. Identify source			
5. State time and place of subject			
6. Relate subject to what class is studying			
7. Give report from notes (no reading)			
8. Write difficult names on board or overhead			
9. Summarize			
10. Be ready for class questions			
11. Comments:			

Observation Scale

3. Oral Report Activity for Elementary or Secondary

ORAL REPORT EVALUATION FORM FOR STUDENTS

when: at time of oral report

what: oral report form for students

how: Students are encouraged to evaluate performance of other students presenting oral reports. The following form will allow students to evaluate an oral report and add comments. Have students fill out form either during or after report.

ORAL REPORT EVALUATION FORM FOR STUDENTS

_____
(student giving report)

_____
(evaluator)

	very weak	fair	good	very good	superior
1. Introduction was interesting.					
2. Student related topic to what we are studying in class.					
3. Student was able to make report interesting with personal opinions yet stuck basically to facts.					
4. Student summarized briefly.					

Comments:

7. DEBATE

Debate, an active teaching technique, is normally used to encourage students to apply the knowledge they have acquired. It is also used to help students develop the skill of preparing arguments for one or another side of an issue. Debate is used in either a formal or informal way. Some teachers like to require their students to learn formal rules of debate. The intent is to teach students the procedures for developing formal argumentation. Most teachers, however, use debate in an informal way--that is with modified rules of debate that are appropriate to the class. The informal technique is intended to prepare students to defend a particular point of view, i.e., argument, stand, or position. The informal technique permits the teacher and students to develop their own set of rules. It is intended that the students be actively involved in preparing and defending an argument. Teachers often use this technique to illustrate that there are many different points of view that can be debated. In short, debate focuses attention and can generate quality time on task.

Debate Activity for Elementary or Secondary

DO WE NEED RULES?

when: as needed to complete activity

what: list of rules suggested by class
     debate and task-oriented small groups

how: Have students think of rules that control their lives, for example, family
   has rules, school has rules, community has rules,
   nation has rules, driving has rules, sports/games
   have rules. List the rules students suggest
   control their lives on the board. Divide the class
   into small debate teams of four or five members.
   Assign one team to defend several of the rules, and
   assign another team to argue that those same rules
   are unnecessary. Continue assigning teams selected
   rules to defend or challenge (argue that rules are
   unnecessary) until all teams have positions to
   defend. Give teams time to prepare. Have one set
   of teams (one team defending and one team challenging
   a specific set of rules) debate their set of rules
   in front of the whole class. For example, each
   team has five minutes to argue for or against a
   rule. Continue allowing sets of teams to debate
   until all teams have had a turn. As a conclusion
   to the activity, ask the class to express their
   opinion by voting for or against each rule listed
   on the board.

**AN EXCITING
TEACHING RESOURCE**

8. PANEL DISCUSSION

Teachers use panel discussions to present information to the class. The panel often consists of a
number of students who are assigned to a specific
topic. Normally the panel orally reports their
findings on the topic to the class. Some teachers
also require that the report be written as well
as orally reported. The panel differs from debate
in that it is not intended as a means of stimulating debate among
the panel members but rather as a systematic way for a group of
students to present their report on a topic. The following is a
sample of a panel discussion technique.

Panel Discussion Activity for Elementary or Secondary

RESEARCHING THE AFRICAN CONTINENT

when: two weeks

what: resource materials, list of African countries,
     panel, small group

how: (1) Divide class into task-oriented small groups
   (each group will act as a panel). Give each
   group a portion of the names from the list.
   (2) Each group will research its own list of
   countries using the following questions:
        a. Where on the map is the country found?
        b. Why is the country important to study?
        c. Suppose you could visit this country,
           what would you want to see?
        d. How would you feel about living in
           this country?
   (3) Each group may be requested to turn in a
   written report on its findings.
   (4) Each group will act as a panel to report
   to the class in an oral presentation. Each
   panel member will deliver some part of the
   panel report so that all panel members have a
   chance to participate.

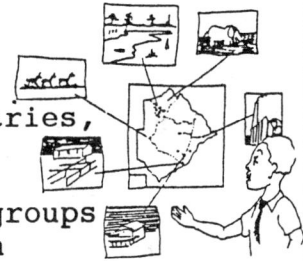

---

9. GAME/SIMULATION

AN EXCITING TEACHING RESOURCE

You know what a game is. That is where people play to win in a contest. But what is a simulation? A simulation is also a game, but it is a game where you do not necessarily win or lose depending on the purpose of the simulation. Simulation is defined as an imitation, a pretending, or a resemblance of an event, person, or thing. For example, students would role-play the process by which legislation in Congress becomes law. The difference between gaming and simulation is that in gaming there is always a winner, but in some simulations there may be neither winners nor losers depending on the purpose of the simulation. In short, most of the time, simulation is role-playing in a game situation. An illustration of that is offered below in the activity "Survival Island."

We include games and simulations as techniques because they can be of value in enriching the effectiveness of your instruction. Simulation also fulfills most

of the practices suggested to achieve effective teaching such as
self-directing, accommodating, integrating, challenging,
feedback, and rewarding. In short, a simulation, when properly
presented, is the most powerful technique for generating
effective learning. Gaming and simulation are motivational
techniques because students enjoy games, meaning they generally
have a positive attitude toward participating. Some of the
advantages of using games and simulations are to (1) review
content as in a quizdown; (2) encourage critical and creative
thinking; (3) offer an opportunity to teach role-playing; (4)
teach content as well as process; and (5) add variety and a
change of pace to your teaching. The following are three
educational games.

1. Game Activity for Elementary

NAME GAME

when: one class period per game

what: maps or globes as aids

how: (1) First student says place name such as "Indiana."
      Second student must say a place name that begins
      with the last letter, "a" of the name said before,
      i.e., "Arkansas." Third student then finds a place
      that begins with "s", i.e., "Syracuse." If student
      cannot find a name, he/she is out. Last person left
      is winner. Could also be played with teams.
      (2) Have one student leave room. Class picks country,
      city, etc. Student returns and tries to guess place
      by asking twenty questions that can only be
      answered by yes or no. For example, Is it small?
      Is it water? If not successful in guessing, then
      another student becomes it.

FAMILIES
THE WORLD

school
SOCIAL
STUDIES

2. Game Activity for Junior High/Middle School

TREASURE HUNT

when: one period

what: no materials necessary

how: Tell students they are going to play a
      game of treasure hunt. Have one or two
      students leave the room and while they are
      gone the class decides on an object to be
      the treasure, i.e., book on teacher's desk,
      poster on wall. Students called back in
      and given clues by the class to tell
      them where the object is. Clues can only
      be given in terms of direction (north, south,
      east, west, front of room, back of room) or in
      distance (for example, two yards from teacher's
      desk). Class members give directions in turn
      until object is located. The object is to give
      such accurate clues that the students looking
      for the treasure will not have to leave their
      chairs to locate treasure. The winner is the
      student or students that find the treasure
      with the least number of questions.

3. Quizdown Gaming Activity for Elementary or Secondary

Quizdown is another example of a game. Quizdowns
are used primarily to involve students in the
recall of information. Some teachers use the
quizdown as a technique for reviewing before a
test, some use it as a technique for
evaluating, and others have used it as a game
to stimulate team spirit and competition
in class. As a review technique it is
intended to stimulate students to
quickly respond to a set of review
questions which the teacher has
prepared, or in some cases which the
students have prepared. In some
quizdowns the students are asked to
stand either along the side of the room
or beside their desks. The teacher asks
a review question to each student in
turn. When a student cannot answer,
he/she must sit down. The student or
students standing at the end of the
review are referred to as the winners.
Some teachers use this technique as a

106

means of evaluating the progress of the class. Some teachers use
a variation of the technique by dividing the students into teams
so that the teams must compete against each other rather than
individuals. The team that answers the most questions correctly
is considered the winner. This technique stimulates
participation and strengthens the students' enthusiasm for
learning, if not for personal satisfaction, then for the welfare
of the team. This technique has various names: quizdown,
baseball or football (the ball is advanced according to the
difficulty of the question). This technique has proved to focus
attention and stimulate high interest for some students.

IMPROVING

TEACHING

4.   Simulation Activity for Junior High/Middle School
     and Senior High.

     The simulation, Survival Island, is an activity that focuses
attention on community development. If you wish students to
think about the problems and issues (and sometimes crises) caused by community development and resource development, this simple
simulation would be a good introduction to
that topic.

SURVIVAL ISLAND

when: one period

what: map of island

how: This can be either an individual
      or a group activity. This activity
      is designed to encourage students
      to consider the problems of estab-
      lishing a colony. What factors
      should be taken into consideration
      when establishing a colony? How
      do you survive in an alien environment?

      You have been elected to lead a group of 500 people
      to begin a new society on an uninhabited island
      200 miles from your nearest neighbor. You want to
      be isolated from the rest of the world. You will
      take with you livestock, seed, and building
      materials. Among your group are people who are
      skilled in almost every necessary trade. As the
      leader you must take all conditions into
      consideration and choose a location for your
      settlement.

How're you going to do it?

SURVIVAL ISLAND

TAKING CONTROL

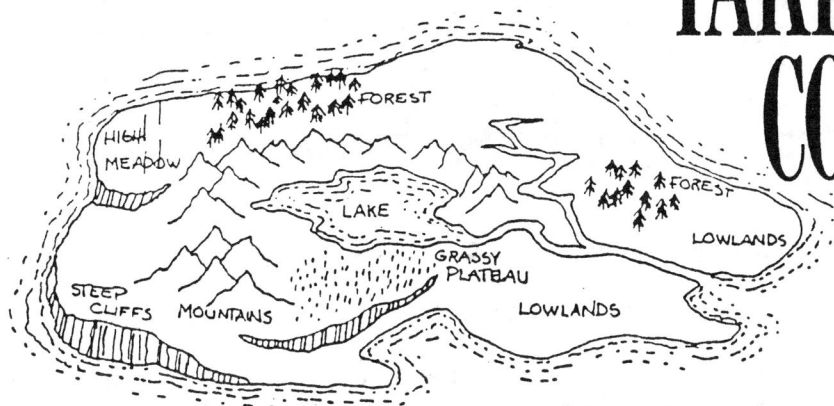

(1) Each student or group of students is to play
the role of the leader of the settlement and as
leader must make a fundamental decision on where
to place the island's one settlement. This
would seem to be a rather simple decision, but
further consideration would suggest that a
decision on where to place the settlement
involves a number of relatively complex problems.
(2) Encourage the students to identify (brainstorm) all of the conditions they can think of
that will be important in choosing a location
for the settlement. Consider these: ecological
problems (disposal of waste, maintenance of
water quality, power), other factors such as
access to other parts of the island, protection
from storms, and finally problems of population
density and population growth, just to mention
a few. Of course, the problems on the island
are exactly the same as living anywhere else.
The issue is quality of life, the question is
survival for what--what will be the quality of
life for which the islanders have survived?
(3) After students or groups of students have
selected and defended their spot on the island,
hold a class discussion in which the class
identifies all the conditions that should be
taken into consideration in choosing an
appropriate site.
(4) Locate where each member of the class
placed his/her settlement and discuss whether
the locations are or are not appropriate in
terms of the considerations identified above.

Commentary

SURVIVAL ISLAND

No matter where the settlement is placed, there will be
severe damage to the environment. Uncontrolled development would
destroy the island. The thoughtful placement of where people

live, which includes the serious problem of waste control, is a quality of life issue--so is it an issue in the United States and on earth. Development, if not carefully planned, can destroy the quality of life itself. Survival Island is actually survival earth.

10. EXTENDING YOURSELF THROUGH TECHNOLOGY AND INSTRUCTIONAL RESOURCES

We have said up to this point that as alternatives to lecturing, recitation, and discussion techniques, you ought to think of grouping, drama/role-playing, oral report, debate, panel discussion, game/simulation. These techniques, if properly applied, should focus attention and help to motivate by encouraging student participation. Active learning through participation may help students learn, but beyond that, one additional way to be effective is through the use of technology and instructional resources. Often it is not enough to involve your students in debates, reports, and groupings; it is equally important to provide them with sights and sounds.

The use of technology and instructional resources is particularly important because much of the content in social studies is abstract, i.e., democracy, freedom, liberty, happiness. It is important to illustrate past history, it is important to visually demonstrate ideas, and it is important to provide models. We need not belabor this argument for few teachers would argue that illustration is not a significant part of teaching and those illustrations which most clearly transmit a clear picture are the most effective. Technology and instructional resources are a means, a technique, by which you extend your thinking to others. An amplifier extends your voice, a chalkboard is an extension of your writing, a tape recorder is an extension of your voice, an opaque projector is an extended projection of your written ideas. A film or videotape is an illustration of ideas you have; slides are specific illustrations of ideas which you wish your students to see, and computers allow student participation and manipulation of programmed materials in the computer-assisted instruction part of your course.

In summary, technology and instructional resources--whether tape recorders, public address system, films, VCR, slides, overhead projector with transparencies, computers or any teaching aids--are merely a means by which you extend yourself. Teachers are limited in the reach of their voice and in their ability to verbally identify meaning. Technology and instructional resources provide teachers with the means to enlarge their capacity to reach others. The use of technology and instructional resources is such an important topic that it deserves special treatment. Though we have introduced the topic of extending yourself through technology and instructional resources here, we will explore their use in Chapter VII, "Technology and Instructional Resources: A Function of Effective Teaching Practices."

Television and Video

Summary

Conclusion

We have attempted in this chapter to distinguish between methods, techniques, and strategies; to provide a rationale for Effective Teaching Practices (Chapter IV); and finally to discuss in depth ten specific techniques from among a list of 150. We have pointed out that there are an infinite number of teaching techniques. A strategy is merely the plan by which the techniques are sequenced (coordinated) to accomplish the method. Research studies on how students learn best as reported in the preceding chapter recommend that teachers use active learning techniques to focus attention on task with, of course, the hope that students will be motivated to learn. Finally, you were asked to identify ten basic techniques that focus attention and generate quality time on task: lecture, recitation, discussion, grouping, drama/role-playing, oral report, debate, panel discussion, game/simulation, and use of technology and instructional resources. When approaching the planning of a lesson you will never be at a loss to recall at least these basic techniques. Being a professional teacher means that you have information on skills that others who are not teachers do not have. Remember that knowing about a variation in methods, and a variety of techniques and strategies are part of what will establish you as a professional teacher.

Coming Events

We turn now to specific classroom skills that are a function of effective teaching practices. The first among them is asking questions.

Have a question

If it's to be heard but not listened to—

1941—SAVE THE WORLD FOR DEMOCRACY!

NOTES

Where Imagination Becomes Reality

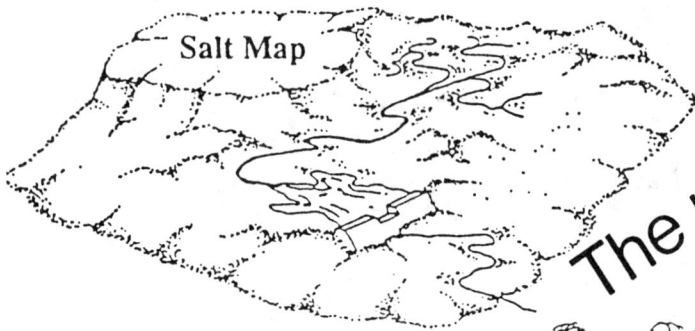

Salt Map

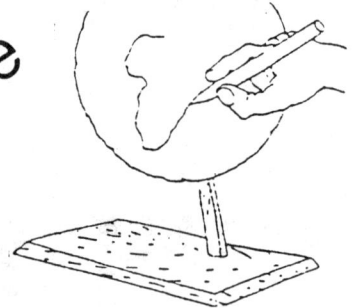

Maps and Globes

The right choice

Sand Table

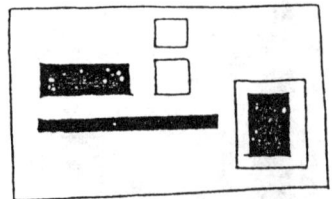

Layout

CHAPTER VI

QUESTIONING:
A FUNCTION OF EFFECTIVE TEACHING PRACTICES

OBJECTIVE: Having completed this chapter on questioning, you should be able to identify the four different levels of questions by demonstrating the ability to correctly construct examples of each and achieve no less than a "good" on the self-test at the end of the chapter.

Questioning is fundamental to learning.
                              Barth/Spencer

AN EXCITING
TEACHING RESOURCE

Questioning is first among teaching skills. Why would this be true? Studies on what social studies teachers actually do in class show that approximately 30% of their class time is verbally asking questions. Another quarter of the time is devoted to reviewing, giving, and grading test questions. In short, on the average about half of social studies class time is devoted to asking questions.

If you are likely to spend up to half of your class time asking questions, then does it not make sense that you learn about and practice the skill of questioning? Of course, your immediate reaction might be that having spent most of your life asking and answering questions, don't you already have the skill? After all isn't asking questions like breathing and walking? Not really, because as a teacher questioning becomes a skill. Asking "good" questions at different levels is a planned strategy. In short, questioning is a teaching skill.

Do you remember the statement in Chapter IV:

Students learn best when they are asked stimulating questions rather than being lectured to? This means students learn best when they are asked different levels of questions, and also by inference, students who ask stimulating questions focus attention and encourage feedback.

Not only should you, the teacher, learn the different levels of questions, it may be equally important that the students you teach also learn the different levels. For you the four different levels are part of your teaching skills. For your students the four levels represent a way to understand the world they live in by testing the reality of that world through the four levels of questions. The goal of social studies is

citizenship education. How better to develop citizens in a
democracy than to equip them with the skill of questioning which
is a required lifelong skill for effective citizenship. Think
about it! Questioning skills are for both you and your students.
As you read about the different levels of questions, consider how
you might teach your students to ask and respond to the four
levels.

In this chapter you will learn how to distinguish between
the four levels of questions and then learn how to use these four
in Chapter XV on "Practice Teaching." The four basic levels of
questions can be divided into lower level and higher level
questions. Lower level questions generally ask for recall,
explanation, and application of information, whereas higher level
questions deal with analyzing, hypothesizing, and making
judgments. They are all part of the process of thinking and
reasoning, and therefore, it is important that both lower and
higher levels be part of a questioning strategy. The four basic
levels of questions are called: (1) **cognitive-memory**, and (2)
convergent (both lower level questions); and (3) **divergent** and
(4) **evaluative** (both higher level questions).

questions yield more questions

I. COGNITIVE-MEMORY QUESTIONS

Cognitive means knowledge,
so congitive-memory
means memorized knowledge.

Cognitive-memory (CM) questions tend to be restricted to the
lowest levels of thinking. Questions of this type seek one right
answer which usually requires students to answer with factual
information or definitions relying on recall or recognition.
Answers tend to be short phrases or merely a single word.
Students respond to cognitive-memory questions by recalling a
fact, defining a term, noting something they observed, or simply
giving an answer based on rote memory. The following questions
are typical of the levels of thinking elicited by cognitive-
memory questions.

  A. In what country is the Mississippi River found?
      (Clearly there is only one right answer--the U.S.)
  B. Which country on the North American continent has the
      largest population? (Clearly the one right answer is--)
  C. Name the countries in Africa that fall along the
      equator.
  D. Recall the name of the highest mountain in Asia.
  E. Is the Nile the longest river in the world?

To help identify cognitive-memory questions the following introductory phrases are to be completed in the form of questions.

Instructions: Complete each sentence.
(for example)
   Label three of the major rivers in the United States.

1.   Recall the name of_____.

2.   Identify the governor of_____.

3.   Is the President of the U.S._____?

4.   Define exactly the meaning of_____.

5.   List the most important_____.

6.   Designate the right name for_____?

   To improve your skill in identifying cognitive-memory (CM) questions, read each of the questions below. In the blank provided write CM if you think the question is cognitive-memory. If you decide that a question is not cognitive-memory, then label it N for no. After labeling each question either CM or N, read the paragraph that follows to check your answers.

Identification Practice: label CM or N in the space provided.

_____A. Name the first person to walk on the moon.

_____B Tell me why you think China is important.

_____C. Explain why acid rain is a pollution problem.

_____D. Recall who was President during the Civil War.

_____E. Identify the country that has the highest suicide rate.

_____F. Did the United States achieve independence in 1776?

   If you marked questions A, D, E, and F as CM for cognitive-memory questions, then you are on the right track. These four questions ask students merely to reproduce short factual information such as names or dates. Although clear distinctions are sometimes difficult to make, questions B and C probably are intended to have the student develop a definition or engage in speculation (higher level questions).

114

Key words when writing cognitive-memory questions are:

COGNITIVE-MEMORY	Recall	Identify	Yes No	Define	Name	Designate

Other key words are:

label	match	recite	tell
list	memorize	spell	write
locate	quote	state	find

For additional key cognitive-memory level words see Knowledge category in Bloom's Taxonomy at the end of this chapter.

Writing Practice
    Time for you to try your hand at writing this level of question. In the space provided below, write three cognitive-memory questions. Choose any topic you wish. Use the chart above as a reference for different key words to write cognitive-memory questions. **RIGHT NOW!**

1.

2.

3.

II. CONVERGENT QUESTIONS

<u>Convergent means coming together as in converging one's thoughts.</u>

    Convergent (C) questions require students to establish a relationship between facts or ideas in order to construct an answer. Convergent questions are aimed at eliciting "right" or "best" answers. Generally the information necessary for answering such questions is assumed to be known by both the teacher and the students such as when the teacher asks you to explain in your words from the homework assignment some event or idea. The question for the student involves recalling certain facts or ideas, organizing or associating them in some manner, and formulating an explanation in the student's own words. To cope with this level of question the student is required to

needed to answer cognitive-memory questions. In short, there is
one best answer or answers which are often stated in the
student's own words. Explaining, comparing, relating, and
associating are the specific levels of thinking behavior
connected with convergent questions. Some examples follow.

    A. Why did explorers want to find the source of the
        Nile?
          (If you had read the textbook assignment on this
          you would probably be able to give a textbook
          answer in your own words. The point of this
          is there is a right answer according to the text.)
    B. How are the states of New England alike?
    C. Explain why the Sahara Desert is growing.
    D. Compare and contrast Great Britain and Japan.
    E. Describe the Battle of Bunker Hill.

To help you identify convergent questions the following
introductory phrases are to be completed in the form of
questions.
1.   Explain the relationship between_____.

2.   Why did the_____?

3.   Compare and contrast_____.

4.   How similar are_____?

5.   State the difference between_____.

    In the set of questions below, use the letters CM, C or N to
indicate whether the question is CM for cognitive-memory, C for
convergent, or N for no. The following paragraph will give you
the correct answers.

Identification Practice: label CM, C, or N in the space
provided.

_____A. Why did the South lose the Civil War?

_____B. What is the name of the longest river in South
        America?

_____C. Should the government put a priority on eliminating
        poverty?

_____D. Name the three branches of the national government.

_____E. Explain why the present economic conditions of
        citizens of Malaysia are different from those of their
        ancestors.

_____F. What was the relationship between English and German monarchies during World War I?

_____G. How are China and Russia alike?

Your task of identifying the different levels of questions in this set was more difficult. If you labeled questions A, E, F, and G as convergent, you are progressing nicely. The use of key words "how," "why," and "explain" should have alerted you on three of these questions. Questions B and D are representative of the cognitive-memory level, while question C should have been marked N for no. If you identified these questions correctly, move on to the next section. If you missed one or two, take a minute to review this section on convergent questions.

Key words when writing convergent questions are:

CONVERGENT		Explain	Describe	Compare	Contrast	Why, How

Other key words are:

change	review	summarize
calculate	reword	offer
account for	paraphrase	interpret

For additional key convergent level words see the Comprehension, Application, and Analysis categories in Bloom's Taxonomy at the end of this chapter.

Writing Practice
    Use the appropriate space below to write out three convergent level questions. The key words for convergent questions might be helpful.   **RIGHT NOW!**

1.

2.

3.

Where have we been?

COGNITIVE-MEMORY		Recall	Identify	Yes No	Define	Name	Designate

CONVERGENT		Explain	Describe	Compare	Contrast	Why, How

Commentary on the use of CM and C

From the examples it is obvious that "how" and "why," "compare and contrast," and "explain" tend to act as key words for identifying convergent level questions. Research studies have found that student thinking can be restricted if cognitive-memory and convergent questions are utilized constantly because students will not think beyond the "right" answer. Students may assume the purpose of instruction is strictly one of finding the right answers and they may become very defensive when challenged to think at a higher level or creatively.

III. DIVERGENT QUESTIONS

<u>Divergent means to hypothesize or inquire to encourage a variety of answers all of which are possible, yet can be supported by evidence.</u>

Divergent (D) questions provide the student with much more freedom and independence in giving answers. Divergent questions allow for a variety of answers that can be supported by objective evidence. It is more difficult to predict the actual answer a student might give. This level of question is often considered to be one that is thought-provoking. Teachers who ask divergent questions of their students are seeking original or creative answers. Divergent questions often confront students with problem situations which force them to combine facts, concepts, and generalizations in new ways to create and develop plausible answers. Designing, evolving, predicting, modifying, reconstructing, hypothesizing, and inferring are the thinking operations typical of this level of question. Below are some examples of divergent questions.

    A.   Might life be changed in this country if life expectancy were to increase by 100 years? (There is no clear answer to this question but the answer would need to include supporting evidence from the past 100 years suggesting changes that have happened because of rising life expectancy.)

    B.   Suggest a number of ways the standard of living could be raised.

C. Imagine what development will do to this country in the future.

D. Predict what would happen to our lives if private automobiles were eliminated.

E. Reconstruct events as they might have happened during the early history of man.

F. Hypothesize about the effect of the space program on the future of the country.

To help identify divergent questions the following introductory phrases are to be completed in the form of questions.

1. Create a lesson plan_____.

2. Hypothesize about the possibility of_____.

3. Predict the outcome of_____.

4. What would happen if_____?

5. Originate a theory for_____.

6. Plan a program for_____.

It is obvious that more imagination and insight is needed to answer divergent questions than is needed to answer cognitive-memory and convergent. The divergent level of questions may tend to stimulate and motivate the interests of students. Questions at this level encourage students to speculate and to explore topics in more depth, the result being focused attention and a more favorable attitude toward the subject matter. Too often teachers become so concerned with covering content using cognitive-memory and convergent questions in recitation that they neglect the divergent questions altogether. Consequently, they miss a valuable opportunity to help students develop higher level thinking by asking them to extend their creative abilities.

By adding another level of questions to the set below, the task of correctly labeling each one becomes more difficult. Read each question carefully and fill in the blanks in the space provided with either CM for cognitive-memory, C for convergent, D for divergent, or N for no. After labeling each question, read the paragraph that follows to check your answer.

Identification Practice: label CM, C, D, or N in the space provided.

_____A. What do you hypothesize the impact of the next drought will be?

_____B. Was Hitler head of the German government during World War II?

_____C. Formulate a plan to combat pollution.

_____D. Why have Polish workers had trouble forming effective labor unions?

_____E. What would you predict would happen if the United States established complete trade barriers against Japan?

_____F. Construct a plan to deal with the expected oil shortage.

_____G. Compare the governments of Spain and Italy.

If you selected questions A, C, E, and F as being divergent, you are correct. These questions would engage the student in hypothesizing and predicting. Question B, however, only requires recall and a yes or no answer as a cognitive-memory question. If you labeled questions D and G as being convergent, you are doing well.

Key words when writing divergent questions are:

DIVERGENT	Predict	Hypothesize	Originate	Create	For-mulate

Other key words are:

combine	develop	suggest
construct	discover	invent
reveal	modify	suppose

For additional key divergent level words see Synthesis category in Bloom's Taxonomy at the end of this chapter.

Writing Practice
    Time to test your questioning skill by rephrasing some of the questions you have already written so that they will fit this new level. Write three divergent questions. Use key words to write your divergent questions.   **RIGHT NOW!**

1.

2.

3.

Where have we been?

COGNITIVE-MEMORY	Recall	Identify	Yes No	Define	Name	Designate

CONVERGENT	Explain	Describe	Compare	Contrast	Why, How

DIVERGENT	Predict	Hypothesize	Originate	Create	Formulate

IV. EVALUATIVE QUESTIONS

Evaluative means to judge, justify or grade; to decide, to offer a personal opinion.

Evaluative (E) questions deal with that area of thinking related to judgment, values, and choices. Evaluative questions tend to force students to organize their thoughts and knowledge to reach their own personal opinion. The students' judgments must be based upon some evidence and standards which the students or some other person or group establishes, but that evidence need not be objective or reliable. The following questions provide examples.

A. Do you think your country is making progress? (The question calls for personal opinion but that personal opinion, in contrast to answers to divergent questions, does not have to be supported by objective evidence, therefore the personal opinion does not necessarily need to be rational or logical.)

B. What is your opinion about the election?

C. What do you believe should be done about the educational system?

D. Defend your position on gun control.

E. Justify your choice for President.

F. Recommend the best way to conserve water.

G. Criticize the plans for urban renewal.

H. What is your ranking of the five top nations in the world?

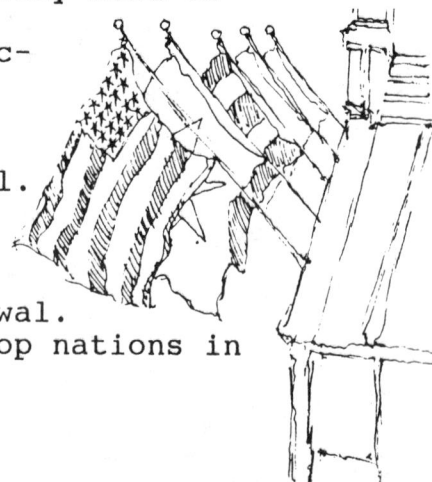

To help identify evaluative questions the following introductory phrases are to be completed in the form of questions.

1. What do you think about_____?

2. In your opinion_____?

3. Do you believe_____?

4. Defend your choice_____.

5. Which is best_____?

6. Recommend the_____.

7. Judge which of the following_____.

You have five different ways of labeling the following questions. In the practice below use CM for cognitive-memory, C for convergent, D for divergent, E for evaluative, or N for no to label each question. Read the paragraph below to check your answers.

Identification Practice: label CM, C, D, E, or N in the space provided.

_____A. If Napoleon had not been defeated at the Battle of Waterloo, how might the position of France in Europe be different today?

_____B. In your opinion what is the best means of enforcing the anti-pollution laws?

_____C. Justify your reaction to limiting the size of families.

_____D. Name the country in which the Black Forest is located.

_____E. How do democratic governments compare?

_____F. In your opinion what should be done to improve public transportation?

If you labeled any of these N, go back and review your mistakes. Only questions B, C, and F should have been labeled with the letter E for evaluative. Question B directs the student to make a best choice between alternatives while questions C and F seek an opinion. The only cognitive-memory question was D. Students must make a series of comparisons in question E, which is one of the thought operations called for in convergent questions. Question A should be labeled divergent because the student is asked to hypothesize. If you labeled these six questions correctly, you are doing excellent work. Recognizing

the different levels of questions is not easy. It takes time to
recognize the key words that indicate the levels of thought. You
may need to continue to review the four levels of questions until
you can actually question and, in fact, think at those different
levels.

Key words when writing evaluative questions are:

EVALUATIVE	Judge	Value	Defend	Select	Opinion	Rank

Other key words are:

assess	decide	rate
choose	grade	recommend
criticize	justify	evaluate

For additional key evaluative level words see Evaluation category
in Bloom's Taxonomy at the end of this chapter.

Writing Practice
        Writing good evaluative questions is not an easy task.
Using the key words for this level question, try phrasing three
evaluative questions in the space provided below. Take notice of
the key words as you write evaluative questions.   **Now**

1.

2.

3.

Where have we been?

COGNITIVE-MEMORY	Recall	Identify	Yes No	Define	Name	Designate

CONVERGENT	Explain	Describe	Compare	Contrast	Why, How

DIVERGENT	Predict	Hypothesize	Originate	Create	For-mulate

EVALUATIVE	Judge	Value	Defend	Select	Opinion	Rank

more questions

Paying attention to the wording of questions is very important. By simply changing a word or phrase questions can require different thinking levels. The sets of questions which follow illustrate this point.

COGNITIVE-MEMORY QUESTIONS
- A. What is the birth rate in the United States?
- B. Tell the number of Senators each state sends to Congress.
- C. State how many degrees north of the equator New York City is.
- D. Did William the Conqueror invade England in 1066?

CONVERGENT QUESTIONS
- A. How does the birth rate of the U.S. compare to that of France?
- B. Explain why states do not have the same number of Senators and Representatives.
- C. Describe the location of the following cities: New York and Los Angeles.
- D. Why was William the Conqueror able to successfully conquer England while Hitler could not?

DIVERGENT QUESTIONS
- A. Imagine what would happen to the standard of living in the U.S. if the birth rate increased from 2.1 to 3.0.
- B. How might our political system be different if each state elected the same number of Senators and Representatives to Congress?
- C. Predict what might happen to New York City in the event of an earthquake.
- D. Suppose Hitler had conquered England, how might that have changed the course of American history?

EVALUATIVE QUESTIONS
- A. Recommend action you think the government should take to reduce the family size of the poor.
- B. Decide whether the seniority system in Congress is beneficial or a deterrent to good government.
- C. Judge whether or not large cities such as New York City should be given the status of a state.
- D. Justify your reasons for thinking that Hitler should have attempted to conquer England before he invaded Russia.

Writing Practice
    It is your turn again. Try taking a single topic and writing one question at each level on that topic: for example,

124

environment, development, economics, crime, living standards, health, or pick your own topic. Once again, space has been provided below. Refer to the key words for help in writing your questions.

UseThis

1. Cognitive-memory:

2. Convergent:

3. Divergent:

4. Evaluative:

Students Who Challenge and Question

Applying Questioning Skills to Effective Teaching Practices

What do we actually know about the relationship of questioning to the achievement of students? Over the past 50 years quite a few studies on questioning do yield some correlation between questioning techniques and student achievement. The following eleven points are a summary of what studies show to be effective teaching practices in questioning.[1]

1. phrasing questions clearly.
2. asking questions of a primarily academic nature.
3. asking questions requiring low cognitive-level responses in elementary settings (and maintaining a high frequency of such questions, particularly with students from low-income families).
4. asking questions requiring high cognitive-level responses in intermediate through high school settings.
5. permitting students to call out responses in classes in which the students come primarily from low-income families.
6. probing students' responses to help them clarify ideas, support a point of view, or extend their thinking.
7. allowing between three and five seconds of wait time after asking a question, particularly when high cognitive-level responses are required.
8. encouraging students to respond in some way to each question asked.
9. balancing responses from volunteering and nonvolunteering students.
10. eliciting a high percentage of correct responses from students and helping students who give incorrect responses.
11. acknowledging correct responses from students using praise specifically and discriminately.

Commentary

Having read this chapter on questioning you now know the differences between the four basic levels of questions. An analysis of social studies textbooks made some years ago revealed that approximately ninety-five percent of all questions asked in the text were cognitive-memory or convergent. Similar studies on teachers' questions in the classroom show the same results. It is not surprising that ninety percent of all questions teachers ask are cognitive-memory or convergent. In other words, social studies teachers have a strong tendency to ask students to recall information either verbatim (cognitive-memory) or in their own words (convergent). But in either case, the results are approximately the same; that is, students believe that social studies is primarily the recalling or recitation of content. Obviously, a pattern of questioning which requires only cognitive-memory or convergent thinking will not ordinarily encourage thinking at all levels.

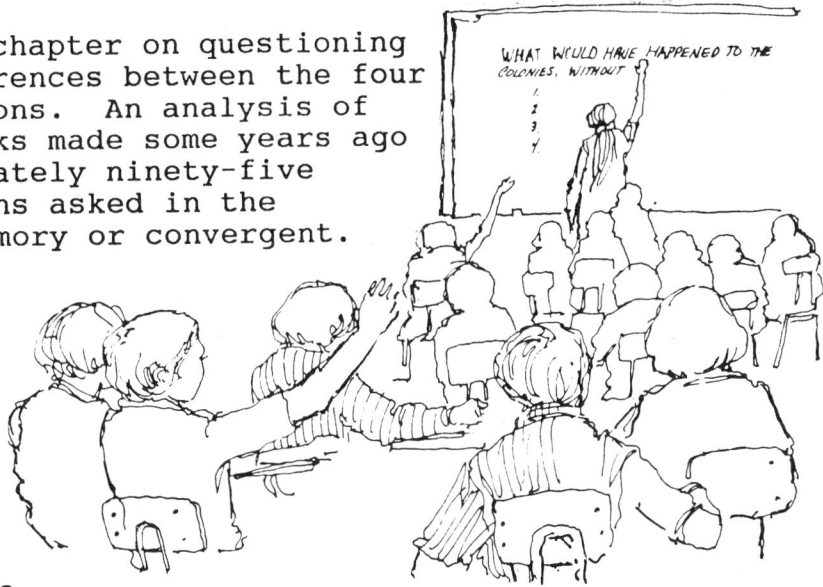

Using All Four Levels

What questioning strategy will encourage all levels of thinking? The answer to this question is very simple and direct. Discussion is stimulated by the use of all four levels of questions. You cannot get students to give thoughtful responses by asking them just to recall, waiting one second, and asking another question, nor are you likely to generate thoughtful responses just by asking evaluative questions. It is equally as important to speculate (divergent) as it is to recall information in one's own words (convergent). It is the accumulated effect of having students evaluate, speculate, recall, and recite that is most likely to excite the students' imaginations. Some teachers choose to start a discussion with cognitive-memory questions and proceed methodically to convergent, divergent, and evaluative questions in that order. Others choose to start with the evaluative level. Frankly, evidence suggests that there is no one best way questions should be asked. How questions are best sequenced depends on the class. Each class is different, thus needing a different approach.

Motivation

We must discuss a very practical problem. Many teachers say that they cannot get their students to answer questions. The students just won't talk and under special demonstrations this obviously is true. Think a minute about the opening remarks above on the levels of questions that teachers and texts ask. You might agree that there is a considerable amount of monotony in asking only cognitive-memory and convergent questions. The students say they are bored according to their reactions in Chapter I. After all, there is an appearance of sameness if, day after day, all questions are pitched at a low level. Asking the same level of questions may lead to student apathy; they just do not want to volunteer anymore. And, finally, what is there to discuss about a recall answer? From the students' point of view the teacher lectures or gives information as an addition to the students' responses. This teaching strategy (recitation, lecture), as research studies show, does not stimulate secondary students to think for themselves. The recitation and lecture-- which seems to be popular with many social studies teachers-- tends to turn off discussion and willingness to participate. That is hard to accept, but it is true.

Different Levels of Questions for Different Students

Not surprisingly, different students seem to respond to different levels of questions. Some students in elementary schools are perfectly happy answering cognitive-memory and convergent questions. Secondary students seem to respond

.The right choice

better to evaluative questions, and even questions that ask for speculation (divergent). When this is pointed out, some teachers are quick to say, "You mean the bright students will answer the speculative and evaluative questions and my slower students will respond to recall questions." That is not necessarily true. Students who have great difficulty recalling specific information might have something to contribute in the form of evaluations, whereas some of the brighter students pick up information easily and recite it but do not respond well to speculating about it. It is true that concrete experiences tend to be appropriate for the slower students, but that does not mean that they will not respond to questioning beyond the recall level. "Well," teachers may say, "that sounds nice, but I tried that strategy last week and it didn't work. I just can't get them to do anything more than sit there. They just want to know what's going to be on the test." You will experience classes that will not want to participate. Do not forget you are teaching citizenship and this requires all four levels of questioning. This includes asking all four levels on tests. Students will not normally respond to a variety of levels in class discussion if your tests are only one level. It takes time to recondition the students to a multi-level questioning strategy. The exchange of ideas at different levels seems to stimulate students and increase their desire to participate. One day, one week, perhaps even one month is not going to make a great difference, but very possibly a semester of multilevel questioning will make the difference, remembering, of course, that social studies teachers are in the thinking and reasoning business.

Applying the Inquiry Method

How're you going to do it?

An inquiry questioning strategy is an absolute necessity if you are going to apply the Reflective Inquiry method. That strategy is not terribly hard; it merely requires that you ask all four different levels of questions. The pattern of questioning that you follow is governed primarily by the type of class that you teach. It is not required that you ask more evaluative questions than you would cognitive-memory questions, nor should they all be asked equally so that a quarter of the class time is devoted to each. One level of questions should lead to another. For example, an evaluative question should lead to some call for evidence--cognitive-memory or convergent questions. It is important that a line of thinking be pursued that follows the steps of the inquiry process. Different students respond to different levels of questions. It is your task as a teacher to discover which questions stimulate responses from your students. Now that you know the four different levels of questions, it is appropriate that you be asked to try a strategy that requires the skill of asking the four different levels of questions.

Your Attitude Toward the Four Levels of Questions

How do you personally feel about the four levels of questions? Yes, you did learn the differences between the four, and you have noted the argument that all four levels of questions should be used in the classroom. Yet you have not had the opportunity to identify your preference. Do you have a preference for one level of questions over another? What is your attitude toward the four levels of questions? It may be possible to identify your preference and your attitude if you fill out the Barth Question Preference Inventory on the following page.

Use This Now

128

BARTH QUESTION PREFERENCE INVENTORY

Instructions:

    PREFERENCE: For each group of questions below, tell which one you would most like to ask by placing a "1" in front of it, a "2" in front of your second choice, a "3" in front of the next, and a "4" in front of the question that you are least interested in.

    STRENGTH OF CHOICE: After each of the questions below, circle how you feel about that question as follows: A = strongly like, B = like, C = neutral, D = dislike, E = strongly dislike.

After you have ranked preference and strength of choice, use the guide following to mark each of the questions in the four sets either CM, C, D, or E so that you can know the type of question you have ranked.

Rank		Strongly Like	Like	Neutral	Dislike	Strongly Dislike	Use this column only after ranking: Type of Question
(Example)							
4	1. How do you feel about ...	A	B	C	(D)	E	E·
2	2. When was the first ...	A	(B)	C	D	E	CM
1	3. What is your ...	A	(B)	C	D	E	C
3	4. Create a lesson on ...	A	B	(C)	D	E	D
____	1. Why did the ...	A	B	C	D	E	____
____	2. In your opinion ...	A	B	C	D	E	____
____	3. Describe the ...	A	B	C	D	E	____
____	4. What would happen ...	A	B	C	D	E	____
____	1. What would you predict ...	A	B	C	D	E	____
____	2. When did ...	A	B	C	D	E	____
____	3. Do you believe ...	A	B	C	D	E	____
____	4. Explain how this ...	A	B	C	D	E	____
____	1. What do you think about ...	A	B	C	D	E	____
____	2. What would it be like if ...	A	B	C	D	E	____
____	3. How are they similar ...	A	B	C	D	E	____
____	4. Identify the ...	A	B	C	D	E	____
____	1. Name the ...	A	B	C	D	E	____
____	2. Compare the ...	A	B	C	D	E	____
____	3. Suppose the ...	A	B	C	D	E	____
____	4. Why do you think ...	A	B	C	D	E	____

Preference Rank Totals:
    Remember, the lower the
    total, the greater your
    preference for that
    level of question.

CM_____
 C_____
 D_____
 E_____

Key to level of questions:

(1) 1. C   (3) 1. E
    2. E   2. D
    3. CM   3. C
    4. D   4. CM

(2) 1. D   (4) 1. CM
    2. CM   2. C
    3. E   3. D
    4. C   4. E

Interpreting Your Response   **IN YOUR HANDS**

This inventory was originally developed for an ESEA Title
IV-C research project with the North Montgomery Community School
Corporation. The form was administered to hundreds of students,
elementary and secondary, with the expectation of measuring their
preference and strength of choice toward the four levels of
questions. Many classroom teachers maintained that students
prefer cognitive-memory and convergent level questions. Students
responding to this form generally favored divergent and
evaluative level questions, which is a direct contradiction to
the beliefs of many teachers.

How did you respond? Inspect the preference side (left
side) of the form. Remember that you ranked your preference with
1 the highest to 4 the lowest. From each group of questions, add
the preference ranks for each level. For example, suppose you
marked the divergent question second in the first set of
questions, third in the second set, first in the third set, and
second in the fourth set. The total would be eight. The lower
the total number, the greater your preference for that level of
question.

Now for strength of choice--in other words, your attitude
toward the different levels of questions. Perhaps all you need
to do at this time is to look at your positive, neutral, or
negative feelings toward certain levels of questions. If you do
have negative feelings toward certain levels of questions, do you
think those feelings will be reflected in your classroom
teaching? Is it possible you might have to change your attitude
if you are to use all four levels of questions? Finally, your
attitude toward questioning is undoubtedly the most important
attitude in the class. Whether students think at all four levels
in your class depends almost entirely on you. A last thought, if
you were a teacher, would it matter what level of questions your
students prefer to answer? If your students' preferences make a
difference to you, then use the above preference inventory--you
might be surprised by the results.

more questions
Self-Test

This is a final check on how well you classify questions using the four levels you have just learned. Answer all the items. If you are unsure about any of them refer to the key words for each level or to Bloom's Taxonomy at the end of the chapter. Place CM for cognitive-memory, C for convergent, D for divergent, or E for evaluative on the line provided before each of the questions.

____ 1. Imagine what might happen to the U.S. economy if there is a major shift to the production of compact cars rather than big cars by the automobile industry.
____ 2. What do you predict will be the position of the U.S. as a world power in the year 2000?
____ 3. In your judgment, who makes the greatest contribution to society, a doctor or a lawyer?
____ 4. What are the similarities and differences between the tribes of East and West Africa?
____ 5. When did Texas join the Union?
____ 6. What are the similarities and differences between the concepts of "status" and "role"?
____ 7. How do the administrations of Nixon and Harding compare and contrast?
____ 8. What is the best way to combat inflation?
____ 9. As the Prime Minister of India, how would you insure that everyone receives an education?
____10. What is the relationship between the production of goods and the standard of living?
____11. Who was the last Stuart King of England?
____12. Plan the steps you would take to insure that each citizen pays his or her equitable share of income tax.
____13. Defend your reasons for deciding to live in the city.
____14. Justify a new position and choose the best person for the job.
____15. What is the name of the highest mountain in the world?
____16. How are countries in the middle latitude north and south of the equator alike and/or different?
____17. How many people live in the Soviet Union?
____18. Suppose that marijuana was legalized; what effect might that have on American society?
____19. Do you think that a person accused of mass murder can receive a fair trial?
____20. Did Hannibal conquer Rome?
____21. Which country was the first to land a man on the moon?
____22. Compare the Democratic and Republican parties.
____23. How do you feel about the issue of a guaranteed annual wage?
____24. Explain the difference between a democratic and socialistic form of government.

Answer Key

1.	D	6.	C	11.	CM	16.	C	21.	CM
2.	D	7.	C	12.	D	17.	CM	22.	C
3.	E	8.	E	13.	E	18.	D	23.	E
4.	C	9.	D	14.	E	19.	E	24.	C
5.	CM	10.	C	15.	CM	20.	CM		

Score: **Good** is a minimum score

23-24   **Excellent.** You have mastered all four levels. You are ready to practice all four levels in micropeer-teaching.

20-22   **Good.** Although you missed a few, your working knowledge is above average and you are ready for micropeer-teaching.

16-19   Take a close look at those you missed. It may be that you are slightly confused on one of the levels. You are not ready to micropeer-teach.

0-15   Check the description of each level carefully and try to determine exactly why you made so many mistakes. Do not even think of practicing the four levels in a micropeer-teach.

INTRODUCTION TO BLOOM'S TAXONOMY

A Reference for All Other Chapters in This Book

You may have developed an interest in different levels of thinking. Perhaps you already know Bloom's six taxonomic levels of thinking: Knowledge, Comprehension, Application, Analysis, Synthesis, and Evaluation.[2] Taxonomy (classification of words) is based on the levels at which people think. The last three pages in this chapter are summaries, including words and examples, of each of the six levels of thinking and are intended as a reference. That is, when reading other chapters such as, "Identifying and Writing Behavioral Objectives," "Identifying and Writing Teacher-Made Test Questions," and "Organizing to Teach: Unit and Daily Lesson Planning," you are encouraged to think of the different levels of knowledge that appear in Bloom's Taxonomy. To examine these different levels, note how thought is advanced from lower level (knowledge) through higher level (evaluation). It is not that we wish to discourage lower level thought, but rather we wish to encourage the use of all six levels of thought, for it is in the application of these levels that citizenship can be promoted.

TEACHING RESOURCE

Commentary on Thinking and Reasoning and Questioning

You could be forgiven if you are now a bit confused about four levels of questions, Bloom's six levels of thinking, and two approaches to reasoning: inductive and deductive. And you know that knowledge can be categorized into facts, concepts, and generalizations. Of course, you are expected to keep all the above in mind when approaching the field of education. Bloom's Taxonomy can be helpful in organizing thoughts on thinking, reasoning, and how knowledge is used. The design of Bloom's categories, knowledge, comprehension, application, analysis, synthesis, and evaluation is only a structure that roughly describes how a group of educators believe mankind uses knowledge: i.e., list, vary, apply, sort, change, rank. Lower level thinking includes knowledge, comprehension, and application, whereas higher level includes analysis, synthesis, and evaluation. When reasoning inductively (from particular to general) one might start with knowledge (facts) and comprehension and proceed to application and analysis levels that might yield concepts, and finally to synthesis and evaluation levels that could yield a generalization. The cognitive-memory level question is equivalent to the knowledge level in Bloom's Taxonomy. Convergent level questions are equivalent to comprehension, application and analysis levels. Divergent level questions are equivalent to the synthesis level, and evaluative level questions are equivalent to Bloom's evaluation level. We will not try to confuse you further, but rather to suggest that the Taxonomy will be useful when looking for key words that trigger a particular level of thinking.

In summary, teachers are in the thinking business. Having some notion of how we think such as the Taxonomy, though imperfect, can help us imagine the levels of thought and what levels of questions will elicit and use those different levels of thought. Why be concerned with levels of thought? You should be thinking, "Citizens who perform the role of decision-makers use these levels to reason through problems. My task as a social studies teacher is to help students practice thinking and reasoning as preparation for citizenship responsibilities."

BLOOM'S CATEGORIES
OF CRITICAL THINKING SKILLS

KNOWLEDGE

Specific information
remembered by students
exactly as they learned it.

To repeat the information
students will:

arrange   pick
check   point to
cite   quote
define   recall
find   recite
group   repeat
identify   reproduce
label   say
list   spell
locate   tally
match   tell
memorize   touch
name   underline
offer   write
omit

For example:

Students will
    -list the 5 major
     rivers in the U.S.
    -repeat the Preamble
     to the Constitution.
    -label the original
     thirteen colonies.
    -define the term
     "Roaring Twenties."
    -recall the date of
     Independence.
    -locate the
     "Continental Divide."

COMPREHENSION

Information learned by
students which they can
explain in their own words.

To explain the information
students will:

account for   group
alter   review
change   summarize
restate   submit
reword   retell
translate   vary
describe   explain
generalize
convert (change, transform)
moderate (make less severe)
paraphrase (restate)
transform (change form)
expound (explain)
interpret (clarify meaning)

For example:

Students will
    -paraphrase Lincoln's
     Gettysburg Address.
    -summarize the
     Emancipation
     Proclamation.
    -submit a proposal for
     a project.
    -rewrite the Preamble
     to the Constitution.
    -describe how a bill
     becomes a law.
    -interpret the Pledge
     of Allegiance.

AN EXCITING
TEACHING RESOURCE

134

APPLICATION	ANALYSIS
Information learned by students and put to a new use.	Information learned by students which they break apart to examine.
To use the information students will:	To examine information students will:

APPLICATION — To use the information students will:

give example	relate
apply	profit by
adopt	show
collect	solve
construct	state rule
consume	try
demonstrate	use
handle	utilize
illustrate	operate
make use of	organize

put into action
put to use
exploit (utilize)
mobilize (assemble, prepare)
devote (apply full atten- tion to)
manipulate (influence)
survey (examine closely)

For example:

Students will
    -organize a new fire
     escape route.
    -apply rules of order
     to a class meeting.
    -operate a new
     computer.

ANALYSIS — To examine information students will:

break down	screen
categorize	search
check	separate
classify	sift
compare	simplify
contrast	sort
deduce	specify
diagnose	subdivide
diagram	survey
divide	take apart
dissect	test for
examine	uncover
inspect	outline

analyze (separate into
        parts to examine)
audit (examine records,
       verify)
canvass (conduct survey
        or poll)
factor (determine, decide)
differentiate (show
        difference between)
scrutinize (examine
        carefully)
section (separate into
        parts)
study (inquire, examine
       closely)
investigate

For example:

Students will
    -compare and contrast
     Lee and Grant.
    -survey the Civil
     Rights Movement in
     the United States.
    -examine the effects
     acid rain.

BLOOM'S CATEGORIES
OF CRITICAL THINKING SKILLS

SYNTHESIS

Information learned by
students which they
formulate in a new way.

To formulate or hypothesize
information students will

formulate   hypothesize
blend   imagine
breed   invent
build   make up
cause   modify
change   originate
combine   plan
compile   predict
compose   produce
construct   rearrange
create   reconstruct
design   reorder
develop   reorganize
discover   revise
evolve   suggest
generate   suppose
find an unusual way
conceive (form, imagine)
effect (cause, bring about)
structure (construct,
              arrange)
visualize (imagine)

For example:

Students will
      -formulate a new
       Constitution.
      -compose a historical
       skit.
      -originate a human
       rights declaration.

BLOOM'S CATEGORIES
OF CRITICAL THINKING SKILLS

EVALUATION

Information learned by
students will allow them to
form their own opinions.

To express their own
opinions students will:

criticize   rate
accept   recommend
award   referee
choose   reject
debate   rule on
decide   select
defend   settle
evaluate   support
grade   umpire
judge   rank
adjudge (determine, decide)
appraise (evaluate,
         estimate)
assess (evaluate, estimate)
arbitrate (judge, decide)
critique (critically
         review)
decree (order, decide)
editorialize (express an
         opinion)
justify (demonstrate,
         prove)
prioritize (establish
         right to importance)
weigh (measure, think
         about)
censure (criticize
         severely)

For example:

Students will
      -choose the best
       person for the job.
      -justify a position
       taken.
      -support a proposed
       recommendation.
      -criticize the new
       dress code.

NOTES

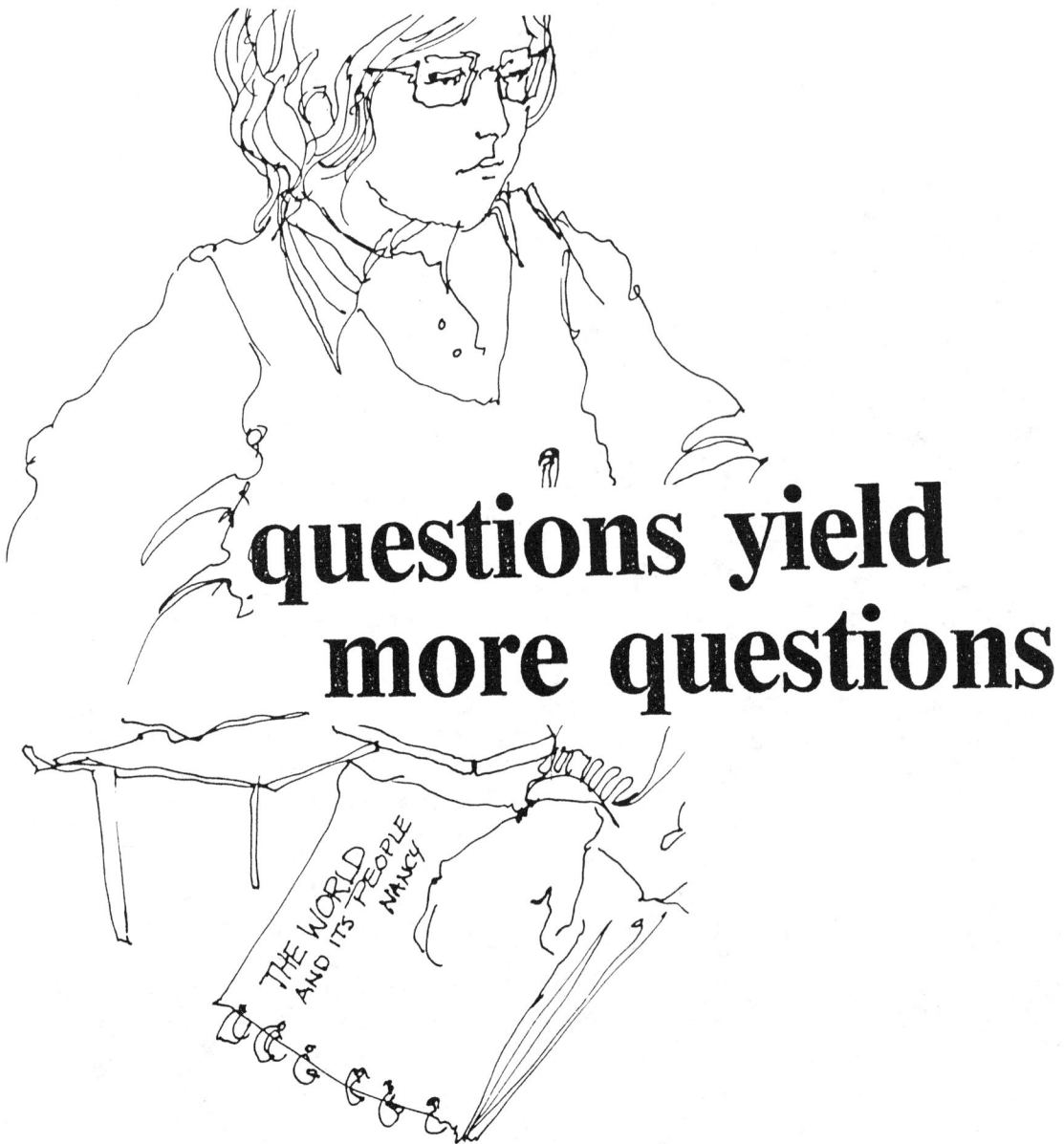

questions yield
more questions

CHAPTER VII

TECHNOLOGY AND INSTRUCTIONAL RESOURCES: A FUNCTION OF EFFECTIVE TEACHING PRACTICES

OBJECTIVE: After reading this chapter you will be able to identify and apply the concepts (concrete and abstract) to the use of technology and instructional resources and systematically plan appropriate use of resources.

In today's social studies classroom, with self-motivation not being what it once was, we teachers need all the tools we can grasp.

Michael Roessler

AN EXCITING TEACHING RESOURCE

Commentary

Within the past 30 years the world has moved from the Industrial Age into the Information Age . . . . Change is neither good nor bad, but it does require that we understand and adapt, otherwise there is no way for us to remain current and prepare students for the office of citizen they will hold in the 21st century . . . . Social studies teachers will need to deliver instruction in new ways . . . . Some of those [new ways] include audio eleconferencing, audio graphic systems, freeze-frame video, satellite transmission of courses, two-way interactive television, and interactive videodisks that extend learning from passive to active modes.[1]

surprise

The use of technology and instructional resources (TIR) has everything to do with learning, remembering, and effective teaching. How do we know that TIR really makes any difference to students' learning and remembering? If you question at all that research supports the use of TIR, please turn back to Chapter IV, "What Research Suggests about Effective Teaching and Learning in Social Studies." You may remember that "studies suggest that students learn and remember at differing rates according to the degree that the students are involved in the lesson." In other words, the more the students are involved with the lesson, actively participating, focused, with quality time on task, the more they will learn and remember what they have studied.

138

Larry Cuban summarizes the research this way:

Yet researchers know that pressures on teachers to cover content swiftly and to raise student test scores have combined to produce classrooms in which teachers lecture for two-thirds of the time, . . . ask most of the questions, and rely on the textbook . . . . Researchers also know that for students to cultivate critical thought, they need to ask questions often and freely, become actively involved for long periods with problems that make sense to them, and engage in activities in which the teacher plays the role of coach.[2]

Cuban identifies how social studies is usually taught in the nation's classrooms. The studies on learning and the Commentary on the previous page strongly suggest that reform and change are necessary. The report of the American Library Association recommends what needs to be done.

an invitation to revolution

What is called for is . . . a restructuring of the learning process. Textbooks, workbooks, and lectures must yield to a learning process based on the information resources available for learning and problem solving throughout people's lifetimes . . . . Such a restructuring of the learning process will not only enhance the critical thinking skills of students but will also empower them for lifelong learning and the effective performance of professional and civic responsibilities.[3]

COMMUNICATIONS, LEARNING AND TECHNOLOGY

This chapter will focus on the use of different types of technology and instructional resources (TIR) with a special section on computers. However, before turning to the application of instructional resources, think about why instructional resources are essential to effective teaching practices.

Using Technology and Instructional Resources to Convert Abstract Ideas to Concrete Examples

Concrete and abstract are opposites. Concrete is something that can be seen, smelled, heard, felt, or tasted. Abstract is a thought (concept or generalization) that cannot be directly sensed. Can you think of something that is

abstract? Words, numbers, symbols of any kind. Can you think of something that is concrete? Perhaps the chair you are sitting on, the desk in front of you, the clothes you wear, all of which are verified facts. TIR will help you to be less abstract and more concrete, but then why would you want to be concrete? There is a good answer to this question.

The more concrete your instruction, the more effective your teaching will be. For example, as you already know, if you are only lecturing with no TIR, students learn and remember approximately 10%. If you include taking notes and writing on a chalkboard and add a visual, you add an additional 10% to make 20% learning and remembering. If you add to the lecture, taking notes, and writing on the chalkboard, either large or small group discussion so that most students participate in a discussion, the learning and remembering increases to 40%. Then if you wish to increase the learning and remembering to 80%, introduce technology through an interactive multimedia computer lesson.

One final thought, do you also remember the research summary that "effective teaching should build in powerful reinforcement of ideas by repeating the same ideas in different forms of presentation"? Of course, repeating the same idea in different forms can be done by offering other verbal examples, but the most effective seems to be a mixture of different TIR that express the meaning of ideas all the way from their most concrete to their most abstract, i.e., "a picture is worth a thousand words."

CONCENTRATE

Concrete and abstract are not the whole story on understanding why one should use TIR. One equally strong argument is expressed as follows:

I know you
BELIEVE
you understand what you
THINK
I said,
but I am NOT sure,
you realize that what you
HEARD is NOT what I MEANT!

The point is that no matter what you say in a concrete or abstract way, you may not be understood. TIR provides a means by which students can know that they may not have understood your meaning. How often have you said, "Yes, that's what I said, but that's not what I meant." The following "Cone of Experience" demonstrates the difference between abstract and concrete on the topic "Early Man."

A PICTURE IS WORTH A THOUSAND WORDS

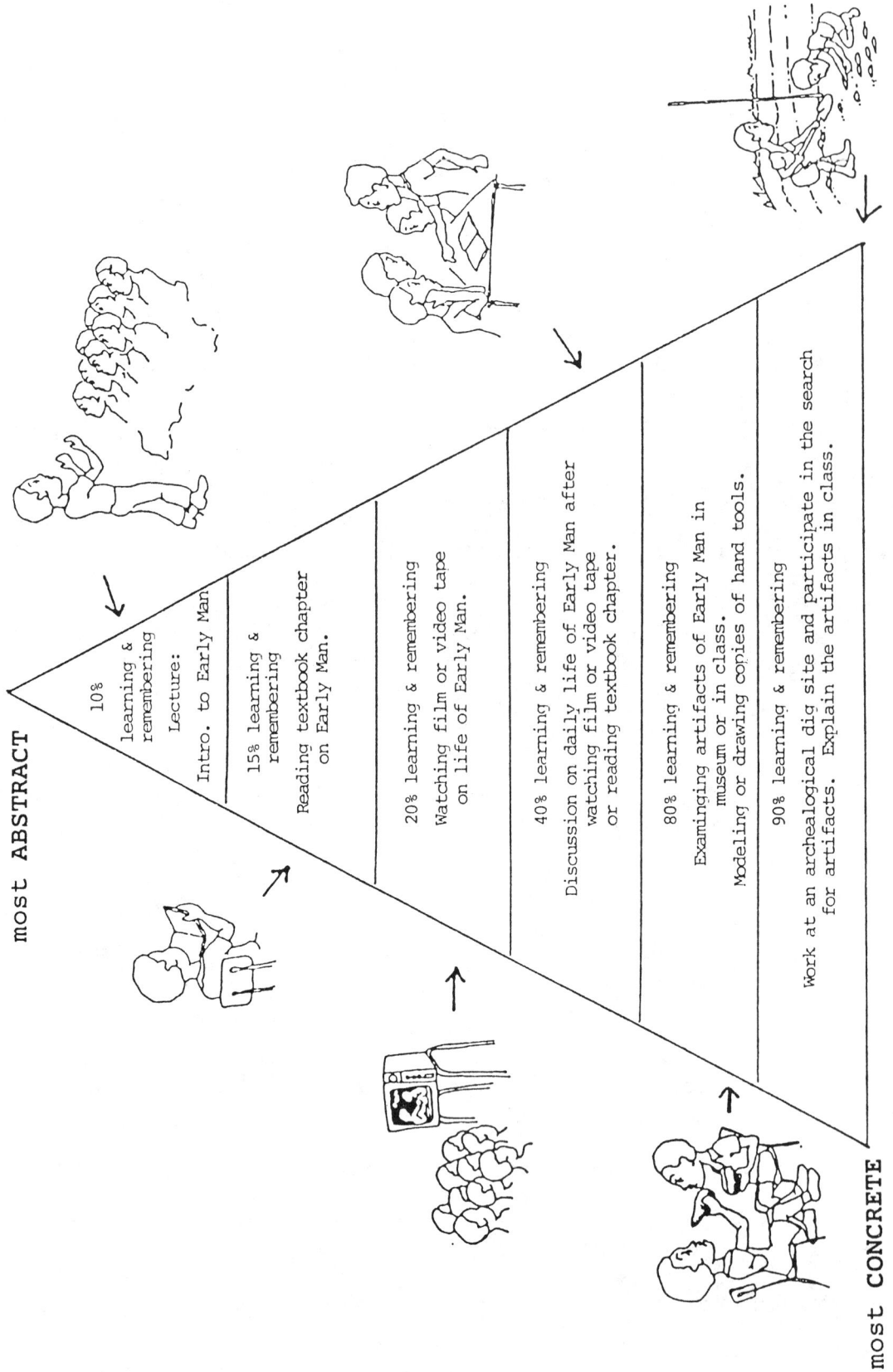

CONE OF EXPERIENCE[4]

as it correlates with

LEARNING AND REMEMBERING

most ABSTRACT

10% learning & remembering
Lecture: Intro. to Early Man.

15% learning & remembering
Reading textbook chapter on Early Man.

20% learning & remembering
Watching film or video tape on life of Early Man.

40% learning & remembering
Discussion on daily life of Early Man after watching film or video tape or reading textbook chapter.

80% learning & remembering
Examining artifacts of Early Man in museum or in class. Modeling or drawing copies of hard tools.

90% learning & remembering
Work at an archealogical dig site and participate in the search for artifacts. Explain the artifacts in class.

most CONCRETE

children learn

lecture

Did you interpret the illustration to mean that lecturing on archaeology is the most abstract, and conversely visiting an archaeological dig and participating in the search for artifacts is the most concrete? Did you note the difference between the top and bottom of the pyramid where students **hear** about archaeology, then read, then **see and hear** a video on archaeology, then **talk** about it, then **practice doing** archaeology, and finally a field trip where students **actually do** archaeology? In short, to do it is to remember, to hear it only is to forget. Are you convinced that practicing and doing are important to learning?

Great abstractions such as democracy, development, self-reliance, freedom, and social justice do not mean the same thing to all people. Historical events, geological landforms, political concepts of power and authority are often difficult to visualize and, therefore, require illustrations and lively descriptions for the events and concepts to come alive. As the report above suggests, "textbooks, workbooks, and lectures must yield to a learning process based on the informational resources." All of the studies are clearly saying that sitting passively listening is the past. Actively doing must be the future. In short, TIR become the means by which the teaching and learning process is to be reformed and changed.

INFORMATION AGE

In summary, when thinking about TIR, keep in mind the words "concrete" and "abstract." Ask yourself how abstract or concrete can I be to achieve learning and remembering? The answer, of course, depends on the past experience of your students. When students have read about and reviewed a concept such as social change, they should be expected to deal with that concept in the abstract. However, if students are just beginning to learn the symbols of language such as an alphabet, math as numbers, social studies as names of geographical land-forms, longitude and latitude on maps, then the instructional resources should be more concrete. Are you convinced that teaching social studies requires TIR? There is really no alternative for the future. Your obligation is to know how to systematically plan the use of resources.

Systematic Planning

Curriculum Development

Systematic planning in the use of resources is often difficult. The reason is that teachers often do not know how to "mix and match" the abstract nature of social studies curriculum with an appropriate choice of TIR. There are important considerations for the use of TIR. These include: (a) the level of abstraction of the content, (b) the age and maturational level of students, (c) the number of students, and (d) the inherent characteristics of the resource itself. The resource used in a class of 200 college students may not be appropriate for a nursery school class of five. A flat picture or a computer program may be better than a moving picture--or vice versa-- depending upon what one is attempting to teach. Keep in mind the following guidelines:

1. Teachers should use a systematic process to select TIR.
2. Teachers should use TIR as a means of extending their ability to communicate, as a means of extending themselves.
3. Teachers should use TIR as a means of making instruction more concrete.

Each of these three points will be explained and applied.

The Systematic Process for Selecting and Using TIR[5]

Ask yourself the following three questions:

1. When do I use TIR?

2. What will TIR do for my students?

3. How do I select the right TIR?

Resources must match needs

The three questions can be sequenced as follows:

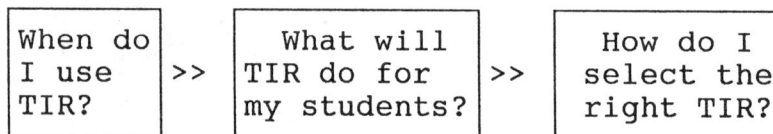

| When do I use TIR? | >> | What will TIR do for my students? | >> | How do I select the right TIR? |

Questions

When Do I Use TIR?   A few suggestions

The answer is when a given piece of TIR helps you to reach a given objective. Imagine a social studies course that you will be certified to teach. Identify a piece of TIR from the given list and describe how you might use the resource to:

***I**ntegrated
learning
environment*

(a) Initiate the lesson _____

_____

_____

(b) Develop the lesson _____

_____

_____

(c) Summarize the lesson _____

_____

_____

Resource

radio
television
film
filmstrip
overhead projector
opaque projector
flannelboard
bulletin board
chalkboard
posters
slides
tape recorder
pictures
chart
diagram
map
globe
videotape
   recorder
interactive multi-
   media computer
   programs

we have to create

What Will TIR Do for My Students?

Using one of the resources identified above, describe how you might use the resource to increase student comprehension/ learning from the lesson.

_____

_____

_____

Use This Now

How Do I Select the Right TIR?

There are two major steps in selecting the right resource. First, you must determine what the instructional objective(s) is(are). For example:

"Having read the booklet Indians of the Midwest, students will be able to identify and name four Indian tribes that lived in the old Midwest Territory."

Second, you must decide which resource will do the best job of meeting those objectives. For example:
"Invite a native-born American Indian to speak to the class; go on a field trip to a local or state museum."
What other resources would be appropriate to the objective above?

In selecting the appropriate resource to meet your instructional objectives (knowledge/skills/attitudes), there are five questions which you should ask yourself:
1. Will the resource be used for group or individual study?
2. Should the given resource be visual, oral, or a combination?
3. What specific purpose must the resource achieve?
4. What resources are available?
5. What one resource or combination of resources will provide the most effective concrete representation of abstract content?

Have Access

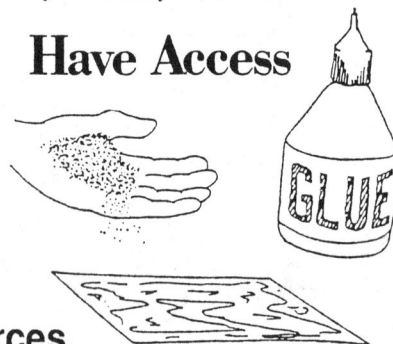

Creating Your Own Resources

In this chapter we are not advising you to become a skilled audio-visual technician or computer programmer, to make your own slides, to shoot your own movie or video film, or to produce your own television or computer programs. This would not be realistic advice given the limited training you will have in the use of TIR and the limited facilities available in some schools.

However, you simply need not accept a school or classroom that does not have resources. You must say to yourself, "There are ways of improving my classroom environment. I can create resources that will make my classroom interesting and challenging." You must first believe in yourself, in your ability to create resources, then you must utilize available materials. This chapter will show you how.

Imagine a classroom with 30 to 40 students. One side has windows, the other walls are blank. There is one entrance door. The room is bare, without any resources. You may very possibly inherit such a room. The task now is to transform a sterile and depressing environment into an interesting, stimulating, aesthetically pleasing classroom, in short, a good place to teach and learn.

Now look carefully at the picture of the room on the next page. Notice the mobile hanging from the ceiling. When there is a breeze through the window the mobile moves, creating constantly changing patterns of light and color. Use the mobile as one might a bulletin board by placing on the mobile illustrations of the topics being studied in class.

The right choice

Innovation

Notice the floor. It is not just a place to walk. It is an excellent location for maps and other kinds of illustrations. Yes, we mean it. The tile squares on some floors can be used to illustrate spatial relations, geometric figures, and measurement, all part of geography. The floor can also be a place for a large paper or cardboard map of a continent.

Note that the lower window has been darkened by a covering of paper. On that paper are illustrations of current events topics. Shining through the paper, the sun illuminates the illustrations in a way impossible to ignore. Notice the posters on the wall opposite the window. Many airlines and travel agencies have colorful posters which they will give you. Better yet, get the class to make their own posters to illustrate the topic under study.

Finally, note that the board at the front of the class is used for two purposes. It can be a bulletin board or a screen against which to project images. We think that this is the beginning of an interesting room. No matter where the students look--at the window, at the ceiling, at the walls, at the floor-- the teacher has provided a stimulating set of visuals. Wherever their eyes turn, they can see some facet of the subject they are studying. The room is both colorful and relevant and should stimulate interest.

we have to create

Creating and Using Concrete Instructional Resources

You or your students are encouraged to create instructional resources. Easily constructed resources can be divided into two types: (a) display boards and three-dimensional materials, and (b) graphic materials. Under the first category are chalkboards, bulletin boards, flannelboards, mobiles, dioramas, sand tables, and salt maps. The category of graphic materials usually includes maps and globes, pictures, diagrams, charts, graphs, posters, and collages. The following is a list of resources, some of which you and your students can create, all of which the class can use as a means of visually expressing ideas.

TEACHING RESOURCE   A few suggestions

Display Boards and Three-Dimensional Materials

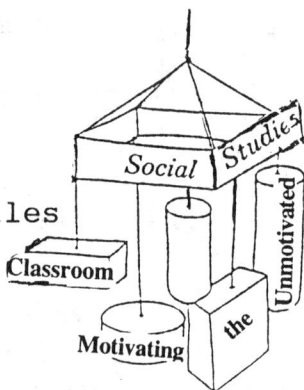

Name	Characteristics
Chalkboards	-most widely used media -easy to write on and erase -effective to highlight or emphasize ideas
Bulletin boards	-excellent place for display of collected materials or student work -good for topical displays
Flannelboards	-often hold your students' attention -good for illustrating stories or problems -materials can be prepared ahead of time -materials can be stored and reused
Mobiles	-good for single topic illustration -make good student construction project
Dioramas (three-dimensional mini-scene)	-usually constructed by elementary students as a project to illustrate some event, location, storyline in book, etc.

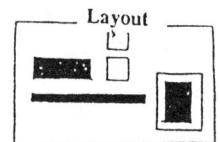

RESOURCES

Sand tables

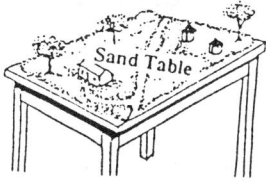

- excellent for modeling or molding
  landscapes and landforms
- may be smoothed and reused

Salt maps
  (1 cup flour,
   1 cup salt
   1/2 cup water)

- mixture excellent for modeling and
  or molding, partic-
  ularly for land-
  forms or top-
  ographical
  maps
- becomes dry when hard
  and can be painted
  and stored for future display

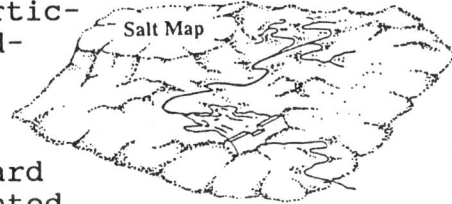

Graphic Materials

Focused Multi-Media

Name	Characteristics
Maps and globes	-visual illustration of relation- ship of one point to another -globe most accurate map form and allows earth to be viewed from many different points
Pictures	-most common form of illustration -enriches oral and written materials
Diagrams, charts, graphs	-used mainly to demonstrate relation- ship between objects, items, events, etc. -the abstractness of these materials and the symbols used call for viewer interpretation
Posters and collages	-often student-created as a project to promote or highlight some topic or event

Effective Teaching Practices Using Instructional Resources

In its broadest sense "motivation" includes all that is known about teaching. Whatever a teacher does can potentially motivate students. Motivation, like the weather, is a perennial topic of teachers, and few teachers need to be convinced that their task--and usually high challenge--is to motivate students.

148

Motivation starts with an interesting lesson and an interesting lesson begins with an attention-getting activity or device that allows students to say, "Huh? What is this? What does that mean? I want to know more." We now want to illustrate just such attention-getting devices that you or your students can make and which we think will focus attention and encourage quality time on task.

1. **Using a flannelboard.** Place a cloth outline map of the United States on a flannelboard. Distribute to the class pieces of cloth shaped and marked as the various states and colonial regions. First ask those students who have colonial regions to place them on the flannelboard so that they resemble our country just before the Revolution. Next, have the students with the states that existed in 1920 place those on the flannelboard. Finally, have students with the states as they appear today place them on the flannelboard. Ask students to identify as many patterns as they can.

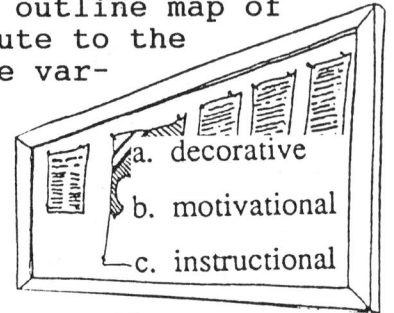

a. decorative
b. motivational
c. instructional

2. **Using maps and objects.** Bring to class a number of objects--small containers of corn oil, pieces of coal, a chocolate bar, a small slab of steel, a container of wheat. Display these items before the students. Ask the class, "Why are these important objects?" If they answer, as they might, "These are created or located in the United States," have students place each of the objects on a map of America at the exact spot where the product is produced, grown, mined, or processed.

3. **Using a chalkboard.** In bold letters write on the chalkboard a startling statement or question such as "Democracy and freedom are dead in America. They simply have not been buried yet." Ask students to comment on this obviously provocative statement. Encourage agreement and disagreement and record the major arguments for and against on the board.

4. **Using globes.** Hold a globe so that only the North Pole and surrounding regions are visible and have students view the world from this polar projection. Now, move the globe to the conventional position. Ask, "If one were to view the earth from the perspective we normally have, which clearly separates continents, would this change one's views?" Change the globe from one perspective to another. Concentrate on what differences in perspectives are created simply by changing the position of the globe.

5. **Using pictures.** Ask students to select the ten most important inventions or discoveries in the history of the world. Once the class identifies ten, assign them to find pictures of each as they are used in the contemporary world. You now have a "Science Hall of Fame." Using a variation of this, you can also create your own "Midwest Hall of Fame" or "Athletes Hall of Fame."

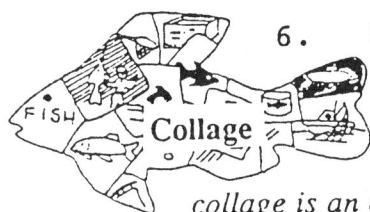

1941 - SAVE THE WORLD FOR DEMOCRACY

collage is an art form

6. **Using a collage.** Each week assign students to bring in a picture from a weekly magazine or newspaper. Then have them put the picture on the class weekly collage and explain why the pictures they chose are important. Store the collages over a period of time, say a month. Use them for a review of current events. Have the class create a collage that represents social problems that they identify, cut pictures from popular magazines. Also list problems on transparency. Post collage and keep transparency, occasionally reviewing both to demonstrate how ideas and problems change over time.

Fish shape overlaid with illustrated food-can labels showing fish or fish names, pictures of rivers and streams, etc.

Can you think of any more ways to use the resources discussed in this chapter? There simply is no limit to the ways that common, ordinary materials in your environment can take on a new life. All you need is imagination. Keep in mind the need to focus attention by doing.

Technology and Instructional Resources

In addition to creating your own resources, look around your school for audio-visual equipment and the software appropriate to each kind of audio-visual device. The following is a list of audio-visual (A-V) equipment which describes the value and limitations of the equipment in the classroom. *Technology is driving the future of Education*

A-V Equipment	Value	Limitations
Opaque projector	-can enlarge almost any picture or object	-projector is heavy -projector gets very warm -room must be darkened

Overhead projector and transparencies	-teacher can face class while using equipment -materials can be prepared ahead of time -transparencies can be wiped clean and reused -materials can be stored for future use -can be used in partially darkened room	-must use trans-parencies (clear plastic sheets) -must use special writing equipment (grease pencil or felt tip pen)
Slide projector and slides	-can be shown to a large group or to one child in individualized instructional program -can control pace of viewing -slides can be arranged or rearranged quickly -can produce own slides	-slides can be easily lost -slides can easily become out of sequence -care must be taken so that slides do not become smudged with fingerprints or dust
Filmstrip projector and film-strips	-film easy to store -film pictures always remain in sequence -can control pace of viewing	-frames (pictures) must be shown in sequence; they can never be rearranged
Motion picture projector and films	-films tend to hold students' atten-tion -can present events and distant places that students would be unlikely to see in person -can speed up or slow down action or objects and thus present what cannot be seen with the naked eye	-film is viewed uninterrupted so you must prepare students to view film and provide them with a follow-up activity

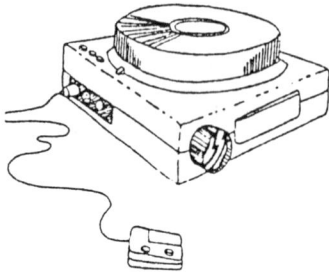

Phonographs and records	-clearness of sound
	-wide variety of
	  materials
		-record storage and
		  maintenance

Tape recorders	-easy to operate
	-can record programs
	  for later listening
	-can tape students'
	  speeches for
	  evaluation
	-tapes can be erased
	  and reused
		-tape storage and
		  maintenance

Television and video-
tape recorder
	-daily news broad-
	  casts
	-record guest
	  speakers for
	  future playback
	-dramatizations and
	  reports recorded
	  for playback or
	  evaluation
		-many pieces of
		  equipment to
		  move and
		  maneuver
		-takes more than
		  one person to
		  operate

Computers will take on importance during 1990s

Microcomputer

Technology and the Computer Revolution

A chapter on the use of technology in social studies would not be complete without recognizing the impact of the computer on social studies. The following reactions by three different social studies teachers help to summarize the impact.

The relationship of social studies to computers is limited only by our imaginations.[6]	We cannot expect the tools to teach the skills, any more than we expect a pencil to teach a child how to write.[7]	By taking charge of data and information in active, creative ways, students may begin to synthesize the knowledge, under-standing and values that are the real goals of social education.[8]

Schools are about to become the way we used to educate our children

SOFTWARE TECHNOLOGY

The statistics are: most people surveyed in the '80s expected that computers would raise the quality of education. By 1980 over 50% of the U.S. school districts were using computers for instructional purposes. By 1984, 89% of the high schools, 81% of the junior highs, and 62% of the elementary schools had computers.[9] By 1990 almost all public schools had computers. This does not mean that all school children are computer literate or that all schools have a sufficient number of computers. It just means that public faith in computers to raise the quality of education was converted, in part, to some or many computing stations. And, of course, some elementary schools are now equipping all students with a take-home computer. Selected colleges are now requiring all students to have their own computers.

the Inevitable

The question is no longer, "Will there be computers in the school and homes?", but rather "What will the computers do in the schools?" So far there are three answers to how they will be applied. Given the demands of a highly technological society, the first application is computer literacy, which simply means learning how to use the computer, perhaps programming the computer in one of the computer languages. A second application is learning to use the computer as a data base, which simply means gaining data information and then processing that information on the computer. The third application is learning to use the computer for computer-assisted instruction.[10]

TAKING CONTROL

The truth is computer software that aims at computer-assisted instruction is developing so rapidly that, if we were to list programs here, those programs would already be obsolete by the time you read this chapter. However, it would be useful if you had an idea of the computer's potential in social studies, for surely within your lifetime textbooks, workbooks, and lecturing as experienced now in the nation's social studies classrooms will practically disappear. One of the replacements might be interactive multimedia. But then let a social studies computer expert tell you about the coming revolution.

Few emerging technologies hold more promise for education than interactive multimedia. When video, text, sound, data and graphics combine in a single program under the control of the user, we can enjoy a powerful teaching and learning experience.

Good teachers of any subject have always taught with voices, with printed texts, with music, with film, with drama. A distinguishing feature of the profession of teaching is the individual art of combining these media into a learning experience with students. We now have technology that allows a teacher to put all these resources in one place, to access them with a touch of a finger, and to make intelligent links between the ideas in one medium and the facts in another. These tools can be delivered at reasonable cost to the teacher's or student's desktop. With it students and teachers can find, display, and produce learning as never before.

In its current form, multimedia teaching uses a Macintosh to drive a laservideodisc, CD-ROM, and HyperCard-based text and graphics. For example the user clicks on a word in text shown on the Mac screen; this brings up a graph and runs a short video clip on the laserdisc, both relevant to the work that was clicked. A cross-reference link to a more detailed text from the CD-ROM might also be made available to the user. Then the user might click on one of the elements in the graph and be shown a still image from the videodisc, in full color, that illustrates that element of the graph.

Like any technology, interactive multimedia can be used in a variety of ways. It can provide drill-and-practice exercises as well as wide-ranging exploratory databases; it can lead the user down a predetermined path or it can allow free access to a myriad of knowledge links.[11]

Remote Access instead of Computer Labs

RESOURCES FOR THE RESOURCEFUL TEACHER

NOTES

Getting Ready

WORD PROCESSOR

I know you
BELIEVE
you understand what you
THINK
I said,
But I am NOT sure,
you realise that what you
HEARD, is NOT what I MEANT!

CHAPTER VIII

READING COMPREHENSION:
A FUNCTION OF EFFECTIVE TEACHING PRACTICES

OBJECTIVE: Having read this chapter you should be able to identify: (1) minimum competencies for developing effective reading, (2) specific types of comprehension problems, (3) coping strategies, and (4) review study skills and complete the Effective Reading Rating.

One of every nine adults in the United States cannot read at all.

Can't read. Can't write. Can't win.

"Can't read. Can't write. Can't win" is a summary of a teacher's responsibilities and this is particularly true when reading comprehension is an important skill in the course. The skills of reading and studying require discipline. What we want to discuss in this chapter is how to improve students' reading comprehension through a disciplined approach to reading and studying. In short, your students need the skill of reading to win, but do you know how to help them win?

Up to one half of American school-age children do not have adequate (grade level) reading comprehension. What you do not know is that the average American is reading at the equivalent of the fifth or sixth grade level. So what of it? Simply put teachers in secondary school face students who do not necessarily read or study very well--yet teaching in social studies is predicated on the assumption that students have the skills to read and study. Frankly, most secondary teachers reject any attempt at an organized, persistent approach to improving the skills of reading and studying. Improving reading comprehension is a real pain. Secondary teachers generally just do not want to deal with that particular pain because other pains have priority. Rejecting students' reading problems has a long history having mostly to do with the traditional job of a secondary teacher.

One hundred years ago students who did not read well and had poor study skills just did not join the 8% to 10% of American children who were allowed to enter senior high school. In fact, the secondary schools of today no longer teach the elite 10%, but rather 95%, of which 75% graduate and herein lies a question. The question is, "Can secondary schools continue to teach the 95% which represents most all American students, yet continue to act as though they were teaching the 10% elite who are ready, willing, and able to study?" Clearly the answer must be that a highly technological, interdependent society such as the United States can not long tolerate a large minority, some claim up to 50%, of nearly illiterate citizens. What are you going to do? Are you going to be part of the problem: "can't read, can't write, can't win," or will you choose to be part of the answer? The remainder of this chapter is written on the assumption that you are interested in being part of the answer.

23 million Americans are functionally illiterate. They can read, but not well enough to function in society.

TAKING CONTROL

Being Part of the Answer Is Improving Reading Comprehension

Let's be clear on what you are being asked to do. No one is asking the secondary social studies teacher to teach reading. In theory, students have practiced reading skills at least since the first grade. What you are asked to do is work on reading comprehension which is simply helping students to effectively use the skill to gain the information you have assigned in your class readings.

41% of the adults who are illiterate in English are English-speaking whites; 22% are English-speaking blacks; 22% speak Spanish.

Research on Effective Teaching with Reading

Social studies is, according to studies, a textbook course, and thus effective reading skills are essential. Do you remember from Chapter IV on research what effective teaching and learning are? Below is a reminder.

1. Students learn best through active rather than passive learning.
2. Students learn best when there is clarity, enthusiasm, and a clear task to perform.
3. Students learn best when there are stimulating questions rather than lectures.
4. Students are better able to learn abstractions through concrete illustrations.

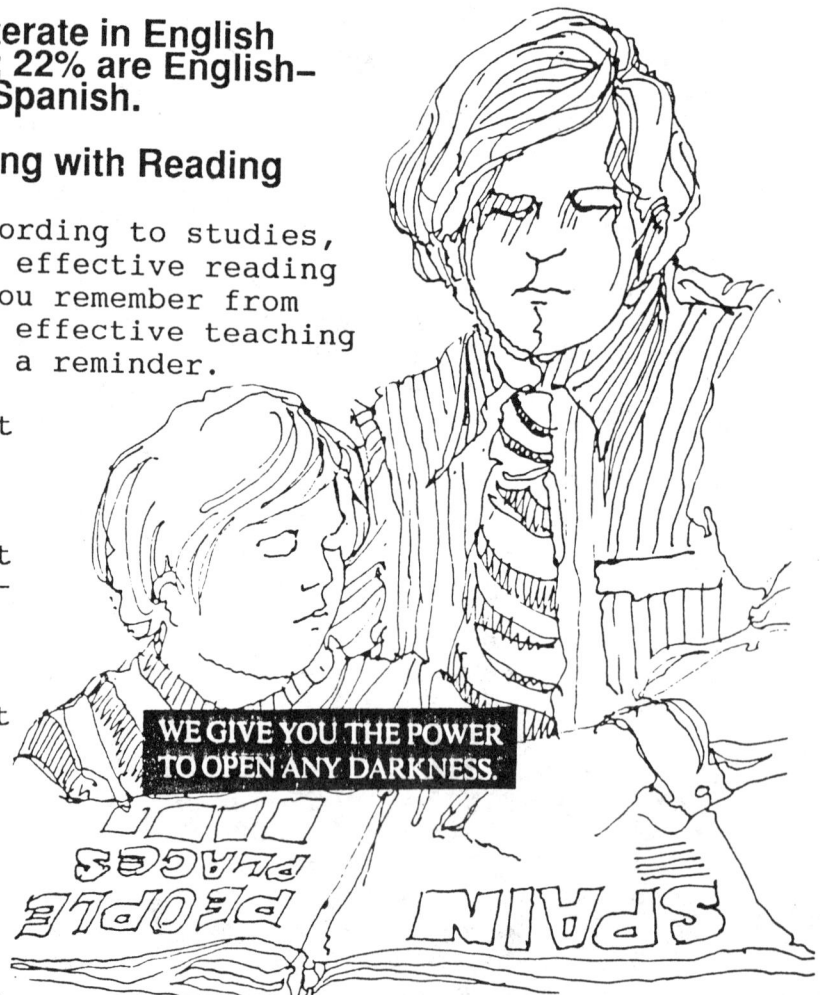

WE GIVE YOU THE POWER TO OPEN ANY DARKNESS.

PEOPLE PLACES

SPAIN

IN YOUR HANDS

Also we know, as you may remember, that if students are asked to just read an assignment, they will learn and remember approximately 15% of what they see. However, if students were to follow a system in which they could enhance their reading comprehension, they would be able to learn and remember at a much higher percentage. But what incentive will you offer so that students will want to read effectively, meaning to increase their reading comprehension? There is a direct relationship between reading comprehension and improved test scores. If students want to improve their class achievement as well as performance on national examinations, they should be concerned with their reading comprehension.

What Are the Social Studies Teachers' Minimum Competencies for Developing Effective Reading Comprehension?

What should a teacher of social studies know and be able to do to improve students' reading? One can argue that every teacher of social studies should also teach reading. But we do not think that every social studies teacher should be a specialist in reading. The assumption is that every teacher should continue to work with students on vocabulary--both pronunciation and spelling--reading comprehension, and study skills. While some teachers, in fact, do just this, it is done in a haphazard and not in a careful and systematic fashion. In short, secondary teachers do not usually encourage systematic reading to improve comprehension. But, of course, you now know that encouraging comprehension is absolutely required for today's students. So what should you know and where do you start?

One of every 10 drivers in the United States cannot read road signs.

Reading Survey Is a Start   TEACHING RESOURCE

This is what you should know. As a minimum, social studies teachers ought to know how to administer two simple surveys: (1) a reading survey that gathers information on students' attitudes and habits toward reading, and (2) a survey that identifies students' reading comprehension on the materials you are using in class.

A typical information survey will have questions such as:
1. Do you do leisure reading outside of school?
2. Do you find reading difficult?
3. Do you find reading social studies materials difficult?
4. Do you ever read the newspaper?
5. Do you have a place outside of school where you generally read?
6. Do you make a careful record of your assignments?
7. Do you normally keep an orderly notebook?

How will the answers to these questions help teachers improve their students' reading? This information survey administered at the beginning of the school year will give you a general picture of your students' overall reading habits. You will know from the survey how your students use reading outside the school and what kind of study skills they practice.

A second competency is to evaluate your students' ability to read and comprehend a text or materials that you are using in the class. To evaluate their reading comprehension you should turn to pages in the middle of your reading materials, then ask each student to read orally several sentences. As the students read, note if they have difficulty pronouncing the words or following the sentence. Select a word or idea from what the students have read and ask them to explain the idea or word. By the time your students have finished the oral reading survey, you should have a good idea of their level of reading comprehension.

Assessing Student Reading Levels   important

Two of the more popular techniques for assessing reading level are the Cloze Inventory and the Maze Technique. The inventory requires students to complete a passage unfamiliar to them from their text or other reading materials at their grade level. Every fifth word should be omitted. The blanks must be completed with the exact words. The scores from this inventory will indicate one of three reading levels: first, independent level meaning students can read on their own; second, instructional level meaning students can read with help; and third, frustration level meaning the reading is unsuitable for the student. The Maze Technique requires the student to circle the correct word to fill in the blank. The passage should be unfamiliar to the students with every fifth word deleted. Multiple choice format is used. For each blank three alternatives are presented in random order: the correct word, an incorrect word of the same grammatical class, and an incorrect word of a different grammatical class.

Identifying the Readability Level of Texts   RIGHT NOW

Though there are many readability formulas, one of the more popular is the "Fry Graph for Estimating Readability." This technique requires the teacher to select three 100-word passages from near the beginning, middle, and end of the reading materials. The teacher counts the total number of sentences in each 100-word passage, then the total number of syllables in each

100-word passage is counted. The final stage is to plot on the Fry Graph the average number of sentences per 100 words and the average number of syllables per 100 words. By plotting these averages on the graph the teacher can determine the grade level at which the book was written.

THE WORLD AND ITS PEOPLE NANCY

Reading Gap

This term refers to the difference between the student's reading comprehension score and the readability of the text. Suppose the student is reading at the 8.5 grade level as measured by an achievement test score and the text used in class is written at the 11.5 grade level. The reading gap for this student is 3.0 years.

65% of prison inmates in the United States cannot read.

The label of a frozen TV dinner is written at an 8th grade level.

The label of an aspirin bottle is written at a 10th grade level.

Can't read

Students' Reading Ability Chart

Secondary social studies teachers might not always be willing to develop a base of information about each student's reading ability considering the 130 to 150 students taught each day. But one could argue that teachers ought to know how a base of information is developed and also be able to interpret organized data from reading scores, anecdotal reports, etc. What minimum base of information should teachers be able to identify and interpret? Most students have taken a battery of achievement tests throughout their schooling. Teachers should be able to interpret a reading score from an achievement test arranged in a reading chart. This sample chart lists all the students in a class and offers an overview of the class's reading ability.

SEVENTH GRADE SOCIAL STUDIES

Reading Scores from Achievement Test Comprehension
Grade Level Scores

4th Grade	5th Grade	6th Grade	7th Grade	8th Grade	9th Grade
Tom White 4.5	Joy Adams 5.6	Ann Smith 6.1	Jim Spencer 7.3	Sue Green 8.0	Bonnie L. Nowakowski 9.1
Sue Price 4.7	Bob Brown 5.9	name____ 6.0	name____ 7.8	name____ 8.2	name____ 9.9
		name____ 6.7	name____ 7.1	name____ 8.9	name____ 9.3
		name____ 6.6	name____ 7.7	name____ 8.2	name____ 9.9
			name____ 7.2		
			name____ 7.9		

Using this chart:
    This chart offers a summary of the reading ability of the class. Using this chart will help the teacher identify the media, resources, materials, reading assignments, and method, techniques, and strategies appropriate to the students' reading ability.

Think about this and respond:
If you were teaching this seventh grade class and you had this chart, what assumptions could be made about the class' reading ability?

_____

_____

_____

What level of social studies reading materials would you request?

_____

_____

_____

To summarize, social studies teachers' competencies should include knowing about and being able to interpret the results from rather standard techniques for developing a reading base of information. As a minimum, teachers should know techniques for content inventory, assessing reading levels (Cloze and Maze), identifying the readability of texts (Fry Graph), and interpreting the meaning of reading gap. Knowing the various techniques for assessment is obviously helpful, but they are by themselves only ways of diagnosing problems. What we need is a strategy for dealing with reading comprehension problems once they are identified.

classroom problems

The Bottom Line: A Simple but Effective Reading Strategy, Pick Your Own--But Pick One!

If there are reading problems, how do I deal with them? That is the bottom line for every teacher. Perhaps social studies teachers can agree that they have an important stake in improving reading comprehension. They can agree that coping skills are needed. Teachers are looking for a reading strategy that does not seriously disrupt their classroom schedule, is easily administered, and not rigid or complex. And if that were not enough, the strategy must make sense and, in fact, actually help students improve their reading. Are there such strategies? If you have taken a reading course such as "Reading in Middle and Secondary School," you know there are many different strategies. Choose any that you think is helpful. The SQ3R strategy cited below is one among many and is intended to serve as an illustration of an easily administered, non-intrusive strategy that has been successful.[1]

A few suggestions

Suppose from the two surveys, information survey and oral readings, you determine that half of your students are unable to successfully comprehend the reading materials. What should you do? We recommend the following strategy. This strategy was originated by F.P. Robinson and remains a standard strategy for increasing reading comprehension. The strategy is called **SQ3R** and is essentially built on Robinson's research which states that the best way to learn and remember what one has read is: to quickly survey (S), glance over the assignment, then turn each heading into a question (Q), then read (R) to answer the question, recite (R) a response in your own words, and finally review (R) your questions and answers. At first this may seem rather tedious and difficult, and require a great deal more time than just skimming though the assignment. But once the strategy disciplines reading behavior, the students' reading comprehension will dramatically increase and the strategy will require very little extra time. The following is an explanation of the **SQ3R** strategy.[2]

AN EXCITING TEACHING RESOURCE

SQ3R Strategy to Improve Reading Comprehension

SURVEY

Glance over the headings in the chapter to identify the main points. Also, read the final paragraph if the chapter has one. This survey should not take more than a few minutes and will show the core ideas around which the chapter is organized. This survey will help you organize the ideas as you read them later.

QUESTION

Now begin to read. Turn the first heading into a question. This will arouse your curiosity and so increase comprehension. It will bring to mind information already known, thus helping you to understand that section more quickly. And the question will make the important points stand out. Turning a heading into a question can be done instantly upon reading the heading, but it demands a conscious effort on the part of the reader to make this a query for which an answer must be found.

READ

Read to answer that question, i.e., to the end of the first headed section. This is not a passive plodding along each line, but rather an active search for the answer.

RECITE

Having read the first section, look away from the book and try briefly to recite the answer to your question. Use your own words and include an example. If you can do this, you know what is in the section. If you can't, glance over the section again. An excellent way to do this reciting from memory is to jot down cue phrases in outline form on a sheet of paper. Make these notes very brief.

Now repeat Question, Read, and Recite on each subsequent headed section. That is, turn the next heading into a question, read to answer that question, and recite the answer by jotting down cue phrases in your outline. Read in this way until the entire lesson is completed.

REVIEW

When the lesson has thus been completely read, look over your notes to get a bird's-eye view of the main points and their relationship and check your memory as to the content by reciting the major subpoints under each heading. This checking of memory can be done by covering up the notes and trying to recall the main points. Then expose each major point and try to recall the subpoints listed under it.

What Comprehension Problems Does SQ3R Help to Solve?

An insurance policy is written at a 12th grade level.
An apartment lease is written at a college level.

TURN BAD

Students read the lesson, but they didn't <u>read</u> it. You know what I mean, you have done it many times yourself. Your eyes played over the words, you turned the pages, but when you finished reading, you hadn't an idea about what you had just read. So, what didn't you do? You didn't focus your attention. If you had applied SQ3R you couldn't have failed to focus attention. In short, SQ3R sharpens concentration and, as we often say, provides quality time on task. Some problems with reading are that students often read without purpose, and they do not discipline themselves to read without supervision. The interpretation of maps, graphs, charts, table, and pictures is nonexistent or ignored when most students read their assignments. Other problems are:

1. Reading just has not become a part of the student's everyday life.
2. The student finds difficulty in expressing thought both orally and in writing.
3. Listening vocabulary is much larger than reading vocabulary.
4. Speaking vocabulary is less varied and there may be difficulties with the meaning of words.
5. The student may show a preference for concrete, specific ideas rather than abstract, general ones.
6. The meaning of facts which become concepts then generalizations are difficult to grasp.

INTO GOOD

SQ3R will help with all of the problems above. We did not say the students aren't going to resist having their comprehension disciplined. They are going to complain, "Why do we have to do this stuff?" The answer is plain. "I want you to focus on the reading and be prepared tomorrow to begin some activities that require information from your readings." The key is FOCUS, FOCUS, FOCUS.

When Do You Use SQ3R Strategy?   What's in it for you

Let there be no mistake. We have said in the most emphatic way that you can improve your students' ability to read effectively if you require them to use a disciplined reading strategy. Teachers often ask, "When should I use SQ3R in class?"

164

Clearly the time to discuss effective reading is when you are giving the reading assignment. Do this: when giving the assignment, practice Survey (S) and Question (Q). Take two to three minutes to survey the headings and any illustrations in the readings. Then with the whole class turn each of the headings into a question. You do some of the turning, the students do some of the turning. In class the next day, complete SQ3R by completing the three Rs--Read (R), Recite (R), and Review (R). It should not take all period. That exercise can take the place of a discussion or recitation. At first the exercise will take some time, but as the students learn to focus on Q (questions), the SQ3R can be done very rapidly to the point where the strategy becomes automatic for the students with only an occasional reminder. Then watch those grades improve.

Pause for a moment and collect your thoughts on suggestions for dealing with reading difficulties. One of the rich places to find suggestions is in Chapter IV in the list of effective teaching practices. The following exercise includes excellent suggestions on how to cope with reading comprehension. Instructions: Read the following suggestions. Which of these suggestions are supported by the research cited in Chapter IV? Write R for research on the line provided before those suggestions for which you can find support.

What's in it for us.

Suggestions for Coping with Reading Comprehension Problems

_____ 1. Use books in which illustrations will help abstract ideas such as concepts and generalizations become concrete.
_____ 2. A good reader could read the material to a group of slow learners; interpreting, commenting, asking, and answering questions. Peer teaching is sometimes very effective.
_____ 3. In many reading activities have students work in pairs or small task oriented groups supporting each other in a common answer or action.
_____ 4. Give special attention to vocabulary growth. Be sure that difficult and new words are on the board.
_____ 5. Visual appeal should be used widely. Much knowledge can come from pictures, and labels and captions provide some reading practice.
_____ 6. Emphasize fewer ideas and repeat the ideas in different forms of presentation.
_____ 7. Keep reading and writing assignments short.
_____ 8. Concentrate on activities that can be completed quickly.
_____ 9. Make sure students know the purpose of the activity.
_____10. Provide checklists or charts to record progress toward goals and check off each item as completed. This provides frequent reinforcement.
_____11. Provide frequent positive reinforcement and de-emphasize comparative evaluation (comparing one student with another). Substitute individual progress whenever possible.

(Numbers 1, 2, 3, 5, 6, 9, 11 are directly supported by research.)

Now we turn to one last set of suggestions on study habits that are important to the achievement of effective learning and remembering.

Study Habits

How're you going to do it?

Knowing how to learn is an important part of lifelong education. Create the proper learning habits with students at an early age and they will definitely have a better chance to achieve. Go over the following suggestions with your students several times during the school year.[3]

(1) Make and keep a study schedule. Set aside certain hours each day for homework. Kept the same schedule from day to day.

(2) Study in a suitable place, the same place each day. Is lack of concentration a study problem? Experts tell us that proper surroundings will help greatly in concentrating. The amount of time is not what counts, it's focused attention and quality time on task that counts.

(3) Collect all the materials you need before you begin. In your study area you should have all your materials at hand so that you can study without distraction or interruption.

(4) Don't wait for inspiration to strike-- it probably won't! We can learn a lesson about studying from observing athletes. Can you imagine seeing an athlete who is in training sitting on the field waiting for inspiration to strike? They train strenuously every day whether they think they want to or not. Like the athlete, we get in training for our tests and examinations by doing the things we're expected to do over a long period of time.

(5) A well-kept notebook can help raise your grades. Teachers know that there's a definite relationship between the orderliness of students' notebooks, and their grades. Set aside a special section for each of the subjects on your schedule.

(6) Make a careful record of your assignments. Put assignments down in your notebook in a special place. Knowing just what you

are expected to do and when you are expected to do it is the first step toward completing important assignments successfully.

(7) Good notes are your insurance against forgetting. Learn to take notes efficiently as your teachers stress important points in class and as you study your assignments. Good notes are a must for without notes you will often need to reread the whole assignment before a test. With them you can recall main points. Following a simple SQ3R will help with good notes.

(8) Perhaps you've asked, "How can I remember what I've studied?" One secret of remembering is over-learning. The secret of learning for the future is over-learning. Over-overlearning is continuing your study after you have learned the materials well enough to just barely recall it. Experts suggest that after you say, "I have learned the materials," you should spend an extra one-fourth of the original study time to over-learn the materials. In an experimental study, students who over-learned the materials remembered the material four times as well after a month than those who did not over-learn.

(9) Frequent reviews will pay off well in knowledge and grades. Without review the average students can forget 80% of what they have read in just two weeks. Your first review should come shortly after you study the material for the first time. This early review acts as a check against forgetting and helps you remember far longer, and this is the reason for using SQ3R which requires a review.

Can't read. Can't write. Can't win.

"Can't read, Can't write, Can't win" is our way of saying there is a reading comprehension problem that is not necessarily being addressed by most secondary social studies teachers. The solution to the problem is in your hands. You can play a role by simply applying a disciplined reading strategy and a suggested disciplined set of study habits. Are you going to be part of the reading problem or are you intent on being part of the solution? One out of every nine Americans can't do what--?

Rating Your Performance on the Use of Effective Reading Ratings

As a final consideration, examine the following rating procedures. We include this rating so that you might check your teaching of reading effectiveness against a standard of excellence. These procedures should act as a guide to the actions you take in the classroom to improve your students' comprehension.

Use This Now

EFFECTIVE READING RATINGS # classroom

Instructions: Circle the number which best represents your performance in teaching your students the procedures listed below. 1 = most always, 2 = sometimes, 3 = rarely.

1. STUDY TECHNIQUES: Are efficient study techniques (SQ3R and study habits) presented and discussed with the class, then gone over and rehearsed from time to time so students will automatically use them?   1 2 3

2. VOCABULARY BUILDING: Are new terms or definitions related to social studies explained to students and their understanding of terms periodically checked?   1 2 3

3. SUPPLEMENTARY MATERIALS: Are materials with different points of view presented so students can learn to distinguish fact from fiction and recognize biased statements, evaluate what they read?   1 2 3

4. SCHOOL RESOURCES: Do you make use of special personnel or services provided by the school when necessary, i.e., library, audio-visual equipment, media, resource people?   1 2 3

5. INDIVIDUALIZED INSTRUCTION: Do you plan for or take into account students who have special needs, i.e., handicapped, gifted, multicultural, disadvantaged?   1 2 3

6. EXAMINING PAST PERFORMANCE: Do you examine past assignments to identify what made them successful or disappointing, i.e., what skills might need more work, what content/concepts were to be learned but were not?   1 2 3

7. EXPLICIT INSTRUCTIONS AND ASSIGNMENTS: Are instructions and assignments worded so as to leave no doubt as to what is expected of students (complete performance objectives)?   1 2 3

8. RELATED READING: Do you suggest outside reading, or AV media, or experiences that relate to class work, i.e., TV specials, historical/political events?   1 2 3

9. APPROPRIATE READING LEVEL: Do you match students' reading level to their ability by providing materials both above and below grade level?   1 2 3

TOTAL _____

Summarizing the ratings: **IN YOUR HANDS**

9-12   Excellent, outstanding. Your teaching procedures include effective reading practices. Keep up the good work.

13-18 Good. Suggests that you are aware of good reading procedures, but not practicing what you know about effective reading.

19-27 Poor. Your students are not going to benefit from your knowledge of effective reading procedures. Identify above the items which you are not practicing and plan them as part of your next lesson.

NOTES

Suggestions for Coping with Reading Comprehension Problems

_____ 1. Us~~~~ PRIORITY ~~bstract
id~~ ~~ecome
co~~

_____ 2. A ~~ ~~roup of
sl~~ ~~ing,
and answering questions. Peer teaching is sometimes
very effective.

_____ 3. In many reading activities have students work in
pairs or small task oriented groups supporting
each other in a com~~~~ answer or action.

_____ 4. Give special att~~ ~~vocabulary growth. Be
sure that diffic~~ ~~w words are on the board.

_____ 5. Visual appeal s~~ ~~d widely. Much knowledge can come ~~ ~~. and labels and captions
provide some ~~ ~~e.

_____ 6. Emphasize f~~ ~~eat the ideas in
different ~~ ~~n.

_____ 7. Keep re~~ ~~ments short.

_____ 8. Concen~~ ~~n be completed
qui~~

_____ ~~ ~~of the activity.
~~rd progress
~~as completed.

~~nt and
~~(comparing one
~~ndividual

CHAPTER IX

DISCIPLINE: A FUNCTION OF EFFECTIVE TEACHING PRACTICES

OBJECTIVE: Having read this chapter and noted Spencer's Principles, Coping with Discipline Problems Chart, and Guidelines you will be able to identify in case studies patterns of disciplinary problems and apply coping strategies.

AN EXCITING TEACHING RESOURCE

Discipline and classroom management were my biggest fears as I entered teaching . . . . After 19 years of teaching . . . each summer before school starts I still have nightmares featuring my class in out-of-control situations.

Betty Clapp

A classroom out-of-control haunts every teacher. Some teachers say that today they face far more students with behavior problems than just ten years ago. Most teachers complain that the last three years are the worst they have experienced. What's going on out there? Why is there an increasing discipline and classroom management problem to the point where veteran teachers are saying that they are no longer free to do the job they were hired to do-- teach? The answer from the teacher's point of view is that the problem arises from the changing American family. The fractured family results in lack of parental interest and support for the school, leaving angry, stressed-out, and frustrated students for the teachers to handle. In short, teachers see class- room discipline as directly related to the larger social concerns outside the school.

Above curriculum and beyond train- ing, salary, working conditions, or almost anything else one could name, teachers concern themselves most with disruptive, insolent, violent, aggressive, uncontrollable, and obnoxious students. This is hardly surprising since the presence of such students can eventually wear teachers down and create symptoms similar to wartime battle fatigue. Disruptive students make teachers wish they had never entered teaching in the first place, and not infrequently send them into early retirement and even chronic physical and emotional disability. Unfortunately, while teacher

170

concerns are entirely real, their understanding of disciplinary
problems often appears to be based upon a number of
misconceptions.

Changing family structure can be directly traced to classroom behavior problems.

DISCIPLINE WITH DIGNITY

The most serious of these misconceptions is that discipline
is something that teachers do in addition to teaching. That is,
teachers tend to separate their curriculum from something called
"discipline." One teaches something and in addition one clamps
down on students. This is a serious misunderstanding of teaching
and discipline. We would like to argue that the title of this
chapter "Discipline: A Function of Effective Teaching
Practices," is what should prevail in schools. That is, good
discipline is the result of effective teaching. However, it
would be naive to believe that in every situation effective
teaching means good discipline. There are situations in which
good teaching makes little difference. The way teachers select,
plan, organize, use technology and instructional resources (TIR),
lead discussions, make assignments, and test, is
usually not separable from the kind of discipline
that prevails.

Educational priorities are second to hunger, abuse (physical and sexual), and neglect which are the first issues in school.

We also believe that there are differences
among students, that some students are docile
and easily teachable and rarely cause trouble
while others tend to be the source of much
teacher unhappiness. We would also maintain
that while there is no magic wand that
teachers can wave over such students, by
understanding their behavior and adopting a
few simple disciplining techniques, teachers
can improve their capacity to deal with
disruptions. We are short of failproof
formulas, but here are some ideas we think you
should consider.

you have to face the critics

The biggest discipline problems are disruptive students--those who interrupt, are rude, leave their seats, are sarcastic and seek attention.

Virtually all normal students will test the limits of a teacher's authority, just as they will test all other aspects of their world. This means that they will "try to get away with" as much as they can. This does not mean--as the conventional wisdom has it--"just don't let them see you smile the first two weeks of school." It does mean that you will need to be firm and to specify what you will and will not accept. It means that there will have to be rules and that students will have to perceive you as a firm but fair human being who cares enough to create a desirable learning climate.

The American Experience

Students lack motivation, responsibility, self-discipline.

There are different kinds of students who present different problems. To be sure, teachers fear the "acting out," noisy, and aggressive student. But the silent, withdrawn, and sullen one can explode and ultimately prove a worse problem. We think teachers label as "problems" those behaviors which may be actually normal for particular ethnic groups. Understanding the meaning of disruptive behavior, such as impulsive talking, may help a teacher ignore it--and this may be a most effective technique. Finally, good discipline comes out of your entire approach to students and to teaching. The implication is that it is much easier to anticipate and prevent disciplinary problems than it is to treat a full-blown, angry, disruptive student.

BAD PUPILS GOOD PUPILS

Other reasons for discipline problems: drugs, alcohol, and lack of respect for teachers or any authority.

A final note for any new teaching situation: it is much preferred that teachers be resolute and determined to enforce classroom discipline. Students will surely test the limits of proper behavior in class. It is much easier to be firm at the beginning of the school year and to modify the rules as you come to know your students. This means that you must first learn in each class what will cause discipline problems. We believe review of the more common causes of discipline problems and suggestions on how to handle those problems will be helpful. The following comments and suggestions for new teachers come from a classroom teacher who has spent almost thirty years trying to get students to do things they didn't want to do. **Good News**

SPENCER'S PRINCIPLES

1. FIND THE SOURCE. There are two sources of behavioral problems, external and internal. Externally, student behavior is strongly influenced by their parents, their home life, other teachers, their peers, physical surroundings, and a myriad of

other things too numerous to mention. Internally, the attitudes
that both the teacher and student bring to the classroom are
paramount to determining what happens. The important
thing is to concentrate on those things
you can change.

2.   **BE PREPARED.** There is no
single factor that will create
more unhappy situations for a
teacher than being unprepared.
It won't eliminate all discipline
problems but it will prevent many
from happening.

3.   **BE YOURSELF.** We understand
that most teachers teach the way in
which they were taught in spite of
the best efforts of teacher education,
and although we expect you to pick
and choose from the best you have seen,

Alternatives

your style of dealing with students must be
consistent with your own personality. You cannot continually
imitate someone else as the students will quickly see through
you. The most important thing is to discover your own
expectations and limits and plan your discipline strategies
accordingly.

4.   **BE CONSISTENT.** The most important thing students perceive
about you is that you are serious about what happens in your
classroom. Convincing them that each of the fifty-five minutes
is equally important is vital in establishing an attitude of
discipline. If you want them to work hard, you will have to work
hard. Inconsistency will destroy classroom atmosphere very
quickly.

5.   **ALWAYS GIVE THE KID A WAY OUT.** The problem with
confrontation situations is that someone has to win which implies
that someone else must lose. The dilemma you face is that <u>you
must win and the student cannot afford to lose.</u> The only viable
alternative, therefore, is to always give the student a way out.
Discipline is a constantly changing, action/reaction type of
thing. There are no pat answers, but trying to find ways for the
student to save face and yet do what you are asking is helpful.

6.   **DON'T KEEP SCORE.** Realizing that student abuse in many
instances is not a personal assault or an indication of failure
on your part is very helpful in allowing you to turn your cheek
with a proper attitude. Teachers who keep track of student's
offenses in order to "get even" are headed for trouble. Students
have more energy than you do and there are more of them.

LIFE BEYOND

In summary, let me point out that discipline problems are not always a sign of failure on your part but are a built-in part of the passage from adolescence to adulthood. Strive to create an attitude of discipline rather than bogging down in policing specific actions. Do not keep score, remembering that to really forgive means to forget. When all else fails and it's time to go to that one class which drives you up the wall every day, keep saying over and over to yourself, "I can endure anything for fifty-five minutes."

Turn with us now to the chart "Coping with Discipline Problems" which summarizes specific problems and suggests coping techniques.

COPING WITH DISCIPLINE PROBLEMS CHART

A few suggestions

Discipline problems may result from:

Coping with the problems:

1. Being too strict or too lenient.

2. Students unsure of how teacher expects them to act.

Be familiar with school rules, set class rules with the help of students, then adhere to those rules.

3. Shouting at students.

Try to relax. (Getting "riled" will only intensify the problem.) "Quiet" control may be the answer. Teach from different parts of the room.

4. Teacher unaware of what is going on in class.

Discuss with the class what is causing the problem and respect their views. Make your physical presence known. Occasionally move about the room.

5. Ineffective or inadequate seating chart.

Rearrange. Try not to reprimand individual students, but rather ask a section of the room to pay attention, quiet down. Stand near that section.

6. Over-excitable, antagonistic student.

Sending a potential troublemaker out of the room on a task may

174

classroom problems

7. Same procedures day after day.

8. No illustrations, demonstrations or concrete experiences.

9. Teacher lacks interest or unable to transmit or demonstrate interest.

10. Lack of planning-- special, disadvantaged, gifted.

11. Lack of specific instructions and/or assignments.

12. Students see no reason for the class, activity or for being in school.

13. Unsatisfactory home environment.

14. Used to different discipline at home.

15. Physical or emotional problems.

16. Teacher too tired to care.

diffuse an imminent problem and consequently be beneficial to all.

Vary teaching techniques and activities including the use of technology and instructional resources to retain student interest or re-interest them. A teacher's task is to focus attention. The research on learning is clear-- focusing during time on task is key to teaching effectiveness.

Planning method, techniques, and strategies that focus attention is the means to achieving positive attitudes. Prepare and plan adequately; this means developing unit and daily lesson plans, taking into consideration individual differences.

How're you going to do it?

Get to know your students so you will be aware of how far you can push them and how to interest them. Allow students to present or express negative feedback.

Be familiar with students' home situations. Not infrequently child abuse is involved. Knowing the home situation is not a solution. However, it can help you, the teacher, cope with classroom behavior.

Punishment inflicted on whole class is rarely effective. Move to trouble spot and carry on class from that spot. Your personal presence will solve many discipline problems.

Creating a Positive Attitude: An Approach to Classroom Discipline

TAKING CONTROL

We truly believe that discipline is a function of effective teaching practices, and by effective teaching we mean creating a positive attitude in the classroom. No one would wish to say that all discipline problems would disappear if we were effective teachers. That will never be true. We have said, and you know, that there are a multitude of reasons why some students will create discipline problems. However, it is also true that you can minimize discipline problems by avoiding an emphasis on (1) student misbehavior and (2) dwelling on students' inadequacies. A rigid puni- tive (meaning castigatory or retaliative) system with a constant emphasis on punishment is built on the assumption that students are essentially bad and that misbehavior could be prevented by strict- ness or treated by punishment. For some stu- dents and their parents the school system appears to be punitive. Punishment for alleged idle- ness and disorder have encour- raged a number of students to leave school. Teachers can do better by reforming their attitudes about how to prevent misbehavior by creating a positive attitude.

How're you going to do it?

Poor performance should not be ignored which means that students do need specific corrective feedback so that they will know what they need to improve. By posi- tive attitude we mean students should expect to learn to receive assistance when they have problems and be supported in their learning efforts. In short, teachers should create a classroom with positive expectations. The following is a list of actions that teachers can take which create positive attitudes and minimize discipline problems.

CREATING A POSITIVE ATTITUDE

1. Identify appropriate instruc- tional goals and discuss them with students so that they are clear about what is to be expected.

2. Insist that students complete work satisfactorily.

3. Refuse to accept excuses for poor work.

4. Convey confidence in the student's ability to do well.

5. Display an encouraging, "can do" attitude that generates student excite- ment and self-confidence.

6. Avoid comparative evaluations of lower- ability students that cause them to conclude that they cannot accom- plish the objectives.

GOOD

A positive classroom also includes praising good performance. When students know that teachers believe them to be capable, then it is easier for students to attempt new tasks and reach higher goals. Do you remember in the research chapter the section on "Effective Teaching Practices" and the practice called the "Self-fulfilling prophecy"? The point was that effective teaching means the accomplishments or success of students will depend, in part, on the teacher's treatment and expectations of them. How does a teacher convey to individual students that positive expectation of success? We recommend public praise, that is an acknowledgement to the student and the class that the student has accomplished a task. However, the public praise should focus on the accomplishment rather than just effort. When a student puts forth considerable effort, you want to acknowledge it, but the praise should also include emphasis on achievement such as, "John, you have worked hard on the project. Your attention to detail and the good organization of your ideas have been quite outstanding." Also, look for ways to provide private praise. Private conversations, written comments on papers, tests, and other assignments give you, the teacher, opportunity for praising accomplishment.

TEACH Canread Canwrite Canwin

Discipline Starts with Expressing Encouragement

The message that teachers deliver to students and how the students receive it has much to do with discipline. Consider the following teachers' comments as examples of ways to provide constructive praise and encourage confidence and acceptance.

1. "I need your help by . . ."
    "The small group needs you help . . ."
    "The class needs your help . . ."

2. "That's what I call improvement" or "I am pleased with your improvement."

3. "I know you want me to believe you can't do it, but I think you can."

4. "We like you, but we don't like what you do."

5. "That's a nice job of . . ."

6. "I can understand how you feel, but you can handle it."

the Brightest
The Best

One last suggestion, extra incentives might be considered to create a positive attitude. If you are looking for performance, achievement, and good participation, you might consider setting incentives such as rewards the class may work towards, i.e., field trips, class party, special privileges like participation in some fun activity which depends on good behavior. In short, provide a common goal which offers the incentive of reward. Rewards are often a visible recognition of success.

Of course, as a teacher you will devise your own classroom management that fits your style and personality. You will want to develop a positive classroom attitude, and this chapter on discipline ends with additional guidelines and case studies that you should consider when devising your own classroom discipline.

Setting the standard for success.

GUIDELINES

At first establish control early in the best way available, hopefully through positive incentives, then consider the following guidelines.

_____a. Have as few rules and regulations as possible.

_____b. Enforce whatever rules and regulations you make.

_____c. Involve students in making and enforcing rules and regulations.

_____d. Do not make threats you cannot carry out.

_____e. Discuss misbehavior in private with the student whenever feasible.

_____f. Vary classroom activities with occasional breaks and change of pace.

_____g. When you use punishment make it as immediate as possible.

_____h. Don't punish the entire class for the misbehavior of a few.

_____i. Be careful with the use of sarcasm in the classroom. Remember you are the model of the behavior you want from your students.

Use This Now

Rank order 1-9
There is always the problem of reading lists of guidelines and not thinking seriously about them. The guidelines above could be useful, but they need to be rank ordered based on your

perception of how you would prepare to provide a disciplined class. You will notice a line in front of each of the nine guidelines. Rank order the nine guidelines based on what you believe to be the most important (1) to the least important (9).

A final thought before asking you to apply what you have learned above to case studies. To be worried about discipline and class management is natural. To know that discipline in the classroom is a top problem for most teachers, and that teachers feel discipline problems are parent and community generated does not help much; in fact, at times it gives one a helpless feeling. We have suggested that teachers can try different strategies. For some students no strategies will work. It is the teacher's job to maintain a learning environment. The Guidelines, Coping Chart, and Spencer's Principles can help.

A discussion about discipline would be incomplete if you just noted the problems, read the Coping Chart, noted Spencer's Principles and positive attitude suggestions and rank ordered the nine guidelines to developing your own classroom discipline. To complete the introduction to discipline you should apply what you have learned to real, live students. No text can give you real live students, but what can be offered are case studies of students who are defined as discipline problems.

Introduction to Case Studies

Before you read the case studies, identify what you might derive from reading them carefully. These case studies are illustrative of discipline problems. They exemplify certain features of common behavior that teachers encounter daily. Before you read each one, prepare yourself by asking the following questions:

TEACHING RESOURCE

1. What problems does this case study illustrate?
2. How did the school--and its personnel--respond to the individual? Does the school identify the student as a problem?
3. How would you as a teacher respond to the student's problem? When responding keep in mind Spencer's Principles, Coping with Discipline Problems Chart, Guidelines, and the positive attitude approach.

The case studies that follow ask that you identify the strengths and weaknesses, strategies, and discipline that might be appropriate for each of the students. As we have said above, teachers should modify their classroom discipline as they come to know the students. Coming to know the students means being able to identify strengths and weaknesses and being able to apply effective teaching practices, strategies, and discipline.

NOW YOUR DECISION

Select those case studies that apply to the level at which you are preparing to teach. Fill in the response box at the end of each of those case studies.

Case Studies CONCENTRATE

Cindy - Kindergarten   Pete - Eighth grade
Jonathan - Third grade   Jimmy - Ninth grade
Steve - Fifth grade   Trudy - Tenth grade
Bob - Sixth grade   Mary - Twelfth grade

CINDY[1]

Age: 5.5
Grade: Kindergarten

Cindy has a relatively short attention span. She is easily distracted and cannot complete tasks without periodic direction or assistance. She can count to five with some prompting and knows the letters in her name. She is able to verbalize her needs and wants in active, declarative, three-word sentences. Her mental age (MA) is approximately 2.6.

Cindy is able to walk and run although she is not coordinated enough to skip or hop on one foot. She is able to hold crayons and pencils but makes random, uncontrolled drawings. Cindy is easily frustrated when given a difficult task. She is frequently noncompliant (refuses to follow directions), has difficulty playing cooperatively, and does not share well with other children.

JONATHAN[2]

Age: 9
Grade: Third

Test Data: Wechsler: Full Scale IQ 64
Bender-Gestalt: Age 6 equivalent
Gray Oral Reading Test: Grade equivalent 1.0

The developmental history indicates that Jonathan was two years old before he walked alone, was not toilet trained until he was four years old, and still needs help in dressing himself.

Jonathan's language development is approximately four years below age expectancy. He speaks in short sentences. When he becomes anxious he either withdraws and refuses to talk or he repeats a word or short sentence over and over. Jonathan is able to recite letter names and sounds, can count to 30, matches numerals to sets, and performs simple addition. He can recognize some words and read fluently in the pre-primer book. His comprehension is very poor. His handwriting is very poor.

Cindy and Jonathan

Write responses here: Check the Principles, Chart an Guidelines.

How would you describe the problems that Cindy and Jonathan have in class?

What techniques and strategies would you suggest using with Cindy and Jonathan?

What would you suggest as appropriate discipline for Cindy and Jonathan?

The remaining case studies appear in unedited form. They were written by teachers about their own students.

STEVE
5th Grade - Non-reader

I.   Steve is considered a "problem child." He is making very poor grades and doesn't seem to care.

   A.   Identifying Data

      1.   Name: Steve Myers Brown
      2.   Address: Logan, Indiana
      3.   School and grade: Logan Elementary School, 5th grade
      4.   Age: 12
      5.   Date of birth: March 24
      6.   Place of birth: Indianapolis
      7.   Sex: male

B.   Description of Problem
      Steve's problem is one of reading. He cannot read
      and therefore makes very poor grades in school.

II. History

   A.   Health and Physical History

      1.   Physical factors:
            There is very little record of his preschool
            development. Steve's mother states that it is
            hard to say when he started to talk because he
            never spoke plainly from the beginning, but with
            a slur. This slur is not so noticeable at the
            present time. His walking age is noted as being
            normal for a baby. Steve's medical history is
            normal with the exception of a mild case of
            scarlatina at age 4. His days absent from school
            are about average. There are no obvious physical
            defects. At present there is only one psychiat-
            ric report available and this was made when Steve
            was in second grade and 9 years old. It was found
            in this report that Steve is partially deaf to
            the degree that he can't hear certain consonant
            endings such as the "d" in "and." It was also
            found that he is a reversal reader--he reads
            "saw" as "was." Steve also showed a slight
            spasmodic eye condition when his eyes moved from
            side to side as they do in reading. There was no
            record of his ever going to a doctor about his
            sight or hearing.
      2.   Personality factors:
            Steve seems always to be talking and interrupting
            the class. He is, however, always very friendly.
            He appears to be rather insecure and tries to get
            attention. Reports show that he has a normal
            relationship with his family, but when discussing
            his parents, such as if one of them would be able
            to help him with his studying, he takes a non-
            committal attitude. Although when asked to do
            something by a teacher Steve will say, "no," he
            always laughs and does it. He seems to want to
            help you and to be helped himself. He will try to
            improve his grades when urged by a teacher and is
            personally helped with something, but when on his
            own he does nothing.

   B.   School History

            Steve is in the 5th grade. His marks are very poor.
            He is failing every subject except math (D). He
            repeated both the first and second grades. Steve never
            hands in homework and the quality of the work done in
            class is very poor--cannot be read. He will answer

182

questions in class, but his answers are usually
incorrect. Steve has always attended fairly small
schools. Most of the teachers consider Steve to be a
troublemaker. Although Steve was always very noisy
in class, the teachers felt that he was a pleasant
person. Steve was seldom seen with any students except
those that had behavior very similar to his own. The
quiet students seemed to shy away from him. There
were no anecdotal records on Steve as the guidance
counselor didn't believe in them. Steve showed an
interest in sports but was barred from these activities
because of his grades. There was no record of plans
for the future as the guidance counselor also did not
believe in autobiographies, and at this age Steve
wasn't having conferences with the counselor about his
future plans.

Steve showed intense interest in performance tests.
On these tests he worked quickly and efficiently, but
became excited and deeply involved in the design itself rather than its completion, and he would attempt
variations of it. In the third grade his WISC scores
showed verbal IQ of 79, a performance IQ of 107, and
full scale IQ of 91. An Otis Quick-Scoring Mental
Ability Test showed an IQ of 71. On a Stanford
Achievement Test that was given to him in the fourth
grade he had a median of 3.5. On the same test he
scored highest in math computation (4.5) and his lowest
score was in work study skills (1.9). On the Durrell
Reading Capacity Test in the fifth grade he scored
5.4. In the same year he scored 2.7 on the D.R.
achievement tests. Steve is classified a non-reader.

C.   Family History

He lives with his parents who both have high school
educations. He has a brother and sister, but older
than him. Both his brother and sister are still in
high school and have very poor grade averages. It
is not known what his father's occupation is, but his
family has a large and beautiful home.

D.   Social History

As far as social history is concerned there was
nothing on record about church affiliation, clubs, or
leisure time.

III. Summary

Unless someone is able to help Steve in the next few years,
it will soon be too late. Although he is only in the fifth
grade, he is 12. And due to his disinterest, he may be a
potential drop-out.

Steve - 5th Grade

Write responses here: Check Principles, Chart, and Guidelines.

Strengths	Appropriate Strategies
1._____	_____
2._____	_____
3._____	_____
Weaknesses	**Discipline**
1._____	_____
2._____	_____
3._____	_____

BOB
6th Grade - Motivation

I.   Bob seemed always to need things explained to him more than "usual," he seemed to need a great deal of attention, and he seemed to have days when he resisted following instructions of the teacher. His general achievements and actions were below what other actions and statements seemed to indicate he could achieve.

    A.   Identifying Data

        1.   Name: Robert Packwood Dietrich
        2.   Address: Wayne, Indiana
        3.   School and grade: Wayne Elementary
            School, 6th grade
        4.   Age: 12
        5.   Date of birth: December 4
        6.   Place of birth: Wayne, Indiana
        7.   Sex: male

    B.   Description of Problem

       Bob is in need of a great deal of attention. He still needs remedial work and external motivation to sustain his interest.

II. History

    A.   Health and Physical History

        1.   Physical factors:
            a.   School Health Record

Grade	Wt.	Ht.	Heart
pre-school	36#	41"	
2	45#	47"	
3	53#	49"	
4	64#	55"	
6	76#	60"	90/60

                 Illnesses: Chicken pox, 3-day measles, whooping cough, mumps.
            b.   No obvious physical defects.
        2.   Personality factors:
            a.   Disposition: amiable, sociable.
            b.   Emotional status: at the present time Bob has an outward well-balanced emotional status in school, except for his need for personal attention.
            c.   Attitudes towards parents and relatives: from talking with Bob's counselor, it seems that Bob has a poor relationship with his mother and one of his sisters who "sides" with the mother. He likes his other sister who "sides" with him. He is now living with his grandparents.
            d.   Attitudes towards teachers and school: he pays attention to those teachers who will give him attention. He seems to enjoy school, especially for a social outlet, and will stay after school to strike up conversations with his teachers.
            e.   Attitudes towards community: refer to Personality-Character Sheet.

    B.   School History

        1.   Test Scores
            a.   Kuder Preference Record--Profile Sheet

Significant at 75%		Age: 11
Outdoor	80	
Mechanical	50	
Computational	1	Note:
Scientific	40	Those who have
Persuasive	50	trouble at home
Artistic	40	very often rate
Literature	40	high in Social
Musical	40	Science.
Soc. Sci.	98	

b.   Other
      Grade   Type
        1   Metropolitan Readiness Score: 59
                 CA 5-9
        2   Kuhlmann-Anderson CA 6-10   MA 7-4
                 IQ 107
        2   Kuhlmann-Anderson CA 7-11   IQ 100
        4   Durrell-Sullivan Score:
                 24   GR EQ 3.0   City 4.0
                 53   4.5   5.2
        4   Metropolitan Readiness Score: 4.4
        5   Kuhlmann-Anderson CA 10-10 MA 9-11
                 IQ 91
        5   Metro-Achievement CA 11-4   GR EQ 5.8
                 City 6.2

2.   Grades Repeated: 2nd

3.   Marks in School

	Grades K	1	2	2	3	4	5
Reading		S	S	S	S	S	S
Language		S	S	S	S	S	S
Spelling			U	S	S	S	S
Writing		S	S	S	S	S	S
Arithmetic		S	U	S	S	S	S
Social Studies		S				S	S
Emotional Development	A	S	U	S	S	S	S

4.   Autobiography
      I, Bob, was born on Dec. 4 at Wayne General
      Hospital in the morning. After that I don't
      remember much until I was five years old. This
      is when I had my first broken bone and this injury
      consisted of a broken collar bone which lasted
      about six weeks. After this broken bones seemed
      to follow me, such as a broken finger, ankle, arm,
      rib, elbow, and one dislocated vertebra. I have
      in my family two older sisters both are married.
      I go to Wayne Elementary School, I have messed
      around for 6 years, until the present day. I am
      now ready to learn and get my education.

5.   Wayne Personal Data Inventory, Fall
      Underline any of the following words which you
      think describe you fairly well: active,
      ambitious, self-confident, persistent, hard-
      working, nervous, impertinent, impulsive, quick-
      tempered, excitable, imaginative, original, witty,
      calm, easily discouraged, shy, submissive, easy-
      going, good-natured, dependable, likeable.

6.   Teachers' Comments
      "Does not take school seriously."

"He still doesn't. Doesn't know when to keep in the background."

"Bob cares little about school. Although he seems fairly intelligent, he rarely applies this to his class work. He has been truant several times this year and absent often. He is pretty clever about getting himself out of a hot spot and will not hesitate to try to put something over on the teacher."

"Bob is basically a good boy but often fails to apply himself. He is more interested in having a good time."

C. Family History

1. Ancestry: American
2. Parents:
    a. Mother: Jane. Born: Muncie, IN Clerk at O.L. White in Wayne.
    b. Father: deceased. Born: Gary, IN Was a war veteran.
       Bob receives a $100 a month benefit as long as he is in school (including college).
       Bob's father died when Bob was approximately 9. Bob's counselor said that boys are closest to their fathers from age 13 through 15.
3. Education of parents: probably not high school.
4. Siblings: two sisters, both married
    a. Sharon lives in Wayne.
    b. Linda lives in Gary. This is the sister who "sides" with Bob.
5. Education of siblings: both high school graduates.
6. Other relatives in the home: Bob lives with his grandparents, not his mother.
7. Socioeconomic status: lower-middle.
8. Cultural resources: TV.

D. Social History

1. Seems to be successful socially.
2. Church attendance: little to none.
3. Associates: seems to associate with the "best girls" and with boys who are easily led.

III. Summary, Additional Information

From my own observation, Bob's need to have personal contact with his teachers is highly evident. I believe his failure in school work stems from two areas: (1) basic tools, and (2) motivation. His reading and organizing of written work need more development. He tends to move his lips while reading, indicating that he needs help with reading skills.

He strongly needs to find internal motivation toward school work. He will perform for a teacher who takes a personal interest and gives him extra time. He virtually gives up when he does not like the teacher, even when the subject matter would seem to be appealing to him.

Bob - 6th Grade

Write responses here: Check Principles, Chart, and Guidelines.

Strengths	Appropriate Strategies
1._____	_____
2._____	_____
3._____	_____
Weaknesses	Discipline
1._____	_____
2._____	_____
3._____	_____

PETE
8th Grade - Slow Learner

I.   Pete is considered to be a slow learner.

   A.   Identifying Data

      1.   Name: Peter John Stuart
      2.   Address: Gary, Indiana
      3.   School and grade: Gary Junior High,
               8th grade
      4.   Age: 15
      5.   Date of birth: May 26
      6.   Place of birth: Gary, Indiana
      7.   Sex: male

II. History

   A. Health and Physical History

      1.   Physical factors:
            The student has no obvious physical defects nor
            has he had any major illness which would have
            affected his physical or mental development.
      2.   Personality factors:
            a.   Emotionally the subject seems to be quite
                  stable, about the same as any adolescent.

        b.   His attitude towards his teachers and school appears to be characterized by apathy and disinterest. It seems to be an attitude of "I could care less."

B.   School History

    1.   8th grade final grades:

Special English	C-	P.E.	B
Math	F	Art	F
Social Studies	D	Industrial Arts	F

    2.   Although it is not reflected in his grade, the student does have ability and interest in art. He has talked with me about it and has shown me some of his sketchings (which he often does during my class).

    3.   He has changed schools a total of eight times since 1st grade. All of these schools are predominately black serving middle to low-income people.

    4.   Suspensions incurred while at Gary Junior High:
        a.   Truancy - September 27
        b.   Tardiness - February 9
        c.   Fighting - April 21

    5.   The quality of the student's school work is generally poor due to the fact that he is disinterested and does not apply himself.

    6.   Vocational and educational plans:
        a.   He has indicated an interest in pursuing a career in commercial art. However, from his past record and my observations I do not believe he has the initiative and motivation needed to prepare for this occupation.
        b.   From his past performance in school and from what I have seen of his general attitude toward school, I do not believe that he will complete his high school education.

    7.   Below are his 8th grade test results from the Long-Thorndike Verbal Achievement Test. The national norm is 8.1.

Subject Area	Grade Equivalent
Vocabulary	5.9
Reading Comprehension	7.1
Total Language	5.0
Spelling	3.5
Capitalization	4.1
Punctuation	5.1
Usage	7.4
Total Work Study Skills	4.5
Map Reading	5.9
Graphs and Tables	3.8
References	3.9

```
        Total Math              6.3
           Concepts             5.6
           Problems             7.0
```

C. Family History

1. Parents were originally from Arkansas.
2. They are divorced and his mother has remarried.
    a. The student could not get along with his stepfather and is now living with his father.
    b. The student has told a teacher that his father is a heavy gambler with card parties often at their home.
    c. The teacher also indicated that the student is not particularly happy living with his father and that there is some friction between the two.
3. His father is employed in the steel mills.
4. The student has one brother and two sisters.

D. Social History

1. I could not confirm his membership in any gangs, but he does have several gang members as close friends. The school social worker indicated that it is very likely the student in question is a member of one of the two local gangs (Kangaroos or Angels).
2. Church attendance is poor to none at all.
3. His social experiences are limited to the school and the city of Gary.

III. Summary

The behavior of the student was fairly consistent in various settings. I would characterize him as a young boy going through the typical problems of adolescence. His scholastic achievement is way below his present grade level, he is bothered by family problems, and he is disinterested in school and lacks motivation. Finally, as with many of my students, that which happens on the street is more relevant and important to them than the classroom.

190

Pete - 8th Grade

Write responses here: Check Principles, Chart, and Guidelines.

Strengths	Appropriate Strategies
1._____	_____
2._____	_____
3._____	_____
Weaknesses	Discipline
1._____	_____
2._____	_____
3._____	_____

JIMMY
9th Grade - Discipline Problem

I.   Jimmy is the biggest problem in the school. He is often in the office for one reason or another, he is a common subject of the teachers' lunch time conversations, and he is notorious even among the students.

   A.   Identifying Data

      1.   Name: Jimmy Walls Carter
      2.   Address: New Hope, Illinois. New Hope, very nice addition to the township.
      3.   School and grade: New Hope Junior High School, 9th grade
      4.   Age: 16
      5.   Date of birth: February 9
      6.   Place of birth: New Hope, Illinois
      7.   Sex: male

   B.   Description of Problem

   Jimmy is a discipline problem, he is failing or close to failing all of his classes, and the number of days he is absent is increasing.

II.   History

   A.   Health and Physical History

      1.   Physical factors:
         a.   Good-looking boy, average height and size.

Developmental and preschool unknown.
   b.   School health record lists no unusual
         injuries or illnesses. In grade 5 there is
         a notation "overactive nervous system"
         on his health record, and an entry said
         "extremely nervous."
   c.   No obvious physical defects, and no
         psychiatric reports.
2. Personality factors:
   a.   Disposition: arrogant, flippant, rude,
         sarcastic, disrespectful, belligerent, and
         stubborn. He is a pest in class, will do
         anything for attention, and often makes
         irrelevant remarks and questions designed
         solely to attract attention or break up the
         class. He can, at times, be pleasant and
         reasonable to talk to personally, but he
         usually reverts back to rudeness.
   b.   Emotional status: blows up easily and talks
         back to teachers. At the same time he is
         conscious of the fact that the other students
         talk about him, and he does not like to be
         known as a hood.
   c.   Attitudes toward family: unknown. He lives
         with his father, mother, and younger brother.
   d.   Attitude toward teachers and school: dis-
         likes school and would like to quit, but
         parents won't let him. He knows he isn't
         very smart. He is rude to all teachers most
         of the time, yet sometimes he appears to
         almost like some of them.
   e.   Attitude toward community: unknown.

B. School History

1. Class in school: 9A
2. Marks in school:

7	$\frac{B}{F}$	$\frac{A}{F}$	$\frac{B}{F}$	$\frac{A}{F}$	8	$\frac{B}{F}$	$\frac{A}{F}$
English							
Soc. St.	F	F	D	F		F	F
Math	D	F	C	D		F	F
Science	F	F	D	D		F	F
Music	D		D		Indust. Arts	F	
P.E.	C	D	C	D		C	B
Health	U	U	S	U			

3. Grades repeated or skipped: seventh. (Note: it
    is a ruling in the township school system that a
    student repeating will automatically be passed his
    second time in the grade.)
4. Quality of work done is very poor. He very often
    does not do the homework assignments.
5. Change in school program or schedule: one week

192

ago all his classes were switched (to another
time) in order to separate him from his best
friend who had been in five of his classes.
6. Type of schools attended: he has attended New
Hope Township schools since the first grade.
(This is a wealthy suburban area with very good
schools.) He changed junior high schools when he
had to repeat the seventh grade.
7. Relationship with teachers: very poor. He is
rude and antagonistic toward all of them, and they
all dislike him.
8. Relationship with students: the majority of the
other students dislike him, but he does have a
small group of friends. He would like to be a
leader, but on the whole he is a follower.
9. Anecdotal records:
"Jimmy's tests indicate that he should be doing
average work. He has many emotional problems.
The family went to the Child Guidance Clinic for
diagnosis, but did not follow up with treatment."
Math: "Some days, for some reason, he just goes
against the classroom atmosphere."
P.E: "He is belligerent and stubborn. He has the
potential, but he has too many demerits to get
good grades."
Music: "He is worse than ever. His choice of
friends hinders his progress."
English: "He disrupts class and has been quite
difficult lately. I look forward to the days
when he is absent."
Counselor: "He has a good attitude while talking
to you, but is hard to handle. He is not very
realistic about his abilities."
Vice-Principal: "He is convinced that he isn't
very bright, so he doesn't try."
Others: "Misuse of study hall, poorly prepared
for class; doesn't try, incessant talker,
inexcusable conduct; can be polite and interested,
but this is very rarely."
10. Interests and hobbies: he is interested in
playing football, but his grades disqualified him
for that this year.
11. Vocational and educational plans: he would like
to quit school.
12. Test records:

Grade	Test	Score
2	Stanford Achievement	2.5
	Scott-Foresman Reading	Very low
3	Iowa Basic Skills	2.5
	Calif. Mental Maturity	3.3
4	Iowa Basic Skills	3.4(norm 4.1)
5	Iowa Basic Skills	4.7(norm 5.2)
6	SRA Ed. Ability	
	language	2nd stanine

```
              reasoning                      1st
              quant. reasoning               3rd
              Total                          1st
         9    Iowa Test of Ed. Development
              Soc. Sci.                      1st stanine
              Nat. Sci.                      4th
              Correctness of Expression      2nd
              Quant.                         4th
              Reading in Soc. Sci.           3rd
                    "      Nat. Sci.         3rd
                    "      Lit.              4th
                    "      Gen. Vocab.       3rd
                    "      Composite         3rd
```

C.   Family History

1.   Lives with both parents and younger brother.
2.   Jimmy's parents have unrealistic expectations for
      his future. They would like him to go to college,
      while it is obvious to even him that it is an
      impossibility. Very little else is known about
      his home life. His mother brought him to school
      one day after he had been expelled for three days,
      and the principal reported that she was overly
      made-up and dressed in skin-tight stretch pants.

D.   Social History

1.   Jimmy is interested in sports, but was academ-
      ically ineligible to play football. He was on the
      wrestling team for a while, but because of his
      size and lack of experience he was not permitted
      to participate in any matches, so he quit the
      team rather than practice to gain the needed
      experience.
2.   He also likes to sing, but he was thrown out of
      the school choir because he constantly disrupted
      the group.
3.   Clubs, church attendance, and sex history unknown.
4.   Use of leisure time: Jimmy has a job in a pizza
      place not far from school from 4-12 on Tuesday,
      Wednesday, Thursday, and Friday, plus Saturday
      and Sunday. His family doesn't need the money,
      but neither do they seem overly concerned about
      his working such long hours when he should be
      concentrating on his studies.
5.   His few friends are also troublemakers, in almost
      as many scrapes as he is. His best friend stole
      a car, hit a woman, and was in the Juvenile
      Detention Center for a few days.
6.   Possible court records: he was thrown out of
      school for three days for destroying a painting
      exhibited at the school.
7.   He is forbidden to ride the school bus anymore

because the bus driver refused to put up with him any longer. His parents bought him a Honda to ride to school, but took it away when his grades did not improve. He probably has the use of it again, however.

III. Summary

Jimmy is a problem in almost every sense of the word. He is not too bright and he knows it, but he no longer even tries. His parents seem to be a cause of a good part of his problem because of their unrealistic expectations. Teachers have tried to bend over backwards giving him extra chances, being especially kind and understanding, and teachers have tried being tough, but nothing seems to help. The principal even paddled him and he quieted down for a few days. He is rude and obnoxious to the teachers, and he disrupts any class he is in. He is failing at least three classes this semester, and has no higher than a D in the others.

Jimmy - 9th Grade

Write responses here: Check Principles, Chart, and Guidelines.

Strengths	Appropriate Strategies
1._____	_____
2._____	_____
3._____	_____
Weaknesses	Discipline
1._____	_____
2._____	_____
3._____	_____

TRUDY
10th Grade - Dropout

I. The reason I chose this particular student is that she exhibited above average intelligence when she participated in the classroom discussions, but she received below average grades consistently on quizzes over the same material. She wants to drop out of school.

A.   Identifying Data

    1.   Name: Trudy Sue Bishop
    2.   Address: Kokomo, Indiana
    3.   School and grade: Kokomo High School, sophomore
    4.   Age: 15 years, 9 1/2 months
    5.   Date of birth: August 5
    6.   Place of birth: Kokomo, Indiana
    7.   Sex: female

B.   Description of Problem

Trudy wants to quit school.

II. History

A.   Health and Physical History

    1.   Physical factors:
      a.   Developmental and preschool illnesses:
        measles, chicken pox, German measles.
      b.   School health record: few cavities in
        teeth, wears glasses - vision correctable
        to L20/25 R20/20.
      c.   Obvious physical defects: none
      d.   Accident defects: none
    2.   Personality factors:
      a.   Disposition: friendly, quiet, unobtrusive.
      b.   Attitudes toward teachers and school: Trudy
        is enduring school until she becomes sixteen
        and can withdraw.

B.   School History

    1.   Class in school: 10th grade.
    2.   Marks in school:

Semester	I	II	III	IV	
Science	C	C			
Home Arts	C				
Language Arts	B	B			
General Math	B	B			
Social Studies	B	B			
Health		C			
Phys. Ed.	S				
Grammar		C			
English			B	BC	(Double grades
Phys. Science			C	DC	indicate the
Bookkeeping			C	CC	first two
Foods			D		grading
Home Management				DF	periods of
					the semester.)

    3.   Promotions: Trudy hasn't ever been retained.
    4.   Quality of school work done: above average in

196

grade school and average to below average in high school.

5. Change of school program or schedule: changed from business-stenographer to straight business course. Bus-steno was too difficult for Trudy.

6. Type of schools attended: all schools in Kokomo, Roosevelt Grade School, transferred to Bon Air Jr. High School, transferred to Kokomo High School (10-12).

7. Relationship with teachers: in grade school excellent; in high school, no interaction.

8. Relationship with students: friendly but not in clique within the class.

9. Anecdotal records:
"These people are making every effort to make a happy home life for their five children. They have built on an extra room to their little house and put on shingle siding. The house is clean and nicely furnished. The backyard has swings, a slide, and other interesting playthings. The place is fenced in for their safety. They have a dog, a cat, and a monkey, also three parakeets. Trudy's mother went one year to high school; Trudy's father only to 8th."
"Trudy is perfect. She does her best at all times. She says her mother wants her to be a singer. Her mother is interested in school. Trudy is pleasant and happy."
"The father had to take a leave of absence from work because of a muscular difficulty; then when again reported for work, his job had not been held for him. They are having a difficult time feeding their family of seven on odd jobs he can pick up. Trudy is a very conscientious worker, always does her best. She accepts new situations slowly, is afraid of anything new--must be encouraged to recite or perform before an audience."
"Trudy is a joy in the room--rated average on sociogram."
"Rapport between Trudy and I was not too good-- she is teacher-shy and felt uncomfortable when I would chat with her. Good girl, pleasant, gets along with group; conscientious student."
"Trudy is a high average student. She is respected by her peers and seems to be well adjusted. She has worked in the cafeteria all year and is an eager room helper. A peach of a student to have around."
"Trudy has worked very hard this year and has tried to do a little more than I ask of her. Very conscientious of her work."
"Above average work, attitude fluctuated--sees

no purpose in school. Family burned out early this year."
10. Interests and hobbies: no activities listed.
11. Vocational and educational plans: Trudy wants to become a secretary, "or something." She plans to drop out of school as soon as she becomes sixteen.
12. Test records:
    a. Intelligence test reports

Grade	Test	GA	MA	IQ
3	Kuhlmann-Finch III	8-2	8-4	103
5	Kuhlmann-Finch V	10-2	12-3	119
7	Kuhlmann-Finch VII	12-3	15-1	117
9	Otis Quick Score AM	14-1		106

    b. Achievement test reports

Grade	Test		
1	Metropolitan Readiness	Numbers C Read: A. T-Score 78 Ave. 68%	
6	California Achievement Form E	Grade Placement 6.4 Percentile Rank 40	
9	Iowa Test of Ed. Development	Percentile 68%	

C. Family History

1. Siblings: Brothers - one older, one younger.
   Sisters - two younger.
2. Education of siblings: older brother dropped out of school at age sixteen.
3. Other relatives in the home: none
4. Socioeconomic status: lower middle class

III. Summary

Before class began Trudy talked and laughed with a couple of girls who sat near her, but after bell rang she remained quiet. Occasionally Trudy volunteered to answer a question, but most of the time she sat listening to the others. One time she had to stay home to take care of her father who had sprained his back. Trudy was usually clean and neat in appearance except that she wore heavy eye make-up. For the most part, Trudy was well-mannered and reserved. She exhibited no hostility toward the teacher, the students, or the assigned homework. By the end of the school year she was 16 and did not intend to return to school.

Trudy - 10th Grade

Write responses here: Check Principles, Chart, and Guidelines.

Strengths	Appropriate Strategies
1._____	_____
2._____	_____
3._____	_____
Weaknesses	Discipline
1._____	_____
2._____	_____
3._____	_____

MARY
12th Grade - Unhappy

I. She was an unresponsive, unhappy looking girl.

   A. Identifying Data

      1. Name: Mary Jane Lott
      2. Address: Lafayette, Indiana
      3. Age: 18 1/2
      4. Date of birth: September 21
      5. Place of birth: Lafayette, Indiana
      6. Sex: female

   B. Description of Problem

      Student is very sullen appearing. Very seldom smiles. Has an unhappy home life. She has an average IQ yet makes Ds and Fs in the Home Ec and general business courses. Seldom will answer in class if called on even if it is a question other than fact.

II. History

   A. Health and Physical History

      1. Physical factors:
         a. No special health record or problems all through grade school. Her health record looks complete and ordinary. Glasses

recommended in the 4th grade. She still wears them occasionally.

   b.   There are no psychiatric reports on her.

2.   Personality factors:

   a.   Disposition appears very unhappy. Seems to have a constant sneer on her face. Never contributes in class. Sometimes talks to the girls she sits with during class. Seems to like to get the class in an uproar. She can do it by chatting with the group of six who sit together.

   b.   Appears to be unemotional since she always has the same unhappy look. She will laugh within her group of friends, but stops when the teacher approaches even if it is a free time.

   c.   Attitude toward family: Is presently living with mother and stepfather. One of her four brothers is also home. He is the youngest in her family. He is 15. She hates her stepfather. In her autobiography she said that the only reason she is still at home (at 15) is because one of her older brothers is still there. That brother is now 20 and gone. She also said she loves her mother and it would hurt her mom if she left. Her real father is living about 40 miles from here. She really likes him. At the time of her autobiography he was serving a one-year term in prison for a "minor offense" she said.

   d.   Attitude toward teachers and school: It is on record that she wants to finish high school and go on perhaps to business college, but with the amount of work she puts out she will be fortunate to graduate. Her attitude toward the Child Development teacher and her Family Living teacher is one of apparent dislike. She refuses to work in either class. She disrupts these discretely when she can. Other teachers have found her uncooperative, but not anything like the other teachers mentioned. On the other hand the librarian says she's the nicest girl in the school and the most helpful.

   e.   Attitude toward community: When asked if she likes where she lives, she said not the house but the community was okay. She would rather live in California or Florida though if she had her choice.

B.   School History

1.   Class in school: Last half senior in the general program.

2. Marks in school: Up until jr. high she was passed without any special comments. At the jr. high level she started getting Cs and Ds. In high school she is getting Cs, Ds, and some Fs. She has at least 10 "yellow slips" in her folder from her three years. She is not particular which course she is flunking; they range from Health to History.

3. No grades were repeated or skipped. She was passed.

4. Has always attended a public school.

5. Health was repeated once.

6. Relationship with students: She seems to get along with a group of girls who are halfway in the status group. Some of these girls have been her friends since jr. high. They all seem to like her and talk with her. When absent for a week straight I asked if Mary were sick. These girls just laughed and said probably not. That's how Mary is. She just wants to stay home and her mother will let her. They were not condemning her. They were just stating a fact.

7. She has had one fight in jr. high that she was required to write a short paragraph about. A girl came up to her in the cafeteria and hit her. Mary turned away and she hit her again. Mary hit her and all heck broke loose. They both had to go to the office. What came of that I don't know.

8. Future interests: Her original interest in business school has not continued for she is now working in a physician's lab and will continue to do so in June when she graduates.

9. Interests and hobbies: Likes to swim, dance, water ski, and ice skate. Yet when asked if she has any hobbies she said no. She also likes to "swing" at the beach and park in the summer. She likes being around people.

10. Test scores:

Otis Quick Scoring-Gamma G	Score 38	IQ 100
Stanford Achievement Form J	%ile 4.0	C.A. 9-7
Stanford Achievement Form K	Score 43	C.A. 10-7
Putner Gen. Ability Form K	Score 154	IQ 108
	M.A. 13-1	C.A. 11-9
Stanford Achievement Form J	Score 4.6	C.A. 11-7
Stanford Achievement Form K	Score 5-9	C.A. 12-7
Hermon Nelson Test on Mental Ability	IQ 91	C.A. 13-1-10

Kudor Preference Record Profile Leaflet

Vocational	%ile	Personal	%ile
Outdoor	12	Group act.	50
Mechanical	86	Stable sit.	15
Scientific	68	Deal with ideas	35
Persuasive	26	Avoids conflict	78
Artistic	78	Directs others	5

```
            Literary          17
            Soc. Service      73
            Clerical          45
```

   C.   Family History
        1.   American born.
        2.   Education of parents: Mother finished 9th grade
                                    Father finished high school
        3.   Four brothers. Two older boys 38 and 29 are
             married and have children. Brother 21 is not
             married. Is gone from home now. One of the boys
             has graduated from high school for sure. The
             others I couldn't find if they did or not.
        4.   Stepfather does not care much what society thinks
             of the way he lives. Mary hates her home because
             it looks like such a mess all the time. Says her
             stepfather is always starting things and never
             finishing them. She is ashamed to bring anyone
             home.
        5.   They appear to be lower middle class people.

   D.   Social History

        1.   Feels her life has not been very interesting or
             exciting yet. Hopes to have something happen to
             her before she dies. Says she hasn't had a real
             happy thing or unhappy experience in her life.
             Everything is just mediocre.
        2.   Has no religious affiliations.
        3.   She was elected to the student council in jr.
             high and feels this was a great achievement.
             She was also on the honor patrol in 6th grade
             and did an excellent job according to reports.
        4.   There is a record of her traits in her file.
             These traits are listed as cooperative,
             industrious, courteous, respect for property,
             reliability, and leadership. She has a good or
             very good listed after each of these for each
             of the years given.

III. Summary

After a great deal of thought and observation on Mary, I
have come to the conclusion that she is a very unhappy
person. She has so many problems that she has no time for
real fun. When she is having fun she probably doesn't
know it anyway. Her counselor finally had a talk with her
about her uncooperative attitude in school. She doesn't
dislike teachers, but she does dislike what we represent
to her. We keep bringing home her unhappy home life.
She can only resist this. She has a way of tuning out the
teacher whenever the subject gets on parents and environment.

202

She tries to keep up with her crowd by buying clothes like they do and going where they go. She had to work long hours after school to have these things. Her counselor finally asked her to stop work in the hope that she would spend a little more time on her school work. This has not seemed to make much of a difference. Mary has possibilities and this is why it bothered me not to be able to make a real dent in her attitude.

Mary - 12th Grade

Write responses here: Check Principles, Chart, and Guidelines.

	Strengths	Appropriate Strategies
1.	_____	_____
2.	_____	_____
3.	_____	_____
	Weaknesses	Discipline
1.	_____	_____
2.	_____	_____
3.	_____	_____

Conclusion

While you may not have run across any of these students while you were in school, if you spend any time in a classroom you will most certainly see students much like these. These case studies may appear to describe unusual students, but they do not. In fact, students like these are becoming more common and are found in every school in the country.

Students at Risk

In summary, we return to the title of this chapter, "Discipline: A Function of Effective Teaching Practices." By effective teaching we mean "prevention is far more important than cure," which suggests that it is important for teachers to accurately interpret discipline situations, and to know different strategies for coping with discipline problems. The case studies are illustrative of discipline problems, and they exemplify certain features of common behavior that teachers encounter. We encourage you to believe that discipline problems arise at times not because of incorrigible students but because of poor

teaching. In the following two chapters--"Social Studies for
Special Students" and "Social Studies for the Disadvantaged"--we
concentrate on those students who have been overlooked because of
their particular handicaps. You are encouraged to continue
thinking about discipline because some of the special students
you are about to discover will appear to be discipline problems.
In some cases they are discipline problems, in all cases they are
handicapped. Remember Spencer's Principles, Coping Chart and
Guidelines, together they offer a good introduction.

DISCIPLINE WITH DIGNITY

TAKING CONTROL

1 out of 2 teens in America has taken drugs. 1 out of 2 parents doesn't see it.

Students at Risk

can be changed But they can never be replaced

CHAPTER X

SOCIAL STUDIES FOR SPECIAL STUDENTS:
A FUNCTION OF EFFECTIVE TEACHING PRACTICES

OBJECTIVE: Having read this chapter you will be able to identify the meaning of the phrase special students, know the national policy on mainstreaming and note coping strategies for integrating special students into regular school programs.

Every American Citizen Should Have Access

Special students are now mainstreamed, which means these exceptional students will be involved in regular classrooms. Who are these special students that are now in every teacher's social studies class? "Handicapped" is probably the shortest definition, but that is a description not a definition and, of course, the range and variety of handicapped conditions are very great. For educational purposes the categories of the special students teachers find mainstreamed in regular classes are: slow learners, learning disabled, physically disabled, emotionally disturbed, gifted and talented, and multicultural.

Who will care

Rationale for Mainstreaming Special Students: Education for All Handicapped Children

By what rationale are these special students, with the handicaps identified above, mainstreamed or provided special facilities within the educational system? The two most powerful arguments tend to be ones based on the country's democratic traditions and enthusiasm for public education. The democratic traditions would suggest that a significant portion of United States youth may in the past have been denied full participation in and benefits from the mainstream of life, and that as a result of past practices have been denied the protection of full citizenship rights. The second strong argument is that among those rights is a public education--an education that must be offered to every child, regardless of the child's handicap. One other point might be that the United States, not unlike other countries of the world, has a significant number of youth who are handicapped, and that those who have handicaps should be a part of the real world that the students will enter as adults. Special students are mainstreamed into regular classes because there is a belief in the dignity and worth of the individual, and democratic ideas which support the protection of full citizenship rights require public education for each child.

For this reason in 1975 Congress passed the "Education for All Handicapped Children Act," often called the Bill of Rights for the handicapped. This law is the basis for what has been called mainstreaming. Mainstreaming is a way of meeting the mandate of P.L. 94-142. It is a means of providing educational services in public schools for those children who have previously been overlooked or hidden away. In short, for all teachers in the public schools it will no longer be acceptable for communities, teachers, and administrators to neglect needed services to the disabled. To teachers who say, "I just don't have the skills," to administrators who say, "I don't have the time," and to school corporations that say, "We don't have the money," the answer is, "It is public law that you must educate all children. Learn the skills necessary. Make the time. Establish the needed programs."

Many teachers are anxious about mainstreaming special students in their classes. Special students have exceptional needs, and this is another way of saying that new kinds of demands and different approaches are placed on the regular classroom teacher. Can we help these teachers to understand and deal in an effective way with their special students? Hopefully, yes. Who are special students, what are their problems and how do teachers make the school an effective place for these exceptional students to learn? As an ideal, most citizens would endorse the notion of educating all children. But the ideal, education for all, has not been easily translated into practice. In practice, schools have done extremely well with students who are ready, willing, and able. Those who were eager to learn, who were eager to read, who could keep still and apply themselves, who could "go along" with the values and beliefs of the community were the students who were considered educable.

But what of the others? What of the multicultural, the ethnic minorities? What of those who were in wheelchairs or who could move only with difficulty? What of the emotionally disturbed, the overactive, the destructive and unhappy? What of the very bright, who quite often found schoolwork unchallenging and dull and sensed the teachers' resentment? What of those who had great difficulty in learning to do the simplest tasks? And how about those with complex neurological diseases, such as muscular dystrophy or cerebral palsy? In fact, this is a list of those whom the schools traditionally overlooked.

POINT OF VIEW

Bill of Rights for the Handicapped

In brief, while as a nation the United States is philosophically committed to basic education for all of the children of all of the people, in fact, we have yet to work out how to accomplish this. While we believe that our aim of education is individual development for self-fulfillment and the betterment of society, teachers have experienced considerable difficulty in identifying, let alone developing, individual fulfillment. While there is agreement and support for equal education for minority children, for the physically and mentally handicapped, and for others who have been overlooked, there remains the task of preparing the school and the teacher to meet this important but difficult challenge.

WHO HAVE WE OVERLOOKED?

We need to identify those who have been overlooked. We shall discuss briefly, the mentally retarded, the emotionally disturbed, the learning disabled, the speech impaired, the hearing impaired, the visually impaired, the physically impaired, the gifted and talented, and students of varied cultural backgrounds (multicultural). The disadvantaged will be discussed in a following chapter.

Mentally Retarded

This term refers to persons with limited intellectual and academic potential who learn less at slower rates. That is, by comparison with their peers, they have difficulty grasping abstract concepts, remembering, writing, reading, and doing basic arithmetic processes and other conventional academic tasks. In addition, they may experience difficulty in learning what is considered "appropriate" social behavior. Thus, in addition to being difficult to teach, parents and teachers maintain that they are hard to control or discipline.

Emotionally Disturbed

Here we are talking about people who, for a variety of reasons, cause emotional conflict within themselves and for others. They may be impulsive, compulsive, fearful, anxious, uncontrollable, angry, unstable (that is, "hyper" [overactive] at one moment and sullen or depressed the next), withdrawn, or violent. We are discussing young people to whom these adjectives apply all or most of the time.

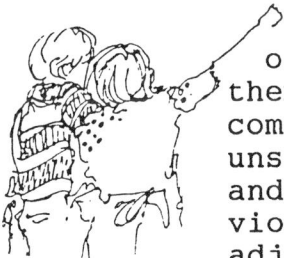

Learning Disabled

As opposed to those who are retarded, a learning disabled person may have average or above average ability to learn. However, for reasons that are often unclear in nature, the learning disabled may have specific disorders in listening, speaking, reading, writing, performing arithmetic operations, or in motor coordination.

Speech Impaired

Often for reasons that are not always clear, those in this category may have difficulties with articulation, fluency, voice quality, or vocabulary. The most common speech impairment is stammering or stuttering. These types of difficulties may have physical or emotional origins.

Hearing Impaired

Students in this category range from the totally deaf to those with mild hearing problems. Those with relatively mild hearing problems can usually be helped with hearing aids or remedial training. Those with a severe hearing loss may require additional special treatment or such aids as an "interpreter," i.e., someone with normal hearing or lip reading skills who translates speech into sign language.

Visually Impaired

Individuals in this category range from the totally blind to those with visual defects correctable by glasses or other forms of magnification. The totally blind might require "Talking Books," materials in Braille, readers, or perhaps Seeing Eye Dogs. The partially sighted may need only slight modifications in the classroom, i.e., sitting next to the chalkboard, or clearer verbal clues from the teacher.

Physically Impaired

In this category can be such students as asthmatics, diabetics, or those with cerebral palsy, muscular dystrophy, or epilepsy. Some of these persons are completely mobile and others are wheelchair-bound. Some require regular medications and injections but otherwise perform in a fairly normal manner. Others may need a change in the environment, i.e., ramps instead of stairs, lowered toilets or drinking fountains. Quite often you will face students with temporary physical handicaps such as broken arms and athletes hobbling about on crutches.

Gifted and Talented

As opposed to all of the above, who have a physical, intellectual, or emotional impairment, the gifted and talented are well above the average in some ability. They may have

musical, kinesthetic, intellectual, dramatic, or artistic talent. They learn rapidly, recall both details and larger concepts, and may also have a creative, imaginative dimension that allows them to be innovative. There is no inherent reason why they must be problems to teachers. They represent one to two percent of the population, and they do have special needs.

Students of Non-Standard Cultures, Multicultural

In this category--often abbreviated as "multi-cultural"--are students who either were born and brought up in another culture or who live in a sort of cultural island that differs from mainstream United States' culture. In this chapter multicultural refers to students who represent a number of different ethnic groups. On the one hand, an ethnic group may not speak one word of English. On the other hand, they may be able to communicate readily enough in Spanish, but their cultural background tends to handicap them in school. For instance, they may be highly vocal, demonstrative, and "emotional," or they may, by comparison, be withdrawn, silent, and uncommunicative. For whatever reasons, they experience problems and have special needs.

School and Teachers' Attitudes Towards Special Students

The point is that while as a teacher you may say to yourself, "I have seen very few of the children who fit these descriptions and I probably will not have many in my class," we should like to convince you otherwise. Of course, in the past it was easy to keep those who were too "different" out of school--either by law or by informal consensus. It was also the practice for schools to ignore and exclude many by erecting architectural barriers, i.e., inaccessible toilets, classrooms and stairs; by expelling those with emotional problems; by insisting that the blind or deaf be turned over to separate schools; by imposing a rigid curriculum that doomed many; or by labeling some as undesirable. However, the days when some ethnic groups were "kept in their place," and teachers could dismiss the problem of special students by admitting that they really didn't know much about "those kinds of kids" are rapidly approaching their end. By moral consensus and will of Congress those who have been overlooked are no longer going to continue to be overlooked.

We need to look at one more point before discussing
techniques of coping with special students. That point has to do
with the objections that teachers have to working with the
handicapped, the culturally different, and the gifted. You
either have heard or will soon hear from some teachers the
following: "I really do not have time to work with (the gifted,
the handicapped, minority children, etc.). I have a state
mandated curriculum to cover. There are certain curriculum items
that I must teach in a certain way. And if I pay much attention
to those children, why then I'll be cheating the rest." This
statement contains within it virtually all of the fallacies and
self-defeating beliefs that create problems for special students.

How You Can Make a Difference

we have to create

First, as we have already said, it is no longer acceptable
to say that teachers do not have time for those students.

Second, education should not consist only of a knowledge
oriented curricula to cover. Social studies objectives call for
skill development in gaining knowledge, processing information,
examining values and beliefs, and participation, all of which are
part of any social studies scope and sequence. If one begins
with knowledge, skills, and attitudes that are spiraled through a
social studies scope and sequence, then it is entirely possible
for any number of different kinds of curricula to meet a given
general objective.

Third, while some teachers believe that they must follow a
state mandated curriculum, they ordinarily have not carefully
thought about how that curriculum could be modified to work with
special students. If they did, they would soon discover that
their curriculum is not strictly mandated day by day. In short,
there is considerable freedom in approaching the subject and the
daily class lessons.

Fourth, we are convinced that as long as teaching is defined
as covering the same materials, at the same rate of speed, and
evaluating all students in the same manner, it is the case that
many students will be ignored. However, just as teaching should
not consist of exactly the same curriculum for everyone, it also
should not consist of teaching the same items in the same way at
the same rate of speed. In short, special needs call for special
planning.

The school and teacher attitudes we have discussed above
often tend to be held at the subconscious level. They are, we
feel, the reasons why teachers have overlooked many young people.
We conclude this section by suggesting that these
traditional school and teacher attitudes towards special students

are changing. To help integrate thoughts about the handicapped,
please respond to the following statements.

Every American Citizen

RIGHT NOW

A multicultural parent says, "I don't see why my child
has to go to school. The teacher hits him and calls
him lazy, and when he's old enough, he's going to join
his dad on the truck."
You respond by saying:

_____

_____

A teacher says, "I'd like to deal with current events,
but I am required, I think, to spend most of this
semester on the Constitution and the structure and
function of the national government.
You respond by saying:

_____

_____

Someone says, "The schools and classrooms are just not
set up for teaching handicapped children."
You respond by saying:

_____

_____

Complete this sentence:
The most important idea I have gotten out of this
section is

_____

_____

What Are Learning Characteristics of These Students Who Cause Problems for Teachers and How Do You Cope with Those Problems?

Since many teaching techniques discussed below can meet the educational needs of many different kinds of students, keep in mind that the headings we use should be interpreted broadly. The headings list some of the common problems and directly below are some of the coping techniques we recommend. At the end of this chapter we ask you to use your imagination by providing a place where you can suggest activities which would be useful in coping with special students. Also, do not forget "Effective Teaching Practices" in Chapter IV as a major source of coping suggestions.

How you can make a difference.

Multicultural and Disadvantaged

While many students with physical disabilities are physically identifiable, one cannot readily identify cultural or ethnic differences by simply looking. Nor are many cultural or subcultural differences especially easy to spot, even for experienced teachers who have known the students for years. Research studies suggest that teachers tend to respond to cultural and subcultural differences by labeling as discipline problems the students who are difficult, uncooperative, or unteachable. As we mentioned in the introductory discussion on multicultural students, some may be demonstrative, expressive, talk a good deal. On the other hand, some are likely to sit unresponsive to the teacher's request to answer questions or contribute, simply answering any question with a shrug.

These kinds of behavior, while baffling, reflect certain subcultures. Those brought up in contact with highly verbal, expressive cultures are expected to respond, to speak out, to argue, to contradict. That is characteristic of life in their home and ethnic culture. However, others have been taught that-- especially when dealing with adults in authority--the best response is as little response as possible. They do not experience physical punishment in their homes nor does their ethnic culture punish them if their behavior does not meet expectations.

Some Asian and Latino cultures exhibit a very different sort of behavior. Their enculturation--that is the way they learned their culture from childhood--stresses deference and respect to adults, compliance with their requests, speaking briefly and to the point when spoken to, avoidance of impulsive behavior, avoiding eye contact, doing one's work quietly and with self-control, and expecting to be punished if their behavior does not meet expectations.

So what learning problems are created by ethnic group membership? The answer: in some cases none. In all cases, it depends upon a number of factors. In many cases, however, some students may not respond to what the teacher considers perfectly reasonable expectations. They may not establish the necessary eye contact. They may talk--teachers would say chatter--constantly, moving about and interacting with others, often to the teacher's distraction. They may experience difficulty in hearing certain sounds or reproducing others in speech. Home living patterns may work against disciplined study--especially if, as in some areas, students have to work or assist parents. In short, be sensitive to cultural differences. When possible build on strength by organizing the class to account for "different" sorts of behavior.

Techniques and Strategies for Coping with Multicultural and Disadvantaged Students

It is a fact that many schools have not been particularly effective in working with the multicultural and the disadvantaged and partly this is because teachers are unprepared to deal with differences in beliefs, values, and learning styles. In some instances the multicultural are also considered the disadvantaged, and because of the number and complex nature of those who are disadvantaged, an entire following chapter is devoted to that topic. For a list of techniques and strategies for coping with multicultural students turn to the chart in the following chapter, "Social Studies for the Disadvantaged: A Function of Effective Teaching Practices."

Gifted and Talented

While it is reasonably obvious that the academically and intellectually gifted who represent on the average one, perhaps two percent in most schools, grasp relationships, have a superior vocabulary, read well, frequently express themselves fluently, possess a large store of information, earn higher grades, make excellent test scores, and achieve at sometimes extraordinary levels; in fact, they may constitute a problem for some teachers. Why? Teachers may resent the fact that the gifted know more about a subject than they do. Teachers may also resent the fact that they cannot claim responsibility for the student's learning, since gifted students are likely to be highly independent learners. Sometimes gifted students are bored and find ingenious and clever ways of getting into mischief. Giftedness may exist in only one or a few areas, further complicating the teacher's lessons. In fact, teachers who teach to--and have traditionally done well with--the "average," often have little patience, tolerance, or sympathy with their gifted students. While "coping with individual differences" is a goal, in reality the teachers' job is defined in such a way that they do not or cannot accommodate differences.

There does persist the cultural perception of gifted students not simply as different, but sometimes even distinctly strange. Gifted students are not necessarily anything of the sort. Some very bright students do develop a sense of loneliness and alienation because they have few friends to whom they can relate on their own level. But, in fact, many have perfectly normal personalities and become some of the nation's elected leaders, inventors, writers, businessmen, scientists, researchers, philosophers, and football players.

How Can I Keep Gifted Students Interested and Focused on Task?

A few suggestions

Almost all the statements on effective teaching practices in Chapter IV are applicable for working with the gifted. Many of the following suggestions are drawn from that research and accompanying practices. However, to summarize, encourage opportunities to: (1) develop abstract thinking, (2) focus reasoning abilities, (3) practice creative problem solving, and (4) emphasize higher cognitive processing. The following are techniques and strategies to provide the opportunities summarized above.[1]

1. Vary the assignments. Consider occasionally allowing special research/library time instead of class time.
2. Center the assignments around self-chosen problems.
3. The new interactive multimedia computer programs would be appropriate.
4. Provide opportunities for individualized research in any given assignment. Thus, while everyone is reading about the "Rise of Industrialism," "The Judiciary," or "Asia," have the gifted student read, compile data, and report on "The Early Flying Machines," or "The History of Hong Kong as a Crown Colony."
5. Have the student help you build a special collection of newspapers, journals, magazines, government pamphlets, etc.
6. Use higher level questioning with emphasis on divergent and evaluative levels.
7. Examine Bloom's higher levels of thinking as found in Chapter VI, particularly note analysis, synthesis, and evaluation levels. These are the challenging levels.

8. Enlist the student as a peer teacher, tutor, or research assistant, a creator of materials, a maker of teaching aids.
9. Identify and use some of the specialized talents of your gifted students, i.e., the musician can play traditional songs, the computer "expert" can create computer programs.

In summary, gifted students have high levels of curiosity, are good guessers, can be intensively focused, and their talents should be used for problem solving, and original work.

Visual, Hearing, and Speech Impairments

With the visually impaired, much depends upon the degree of impairment. The central problem, of course, is that if the impairment began early or at birth, there are difficulties associated with reading, writing, and most other school activities that require sight. In some cases there may be problems discriminating colors or shapes. In some cases a difficulty is mobility. Without training, a person with serious visual handicaps can get around only with difficulty and is afraid of bumping into things. They therefore experience problems on the playground, in halls, looking for books in the library, or finding toys. These problems are not usually unconquerable. In some cases technology in the form of computers with large screen displays have made independent reading and responding possible for the partially sighted.

Many of the same points may be made about the hearing impaired. Much depends upon how long they have been impaired and to what extent. There does seem to be agreement that severe hearing problems are perhaps more incapacitating than blindness. Totally deaf students and adults seem to have more sensory deprivation and seem to experience problems relating to their peers. In addition, if the handicap has been present since birth, hearing disabled students not only have difficulty with speech, they also have serious problems learning how to read. It also follows that they do not hear directions, lectures, discussions, and other oral activities. These deficiencies can be compensated for in class, but the teacher needs awareness, sensitivity, and some ideas about coping with the problems. Again, technology in the form of interactive multimedia computer programs that are now available will prove to be particularly helpful because the student can choose and control the medium that is best.

Those with mild or severe speech problems may have all of their sensory equipment in good order and a perfectly normal IQ.

However, the existence of their speech defect is also the basis for their primary learning problem--fear of response to their vocal sounds and production. Many persons with severe speech problems report that speaking is often a nightmare--accompanied by cold sweats, pounding heart, and muscular spasms. This obviously limits them in such tasks as reading out loud, classroom discussion, and the asking and answering of oral questions. It also has a depressive effect on their self-image and sometimes imposes barriers to the usual formation of friendships.

How Can I Cope with Visual, Hearing, and Speech Impaired Students?

A few suggestions

For the visually-impaired student[2]

1. If the chalkboard is situated at the front of the classroom, the center of the front row is usually a good seat for a visually impaired student. Because glare may cause discomfort or inability to read, some students prefer seats away from the window. Don't stand with your back to the window. Glare and light will make it difficult to see your demonstration and eye fatigue may occur.

2. Say the notes aloud as you write them on the board. The visually impaired student can take them down as dictation. Lend the visually impaired student your copy of the notes you put on the board or the book from which you have taken them.

3. Let the visually impaired student stand close to or next to any demonstration, map or chart being used, perhaps taking a seat on the floor at the front of the class. Let the student help with the demonstration, handle the materials you use or make a desk copy for that student's personal use.

4. All students are sensitive to peer criticism. Your own acceptance of a visually impaired student will serve as a positive example to the class. Introduce the visually impaired student as you would any other student. The other students will ask questions. Try to get the visually impaired student to answer the questions by him/herself.

5. Include the visually impaired student in all activities as far as possible, i.e., debates, panels, oral reports. The same rules that apply to the rest of the class should also apply to the visually impaired student. Encourage the student to take leadership positions in the same way that other students do.

6. Provide additional space for any special materials the visually impaired student needs. Let the visually impaired student move around the classroom to obtain materials or

to get visual information. The student will know his/her
own needs and the student's methods of compensating will
soon become part of the classroom routine.

7. When you approach a visually impaired student, unless
the student knows you well, always state your name.
Voices are not always easy to identify, particularly
in crowds or stressful situations.

8. Remember, for the safety of the visually impaired student
(and other students) doors and cupboards should be all
the way open or all the way shut. Always tell the
visually impaired student about any changes in the
position of the classroom furniture.

Recorded Books

For the hearing impaired student[3]

1. Background noises (such as other people talking) are
confusing for hearing impaired students. The student
should sit as close to the teacher as possible (i.e., at the front of the class)
when the teacher is talking. Other
students should be kept as quiet as
possible.

2. Before speaking, get the student's
attention. Wave your arms, touch the
student gently, or call the student's
name (if some hearing exists) but
do not begin talking until the
student is focused on you.

3. Face the student when speaking. Do
not turn your back or lower your head
since these actions lower the volume of
sound and make lip reading impossible.

4. Stand as close as possible to the student when speaking. One to two yards is a reasonable
distance to make lip reading easy and to minimize
interfering sounds.

5. Do not stand in front of a window or light. The glare
makes lip reading difficult because of shadows on
your face.

6. Do not cover your mouth with your hand or anything
else. This distorts speech sounds and interferes
with lip reading.

7. Speak slowly, clearly, and if it is helpful, loudly.
This does not mean you should exaggerate mouth movements
nor does it mean you should shout. Simply concentrate
on enunciating words carefully.

8. Use your face, hands, and body to help express what you
wish to communicate. For example, an enquiring look
on your face will help to emphasize that you have asked
a question. You may wish to use special signs with
specific meaning for some things. Sign languages are

very effective communication forms.

9. If at first you don't succeed, try again, if necessary. Rephrase your sentence or try a different expression or a new gesture. Do not be embarrassed or frustrated and do not let the student become impatient. Remember, even hearing students do not always understand the first time and a hearing impairment makes communication even more difficult.

10. When the hearing impaired student tries to communicate with you, particularly if speech is impaired also, you must be patient and creative. The important thing is for communication to occur so that both of you share each other's thoughts and feelings.

The hearing impaired student is like all other students in this regard, although the hearing impaired students may need extra time to think about what you have said and to organize a reply.

Physical Disability

The points above are applicable to the physically disabled. What kind of learning difficulty they may have and how much of a problem it constitutes for the student and for teachers depends on many factors. We can give you a few ideas, but as is true of each of the categories we are describing here, you will have to inquire into the specifics. Thus, while an orthopedically handicapped (physically disabled) student is obviously not as mobile as one without such a handicap, it does not follow that they cannot move. They can. How much mobility they have depends upon the nature of their handicap, the kind of device they must use (i.e., crutches, canes, braces, etc.), upon the adaptive training they have received, and upon their adjustment.

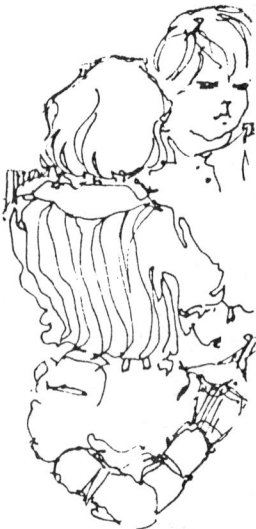

Physical handicaps may or may not be accompanied by learning disabilities. Obviously, the pain a student suffers may prevent him or her from concentrating. An orthopedically handicapped student cannot engage in the running and jumping activities of most students--but many, in fact, can participate in some physical activities, and sometimes at a proficient level. Some may need to be excused for medications, injections, physical therapy, etc., at inconvenient times. Some may have a higher absentee rate than is normal. Some must have some aspects of their physical environment altered.

Emotional Disturbance

There is a wide variety in emotional disturbances. These range from the withdrawn to the "acting out," from the hostile to the timid, from a student whose conflict is largely within him/herself to the student who creates disturbances and confusion among others constantly.

What kind of learning problems might teachers of all age groups expect from emotionally disturbed students? A student may succeed quite well in relationship to others but be unable to deal with even the slightest failure. This student may cry or sob, become angry or morose, or "take it out" on the teacher or other students. A student may perform erratically, now doing acceptable work but later unable to understand instructions, comply with them, finish work or hand it in. Another student may be "absent-minded," unable to focus attention on an assignment. A hyperactive (highly active and excitable) student may be unable to sit still long enough to accomplish more than a small fraction of an assignment. An angry or hostile student may divert most of his or her energy to expressing anger and very little to actually doing the work. A fearful, timid, withdrawn student may be too upset to begin or too insecure to risk failure. In some cases, the behavior may be predominantly verbal and in other cases it may be physical, i.e., hitting, throwing, pushing, shoving, etc. This paragraph does not even come close to describing the range of behavior. But it should give you a sense of what kinds of behaviors to expect and why they are likely to create problems for teachers.

Learning Disabilities and Impairments

This is the most confusing sort of category. As we have said, little is known about them, their causes, or their cures. A student with a learning disability may not have any obvious physical impairment and may be of normal or above normal intelligence; however, some kinds of learning are difficult and perhaps impossible. Some students can read and write well, but may be unable to perform acceptable arithmetic. Some students with what is known as "dyslexia" do not read from left to right; they may begin to the right of the line of print, continue reading to the left, and then begin in a circular fashion. Other dyslexics reverse letters, reading or writing a "b" for a "d," for example. In some cases, the math and language learning is perfectly acceptable, but the student is somewhat uncoordinated and cannot perform many physical motions normally. Needless to say, much of the difficulty is that in all of the cases we have described, a student may be too self-conscious or embarrassed to learn or may fear cruel teasing from classmates.

Mental Retardation

Again, we make the same point; "retardation" is
not an unqualified term. It may refer to something
that causes some problems in learning how to read.
For example, it may also prevent a student from
performing competently any learning task--writing,
complex concept attainment, speaking, understanding rules and regulations, learning ordinarily appropriate behavioral patterns and the
rest. Students with some degree of retardation experience difficulty in repeating the
proper sounds, acquiring verbal learning, building
concepts, and acquiring higher level intellectual
skills. They usually lack insight into cause and
effect situations and into consequences and cannot
easily make inferences or see wider implications and
applications.

Some severe forms of retardation mean that the student can
only function with assistance in an institutional setting. While
some schools have special education teachers with their own
rooms, the fact is that many schools have no such resources.
Individual teachers need to learn how to incorporate students
with mild and moderate forms of retardation--as well as the other
categories we have discussed--into regular "mainstreamed"
classrooms.

Improving

Worried about the Low Self-Concept of Certain Students

With some emotionally disturbed, learning disabled, and slow
learners, a squeeze, a pat on the head, a hug communicates
acceptance. Try to reinforce good behavior not just by verbally
saying "Right!" or "That's good!" but in other ways. Here is an
example, a "one-liner" that you can leave on a student's desk or
give to him/her:

Dear Mike/Nancy (student's name),

Your participation in today's discussion (or nice behavior on the
playground, help in the student
project, written paper you handed
in, etc.) was really helpful (or
very nice, most useful, made a
good contribution, etc.).
Thanks.

Teacher's signature

On the other hand, try to downplay, perhaps even ignore,
negative, antisocial, or maladaptive behavior, if this is at all

possible. In any event, keep your voice low, don't lose your "cool" (patience), and don't magnify the problem out of proportion. Attempt to include the students in a general class discussion. Use personal progress charts. Build or create activities which have the individual student as the subject, for instance:

> "Everybody does something really well. The thing that I do quite well is (hunt, cook, read, repair broken household items, sing, etc.). What do you do really well?"

For further discussion on building student self-confidence see the preceding chapter on "Discipline: A Function of Effective Teaching Practices," the section on "Creating a Positive Attitude" and "Discipline Starts with Expressing Encouragement."

A few suggestions

How Can I Teach the Slow Learner and Learning Disabled?[4]

You can give shorter writing assignments. You can provide more time to finish assignments. You can arrange for extra help with writing assignments--either yourself or an able student. You can integrate a writing assignment into a project such as requesting some students to do captions, write a story line, print titles in a student project. You can create more imaginative assignments using themes from contemporary films, rock and roll or other popular songs, cartoons, poems. You can combine writing assignments with other activities, i.e., reading, discussion, role-playing, and outside research. The following are coping techniques.

1. A good relationship with the student's parents or guardian is very important. Talk with the parents in an understanding way about the learning difficulties as well as the successes that the student is having at school. Find out how they view the student and what they are able to do to assist. Using what you have found out about the student's strengths and interests work with the parents or guardian to plan so that the student can experience success in both school activities and home activities.

2. Find out as much as you can about the student and his/her learning through observation. Which skills does the student have and which one does the student lack. Try different methods of teaching. Does the student learn best by seeing, by hearing, by writing, or by a combination of these?

222

3. Plan for a successful learning experience for the student. Starting from what the student already knows, what are the very next things which should be taught? List the learning tasks in order so that each one builds upon the task which the student has just learned. Plan small steps making sure that the student has learned one step very well before introducing the next step. Plan the method of teaching, using the method by which the student seems to learn best.

4. Plan how you will organize to provide teaching at the student's level of ability. You may need to teach the student individually or in a small group. Other students in the classroom can help by working with the slower student in activities.

5. Plan with the student a few simple rules of behavior for the class and be consistent and fair in enforcing these rules. A student with a learning difficulty feels more confident if he/she knows what is expected of him or her.

6. Give clear instructions and make sure that they are understood. Face the student to get attention. Give instructions in short simple sentences. Make sure the student has understood by having the student tell or show you what he/she is to do.

7. Teach using all the senses. For example, a student who has difficulties in remembering a new word can be helped by using techniques (see 150 suggestions in Chapter V) which combine hearing, touch, and movement with sight--tracing the word with fingers while looking at it and saying it.

8. Praise and encourage the student as often as possible. Clap hands, smile, pat on the shoulder, say "very good," present a small prize, allow student to play a game.

9. Always respond to a good answer. The student needs to know if he/she has answered correctly so that he/she does not continue the wrong response.

10. Try to help the student achieve success so that he/she will feel good about him/herself and the learning situation. Avoid situations in which the student is made to feel a failure in front of the other students. Praise the student for trying, even if he/she does not have the right answer.

11. Use real objects and situations to give meaning to what the student is learning. Let the student actually do things while seeing and hearing them. Relate things the student is learning to real life.

12. Change teaching procedures to fit the learning needs of the student. Introduce a new thing at the beginning of the day before the student tires. Limit the number of new ideas presented in a lesson. Do not teach things together which can easily be confused.

13. Encourage the other students to accept the student with learning difficulties as a valued member of the class.

Show by your positive attitude that you value the student
as a member of the class. Arrange situations for the
student to work with other students in a positive and
cooperative fashion.

RIGHT NOW

We would like you to integrate what you have learned in this
chapter on special students with what you may remember from
Chapter VII on "Technology and Instructional Resources," and
Chapter V on "Methods, Techniques and Strategies".

List five techniques and/or technology and instructional
resources that have been identified in this chapter on coping
with special students that would also work for "normal" students.
(This listing requires you to look back over the various
suggestions on coping with handicaps.)
1.

2.

3.

4.

5.

COMMUNICATIONS, LEARNING AND TECHNOLOGY

Now would you list five techniques you have learned in the
chapter on methods, techniques and strategies and the chapter on
technology and learning resources which might be appropriate for
special students?
1.

2.

3.

4.

5.

Summary

To summarize, this chapter offers observations about what
teachers are likely to experience as problems when teaching
special students. However, what you have read should be
considered only an introduction to the problems and needs of
special students. Even if you had mastered what was written

here, you would just begin to understand the requirements for
effectively teaching special students. We would like you to
believe that all of the students we have described are teachable.
With some effort and imagination there is no reason why the
majority of these students cannot be educated. We hope you will
find what many teachers have discovered: succeeding with
sometimes troublesome, often hard-to-reach students is a
challenge. But if you succeed, the rewards and gratifications
are extraordinary. Finally, if the appeal to your sense of
challenge is not sufficient, then remember P.L. 94-142, it's the
law.

We turn now to one other category of special student in
Chapter XI, the disadvantaged and deprived. This category is
especially important not just because the students who fit this
category are continuing to increase in number, but also because
they represent a strata of United States' society that is not
achieving substantial benefits from education.

Good things happening

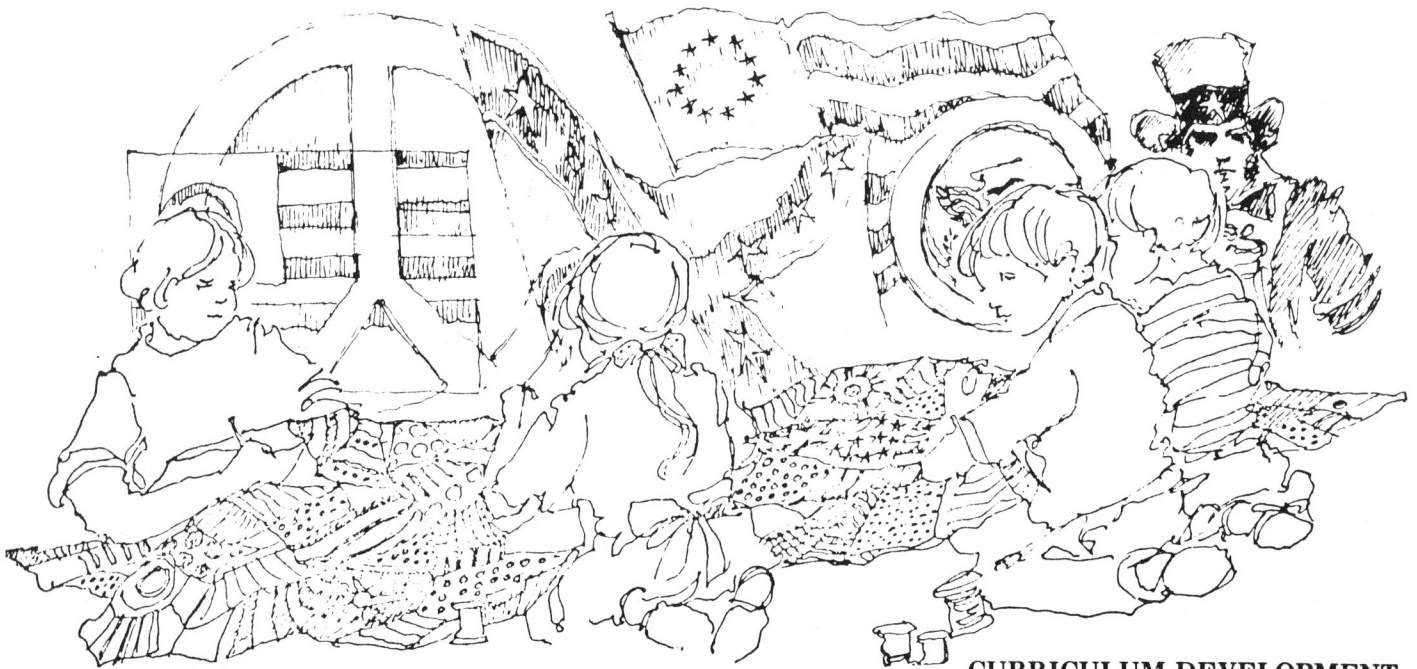

CURRICULUM DEVELOPMENT

CHAPTER XI

SOCIAL STUDIES FOR THE DISADVANTAGED:
A FUNCTION OF EFFECTIVE TEACHING PRACTICES

OBJECTIVE: Having read this chapter, you should be able to identify the general characteristics of an educationally deprived and culturally disadvantaged student. Analyze a case study using the "Cultural Chasm" exercise, and demonstrate knowledge of coping techniques and strategies in written responses.

> We were not educating all of the children of all the people. Then we began to ask, "Who are these children?" The answer came back: The educationally deprived and culturally disadvantaged. The poor--to use the older but still accurate term--often did not "fit in." Precisely because they were poor and had difficulty coping with an institution that was destined for middle-class children, the offspring of migrant families, ghetto dwellers, and those from isolated mountain towns, for example, were overlooked.
>
> Barth/Shermis

Rationale

Why make a case for educationally deprived and culturally disadvantaged students? After all, are they not just another group of multicultural, special students who in this case typically fail in their schoolwork? The answer is teachers are expected to be effective with special students. Remember P.L. 94-142, it's the law. Just as teachers are expected to cope with the multicultural, gifted, the physically and mentally handicapped, and the others identified in the last chapter, the growing expectation is that they ought to succeed with those defined as "disadvantaged and deprived."

Educating all of the children of all of the people.

But why a special chapter on the disadvantaged? The substantial number of disadvantaged, approximately one out of every four or five students now in school, is surely a sufficient reason to justify special attention. One additional startling fact is that the percentage of disadvantaged is growing. We are talking here about one-fourth of all school age students in the near future qualifying as disadvantaged if not deprived. With perhaps a few exceptions, almost every public school teacher will be working with substantial numbers of disadvantaged. One other disconcerting point, the public school system has not generally been particularly successful with disadvantaged students. Why? This is an important question because the answer should help you cope with the problems of the special students who are disadvantaged.

Handicaps of the Disadvantaged

Disadvantaged students in the past either would not have been sent to school or if sent would have "dropped out" immediately--actually "pushed out" is a more accurate term. Why? Because in the past the assumption was that either students could accommodate themselves to the curriculum and procedures of the school, in short, be ready, willing, and able, or they could drop out. The notion that a nation can simply waste the lives of those who don't quite "fit in," however, is becoming unacceptable. If you grant that the present is unacceptable, what can you do? What do you need to know? Start with, "What are the classroom handicaps of the disadvantaged?"

Classroom Problems

All or some of the following are handicaps:

1. Inability to read at grade level.

2. An obvious lack of interest in the subject.

3. Inability or unwillingness to engage in meaningful dialogue with the teacher or with peers.

4. Varying degrees of inability to write in English.

5. An apparent low level of development in speaking English and listening skills.

6. An apparent unwillingness to engage in activities which require reflection or thought.[1]

Many teachers, noting one or more of these six handicaps, have been inclined to assume that disadvantaged students were incapable of achievement, and so consigned them to the category of low achievers who could not generally benefit from school. Many teachers believe that only those students who are able can achieve and teachers, therefore, aim their instruction at just those--who, in fact, constitute the majority. This means that the disadvantaged--who with a few exceptions are a minority in some classes but an overwhelming majority in others--do not have their educational needs met. Indeed, one author, Daniel Selakovich, believes that if". . . the children of the poor constitute the greatest single group of failures in the secondary school social studies program [then] we should attempt to determine . . . who they are . . . ."[2] In fact, the students we are talking about, along with their families, are referred to as a "permanent underclass" that either cannot or will not use the traditional means of overcoming poverty. They are, generation after generation, locked into the low achievement, low status, low pay lifestyle defined as the cycle of poverty.

At Risk

Who Are the Disadvantaged?

What do they look like in school? Let us begin by identifying actual students whom we will name Judy and John, described by their schools as both deprived and disadvantaged. As you read the case studies, determine whether Judy or John demonstrate any of the six handicaps identified above. Be prepared to define disadvantaged and note handicaps in the response box at the end of each case study.

can't protect you

JUDY

I. Judy is considered a "problem child." The school administration and teachers have had much difficulty in relating to her.

    A. Identifying Data
        1. Name: Judy Lou Stevenson
        2. School: Middle School
        3. Age: 12 1/2
        4. Grade: Grade 6 repeater
        5. Born: Cleveland, Ohio
        6. Sex: Female

    B. Description of Problem
    Difficulty in adjusting to teachers, pupils, administration (school, motivation, achievement). Sex adjustment: precocious.

II. History

    A. Health and Physical Factors
        1. Physical factors:
            a. Stocky build, mature physically beyond years, very slow walk and speech patterns. Developmental and preschool (speech, walking, early illness): unknown.
            b. School health record: 32 days absent, 57 days present.

Guidance counselor: "I noted a strong odor of perspiration emanating from her that was quite offensive. I took Judy to the nurse and asked her to discuss personal hygiene with her."

   c. No obvious physical defects, no psychiatric reports at present.

2. Personality factors:

   a. Disposition: Mood sullen, quiet, defensive--easily angered. Difficult to communicate with.

   b. Emotional status: Given to sudden outbursts of emotion in defensive reactions to teachers and students--"My mother tells me to go to school. I wish I had an older brother instead of an older sister. Her husband [brother-in-law] treats me like he was my older brother."

   c. Attitudes toward teachers and school: Defensive. "Teachers sometimes get in my way when I want to do something. I like some when they don't pick on me. Some day I sort of don't feel like going to school."

B. School History

1. Marks in school (letter indicates grade, number indicates attitude: 1 = excellent, 2 = average, 3 = poor):

    English D3; Social Studies F3; Science F2; Guidance U3; Home Ec D3; Music C1, Gym D3.

2. Test records:

    Intelligence test reports: Group tests--GR 61.

    Cleveland Intelligence (Probable Learning Rate IQ) 75.

    Achievement test reports: Stanford Achievement: Reading 5.9; Arithmetic 7.3.

3. Grade repeated: 6th.

4. Quality of work:

    English teacher: "She rarely comes to class prepared. I see her borrowing pencils, paper, etc. from other students. She is reluctant to do her work and wastes time."

    Math teacher: "Judy has not handed in one assignment or class work or anything else in the last three months. She sits in the back of the room and does nothing."

5. Schools attended: Inner-city elementary school.

6. Relationship with teachers:

    English teacher: "She is often disrespectful and answers back when spoken to or corrected."

Home Ec teacher: "I will not take Judy back into my class until she has done something with her hair. I had already corrected her for writing party invitations; she yelled at me in a most disrespectful tone."

7. Relationship with students: "I guess the other girls look up to me because I'm older."
Homeroom teacher: "Judy has been involved in several disturbances in the movies during the early part of the semester. She somehow became involved in a fight between two girls. She is a leader of the troubled 6th grade section. She represents a symbol of disrespect to school rules, in many cases."

8. Anecdotal records: Breaking school rules. Teacher reported Judy smoking in lavatory. Principal suspended student (Oct. 1). Another teacher saw Judy smoking at the close of school, 50 yards from premises (Nov.). Principal observed Judy in corridor with her heavy hairdo sprayed white. Judy sent home. Judy returned with hair brushed but no other improvement. I [author] asked Judy about her excessive tardiness and failure to make up eight detentions. Judy replied to me, "I'm absent a lot because I'm suspended a lot." I might add that the great amount of time spent in the office keeps her away from class (a vicious circle).

9. Interests and hobbies: Artwork. "I like to go to the Museum and look around. I sometimes go by myself." I asked her how she got there and she replied, "I walk. It's not that far. I would like to see the World's Fair."

10. Vocational and educational plans: Judy has made no concrete plans for her artwork. She just likes art but has not discussed this with her mother.

C. Family History
1. Ancestry: American (from Salem, Mississippi).
2. Judy comes from a split home. Mother on relief while whereabouts of father unknown. Mother supposedly completed grade school. Judy has a younger brother and a sister in elementary school and an older sister (married) who attended school until age 16. Sister's husband is a construction worker and helps the family. He likes job since it is good pay. They live

separate but visit Judy's home often. Brother-
in-law acts as "big brother."

3. Attitude of parent toward society:
Mother's reaction to school prob-
lems--Judy is told to go to
school.

Mother: "She's late because I
had to locate her some
overshoes before she came
to school. I hope she
will settle down and cause
the school authorities no
more trouble."

Homeroom teacher: "Judy's
mother had an abusive attitude. She informed me that
she would come (conference) at her own
convenience and not before she was good
and ready."

(See sex history problem.)

4. Socioeconomic status: Lower-lower class, yet
Judy has enough money for cigarettes, good skirts
and sweaters. (See sex history.)

5. Cultural resources at home: Minimal--TV; no
books, papers, or magazines.

6. Adjustment of parent: Defends daughter when
cause seems just. Very aggressive when defensive
(much like daughter) yet respects school authority
and tells daughter to be good.

D. Social History
1. Extent: Social activity limited to small group
activities, parties. (Judy states that she dates
in groups. See sex history.) She relates well
to those who are in her social group. She is
very hesitant to mix with others.

2. Church: Sunday School, minimum attendance.

3. Clubs: Judy is leader of the "In-Crowd." She
told me that the name came from a record. The
record states that the in-crowd is the one which
is looked up to and has gained respect from social
know-how. It seems that the "in-crowd" membership, a clique, is an honored group.

4. Leisure time: TV, records, art. Associates
include girls who are now in 7th grade. Judy
associates with two girls who have had trouble
with school authorities. Her 6th grade classmates look up to her.

5. Sex history:
Guidance counselor: "Her skirts tend to be
extreme, short and tight, her hair
bouffant--extreme in its high fashion."

Judy has earrings on most days and wears heavy
make-up.

Teacher: "Judy was seen on the street during
an eighth period which she cut. She was
also seen at another time talking to a
group of men in a car.
This was an attempted
pickup."

The administration feels
that this abnormal sex
history, "beyond her
tender years," without
emotional maturity is a
prime factor for Judy's
failure to adjust to
school life.

6. Court records: Judy was
assigned to the N.E.
Attendance Center. If progress is not made,
Juvenile Court proceedings may start. Judy
will report to the Center this month; her
progress will then be evaluated.

III. Summary

Judy presents a good case study for noting individual
differences. Her emotional make-up is certainly not
"normal." Her aggressive patterns reflect much frustration in her adjustment in school. She is a paragon among
the "problem" peers. She can be seen in the halls and
movies as a very quiet, sullen, and, for the most part, a
lonely girl. She walks alone at a very slow pace. She
sometimes claims that "she doesn't know where to go."
Judy really doesn't. She is 12 1/2 and appears older;
it is indeed unfortunate that she is in an all-girls'
school. Her sexual frustration during the day is
apparently relieved in abnormal contacts out of school.
Although Judy can be noted for her individual differences,
she is characteristic of the culturally deprived child.
Judy "doesn't know where to go" since society has not
really aided her by showing her alternative paths.

Judy - 6th Grade

Of the 6 handicaps noted at the beginning of the chapter, list those which would most appropriately fit Judy's case.

_____

_____

_____

_____

_____

_____

_____

_____

_____

Judy has special handicaps which translate in school to special needs. How would you suggest the school cope with those needs?
(You may wish to delay answering this question until you have reviewed the chart on the following page entitled "Teaching Techniques and Strategies for Coping with Handicaps of the Multicultural and Disadvantaged."

_____

_____

_____

_____

_____

_____

How're you going to do it?

Imagine that Judy is in your social studies class. You have identified the learning handicaps she now demonstrates as a disadvantaged student. How would you cope with this young lady? The following are suggestions on techniques and strategies for coping. Other sources of reference are: "Effective Teaching Practices" in Chapter IV, always a rich place to find excellent suggestions; also Chapter VI, "Questioning," the summary on research on questioning where several studies suggest in particular an effective style of questioning for students like Judy. In addition, Chapter VII on "Technology and Instructional Resources" also could be important because of the discussion on abstract to concrete which is particularly pertinent to Judy.

A few suggestions

Handicaps of the Multicultural and Disadvantaged	Techniques and Strategies for Coping

school

classroom problems

General school handicaps:

1. School viewed as a place to be endured until old enough to leave.

(a) Teachers enthusiastic about subject.
(b) Social studies which is relevant to present values.
(c) Variety of media, techniques, and strategies, i.e., collage/mobile, small group debates.
(d) Explicit short and long-term goals.

2. Disinterest and often antagonism on part of teachers.

(a) Teachers demonstrate through their actions genuine interest in education.
(b) Strong personal interest in student.

3. Language use limited because of inexperience in various social situations.

(a) Teachers and students read aloud in class.
(b) Oral vocabulary building.
(c) Active participation through the use of panels, discussions, extemporaneous plays, sociodrama, etc., with emphasis on high interest topics.
(d) Record with play-back above activities.

Classroom handicaps:

4. School skills underdeveloped.

(a) Much attention to skill development: reading, writing, studying.
(b) Upgrading pretests.
(c) Emphasize achievement, accomplishment; de-emphasize grades.

5. Limited attention span.

(a) During each class period, teaching strategies should include at least 2 or 3 different activities including use of media.
(b) Emphasis on concrete examples, illustrate the abstract.

6. Motivation through delayed satisfaction/reward is unacceptable. Must receive immediate, concrete satisfaction/reward.

(a) Frequent use of praise, upgraded evaluation aimed at identifying achievement and progress.
(b) Students' frequent evaluation of papers in class.
(c) Frequent display of student's work.
(d) Immediate feedback.

7. Answering questions in a discussion.

(a) Asking questions requiring low cognitive level responses in elementary settings.
(b) Permitting students to call out responses in classes.
(c) Encouraging students to respond in some way to each question asked.

questions yield

Social/personal handicaps:

8. Lack of self-esteem

   (a) Plan daily activities that can be successfully completed.
   (b) Frequent praise and encouragement.
   (c) Personal attention with emphasis on achieving goals, both short and long-term.

9. A need for successful adult role models.

   (a) Teachers are role models.
   (b) Successful models identified from their own community and cultural group.
   (c) Bring resource persons into the school environment.

10. Outside experiences limited.

    CONCRETE

    (a) Field trips to ameliorate cultural isolation.
    (b) The use of media to provide visual, concrete experiences.
    (c) Bring resource persons into the school environment.

11. Lives for the present, probably lacks a sense of personal or family history.

    (a) Include materials that focus on historical contributions of relevant ethnic or cultural group.
    (b) Relate contemporary events to relevant ethnic or cultural group.
    (c) Emphasize historical as well as contemporary time and place to relevant ethnic or cultural group.

12. Expectations poor, lacks a strong future concept.

    (a) Emphasize the potential to achieve and accomplish short and long-term goals.
    (b) Project a future goal by exploring through resource persons, media, and trips to locations that promise alternative careers, i.e., college campus, business, industry.

Have Access

13. Physical activity is valued and expressed through aggressive and occasionally violent behavior.

    (a) Plan for active participation.
    (b) Plan for variety of teaching techniques during each period.
    (c) Emphasize audio and visual media both to be seen and to be made.
    (d) Emphasize appropriate means for relieving aggressive feelings, i.e., debates, discussions, projects, role-playing.

JOHN

The Wrong Image

Having read the case study on Judy and noted the handicaps and coping techniques in the chart, apply what you have learned about handicaps and coping to the case study on John. Which, if any, of these handicaps does John experience? Why might you have difficulty coping with him in your social studies class?

I. Student is very short, has an inferiority complex as a result of this, and uses a "shorty complex" cover-up--is very vain and cocky. Has a Probable Learning Rate (IQ) of 121 yet has an extremely poor academic record.

   A. Identifying Data
       1. Name: John Small Jackson
       2. School and Grade: High School, Grade 11B
       3. Age: 15
       4. Born: Pittsburgh, Pennsylvania
       5. Sex: Male
   B. Description of Problem
       See introduction.

II. History

   A. Health and Physical History
       1. Physical factors:
           Nothing outstanding about health, except the size problem. He is about 5'1" and is of slight build. For a 15-year-old boy this is of great importance. He freely admits he feels inferior because of his size and feels he must compensate in other areas.
       2. Personality factors:
           a. Disposition is amicable, very demanding of constant attention and/or approval. Cannot stay out of the limelight for more than a few minutes. If the class hits a lull, he must force attention to himself. Is cooperative to a degree (provided he likes you) and will try within his limitations to be helpful. Is extremely lazy--and admits this, too--but constantly complains he can do nothing about this, believes it is there to stay.
           b. Emotional status: Remains on a fairly even keel, does not vacillate more than the average 15-year-old boy. Is bright enough to know he is capable of doing far more than he is currently doing.
           c. Attitude toward family: Is living with mother and brother. Shows verbal antagonism

toward father who does not live with them. Is attached to younger brother.

d. Attitude toward school and faculty: Dislikes school intensely except for the social contacts. Is capable of doing a very high level of work but is "too lazy" to bother.

e. Attitudes toward the community: His ambition is to be a pimp. He believes this is an excellent profession for several reasons: (1) lots of money is involved, (2) it would bring status with the money, (3) he believes every job must be done--even the more unpleasant ones--and is willing to "stoop." Is looking for a degree of status attached to certain material things beyond the grasp of most lower-class Americans--large bankroll, sharp clothes.

B. School History

1. Marks in school:

	Sems.			Sems.	
9th Grade	A	B	**10th Grade**	A	B
English	C	D	English	F	C
Social Studies	C	D	World History	D	D
General Science	C	B	French I	C	F
Algebra I	C	C	Geometry	F	D
P.E.	C	B	Typing I	C	A
			P.E.	B	D

2. Test records (tests administered in middle school years):

California Mental Maturity	Language IQ	119
	Non-Language IQ	117
	Total IQ	117
	Language %ile	90%
	Non-Lang. %ile	90%
Pittsburgh, Intelligence	PLR	119
Terman-McNemar	PLR	121
Otis Gamma	PLR	113
Stanford Achievement	Reading	8.9
	Arithmetic	8.6

Iowa Algebra Aptitude   Score 64   87%ile
Iowa Geometry Aptitude   Score 213   85%ile
Nelson-Denny Reading (Form A) Vocab. 11.6
                              Comp. 11.1
                              Total 11.4

3. Has repeated two subjects: English and Geometry.

4. Quality of work done by this student is very poor considering the boy's capabilities. He is very quick and will pick up the slightest detail in class. His reasoning abilities seem to be fairly well developed and he is capable of doing much, much more than he does. About this, too, he

is very frank and admits that he is unbelievably lazy.

5.   Student is on academic program but has not maintained academic level work.
6.   Student has always attended public school.
7.   Relationship with teachers: Those teachers who have worked with him say he is a bright kid and could do so much more. He's very likeable and, in spite of his antics, he is a fairly nice boy.
8.   Relationship with students: Seems to get along fairly well with others, particularly girls, loves showing off for them.
9.   Interests and hobbies: Enjoys girls and shooting pool. Spends good deal of his time hanging around the pool halls.
10. Vocational interest as previously stated is to become a pimp. He feels this is the only way he can be "cool." He wears expensive "sharp" clothes, and the only way he can see to obtain this money is to pimp. He also said he has spent a lot of time hanging around them and likes their style.

C.   Family History
1.   American.
2.   Lives with mother and younger brother (age 11).
3.   Mother divorced father when subject was about 5. Says father has never paid support for the children, nor does he pay alimony. Mother is on public welfare and is receiving ADC (Aid to Dependent Children). Obviously the socioeconomic status is very low.
4.   Subject spoke of father in hostile manner and was indifferent about his mother. Seems to like younger brother and expresses concern for him.

III. Summary of Case Study

After a great deal of observation of subject, I have come to the conclusion that he could be helped to realize his potential if he had a strong older man or father image with whom he could identify. He feels inferior because of his size and needs other means of bolstering his ego than wearing expensive clothes and hanging around pimps. His ego is outstanding and he requires constant attention as well as approval for his actions. All of this is very evident in everything he does. His manner is very swaggering an

238

cocky, he dresses as "sharp" as possible, he always demands attention in one way or another.

Use This Now

JOHN - 11th Grade

Of the 6 handicaps noted at the beginning of the chapter, list those which would most appropriately fit John's case.

John has special handicaps which translate in school to special needs. How would you suggest the school cope with those needs?

_____   _____

_____   _____

_____   _____

_____   _____

_____   _____

_____   _____

Given Judy's and John's list of handicaps and the chart on coping techniques and strategies, can you now define what disadvantaged and deprived means? Finish this sentence: Disadvantaged (how) and deprived (of what) mean: _____

_____

_____

_____

This introductory chapter on special students, disadvantaged and deprived, has not yet ended, one last consideration. How well did you relate to Judy and John? Did their experience as related in the case studies seem a bit unusual, perhaps unreal and a bit disconcerting? What evidence we have seems to show that to work with disadvantaged and deprived students you will need to understand, if not relate to, "where they are coming from." Well, how do you relate? The following ought to help.

TAKING CONTROL

Identifying Your Values

Have you ever wondered whether your values might prevent you from effectively working with students such as Judy and John who

have values different from yours? For example, if you held one
set of values and your students held another set, might you have
difficulty communicating with those students? This chapter
suggests that cultural patterns and values held do, in fact,
prevent teachers, administrators, and school systems from
identifying with students who hold different patterns of values.
But to say this is not to make it so. We need to demonstrate
that there are conflicting patterns and values between teachers
and students and that those conflicts may lead to forms of
teacher dissatisfaction and student alienation.

Instructions: Note in a word or two your feelings about or
concept of each of the following 12 items. This is important,
please respond.   **AN EXCITING**   **RIGHT NOW**
                   TEACHING RESOURCE

Authority (courts,
police, principal)_____   The Future_____

Education_____   "The Street"_____

Joining a Church_____   Liquor_____

Ideal Goal_____   Violence_____

Society_____   Sex_____

Delinquency_____   Money_____

On the following page is a chart called "The Cultural
Chasm."[3] This chart identifies in a simplified form the
different interpretations between middle-class and lower-class
understanding of the 12 items above. Please compare your concept
with the concepts found on the chart, in short, where do you fit?

240

THE CULTURAL CHASM[4]
Where Do You Fit?

The concept of .	In socioeconomic middle-class terms stands for . . .	But to the socioeconomic lower class is . . .
Authority (courts, police, school principal)	Security to be taken for granted, wooed	Something hated, to be avoided
Education	The road to better things for one's children and oneself	An obstacle course to be surmounted until the children can go to work
Joining a Church	A step necessary for social acceptance	An emotional release
Ideal Goal	Money; property; to be accepted by the successful	"Coolness"; to "make out" without attracting attention of the authorities
Society	The pattern one conforms to in the interests of security and being "popular"	"The Man"--an enemy to be resisted and suspected
Delinquency	An evil originating outside the middle-class home	One of life's inevitable events; to be ignored unless the police get into the act
The Future	A rosy horizon	Nonexistent; so live each moment fully
"The Street"	A path for cars	A meeting place; an escape from a crowded home
Liquor	Sociability, cocktail parties, "party"	A means to welcome oblivion
Violence	The last resort of authorities for protecting the law-abiding	A tool for living and getting on
Sex	An adventure and a binding force for the family; creating problems of birth control	One of life's few free pleasures
Money	A resource to be cautiously spent and saved for the future	Something to be used now before it disappears, there is no tomorrow

will take on importance

What's in it for you

TEST YOUR UNDERSTANDING

Some questions to think about:

1. When you compared your concept of the 12 items with those on The Cultural Chasm chart, which pattern of values (middle or lower) did you follow?

    _____

2. Turn back to the Chasm chart: Where do Judy and John fit? Briefly explain why they fit the pattern of values you have assigned them?

    _____

    _____

    _____

3. Suppose for the moment you held middle-class values and were teaching students who held a different pattern of values, i.e., Judy and John. Would that make a difference in discussions on education, authority, the future, free-dom, democracy, the American way?
    Yes_____   No_____
    Explain your answer:

    THINK _____

    _____

    _____

    _____

    _____

We have discussed so far in this chapter why we care about the disadvantaged, and we have asked you to read and comment on Judy and John, two actual students who illustrate the meaning of disadvantaged. In addition we have suggested that a difference in values, in part, explains why teachers and Judy and John are living in different social and cultural worlds. Given the section just completed on identifying your and Judy's/John's patterns of values, would you add to or change your previous definition of disadvantaged and deprived?

What's in it for us

_____

_____

_____

Conclusion

You may be thinking that Judy and John are not going to be in your class because they are really severely disadvantaged inner-city students. Not so! Judy and John may illustrate extremes, but it is now common to find a portion of these disadvantaged and deprived students in most classrooms. One does not have to be inner-city ghetto, one can just as well be rural or urban alienated and disadvantaged. By the turn of the twenty-first century public schools may well be looking at 30% of their students who fit this category. If you plan to be a professional teacher for the next thirty years, the Judys and Johns will occupy one third of the chairs in your room.

We leave you with this final thought: educate all of the children of all of the people. That's a teacher's responsibility.

Putting you first

programs to help
Every American Citizen

CHAPTER XII

IDENTIFYING AND WRITING BEHAVIORAL OBJECTIVES

OBJECTIVE: Having completed this chapter you should be able to identify the three criteria that guide the writing of behavioral objectives and be able to identify and write complete knowledge, skill, and attitude behavioral objectives.

Why We Care About Objectives:
An objective is . . . a statement of what the learner is to be like when he has successfully completed a learning experience.

Robert F. Mager

Introducing Evaluation

plan

This chapter on behavioral objectives and the following chapter on writing test items from objectives should be considered essential for planning and evaluation. Objectives should guide the creation of test items for the simple reason that teachers should have objectives that give direction to their teaching and thus a basis for evaluation.

Rationale

The first task is to identify how to write complete behavioral objectives that specify the knowledge, skills, and attitudes which we expect students to learn. In the succeeding chapter we will learn about the construction of tests that can be used to evaluate the objectives. By evaluation we mean to judge or determine the worth or quality of whatever we are evaluating. All evaluation is not testing. In fact, most of the evaluations we make in our daily lives are not based upon test items, but rather are about events that we pass judgement on based on our beliefs and values. The emphasis on evaluation in formal education is becoming more important as the years pass. Examinations and passing examinations sometimes seem to be all that counts. Examinations determine the curriculum, the curriculum determines the text, the student learns and remembers the text only for the purpose of passing the exam. Many believe that examinations are schooling but have little to do with education.

Continuous Assessment (Evaluation)

Evaluating

Some educators have argued that one way to modify a curriculum that ends with only one assessment, i.e., final examination on paper, is to encourage teachers to adopt continuous assessment. Continuous means that throughout the school year students will be continuously evaluated by testing, through observation, and on attitude and participation, which indicates that student achievement is not measured by test items alone. Perhaps it is the recent emphasis upon continuous assessment that has caused educators to emphasize the writing of specific behavioral objectives. Such specific objectives tend to force teachers to divide the year's study into units of instruction, then teachers are asked to evaluate continuously those objectives that guide the teaching of the unit.

Classroom Problems

In summary, assessment is very important in formal education. Teachers, students, and parents are all very much concerned with progress and achievement. Many educational systems in the past have been aimed at passing tests which allow some to go on and force others to drop out. In recent years, ideas about continuous assessment hold some promise on modifying the past practices of evaluation. Therefore the modern teacher is expected to know how to write objectives, including specific behavioral objectives which should guide instruction and evaluation in the classroom.

Nobody Asked Me

You may be wondering why there is a chapter on objectives. Surely you expected examples of test questions. But think for a moment, which comes first when planning a lesson, objectives or test questions? Imagine, do teachers normally start planning to teach by writing test questions? No. Normally teachers start with thoughts about why they are teaching--the purpose; what they will teach--the content; and how they will teach--the method. Usually the topic of evaluation is the last to be considered when planning. This chapter will illustrate the role of objectives as they relate to evaluation.

What Are the Purposes of Having Objectives for Any Activity?

One answer is objectives are specific directions on the use of method, technique and strategy. Are there other reasons for objectives? Can you express the purpose for objectives in your own words?

_____

_____

For example, can you think of one objective for teaching social studies? Perhaps helping your students to be good

citizens would be an objective.   What would one other objective
be for teaching social studies?

(write your response here)

```




```

What are objectives?   Why are they necessary?   Imagine that
the Jones family wanted to go on vacation, but they
could not decide where to go.   If they packed
the car and left on their vacation without
having picked a destination, in what direction
would they go?   What road would they take?   Of
course, this is a ridiculous situation, as
ridiculous as the Jones family deciding that
they were going "east" for a vacation.   "East"
could be anywhere from the Florida Keys to
Maine.   Although a general direction would be of
some help in planning a trip, it certainly would
not help them in making advance hotel reservations or in deciding the proper clothes and
sports equipment to pack.   On the other hand,
if the Jones family decided to go to New York
City to shop on Fifth Avenue and to attend Broadway plays, then
they would be able to select a specific route, make reservations,
and take the proper clothes and equipment.

How does this example compare with writing teaching
objectives for a class?   Why does a teacher need objectives?
General objectives give direction but do not tell what content,
methods, skills, or attitudes are necessary for the successful
completion of the lesson.   Many social studies teachers consider
the development of "good citizenship" a general objective.   Write
what you believe teachers mean by this term--that is, what are
some of the characteristics of "good citizenship."

(write your response here)

```




```

246

Do the characteristics you have listed above actually help you select content or determine how you will teach and what your students will learn? Circle either **YES** or **NO** . Explain.

(write your response here)

A general objective of many social studies teachers is: "I'd like my students to understand and appreciate the Industrial Revolution in this country." Do the words understand and appreciate as used above have a precise meaning? Circle either **YES** or **NO** . If I said "You should understand and appreciate the Industrial Revolution," would you know precisely what was expected of you? That is (1) what knowledge you should have, (2) what skills you should practice, and (3) what attitudes you should have about the historical event commonly called the Industrial Revolution?" Explain.

(write your response here)

General Objectives vs. Specific Behavioral Objectives

Teachers usually have objectives for teaching their courses though often those objectives are neither spoken nor written down. Teachers' objectives are often very general and sometimes these objectives are in conflict. If the social studies general objective is to "develop good citizens," this is somewhat like the Jones family saying they are going "east." The general objective provides the teacher with no specific guide as to what content to select, what methods or techniques to use, what assignments to give the students, or how to evaluate the students in relation to the objectives. As the Jones family might spend their vacation wandering all around the "East" without much satisfaction because they do not know where they are going or how to get there, the teacher might spend the year wandering all around "good citizenship" with an equal lack of achievement.

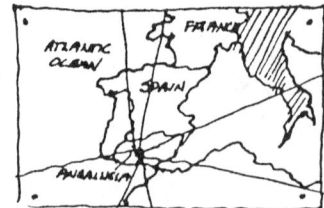

IN SUMMARY, GENERAL OBJECTIVES WOULD BE STATED LIKE THIS:

In this course students will learn to appreciate the values of a democratic country.

or One of the major objective of this course will be to develop students' positive attitudes toward social justice.

or As part of this course students will improve their reading comprehension using the social studies textbook.

But none of these general objectives give guidance to planning or evaluation.

HOWEVER, SPECIFIC BEHAVIORAL OBJECTIVES MIGHT BE STATED LIKE THIS:

Having read the assignment in Chapter 4 of the social studies text students will be able to identify in a class discussion the three reasons why the Continental Congress adopted democracy.

or Having read Chapter 4 in the social studies text students will demonstrate on a post-attitude survey a postive attitude toward the national aim of social justice.

or Students will apply SQ3R strategy to their reading assignment to improve their reading comprehension which will be evaluated in class through an oral reading survey.

These objectives give specific guidance to planning and evaluation.

Setting the Standard for Success

Behavioral Objectives

Characteristics of any good behavioral objectives:

1. They should give both the teacher and the students a sense of direction.
2. They should guide the teacher in selecting materials, techniques and strategies of teaching.
3. They should provide guides for teaching behavior.
4. The should not be in conflict with one another.

There is a fifth characteristic. In order to determine whether the students have reached the objective or not, the objective should be stated in such a way that the teacher can objectively measure student behavior. Objectives of this type are called specific behavioral objectives. What is the sense of having an objective that cannot be evaluated? How can the teacher determine whether the student has become a "good citizen" or an "independent thinker" if there is no specific criteria by which to judge the performance of the student?

Writing Your Own Behavioral Objectives

Perhaps you already know how to write a complete behavioral objective. You should have a chance to demonstrate your knowledge and skill.

Instructions: Please circle the response that best fits your knowledge of writing behavioral objectives.

(a)   I don't know anything about writing a complete behavioral objective, but I will try to write one in the box below.

(b)   I know something about writing objectives, but I am not sure I can write a complete behavioral objective. I will try to write an objective in the box below anyway.

(c)   Yes, I know how to write a complete behavioral objective and just to prove the point, I will write one in the box below.

If you have attempted to write a complete behavioral objective, then check your objective against the three criteria listed below.[1] Any complete behavioral objective fulfills these three criteria. Check the criterion if you have fulfilled it in your written objective above.

_____ Criterion 1: Is there an **observable behavior**?

_____ Criterion 2: Are the **conditions for behavior** specified?

_____ Criterion 3: Is there **acceptable performance** included?

For example: here is an objective with the three criteria.

Having <u>viewed</u> the filmstrip "Westward Ho" and <u>read</u>
     _____(conditions for behavior)_____/

Chapter 4 of the text, students <u>will be able to identify</u>
                    (observable behavior)

in small discussion groups <u>two or three reasons</u> for the
                   (acceptable performance)

westward movement.

If you have not included all three criteria--observable behavior, conditions, and acceptable performance--then your objective is not complete. If you have not written a complete objective, what you should do now is review the following explanation of each of the three criterion. Keep in mind you are learning the skill of writing a complete behavioral objective. Learning the skill will take practice.

Criterion 1: Observable Behavior

Does your objective include a behavior you want to observe when the student has completed the lesson? For example:

The students <u>will be able to identify</u> through discussion . . . (this is observable behavior)

The students <u>will be able to write</u> . . .
        (this is observable behavior)

Observable behaviors other than <u>identifying</u> and <u>writing</u> are:

analyze	classify	examine	survey	construct
hypothesize	suggest	defend	evaluate	justify
support	define	list	locate	name
describe	explain	summarize	apply	illustrate
discover	reject	recall	organize	

For other words on knowledge objectives see Bloom's Taxonomy in Chapter VI, "Questioning: A Function of Effective Teaching Practices."

Instructions: Now try your skill at writing out an observable behavior using one of the suggested words above.

For example: the students <u>will be able to summarize</u> the ideas
about death among the San People...

(write two examples here)

1.
2.

Criterion 2: Conditions

Does your behavioral objective include the conditions under
which the student is expected to perform the desired behavior?
For example:

<u>After listening in class to the audio-tape</u> with
        (this is a condition)
statements by the Supreme Court Justices, the
students will be able to identify through class
discussion . . .

<u>After completing one of the selected readings</u> in
          (this is a condition)
the class list, the students will be able to
write . . .

Instructions: Now try your skill at writing out
the conditions under which the students are
expected to perform.

For example: <u>After reading Chapter 4</u> in the text, the students
will be able to summarize the ideas about death
among the San People . . .

(write two examples here)

1.
2.

Have you tried?

Criterion 3: Acceptable Performance

Finally, does your objective specify acceptable performance? For example:

After listening in class, to the audio-tape with statements by the Supreme Court Justices, the students will be able to identify through class discussion, <u>three of the four judges' opinions</u> concerning wire-tapping.   (this is acceptable performance)

After completing one of the selected readings on the class list, the students will be able to write a one page paper noting <u>at least two reasons that justify</u> the aim of social justice. (this is acceptable performance)

Instructions: Now try your skill at writing acceptable performance.

For example: After reading Chapter 4 in the text, the students will be able to summarize the ideas about death among the San People in a small group report which will cite <u>at least two ideas</u> that will be discussed in class.

(write two examples here)

1.

2.

The following are a series of complete, correctly stated behavioral objectives. Please carefully read the examples in preparation for writing your own complete objective. As you read through the examples identify each of the three criterion in each example: Is there **observable behavior**? Are there **conditions** under which the student is to perform? Is there **acceptable performance**?

Instructions: Underline the three criteria in each example. Label the criteria O for observable behavior, C for conditions, and A for acceptable performance.

For example: <u>After listening</u> to the speaker, our representative
                     C

in congress, each students <u>will write out</u> at least
                           O

<u>one question</u> to ask the speaker.
   A

1. Having read the chapter on "Passing State Laws" the class will participate in a field trip to the State House after which each student will write a personal account of his/her experience according to the outline provided in class.

2. The students will be able to participate in a mock national convention by role-playing accurately a delegate, having read and discussed the chapter on "National Elections."

3. Given the experience of having visited the State House on a field trip, students will be placed in small groups and each group will prepare to debate the other groups on how best to spend the State's budget. The students' performance will be evaluated by the teacher on a rating form based on the quality of the groups' presentations.

Instructions: Now try your skill at writing out two complete behavioral objectives. **REACH**

```
+------------------------------------------------------------+
|  1.                                                        |
|                                                            |
|  2.                                                        |
|                                                            |
|                                                            |
+------------------------------------------------------------+
```

Checking Yourself Out

Can you identify complete behavioral objectives? Let's find out. Read the following six objectives. Mark each one either complete or incomplete on the line provided. If the objective is incomplete, explain why.

1._____After participating in the "trust walk," each student will write a definition of trust in one sentence. (Explain if incomplete.)

2._____Having viewed the film "Black Prophets," students
will be able to discuss in a small group three of
the four black leaders and their views.
(Explain if incomplete.)

3._____The students will be able to define 80% of the
history terms.
(Explain if incomplete.)

4._____Given the latest issue of <u>Know Your World</u>, the
student will write and present a mock newscast
according to the criteria discussed in class.
(Explain if incomplete.)

5._____Given the in-class reading, "Voices in the Soviet,"
the students will understand three of the five
Russian authors known for their dissent.
(Explain if incomplete)

6._____After hearing the audio-taped speeches of two
opposing candidates, the students will list three
differences between the candidates views with 80%
accuracy.
(Explain if incomplete.)

The following are answers to Check Yourself Out.
    1, 2, 4, and 6 are complete.
    3 is incomplete because Criterion 2 (conditions under
which the student is expected to perform) is missing.
    5 is incomplete because Criterion 1 (observable
        behavior) is improperly stated. "Understand"
        cannot be measured or observed.

To summarize what you have already learned and what you are
about to learn, examine the following chart.

skills

WHAT YOU HAVE LEARNED	WHAT YOUR ARE ABOUT TO LEARN
Complete behavioral objectives are evaluated in terms of their construction based on 3 criteria. 1. Is there an **observable behavior**? 2. Are there **conditions** under which the student is to perform? 3. Is there specified **acceptable performance**?	Behavioral objectives are written on three levels: 1. **Knowledge**, which is a body of facts and principles. 2. **Skill**, which is acquiring an ability through experience or training. 3. **Attitude**, which is one's opinion, feeling, or mental set as demonstrated by one's actions.

THREE LEVELS OF OBJECTIVES:

KNOWLEDGE, SKILL, ATTITUDE

If you have mastered the skill of writing complete behavioral objectives, then you ought to feel a sense of accomplishment, for now you are almost ready to write good lesson plans and good test questions. You are almost ready because you still must master the skill of identifying and writing the three different levels of behavioral objectives. Do you remember in the introduction to this chapter the discussion on the three levels of objectives: knowledge, skill, and attitude? In this final section of the chapter you are expected to identify and write objectives that are classified as one of the three levels. For example:

Knowledge objective: Having read Chapter Three in the history text, students will <u>identify and list</u> on a class quiz three of the five generals named. (This calls for knowledge.)

Skill objective: Having selected an individual topic, students will <u>demonstrate research skills</u> by completing the required topic outline. (This calls for skills.)

Attitude objective: Students, having studied the American Revolution, will demonstrate a <u>critical (open-minded) attitude</u> toward revolutions in a short written exercise. (This calls for attitude.)

Did you notice how the three levels of objectives differ from each other? All three levels meet the criteria of complete behavioral objectives, but they differ on the behavior called for. The knowledge objective calls for the listing of information (cognitive-memory), the skill objective calls for the

demonstration of a research skill, and the attitude objective
requires the demonstration of a critical attitude.

Knowledge Behavioral Objectives

Knowledge objectives normally call for recall, explanation,
and application of information, so this objective often includes
such words as recite, restate, organize and compare. This level
of objective often calls for lower levels of thinking such as
cognitive-memory and convergent. (For an extensive listing and
explanation of these different cognitive levels of thought be
sure to see Bloom's Taxonomy that explains those levels of
thought in Chapter VI, "Questioning: A Function of Effective
Teaching Practices.") Examples of knowledge behavioral
objectives are:
1. After reading the article "Poor Rains a Concern," in the
    Daily News, the students will be able to cite two reasons
    for the continued concern in a class recitation.

2. After seeing the film, "Nicholas and Alexandra," the
    students will identify a personality characteristic of
    Nicholas and compare it with the characteristic of one
    other European monarch (student choice) in a brief,
    written paragraph.

Instructions: Now try writing a knowledge behavioral objective.

Skill Behavioral Objectives

Do you recall in Chapter V, "Methods, Techniques, and
Strategies," a discussion on using different techniques? The
point was made that techniques requiring skills, i.e., debate,
research, oral report, grouping, etc., would not be effective
unless the necessary skills were developed. For example, if you
ask the student to read a paragraph and identify the main idea,
you are literally asking the student to practice the skill of
reading comprehension. Other skills which have been
traditionally practiced are writing (which includes note-taking,
papers, essays, research), speaking, studying, and grouping.
Examples of skill behavioral objectives are:
1. Having reviewed the SQ3R strategy, students will demonstrate
    reading comprehension skills by orally reading in class
    following the SQ3R strategy.

2. Using the library, the students will demonstrate <u>research</u> skills by selecting three sources and writing a 200-word theme noting two environmental problems in the northern hemisphere.

3. Given a lecture on the chapter assigned, students will <u>take notes</u> on the lecture which will be handed to the teacher and evaluated based on the criteria in the handout, "Taking Effective Notes in Social Studies."

<u>Instructions</u>: Now try writing a skill behavioral objective.

Attitude Behavioral Objectives

YOU HAVE

Your lessons not only call for knowledge and skill, but often call for students to acquire a particular attitude. For example, social studies teachers often say, "I want my students to like social studies." In precise behavioral terms the social studies teacher in reality means, "I want my students to have a positive attitude toward social studies." In fact, one can measure whether students have a positive or negative attitude toward social studies or for that matter toward any subject. Attitudes other than positive which teachers wish students to acquire are open-mindedness (critical thinking), willingness, self-respect, tolerance, cooperativeness, receptiveness, impartiality, unbiasedness, and readiness. Examples of attitude behavioral objectives are:

1. Having been placed into small groups for the study of Chapter III, students will demonstrate in their small groups a <u>cooperative attitude</u> as measured on a small group self-evaluation check list.

2. While a student is showing an individual project, students will demonstrate an <u>attitude of respect</u> for others by listening to the presentation. The attitudes will be evaluated by teacher observation.

3. After studying conflicting historical evidence found in the Jackdaw Kit, the students will demonstrate in class discussion a <u>critical attitude</u> toward historical events as evaluated by the teacher observing students' level of critical questions.

Instructions: Now try writing an attitude behavioral objective.

     Did you remember to check each of your objectives with the three criteria: observable behavior, conditions and acceptable performance? Just remember, if you are having problems writing knowledge, skill, and attitude objectives that include the three criteria, be patient and persistent. Go back over the lesson until you have mastered the skill.

Some Behavior Objectives Contain All Three Levels: Knowledge, Skill, and Attitude

     Have you made a discovery? You may have discovered by now that one complete behavioral objective may contain several levels of behavior. It is not uncommon to find knowledge, skill, and attitude behaviors in a single objective. For example:

Students will name (knowledge) in class discussion the three important points from a lecture after following the proper note-taking form (skill).
    [This behavioral objective includes both knowledge (name) and skill (note-taking)]

While working in small groups (skill), the students will demonstrate the attitude of respect for others by adopting a cooperative attitude (attitude) as evaluated on a post-attitude survey.
    [In this case both group skills and attitudes of respect and cooperation are combined in a single objective.]

     So what should you conclude? You should conclude that the three levels of objectives (knowledge, skill, attitude) can be stated separately or they can be combined in one objective. For example, the following is a complete knowledge, skill, and attitude objective written using the three criteria.

Having <u>watched</u> a TV program and <u>read</u> several
       (Criterion 2-conditions)
articles on SADCC, each student will <u>recall</u> in a
       [knowledge obj.]
short paragraph <u>two benefits</u> of the SADCC organ-
       (Criterion 3-acceptable performance)
ization and will <u>practice research and oral</u>
       [skill obj.]
<u>presentation skills</u> by <u>preparing</u> a brief in-class
       (Criterion 1-observable behavior)
presentation and in that presentation will <u>demonstrate</u>
       (Criterion 1-observable behavior)
<u>an open-minded attitude</u> toward SADCC as <u>evaluated</u>
       [attitude obj.]
<u>through teacher observation</u>.
(Criterion 3-acceptable performance)

You may wish to try writing your own complete behavioral objective that fulfills all the criteria and contains knowledge, skill, and attitude levels just for practice. However, you will probably never be asked to write such a complex objective. We merely presented an example to demonstrate that one could be successfully written.

The Final Check on Your Skills at Identifying
Complete Behavioral Objectives

Listed below are eight objectives on the topic of "developing good citizenship." Mark each one by writing <u>complete</u> or <u>incomplete</u> above the line in front of the objective. Circle the appropriate level or levels: K = knowlege, S = skill, A = attitude.

For example:

   <u>complete</u>

(K) (S) A   Having studied the map of Africa in their class atlas students will locate and name on an outline map 5 of the longest rivers on the continent.

---

1. _____
  K   S   A   Having studied the Constitution, students will know the duties of the Chief Justice. (Explain and rewrite if incomplete.)

2. _____
  K   S   A   Having studiedthe Bill of Rights, students will demonstrate in their pesonal relations with others the attitude of respect, and the demonstration of this attitude in class will be evaluated through observation by the teacher. (Explain and rewrite if incomplete.)

3. _____ Students from their study of democracy in Unit 5,
    K   S   A   will demonstrate their research skills by listing
                     a brief bibliography on the subject on an in-class
                     exercise. (Explain and rewrite if incomplete.)

4. _____ Students will learn to appreciate the advantages
    K   S   A   of being a citizen in this country. (Explain and
                     rewrite if incomplete.)

5. _____ The values of a democratic system will become
    K   S   A   known as students think about the benefits they
                     have come to enjoy. (Explain and rewrite if
                     incomplete.)

6. _____ Students in small groups while studying the Bill
    K   S   A   of Rights will show by their rating on an
                     evaluation form their positive attitude toward
                     group cooperation. (Explain and rewrite if
                     incomplete.)

7. _____ In Chapter Seven of the social studies text,
    K   S   A   students will identify and explain two of the
                     three major concepts as part of a unit test.
                     (Explain and rewrite if incomplete.)

8. _____ Students, having studied the Constitution, should
    K   S   A   really understand, fully appreciate, and finally
                     have faith in the wisdom of those who fought for
                     independence. (Explain and rewrite if incomplete.)

have to

Final Check Answers: Check your responses against the answers
below.
1. Incomplete (K) because Criterion 1 (observable behavior)
    is improperly stated. What does "know" mean? Also
    Criterion 3 (acceptable performance) is not stated. Rewrite
    number 1 so that it is a complete behavioral objective.
2. Complete (A)
3. Complete (S)
4. Incomplete (A) because Criterion 1 (observable behavior)
    is improperly stated. "To appreciate" cannot be measured
    or observed. Criterion 2 (conditions) and Criterion 3
    (acceptable performance) are missing. Rewrite number 4 so
    that it is a complete behavioral objective.
5. Incomplete (A) because Criterion 1 (observable behavior)
    is improperly stated. "Become known" cannot be measured
    or observed. Criterion 2 (conditions) and Criterion 3

(acceptable performance) are missing. Rewrite number 5 so that it is a complete behavioral objective.
6. Complete (A)
7. Complete (K)
8. Incomplete (K,A) because Criterion 1 (observable behavior) is improperly stated. "Really understand, fully appreciate," and "have faith" cannot be measured or observed. Criterion 3 (acceptable performance) is missing. Rewrite number 8 so that it is a complete behavioral objective.

Conclusion

TAKING CONTROL

Return to the Jones family who at the beginning of the chapter were heading "east" on vacation but without any objective in mind. Exactly what is "east?" Where is it? What is there to see, do, and wonder at? Some social studies teachers, just like the Jones family, are wandering about their subject without a clear idea as to the purpose. You know now how to turn your meaning of social studies into clear behavioral objectives, in short, you know how to think about teaching. The task ahead is to apply that skill to testing, planning, and practice teaching.

A Suggestion

Congratulations if you have successfully fininshed this chapter on writing objectives. However, please keep in mind that learning to write good objectives is diffi- cult. Writing objectives is also a skill and just because one can recall the three criteria and the three levels (knowledge, skill, and attitude) does not mean that one has mastery of that skill. You may need to read over the chapter a number of times. The only way you can improve your ability to write objectives is to practice until finally you have disciplined yourself to think in specific terms about objectives. If you have mastered both the theory and the practice of writing objectives, then turn to the next chapter on evaluation and testing. In that chapter you will learn how to convert behavioral objectives into different types of test questions. In Chapter XIV, "Organizing to Teach: Unit and Daily Lesson Planning," you are required to plan by stating complete behavioral objectives. Testing and planning require clearly stated objectives, a skill that you have now mastered.

CHAPTER XIII

IDENTIFYING AND WRITING TEACHER–MADE TEST QUESTIONS

OBJECTIVE: Having read this chapter you should be able to identify the five different categories of teacher-made tests, write valid objective test items, and demonstrate on the Final Test your knowledge of the general basic rules for test construction.

Facts, concepts, and generalizations drive the curriculum, which drives the textbooks and other classroom instructional materials which along with objectives drive the evaluation--and that's testing.

**YOU HAVE
AN EXCITING
TEACHING RESOURCE**

If you have read Chapters VI on "Questioning: A Function of Effective Teaching Practices" and XII on "Identifying and Writing Behavioral Objectives," you have two of the pieces of information necessary to construct good test questions. The third piece of information concerns the actual construction of specific test questions. The chapter on questioning identified the four different levels of questions: cognitive-memory, convergent, divergent, and evaluative. The chapter on behavioral objectives taught you how to write complete knowledge, skill, and attitude behavioral objectives. This chapter on test construction will demonstrate how to convert the levels of questions and the behavioral objectives into teacher-made tests that can be helpful in evaluating continuous progress.

Suppose you were to write this objective, "Having read chapter three on discovery and colonization, students will identify on a written test six of eight explorers and explain what each discovered." Given this objective which calls for cognitive-memory and convergent learning, what should you be testing? Obviously, you would say the identification of six people and why they were important. How should this objective be tested? Well, the answer depends on the type of test you wish to grade. Perhaps, "short answer" (several sentences or a paragraph) might be the first test to come to mind, requiring an answer that identifies a person and explaining in a sentence why that person was important. However, alternative types of objective tests, matching, multiple choice, fill-in, or true-false, could also be effective.

Evaluation
Alternatives

Assume for the moment that you have developed an acceptable set of behavioral objectives, and that you have taught in ways you think have helped students achieve your objectives. You want to determine how well your students have done. In short, you are going to evaluate the performance of your students. But what kind of evaluation? There are five general categories of teacher-made evaluations. You are on familiar terms with paper and pencil essay and objective examinations. Another type is the formal oral examination, for example, an oral presentation in class, speech, debate, or panel discussion. There is also testing through the creation of an object, i.e., building a model, drawing a picture, writing a play, creating a poster, making a map, creating an audio-visual display. And finally there is attitude testing.

How long have you been taking tests? Perhaps it goes without repeating, but the occasion calls for it: "Taking a test is one thing, giving it is quite another." You have spent much of your life in school thinking about tests, trying to figure out the best way to study for and be successful on different types of tests. So, you know about taking tests, but now think about giving tests. The most popular tests are objective (multiple choice) and subjective (essay). You are asked in this chapter to identify the five different categories, practice writing some of them, and demonstrate that you know how to use them.

Evaluation (testing) categories can be:

A.   **Objective Tests: 7 types**
   1. true-false   5. sequencing
   2. fill-in   6. labeling
   3. short answer   7. multiple choice
   4. matching

B.   **Essay Tests: 4 levels**
   (examples)
   1. (cognitive-memory) Describe the Battle of
        Gettysburg.
   2. (convergent) Compare and contrast the Northern
        strategy with the Southern at the Battle of
        Gettysburg.
   3. (divergent) Suppose the North had lost the Battle
        of Gettysburg, what effect might this have had
        on the final outcome of the Civil War?
   4. (evaluative) What do you believe are the most
        important events to remember about the Battle
        of Gettysburg?

SPECIAL STUDENTS
Evaluation

new tests to help us
Imagine

C.   Testing through the Creation of Objects:
   An evaluation technique used for social studies
   projects, for example, visual aids that students have
   created such as maps and globes; posters including
   collages, mobiles, pictures, diagrams, charts, graphs;

and models including dioramas, sand table, salt maps. (See Chapter VII on "Technology and Instructional Resources: A Function of Effective Teaching Practices" where creation of these objects is discussed.)

D. **Attitude Testing:** Measuring how students feel can be done by using positive vs. negative attitude strength scales (strongly agree, mostly agree, uncertain, mostly disagree, strongly disagree). Teachers often wish to affect students' attitudes. Obviously, attitude and attitude change can be measured on a pre and post-attitude inventory.

E. **Oral Examination.** Some students for special reasons require oral examinations. Oral examinations also refer to speeches, debates, panels, discussions, participating in a dramatization, play, or simulation. For examples of forms used to evaluate oral reports see Chapter V, "Social Studies Methods, Techniques, and Strategies."

Strengths and Weaknesses of Objective and Essay Tests

Objective and essay tests have advantages and disadvantages. Below are listed some strengths and some weaknesses of essay and objective examinations. See if you can match them with the category of test they bet fit. Put O if you think the statement best fits objective tests, and E if you believe the statement is most characteristic of an essay question. Write O for objective or E for essay on the line before each statement.

STRENGTHS

_____ 1. Gives an extensive test sample.
_____ 2. Is easy to construct.
_____ 3. Promotes more intensive and comprehensive type of study.
_____ 4. Can be made highly reliable.
_____ 5. Can be graded objectively.
_____ 6. Measures writing, organizational ability, and creativeness.
_____ 7. Can be subjected to item analysis and further refinement.
_____ 8. Can be made highly valid. (Does it measure what it is supposed to measure, is it precise, well-defined, accurate?)

WEAKNESSES

_____1.   Encourages guessing.
_____2.   Is difficult to prepare (construct).
_____3.   Gives limited test sample.
_____4.   Is difficult to grade.
_____5.   Favors the verbally inclined student.
_____6.   Has low reliability. (Reliability means trustworthy,
            in short, how well a test measures what it is supposed
            to measure.)
_____7.   Encourages bluffing, "throwing the bull!"
_____8.   Frequently neglects measurement of higher thought
            processes.

(See key below for right answers.)

Validity and Reliability   *educational*

You can grade yourself in a moment; but before you do,
consider two terms--validity and reliability. These are
important terms because they reflect the quality of the test.
Validity refers to whether a test measures <u>what</u> it is supposed to
measure. In other words, is it precise, well-defined, accurate,
well-written? Reliability refers to <u>how well</u> a test measures
what it is supposed to measure. In other words, is it
trustworthy, dependable, did the test achieve its purpose? What
you should know is that objective tests such as multiple choice,
true-false, fill-ins, sequencing, labeling, short answer, and
matching can more easily be developed to insure good validity
(precision) and reliability (purpose) just because these types of
questions tend to yield right answers or short correct responses
that can be objectively analyzed. Validity and reliability are
much more difficult to establish with essay questions which are
more subjective, that is, evaluated at the grader's discretion.

Objective tests will give you a much more extensive test
sample than will an essay exam. Unfortunately, good objective
tests such as true-false and multiple choice are quite difficult
to prepare, encourage guessing, and frequently neglect
measurement of organizational ability and higher thought
processes. Essay tests, on the other hand, are easy to construct
and can measure writing, organizational ability and creativeness.
But essay questions have liabilities, too. They give you a
limited test sample, are difficult to grade objectively, favor
the verbally inclined students, and encourage bluffing--throwing
the bull!

Key to Strengths and Weaknesses:
     O - 1, 4, 5, 7, 8   (strengths)
         1, 2, 8   (weaknesses)   **Use This**
     E - 2, 3, 6,   (strengths)
         3, 4, 5, 6, 7   (weaknesses)

Other Factors: Types of Students

Other factors must be considered before you begin construction of a test. (1) What is the nature of the group to be tested? Evaluation of a "top" group will call for a different kind of test than would, say, a group of students who had serious reading or learning disabilities. (2) Certain kinds of measurements are best attempted through the use of certain types of questions. For example, when thinking about objective type questions, true-false questions are best when there is one correct response. Completion or short answer questions are useful for drill exercises. Matching exercises are probably best for testing knowledge of names, terms, and places. Multiple choice questions, properly constructed, can measure all six levels of thought as organized by Bloom's Taxonomy (see chapter on questioning). The essay question, you will recall, is a good index of writing, organizational ability, and creativeness, all of which may call, in part, for a subjective evaluation.

Use This

General Rules on Test Construction

The following are some general rules on test construction that you should consider.

1. **Have something for everyone in the class,** and begin the test with the easiest items. A test is a real threat to many students. It helps to ease tensions if the first items are easy, and this ensures that everyone will achieve some degree of success.
2. **The test should sample all the content of the unit.** Any emphasis in the test should be a reflection of what you have emphasized in class.
3. **Authorities on test design recommend that no more than four different types of test items be used in** any one test: i.e., (1) true-false, (2) multiple choice, (3) matching, and (4) essay. More than four tend to confuse students.
4. **Be sure to give instructions,** including point values, at the beginning of each different type of test item so there will be no misunderstanding as to how the test is to be answered or how much time to spend on any one section.
5. **If you are going to penalize a student for guessing, say so.**
6. When you have completed constructing the test items, let the items "cool off" for a day or so, then **take the test yourself.** Your test errors are best caught by you.

Setting the standard for success

Reviewing and Constructing Seven Types of
Objective Questions

True-False	Sequencing
Fill-In	Labeling
Short Answer	Multiple Choice
Matching	

True-False Questions

True-false is the most deservedly criticized type of question because it encourages guessing. After all, there is a fifty/fifty chance of guessing the right answer. However, this type of question calls for cognitive-memory thinking--recall of specific information--and can be useful if you follow a few basic rules.

1. Keep the language simple and precise. Test authorities suggest that about five true-false questions should be answered per minute.
2. The question should be entirely true or entirely false. If the questions are not entirely true or false, then in the instructions state, "If any part of the question is wrong, then mark the question as false."
3. The answer to the question should not hinge on some trivial detail.
4. Don't quote from the textbook. Change the wording to thwart the student who recognizes without understanding.
5. Avoid a pattern of answers. One useful way to do this is to arrange true-false questions on the basis of a flip of a coin.

The following is an example of a behavioral objective from which the true-false test items have been drawn.

Having studied the different ethnic groups in the United States in the chapter on the history of ethnic groups, the students will be able to identify on a test where these groups settled and even today continue to live.

Example of instructions and questions for true-false.

Circle T for true and F for false. If the statement is partly false, it should be considered totally false.

T F 1. The Scandinavian people live mainly in the northern Midwest.

T F 2. The Scandinavian people today live mostly in Texas.

(Create a true-false **question** including **instructions.**)

Fill–In Questions

Coming Event

A properly constructed fill-in (completion) question can prevent guessing. Multiple choice, and true-false cannot. This type of question calls for cognitive-memory level thinking--one right answer response. The following are some basic rules for constructing fill-in the blank test questions that may help.

1. Omit only significant words, but don't omit too many. A chopped-up sentence may only confuse students.
2. Keep the blanks uniform in length (this lessens the possibility of guessing), and allow an equal amount of credit for each blank.
3. Ideally there is only one possible right answer to any fill-in question.
4. Avoid verbatim quotes from the text for reasons given previously--it encourages empty word memorization.

The following is an example of a behavioral objective from which the fill-in test items have been drawn.

Having listened to a lecture on the structure of the national government, students will name the first President and Vice President and will list the two parts of the legislature on a test.

Example of instructions and questions for fill-in.

Fill in the blanks to complete the sentence.

1. The first President of the United States was_____ and the first Vice President was_____.

2. Under the Constitution the Congress consists of the House of Representatives and _____.

(Create a fill-in question including instructions.)   **RIGHT NOW**

```

```

Short Answer Questions

Coming Event

Short answer is a popular type of test question for many social studies teachers. It is easier to grade than an essay, yet it establishes whether the student has learned and remembered the required information. This type of question calls for convergent level thinking--a correct answer but in the students own words. The following are some basic rules for constructing brief, written, short answer response questions that may help.

1. Be sure to tell students in your instructions whether they are to write their answers in sentence or paragraph form. Often students write short written response answers in fragmented sentences. Be sure to suggest how you want the answers written.
2. Does spelling and punctuation count? Students ought to know ahead of time if they will be penalized for guessing on spelling or punctuation.

The following is an example of a behavioral objective from which the brief, written, short answer response test items have been drawn.

Having read Chapter Six in the text students will define the aim of industrial development and identify positive and negative reasons for development in a brief, written, response.

Example of instructions and questions for brief, written, short answer response.

Define the following in no more than two complete sentences. Mistakes in spelling and punctuation will not be counted off.

1. The aims of industrial development.

2. The positive and negative reasons for industrial development.

(Create a brief, written, short answer response **question**
including **instructions**.) **_RIGHT NOW_**

```
┌─────────────────────────────────────────────────────────────────┐
│                                                                   │
│                                                                   │
│                                                                   │
│                                                                   │
│                                                                   │
│                                                                   │
│                                                                   │
└─────────────────────────────────────────────────────────────────┘
```

Matching Questions

Coming Event

The matching form of examination question is frequently used
by teachers to measure recognition and recall. Properly
constructed, this type of testing makes guessing difficult. This
type of question calls for cognitive-memory level thinking--
correct association of known facts. The following are some basic
rules for constructing matching questions that may help.

1. Don't use more than fifteen items or less than five items.
    More than fifteen tends to confuse students. Less than
    five encourages guessing. If you want to use more than
    fifteen in your test, break them up into two or more
    sections.
2. All items in any one section should be on the same page.
    Don't let the test itself be a handicap.
3. Arrange the premises on the left-hand side of the page
    and the responses on the right. Number or letter these
    chronologically and alphabetically. If you are using an
    answer sheet, both numbers and letters are necessary.
4. Include more responses than premises or have one response
    match more than one premise. This cuts down on guessing.
5. Avoid patterns in the location of your responses.

The following is an example of a behavioral objective from
which the matching test item was drawn.
    Students, having surveyed the first twenty years
    after Independence, will be able to identify a
    list of prominent Americans during that period
    on a written test.

Example of instructions and questions for matching.

    Match items by writing the letter for the
    correct response from the right column next
    to the correct premise on the left.

_____1. Was President of the U.S. a. John Marshall
_____2. An author during the   b. Aaron Burr
      colonial period who wrote c. Millard Fillmore
      about Indians.   d. John Quincy Adams
_____3. Was Chief Justice of the e. James Fenimore Cooper
      Supreme Court.   f. Walker T. Grant
_____4. His father was President. g. James L. Lee
_____5. He shot Hamilton in a duel. h. Thomas Jefferson

(Create a matching question including instructions.)

(empty box)

Sequencing Questions

Coming Event

    Sequencing is quite a popular type of social studies teacher-made test, but it is also one of the most disliked by students because if they miss one item by sequencing a response in the wrong place, then surely there is a second error. Sequencing is a particularly good type of test for evaluating students' sense of time and place. This type of question calls for cognitive-memory level thinking--the order in which events or steps in a process occur. The following are some basic rules for constructing sequencing questions that may help.

1.   Be sure that the instructions state how the items are to be sequenced, i.e., time (chronologically), importance, according to some authority, the text, etc.
2.   Sequencing encourages guessing. Suppose there are five items to the sequence. If one knows three items, the other two items' placement can often be accurately guessed at. Keep this in mind when thinking about using sequencing, for there is no way to cut down on guessing with this type of test question.
3.   Be careful of creating long lists of items to sequence. It is best to divide a long (fifteen items) list into two sections and, as in matching, place all items to be sequenced on one page.

The following is an example of a behavioral objective from which the sequencing test item was drawn.
    Having studied the inquiry process in The Nature of the Social Studies, students will be able to construct the sequential steps of the process with 100% accuracy on a test.

Example of instructions and questions for sequencing.

Sequence the steps of the inquiry process according to
the methods book by placing 1-6 in the brackets: 1 for
the first step and so on up to 6 for the last step.

(4) formulating hypotheses
(2) state of certainty
(6) generalization
(5) exploring and evidencing
(1) experience
(3) framing the problem

The following is an example of a behavioral objective from which
the sequencing test item was drawn.
After constructing a time line of major United States
historical events as a class project, students will be
able to recall the chronological order of those events
on a written test.

Instructions and question.

Sequence these events in historical chronological order,
1 for the oldest event and 5 for the most recent.

(3) Jackson Presidency
(2) Monroe Doctrine
(5) Spanish American War
(1) War of 1812
(4) Civil War

(Create a sequencing question including instructions.) **RIGHT NOW**

Labeling Questions

You know labeling. Remember the blank map of the United
States with instructions to fill in the states and capitals?
Labeling is a favorite technique for a limited number of topics.
What can be labeled? Maps, pictures, diagrams, graphs, charts,
time lines, etc. This type of question calls for cognitive-
memory level thinking--label, find, locate, name.

The following is an example of a behavioral objective from which the labeling test item was drawn.

After researching the major wars fought by the United States, students will be able to correctly place those wars on a time line as part of a final test.

Example of instructions and question for labeling.

Label the time line with the wars and the dates each began and ended in the order they were fought.

Spanish American War
Civil War
World War I
American Revolution

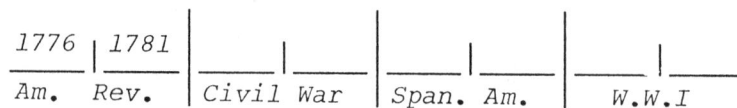

```
    1776 | 1781    |____|    |____|    |____|
    _____|____|____|____|____|____|____
    Am.   Rev. | Civil  War | Span.  Am. | W.W.I
```

The following is an example of a behavioral objective from which the labeling test item was drawn.

After reading a chapter on the use and construction of a bell curve, students will be able to label the parts of the curve on a unit test.

Example of instructions and question for labeling.

This is a normal bell curve. Label the various parts.

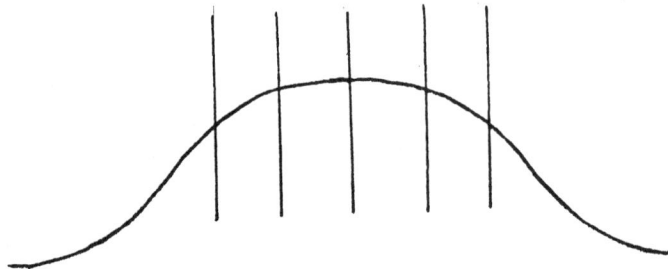

(Create a labeling question including instructions.) **Now**

Multiple Choice Questions

The multiple choice question is generally considered to be the most versatile type of objective question. It is also the most difficult to construct properly for it can be written to measure different levels of student response. There are six Bloom's Taxonomic levels on which multiple choice questions can be written. Needless to say, learning to incorporate the six levels (knowledge, comprehension, application, analysis, synthesis, evaluation) in your questions requires considerable test construction sophistication. To refresh your memory on the meaning of these different levels, see the discussion on the six levels at the end of Chapter VI on "Questioning." For the purpose of preparing you to write multiple choice test items, two general categories have been chosen rather than the six specific levels. The two levels are (1) knowledge (lower level recognition and recall) and (2) application (higher level interpretation and problem solving).

Note there is a hierarchy here. Recognition and recall multiple choice questions are much easier to write than are problem solving and interpretation questions. If your objectives include measurement of the recall level (name, identify, state), the type of test questions previously discussed (true-false, fill-in, labeling, short answer) might be more applicable. If you desire to measure thinking at the level of interpretation, be prepared to spend time constructing the multiple choice questions.

A multiple choice question consists of two parts: a stem and the responses. The stem is the statement at the beginning of the question. The responses are the 3 (elementary), 4 (secondary), or 5 (higher education) choices that follow the statement. The composition of both is crucial for effective use of this kind of question. The following are some basic rules on constructing multiple choice questions that may help.

1. The question should be written in a way that justifies only one best answer.
2. The choices should be as brief as possible, and all should be about the same length.
3. Make the choices as plausible as possible. The student should have to consider all the choices.
4. It is suggested practice that elementary students be given three responses to choose from, secondary four responses, and higher education five responses.

Setting the standard for success

5.   When giving instructions be sure to say, "the answer that best fits the statement" (stem). The reason for this instruction is that all or part of the responses to a statement could be true, but there is only one best response. You will save yourself from students arguing that all the responses are correct.

The following is an example of a behavioral objective from which the multiple choice test items have been drawn that demand lower level recall and recognition of information.
     Having read about and discussed the Constitution and Amendments in class, students will be able to identify the important points discussed on a unit test.

Example of instructions and questions for multiple choice.

     Circle the letter representing the answer that best fits the statement. (sample 3 responses for elementary)

     1.   The Amendment which guarantees freedom of speech and assembly is:
          a.   The Preamble to the Constitution
          b.   The First Amendment
          c.   The Tenth Amendment

     (sample 4 responses for secondary)

     2.   Which of the following is not required by the Constitution?
          a.   The President must be 35 years of age.
          b.   The Senate members must be 42 years of age.
          c.   The Supreme Court Justices can be of any age.
          d.   The House members must be 25 years of age.

RIGHT NOW

(Create a multiple choice **question**, including **instructions,** which demands recall and recognition.)

```



```

The following is an example of a behavioral objective from which the multiple choice test item was drawn that demands higher level problem solving and interpretation.

Having studied in the first chapter the philosophy of social justice in the United States, students will be able to apply the national aims to that philosophy on an objective examination.

1. Which of the following best characterizes the philosophy behind social justice in the United States?
   a. the national aim of redistribution of wealth
   b. the national aim of providing free enterprise
   c. the national aim of egalitarianism
   d. none of the above

the Inevitable

(Create a multiple choice question, including instructions, which demands problem solving and interpretation. Remember 3 responses for elementary, 4 for secondary, and 5 for higher education.)

RIGHT NOW

Essay Examinations

CREATIVE MINDS

Remember what was said earlier--that essay exams can measure (1) writing, (2) organizational ability, and (3) creativeness, but the liabilities are that essays are unreliable, favor the verbally inclined, encourage bluffing, and are often hard to grade objectively. One advantage may appeal to the overworked teacher, the essay examination does take less time to construct. A few essay questions could occupy students for an entire test. You would probably need fifty to seventy-five objective test items for a similar time period. However, constructing essay questions does take time and careful thought, and of course, the grading time for essay tests is one of the major drawbacks for teachers with large classes. The following should be considered when constructing an essay exam.

Is an essay test appropriate for measurement of the course's stated objectives? Obviously it can be, even if you just want students to demonstrate cognitive-memory and convergent levels of thinking. After all, an essay question can call for the recall and proper sequence of events, i.e., "Describe the Battle of Gettysburg." Probably we would urge that this level of thinking (cognitive-memory and convergent) would be better tested by objective type questions, i.e., true-false, multiple choice, fill-in, matching, etc. In short, if the objectives call for the lowest levels of thought, then think of using objective type test questions. However, if the objectives call for higher levels of thinking such as divergent and evaluative and require analysis, synthesis, and evaluation, then consider using essay type questions that call for more than simple recall. Divergent and evaluative levels of thinking can be encouraged and evaluated with questions such as (divergent) "Suppose the North had lost the Civil War? How might that have changed the United States approach to Manifest Destiny?" and (evaluative) "Inflation is a serious problem. What do you judge are the best measures to take to cope with inflation?"

If you choose to use essay type questions, what should you keep in mind? You should consider two items of crucial importance, the content (what the question is about) and the structure (how the question is written). Content determines what you are going to measure--validity. Structure determines how well the question measures--reliability.

Setting the Standard for Success

With this in mind, here are a few basic rules for writing essay questions.

1. Keep the language simple and precise. An essay question should tell the student exactly what is required for a good answer. Words like discuss, analyze, or react are confusing unless they are qualified by some kind of criteria. If students are asked to discuss something by illustrating, defending, comparing, defining, outlining, or summarizing, they have a little better idea of what you have in mind.
2. Several shorter essay questions are better for evaluation purposes than one or two long ones. Shorter essays give you a more extensive sample of student achievement.
3. Require the students to answer all the questions. A common procedure among teachers using essay questions is to permit the students to select from a variety of questions those they feel they are best equipped to handle. There are two reasons why you should not do this. It is very difficult to write essay questions of equal difficulty. Moreover, the available evidence indicates that students do not select the questions best suited to their preparation.
4. Do not assume that students know how to answer an essay exam for you. Expectations differ on just what ought to be included in a "good" essay. Be sure you review how to answer a "successful" essay question if you intend to use essay questions.

The four different types of essay questions illustrated below are based on the four levels of questions found in Chapter VI on "Questioning."

The following is an example of a behavioral objective from which the cognitive-memory, convergent, divergent, and evaluative essay questions have been drawn.

> After a unit study on the Civil War, students should be able to discuss, describe, hypothesize, and appraise that period in American History on a unit test.

(Cognitive-memory level essay question--recall)
1. Reproduce the arguments as discussed in the text for the South's secession from the Union.

(Create a cognitive-memory essay **question**.)

```



```

(Convergent level essay question--compare and contrast)
2. Compare Lee's strategy with that of Grant.

create

(Create a convergent essay **question**.)

```



```

(Divergent level essay question--speculation)
3. Suppose you had been President of the U.S. at the time Lee surrendered to Grant; what action might you have taken toward reuniting the North with the South?

(Create a divergent essay **question**.)

```



```

(Evaluative level essay question--personal judgment)
4. What do you believe was the purpose of the Civil War?

(Create an evaluative essay question.)

```

```

can be changed But they can never be replaced

Attitude Testing

Attitude testing could perhaps better be called attitude surveying. Do you recall in the preceding chapter the heading, "Attitude Behavioral Objectives"? By now you know that you can state attitude objectives, but as yet you have not learned how to evaluate or survey those attitude objectives. Perhaps you think that attitude testing really cannot be done, but of course it can. And we suspect over the years you have taken a good many attitude tests even though you may not have recognized them at the time. Suppose you wish to check your students' attitudes about their own self-concept, which is an attitude toward oneself. How would you do that? An attitude objective might be stated as:

Students, having studied a first grade unit on self, family, and school would, after class dis- cussion and small group projects, demonstrate positive attitudes toward the aim of self- reliance as measured on a pre and post-attitude survey.

Example of attitude survey based on the objective above.

Attitude Survey

Instructions: Circle the word or words that best fit your attitude about the following statements.

1. I feel good about myself.

    always   sometimes   neutral   almost never   never

2. I feel good about myself in school.

    always   sometimes   neutral   almost never   never

3. I feel good about myself when I am able to accomplish my own projects.

    always   sometimes   neutral   almost never   never

4. I feel good about myself when I am working.

    always   sometimes   neutral   almost never   never

Suppose you wished to improve Judy's and John's, the disadvantaged students, self-concept attitude so that at least they would feel more confident at school. Very simply, you would give a pretest on the students' self-concept attitude, then teach your unit of material, and finally, as part of the evaluation, post-test the students' self-concept attitude again. The difference between the pre and post-test shows you whether you have achieved the attitude objective, which was to improve the students' self-concept. So attitude objectives such as open-mindedness (critical thinking), willingness, self-concept, respect for others, tolerance, cooperativeness can be measured by pre and post-testing. The following is one example of sample instructions and test questions. The testing can be done orally, by paper and pencil, or through the teacher's observation of student behavior.

IMPROVING TEACHING

Example

Instructions:
    The following statements are designed to provide information on how you feel. You may find yourself agreeing with some statements, disagreeing with others. Whatever your response, you can be certain that many other people feel the same way you do.
    There are no right or wrong answers to these statements; rather, your response simply indicates how you feel about each statement. Remember, your response to any statement should indicate how you usually feel.
    Your response to each statement can range from strongly agree to strongly disagree as follows: 1 = strongly agree, 2 = mostly agree, 3 = uncertain, 4 = mostly disagree, 5 = strongly disagree. Circle the number which best represents your feeling.

EVALUATION OF STUDENTS' ATTITUDES TOWARD SMALL GROUP COOPERATION

1 2 3 4 5   1. I feel that cooperation in a small group is important.

1 2 3 4 5   2. Students in my small group contributed to the group's effort.

1 2 3 4 5   3. I believe that I should respect others in my small group.

Example  create

Instructions: Circle the word that best represents your feeling.

1. ALL MOST MANY SOME NONE of South Africa's leaders are immoral people.

2. Life, liberty, and property are rights due everyone ALL MOST MANY SOME NONE of the time.

3. Inflation is bad for the country ALL MOST MANY SOME NONE of the time.

4. Civil rights should be guaranteed to ALL MOST MANY SOME NONE of the citizens of the United States.

(Using the illustrations above as a guide try your skill at developing a simple set of attitude test survey items.)

THE FINAL TEST

This will be your final test. If you have worked your way through this chapter, noting each of the different types of test questions and trying your skill at writing each of these questions, then you are prepared for this final test. This is going to be a different kind of test from what you have had before. You will not be expected to answer the test questions, but rather to judge whether the test questions are well written. In fact, on this final exam many of the test questions were purposely made faulty. In short, there are a number of poorly written test questions which you are asked to identify and correct. After each type of test question a space will be provided for you to note what is faulty with that series of questions. Frankly, if you are able to successfully identify the problems with this test, you probably are capable of creating your own test without repeating the errors you will find here. Good luck on this final exam--may you not repeat the errors found here. A final reminder: as you go through this final exam, you may wish to refer back to the basic rules for each type of question. Undoubtedly the faulty questions violate some of those rules.

EITHER YOU HAVE IT...
OR YOU DON'T.

WRITTEN TEST OVER THE ENTIRE TEXT

Instructions: This is a take-home written test over the entire text. Take all the time you need to answer all of the questions.

True-False: 20 points

    T F   1. Students' reactions to school in Chapter I were usually negative toward school teachers but positive toward school administrators.

    T F   2. One of the major problems identified in Chapter I was lack of student enthusiasm.

    T F   3. Seven different types of small groupings were identified in Chapter V.

    T F   4. Teaching strategy and teaching method are actually the same as a teaching technique.

    T F   5. The poor are generally without money.

(Identify the faults, if any, in the true-false questions above.)

Multiple Choice: 6 points

1. The research on learning and remembering supports one of the following statements:
   a. We learn and remember 10% of what we both see and hear.
   b. We learn and remember 40% of what we discuss with others.
   c. We learn and remember 80% of what we hear.

2. The chapter on questioning emphasized the following:
   a. cognitive-memory questions
   b. convergent questions
   c. divergent questions
   d. evaluative questions
   e. all of the above
   f. none of the above

3. Select the answer which best supports the following statement. Active learning is favored by virtually all educational psychologists because:
   a. students learn faster, remember more, and derive greater enjoyment.
   b. passive learning is negative and therefore is to be avoided.

    c.   active learning is always preferred over passive
         learning.
    d.   any teaching techniques can be either active or
         passive.

(Identify the faults, if any, in the multiple choice questions
above.)

```



```

Matching: 15 points

    ____Task oriented small group a. specific project or
    ____Tutorial small group   proposal
    ____Brain storming small group b. individual instruction
    ____Discussion small group   c. free and unencumbered
    ____Socratic small group   discussion of an
                          assigned topic
                        d. discuss problem posed
                          by teacher
                        e. discuss freely and
                          uninhibitedly

(Identify the faults, if any, in the matching question above.)

```



```

Completion, Fill-In: 22 points

  1. The four levels of questions are _____,_____,
     _____, and evaluative.

  2. _____, according to the text emphasizes
     _____,_____, and _____.

284

(Identify the faults, if any, in the fill-in questions above.)

```
┌─────────────────────────────────────────────────────────────┐
│                                                             │
│                                                             │
│                                                             │
│                                                             │
│                                                             │
│                                                             │
│                                                             │
└─────────────────────────────────────────────────────────────┘
```

Sequencing: 6 points

    ____what we see
    ____what we experience directly or practice
    ____what we discuss with others
    ____what we hear
    ____what we attempt to teach others
    ____what we both see and hear

(Identify the faults, if any, in the sequencing question above.)

```
┌─────────────────────────────────────────────────────────────┐
│                                                             │
│                                                             │
│                                                             │
│                                                             │
│                                                             │
│                                                             │
│                                                             │
└─────────────────────────────────────────────────────────────┘
```

Labeling: 14 points

Instructions: Place T for traditional or P for progressive
on the line by the statement which best represents that
tradition.

    ____based on needs of students   ____much use of testing
    ____use of group work   ____use of problem solving
    ____much emphasis on drill   ____concerned more with
    ____use of evaluation rather   transmission of culture
    than grades

(Identify the faults, if any, in the labeling question above.)

```
┌─────────────────────────────────────────────────────────────┐
│                                                             │
│                                                             │
│                                                             │
│                                                             │
│                                                             │
│                                                             │
│                                                             │
└─────────────────────────────────────────────────────────────┘
```

Essay: 14 points

    Recall in the chapter on methods, techniques, and strategies that ten techniques were identified which you ought to know. Identify and list the ten techniques.

(Identify the faults, if any, in the essay question above.)

TAKING CONTROL

OVERALL CRITICISM OF THE TEST

1.   What would you say about the values assigned to each set of test questions, i.e., T-F (20 points), multiple choice (6 points), etc.? What values would you have assigned?

2.   How many different types of test questions were used in this test? How many types of questions are supposed to be used in a "good" test?

3.   This was a test over the entire text. Did the test questions reflect a general coverage of the text? Were there chapters that were not covered at all in the test?

Critique of the Test

    The old adage is that you can learn from your mistakes. In this case, you can learn a good deal from a bad test. Turn with us to a general criticism of the test and then examine each type of test question.

The values assigned to each section were not appropriate. For example, true-false questions were worth 20 points; that means each true-false question was worth 4 points. Remember that five true-false questions on the average should be answered in one minute. This means in one minute almost one-quarter of the test was answered. The three multiple choice questions were worth only 6 points, making each multiple choice question worth only 2 points. You know that it takes longer to answer multiple choice questions than true-false questions. Each part of the matching question was worth 3 points for a total of 15, whereas two fill-ins were worth 22 points. Obviously, they should not be worth more than the essay which is only 14 points and usually calls for a good deal more work than does the matching or fill-in. Each sequencing item is worth 1 point, whereas each labeling item is worth 2. Why? Surely sequencing should be equal to the worth of labeling. Remember, points assigned reflect the amount of time you wish the test taker to spend on a particular type of question. If you were to take the above test seriously, you would spend more time on the true-false (20 points) than you would on the essay (14 points). That, of course, makes no sense at all. In fact, none of the points assigned are appropriate.

Seven different types of test questions were used in this test. You may recall that authorities on testing recommend that no more than four different types of questions should appear on any one test. There can be no excuse for using seven different types, most of which were cognitive-memory level calling only for recall of knowledge. Surely four different types would have been sufficient.

The test did not adequately cover the text. Certain chapters received special attention while others received no attention at all. In other words, the test was uneven, for though the title "Test Over the Entire Text" suggests questions about each chapter, it is obvious that half the text was not covered.

A final general criticism: the test lacked explicit directions for each section. Only the labeling and essay questions had instructions. Anyone taking this test could rightfully complain that they did not know what to do, for there were no instructions on true-false, multiple choice, matching, fill-ins, or sequencing questions. The failure of stating instructions alone would have condemned this test.

Examining Types of Test Questions

True-False. The first true-false statement is half right and half wrong, so this means that the instructions should have contained the statement, "If the question is partly wrong, it should be considered false." All five of the items were false. Certainly that is easy to grade, but it is poor test organization. True-false questions should be organized so that they do not suggest a pattern. Finally, item 5 was not covered in the text, and without special knowledge could not be answered and, therefore, should not have been asked. Now look back to your criticism following the true-false questions; did you identify what was faulty?

Multiple choice. Question 1 had three responses and question 2 had six responses. Test authorities suggest four responses for secondary and five for higher education. The answer to question 3, "students learn faster, remember more, and derive greater enjoyment," is a direct quote from the text. This question could be measuring students' ability to recall this phrase, when the intent of the question was to encourage problem solving and interpreting. The answer should have been a paraphrase rather than a direct quote. Now look back to your criticism following the multiple choice questions; did you identify what was faulty?

Matching. The major fault with the matching is that there were five matches. A good matching would have had 5 premises on the left side and six or more responses on the right side. In this case, if the students knew three matches, they could have guessed without knowledge at the remaining matches. Now look back to your criticism following the matching question; did you identify what was faulty?

Fill-Ins. The first question has three uneven spaces which encourages students to guess at what would fit those three spaces. Keep the spaces uniform. The second question clearly violates the rules that "a chopped-up sentence may only confuse students" and "ideally there is only one possible right answer." Now look back to your criticism following the fill-in questions; did you identify what was faulty?

Sequencing. The obvious main fault is that no instructions are given as to how and according to what the items are to be sequenced. Instructions for the sequencing should have mentioned that the items were research findings on learning and remembering and that the items should be sequenced from the least (1) to the most (6) productive learning experience. Now look back to your criticism following the sequencing question; did you identify what was faulty?

Labeling. For the most part the statements are too generally stated to be labeled either traditional or progressive. The statements could be either "T" or "P" depending upon how one wished to interpret the statements. Each of the statements would need to be much more precisely worded if they are to be labeled. Now look back to your criticism following the labeling question; did you identify what was faulty?

Essay. This essay question calls for the lowest level of cognitive-memory thinking. The students merely need to recall ten techniques. An essay question should encourage organizational ability, writing, and creativeness. The information asked for in this essay question could better be measured by one of the objective type questions. In short, the essay question is inappropriate. Now look back to your criticism following the essay question; did you identify what was faulty?

SUMMARY

In summary, a good teacher-made test requires that you think at least about the following points. You may wish to use this as a checklist when constructing your own tests.

Checklist

_____1. No more than four different types of questions.

_____2. The values assigned to each question should be determined by the estimation of student time spent answering each question.

_____3. Construct test questions that reflect the objectives of the course and class time spent on a given topic.

_____4. Give instructions for each of the different types of questions. Over the long run, instructions will reduce students' arguments about how they were intended to answer the questions. Remember when writing out instructions to include the point values, because points represent time spent on the task. Students will figure out how to apportion their time.

The beginning of a new world

Congratulations, you have finished a most difficult chapter. Having finished the chapter, however, does not mean that you are proficient at writing the different types of test questions, nor have you probably considered the use of the five categories of teacher-made evaluations. Hopefully you have identified how different types of tests are written based on behavioral objectives. You have become sensitive to what is good and bad about test questions. In short, you are ready now to practice the skill of writing good tests. We do urge you to review the chapter as you practice creating test questions in the future. We hope that your achievement in writing good test questions will be matched by your students' achievement in answering those questions. YOUR FUTURE

CHAPTER XIV

ORGANIZING TO TEACH: UNIT AND DAILY LESSON PLANNING

OBJECTIVE: Having read this chapter you will be able to identify in class discussion the three types of planning outlined and demonstrate knowledge of unit and daily lesson planning by constructing both types of plans.

> You either affect the world or
> you are the effect of it.

One can almost claim that many of the breakdowns, failures, and inadequacies identified by all the students and teachers in the first chapter flow from teachers' inability to plan and to reach objectives. And this raises the next question: Why don't teachers do an adequate job of planning? In fact, we must say in all honesty that teachers typically do not plan--not at all. They let the book and the school's curriculum guide do their planning for them. They don't own the courses they teach, the book does.

This is defended by teachers who reply that they do not need to plan, that they carry their objective with them--in their heads. And, of course, since most techniques have been reduced to textbook coverage through recitation, in-class reading, lectures and tests, they do not feel a need to plan strategies, nor do they need to even plan a test which comes compliments of the textbook teacher's guide. However, many schools require teachers to fill out a Lesson Plan Book for each day's instruction in case a teacher might be absent and the substitute would need to know what was to be covered and assigned. But the "Plan Book" represents only a brief set of notes and is in no way comparable to what is considered a daily lesson plan.

You may be asking, "If experienced, professional, certified social studies teachers generally do not have unit plans or even daily lesson plans, then why should I?" The answer is, do not assume in advance that you can project a set of plans and carry them out successfully. In short, learn to be systematic in your planning particularly given that you have not taught the subject. You need to practice good habits of ownership by learning to develop on paper, not just in your head, and in careful and sequential fashion, just what and how you want to teach. The following course plan organization will help you own the course you teach.

Resource Plan, Unit Plan, Daily Lesson Plan

plan

Over the last half decade educators have identified at least three levels of curriculum planning. They are the resource plan, the unit plan, and the daily lesson plan. Let us first consider the resource plan as a guide to social studies curriculum development.

A **resource plan** is often thought of as a teacher's brainstorming and planning for one term, or semester, or grading period, or an entire year. The resource plan is an organizing plan to pull together all of the resources that might be available to teach subjects or topics. Normally the teacher or team of teachers developing a resource plan would identify content, method, and resources. They would list alternative series of methods, techniques, and strategies and include appropriate media and a bibliography. When a team of teachers in a specific subject area develop a resource plan together, it gives departmental unity to the teaching of that subject. Each teacher on the team then develops his/her own unique unit plans and daily lessons based on alternatives offered in the resource plan.

A **unit plan** is thought to be any planning that includes more than one day. It can encompass any amount of time from two days to a year, but normally a plan covers one to three weeks of work. As mentioned above, a unit plan usually is drawn from alternatives offered in the resource unit.

The **daily lesson plan** is what the name implies--a plan for a single day's lesson. The assumption is that the teacher ought to know how the class is to proceed day by day through a unit. The daily lesson plan, therefore, is a breakdown of the unit into brief specific notations to yourself on what in particular the class will do that day.

In summary, a complete set of curriculum plans for the school year is organized this way: resource plans (i.e., "America Becomes a World Power") from which a number of unit plans are drawn (i.e., "Spanish-American War") from which in turn daily lesson plans are drawn (i.e., "Roosevelt and the Rough Riders").

MAKE THE WORLD SAFE FOR DEMOCRACY!

THINK Imagine plan

PLANNING CHART

example: your plans:

```
┌─────────────────────────────┐        ┌─────────────────────────────┐
│      RESOURCE PLAN          │        │  RESOURCE PLAN              │
│                             │        │                             │
│ "America Becomes a World    │        │                             │
│ Power"                      │        │                             │
│      (1870-1914)            │        │              (length)       │
│              (length)       │        │          _____      │
│       one semester          │        │                             │
└─────────────────────────────┘        └─────────────────────────────┘
              │                                        │
┌─────────────────────────────┐        ┌─────────────────────────────┐
│      UNIT PLAN              │        │  UNIT PLAN                  │
│                             │        │                             │
│ "Spanish-American War"      │        │                             │
│        (length)            │        │              (length)       │
│        2 weeks             │        │          _____      │
└─────────────────────────────┘        └─────────────────────────────┘
              │                                        │
┌─────────────────────────────┐        ┌─────────────────────────────┐
│    DAILY LESSON            │        │  DAILY LESSON              │
│       PLAN                 │        │     PLAN                   │
│ "Roosevelt and             │        │                             │
│ the Rough Riders"          │        │              (length)       │
│       (length)             │        │          _____      │
│        1 day               │        │                             │
└─────────────────────────────┘        └─────────────────────────────┘
```

Can you think of your own examples? Fill out the spaces in the resource unit, unit plan and daily lesson plan above.

Having completed the chart above, test your ability to label topic headings.

Instructions: Before each topic heading place the label that best fits the heading: RP = resource plan, UP = unit plan, DLP = daily lesson plan. On the line provided briefly justify your choice.

_____1. America Becomes a Nation: 1600-1850

_____
(justify your choice)

_____2. Indians in Indiana

_____

_____3. The Mayflower Compact

_____

_____4. Presidential Elections: 1932

_____

_____5. Survey of American History: 1900 to present

_____

_____6. Emancipation Proclamation

_____

Answer Key to Topic Labels

1. RP - Large scope of topics
2. UP - Clearly more than a
         one-day topic
3. DLP - Clearly a one-day
         topic

4. UP - Obviously would take
         more than one day to
         cover different
         candidates
5. RP - Large scope of topics
6. DLP - One-day topic

Planning Outlines

       While it is obviously useful to know the differences between
different ways of organizing both information and large and small
scale planning, you do not necessarily know how to plan. In
order to identify different planning tasks, outlines of the three
different kinds of plans, resource, unit, and daily lesson, are
included. First is an outline for a resource plan, then the unit
plan and daily lesson plan.

Resource Plan Outline
for several terms, a semester or a school year

1.   **STATEMENT OF THE GENERAL PURPOSES** for which the course is
     taught. This statement of purpose is intended as an over-
     view that identifies how the teacher is intending to treat
     the subject. For example, the statement covers such
     questions as whether the course will be treated essen-
     tially as transmission of content or as a means to
     encourage problem solving, or if the course is intended
     to be fine arts oriented or directed toward a special
     objective such as citizenship training.
2.   **THE LISTING OF BROAD TOPICS** and a suggestion of topics and
     questions.
3.   **LEARNING ACTIVITIES, METHODS, TECHNIQUES, AND STRATEGIES.**
     The method would be identified with an extensive listing
     of possible alternative techniques. Often it is in this
     category where a set of strategies is developed.
4.   **TECHNOLOGY AND INSTRUCTIONAL RESOURCES.** All the resources
     for teaching this course are noted. These include all
     films, filmstrips, tapes, slides, maps, pictures, TV
     programs, programmed lessons, and any other appropriate
     resources that could possibly add to the teaching of a
     lesson.
5.   **BIBLIOGRAPHY.** A listing of all the appropriate reading

materials: books, magazines, pamphlets, newspapers, and journals.
6. **EVALUATION.** Suggestions for alternative types of teacher-made tests to evaluate the content covered in the resource unit.

This resource plan is in outline form only to suggest the categories that would help organize a semester's work. A unit plan outline follows.

```
┌─────────────────────────────────────────────────────────────┐
│  REMEMBER, FROM THE LARGER RESOURCE PLAN COMES THE UNIT PLAN  │
└─────────────────────────────────────────────────────────────┘
```

Unit Plan Outline   Setting the standard for success

I. Introductory Statement
  A. State the age and grade level for which the unit is planned.
  B. Indicate the length of time needed to carry out the unit.
  C. Briefly state how this unit fits into the overall plan.

II. Objectives Stated as Performance or Behavioral Objectives (For training on writing objectives, see Chapter XII entitled "Identifying and Writing Behavioral Objectives.")
  A. Outline the specific knowledge which students are expected to master (know the 3 major reasons . . . . recall the name of . . .).
  B. State the specific skills which students will build (research, note-taking, writing, etc.).
  C. Outline the specific attitudes which students will develop (cooperative, open-minded, critical, respectful, self-confident).

                              Concepts

III. Content Outline
  A. Outline the major subject matter content, or
  B. Outline a statement of problems to be solved, or
  C. Outline a series of projects to be completed.

IV. Activities in Which Students Will Engage to Achieve Objectives
  A. Initiating activities
    1. Outline a series of activities in which students will engage to make a successful beginning. Indicate the sequence of these activities. The activities should be constructed to stimulate interest in and call attention to the topic.
    2. Indicate the time anticipated for initiating the unit.
  B. Developmental activities
    1. Outline activities in which the students will engage to acquire knowledge, skills, and attitudes. Indicate sequence in terms of how

TEACHING RESOURCE

OUR WORK

the knowledge, skills, attitudes, etc. are to be
learned.
2. Estimate the time needed to carry out this phase.
C. Summarizing activities
Outline a summarizing activity or group of activities
toward which the whole group will direct effort
throughout the major portion of the learning period,
and which may serve as a basis for evaluating
individual student achievement.

RESOURCES
TECHNOLOGY

V. Materials and Resources
A. Locate reading materials, audio-visual instructional
aids, and materials for demonstration and experimenta-
tion which are needed to make the activities most
worthwhile.
B. Locate and outline types of facilities outside the
classroom in the school and community which will be
used.
C. Locate and identify procedures for bringing community
persons into the classroom and for taking the students
into the community.
D. When students are to make contacts with persons outside the classroom or are to secure materials, outline
procedures which will be employed to facilitate such
activities.

VI. Evaluation Procedures
A. Outline the procedures which will be employed to
determine where students are at the beginning--a pretest or activity which measures the students' knowledge about the content and topics to be covered.
B. Outline techniques to be used in assisting students
to measure their own progress.
C. Outline procedures to measure student growth in
knowledge, skills, and attitudes throughout the unit.

FROM UNIT PLANS COME DAILY LESSON PLANS

Daily Lesson Plan Outline

Each daily lesson plan should contain as minimum
requirements:
1. objectives
2. content
3. techniques and strategies
4. summary and assignment

Objectives. An objective is simply a statement of what the
teacher would like to see students do by the end of the period.

There is a distinction between "general objectives" and "behavioral objectives." The former are general statements of aims or goals. The latter are similar statements spelled out in specific behavioral terms. General objectives are usually not very useful as discussed in Chapter XII, "Identifying amd Writing Behavioral Objectives." Objectives should suggest what specific knowledge, skills, or attitudes are to be learned. For example:

Given the in-class reading "Voices of the Soviet," the students will identify three of the five Russia authors known for their dissent in a short in-class essay.

Behavioral objectives will help teachers and their students identify specifically what is meant by the term "general objectives." (If there are questions on how to write specific behavioral objectives, see Chapter XII entitled, "Identifying and Writing Behavioral Objectives.")

Content. Content is essential, but it is not the only part of planning. By content we mean the facts, concepts, generalizations, terms, ideas, and beliefs that the teacher will present in class, in short, what is to be covered that day.

Techniques and Strategies. There are an infinite number of teaching techniques that could involve students in active learning, i.e., grouping, role-playing, debates, panels and any of the other 150 techniques in Chapter V, "Social Studies Methods, Techniques, and Strategies." The strategy states how the techniques are to be sequenced.

Summary and Assignment. Teachers frequently fail to "pull together" the major idea discussed during the class period. An adequate summarization and a well-explained assignment (SQ3R) help students understand "where they have been" and "where they are going."

How're you going to do it?

Examples of Unit Plans and Daily Lesson Plans

What follows are examples of unit plans designed for a particular grade. Included with some plans are daily lesson plans drawn from the units. Use the units as examples of how to plan using both the "Unit Plan Outline" and the "Daily Lesson Plan Outline." The exemplary units by grade level and topics are:

YOU HAVE

Grade	Topic
Kindergarten and First Grade	"Feelings"
Third and Fourth Grades	"Mapping Skills"
Sixth and Seventh Grades	"Africa--The People South of the Sahara"
Eighth and Eleventh Grades	"Civil War"
Twelfth Grade	"Minorities"

a guide for curriculum development

Unit Plan Designed for Kindergarten and First Grade
FEELINGS

Ellen Thamy
Kindergarten and
First Grade
Teacher

I.   Introductory Statement
    A.   This unit is planned for 5 or 6-year-olds in kinder-
        garten or first grade.
    B.   The unit should begin on Monday and culminate
        on Friday and take five days to complete,
        allowing half an hour per day.
    C.   The unit should be taught between other
        units concerning the self. Learning
        about feelings can help children form
        positive attitudes about themselves and
        others.

II. Objectives Stated as Performance or Behavioral Objectives
    A.   Knowledge
        The students will be able to distinguish between
        different feelings by matching a picture of a feeling
        to the word. The words will be written on the board
        and the students will display the picture in front
        of the correct feeling.
    B.   Specific skills
        1.   Following a discussion on what feelings are, the
            students will demonstrate brainstorming tech-
            niques by adding some additional examples of
            feelings to those already written on the board.
        2.   Students will demonstrate good listening skills
            and identify how feelings are expressed by
            making their faces show the correct expression
            that is asked for by a tape recording.
        3.   Students will demonstrate good listening skills
            by describing the feeling they have while
            listening to various selections of recorded music.
        4.   After choosing a feeling, the children will
            demonstrate how feelings relate to their lives
            by drawing a picture of a time when they
            experienced this feeling. They will then be
            asked to dictate a story to go along with the
            picture and thus demonstrate communication skills.
    C.   Specific attitudes
        1.   After being placed in small groups, the students
            will demonstrate role-playing techniques by acting

out various people's feelings. In the small group the students will display a cooperative attitude as measured by teacher observation.

2. In an informal discussion with the teacher, students will explain why there is nothing wrong with showing feelings. This discussion will allow students to exhibit verbal communication as well as demonstrate positive attitudes toward themselves and others.

III. Content Outline

children learn about

A. What are feelings?
B. How do I show or express my feelings?
C. Why do I feel that way?
D. Who has feelings?
E. Is it all right to show or express your feelings?

IV. Activities
A. Initiating activities (Monday - 1/2 hour) - What are feelings?
1. Show film "The Red Balloon." This film will be used to catch the students' attention. It will expose the children to several different feelings and emotions.
2. Discussion.
a. The teacher will begin a classroom discussion by asking questions (convergent and divergent) about the film, i.e., "How did the boy in the movie feel?" "Would you feel that way too?"
b. The teacher will give students examples of feelings and write them on the board (i.e., happy, sad, mad, nervous, etc.).
c. The teacher will have the students brainstorm and come up with additional feelings. These will be added to the list on the board.

like or agree   dislike or disagree   neutral or mild feelings

3. Activity - The teacher will read some unfinished sentences and ask the students to respond orally with the correct feeling (i.e., "When someone loses their best friend, they feel _____." "When I play with my friend after school, I feel _____.").

B.   Developmental activities (Tuesday-Thursday, 1 1/2 hours)

How do I show or express my feelings? (Tuesday)
1.   Discussion - The teacher will lead a discussion on how people express feelings. She should include expressions given by face, walking, standing, body language, etc. The teacher should demonstrate some expressions.
2.   Activity - The teacher will play a tape which asks students to express different feelings (i.e., when the tape says, "I am happy," the students will smile).

Why do I feel that way? (Wednesday)
1.   Discussion - The teacher will lead a discussion on the various things which can cause emotion (i.e., people, objects, situations, sounds, smells, etc.).
2.   Activity - The teacher will play various musical selections and ask the students how the music makes them feel and why.
3.   Activity - The children will choose a feeling and draw a picture of themselves when they experienced the feeling. The students will then dictate the story that goes with the picture.

Who has feelings? (Thursday)
1.   Discussion - The teacher will lead a discussion on who has feelings. She should include brothers, sisters, parents, friends, teachers, and others.
2.   Activity - The students will break into small groups and be given pictures of people expressing different feelings. The feelings will be written on the board and the students will decide to which feeling the pictures belong.
3.   Activity - While in the same groups the students will be given a situation and asked to role-play the different characters (i.e., situation - child breaks a window. How would the father feel? Mother? Child?).

C.   Summarizing activities (Friday - 1/2 hour)
Is it all right to show or express your feelings?
1.   Story - The teacher will read the students a story in which the characters discuss emotion. Such questions will be raised as "Why did the boy feel that way?" "Was it all right for the boy to cry?" "Why?"
2.   Discussion - The teacher will lead a discussion on why it is all right to express your feelings.
3.   One-on-One Discussion - The teacher will meet with each student and discuss the subject of feelings.

V.   Materials and Resources
   A.   "Feelings" Books
        Keats, Ezra Jack, The Snowy Day (Viking Press, 1962).
             [Joy]
        Alexander, Martha, Nobody Asked Me If I Wanted a Baby
             Sister (Dial Press, 1971). [Jealousy]
        Klein, Norma, If I Had My Way (Pantheon Books, 1974).
             [Jealousy]
        Brown, Margaret Wise, The Dead Bird (W.R. Scott, 1974).
             [Sorrow]
        LeShaw, E., What's Going to Happen to Me? When Parents
             Separate or Divorce (Four Winds, 1979). [Sadness]
        Sendak, Maurice, Where the Wild Things Are (Harper &
             Row, 1963). [Fear]
        Mayer, Mercer, There's a Nightmare in My Closet (Dial
             Press, 1968). [Fear]
        Rockwell, H., My Doctor (Macmillan Publishing Co.,
             1973). [Fear]
        Udry, Janice, Let's Be Enemies (Harper & Row, 1961).
             [Anger]
        Zolotow, Charlotte, The Quarreling Book (Harper & Row,
             1963). [Anger]

   B.   "Feelings" Media
        Lamorisse, Albert, The Red Balloon (Macmillan Films).
             [Film]
        Piper, Watty, The Little Engine That Could (Society
             for Visual Education). [Filmstrip]
        Palmer, Hap, Getting to Know Myself (Activity Records,
             Educational Activities, Inc.). [Record]

WORTH A THOUSAND WORDS

VI. Evaluation Procedures
   A.   The students will have no formal pretesting since
        the students in kindergarten and/or first grade may
        have had no past formal training. There are no
        prerequisite skills to the unit.
   B.   Evaluation will be informal in nature and in the form
        of a checklist.
        1.   In the brainstorming exercise, the teacher will
             look for student ability and participation.
        2.   In the tape recorded activity, the teacher will
             look for participation as well as the correct
             facial response.
        3.   In the music activity, the teacher will look for
             participation.
        4.   In the picture drawing exercise, the teacher will
             evaluate both the students' ability to understand
             which feeling they are drawing and their ability
             to explain their drawing.
        5.   In the small group activities, the teacher will
             look for the ability to distinguish feelings,
             act out feelings, and work in a cooperative way.

C.   The conference will be the final means for evaluation. At this time, the teacher will look at the checklist and see if and where any problems occurred. In the discussion, students will explain their attitudes toward the unit. If remediation is needed, the teacher can diagnose which area is troubling the student and proceed from that point.

Below are daily lesson plans for the unit on "Feelings." The first three daily lesson plans are filled in.

Instructions: fill in the remaining two days demonstrating your ability to turn unit plans into daily lesson plans.

FEELINGS

First Day -	Second Day -
OBJECTIVE: Having watched the film and thought about their own feelings, students in class discussion will brainstorm words for different feelings as teacher lists these feelings on board.	OBJECTIVE: Students will demonstrate good listening skills and identify how feelings are expressed by making their faces show the correct expression that is asked for by tape recording.
CONTENT: What are feelings?--Define.	CONTENT: How do I show or express my feelings?
TECHNIQUES & STRATEGIES: Show film, "The Red Balloon." Brainstorming class discussion on identifying what are feelings.	TECHNIQUES & STRATEGIES: During class discussion on feelings teacher will role-play how feelings are expressed. Tape recording asking for different emotions.
SUMMARY & ASSIGNMENT: Summarize by pointing to board and naming and defining each of the feelings that are listed. Leave words on board for the rest of day as preparation for next day's lesson which is on expressing feelings.	SUMMARY & ASSIGNMENT: Summarize by reminding students about what feelings are by pointing to words on board and discussing expressing feelings to get ready for next day's lesson on, "Why do I feel that way?"

THINK Imagine plan

(Fill in last two days using unit plan.)

Third Day –	Fourth Day –	Fifth Day –
OBJECTIVE: Students will demonstrate good listening skills by describing the feelings they have while listening to various selections of recorded music. After choosing a feeling, the children will demonstrate how feelings relate to their lives by drawing a picture of a time when they experienced this feeling. They will then dictate a story to go along with the picture to demonstrate communication skills.	OBJECTIVE:	OBJECTIVE:
CONTENT: Why do I feel that way?	CONTENT:	CONTENT:
TECHNIQUES & STRATEGIES: Recorded music to respond to. Class discussion on what causes emotions. Drawing pictures of emotional situations.	TECHNIQUES & STRATEGIES:	TECHNIQUES & STRATEGIES
SUMMARY & ASSIGNMENT: Summarize by pointing to words on board that identify feelings, discuss expressing feelings (Why do I feel that way?) in preparation for fourth day's lesson on who has feelings.	SUMMARY & ASSIGNMENT:	SUMMARY & ASSIGMENT:

Unit Plan Designed for Third and Fourth Grades
MAPPING SKILLS

Lisa Luken
Third Grade
Teacher

I. Introductory Statement
    A. This unit will be taught to third or fourth grade students.
    B. This unit will take 13 class periods to complete.
    C. This unit focuses on developing mapping skills. The unit will encourage exploration of their community and will show the importance of mapping as a means of communication. This unit is a part of a continuing investigation of the use of maps and should be followed by a unit in map reading in fourth grade Indiana history.

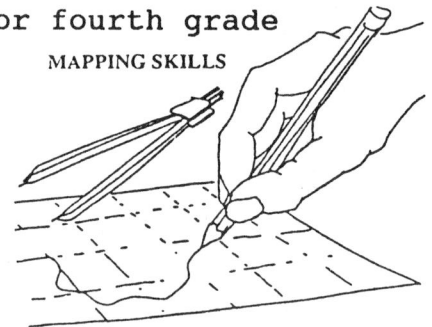

II. Objectives Stated as Performance or Behavioral Objectives
    A. Knowledge
        1. After participating in class discussions on "What makes a map?," the students will identify and explain orally in small group discussions all the parts of a map previously discussed.
        2. After viewing the film "Maps and Their Uses," the students will identify in a written response six uses of maps.

    B. Specific skills
        1. After discussing as a class how to map the class-room, the students will individually construct with 100% accuracy a map of the classroom.
        2. After making their own classroom map scales, the students will individually, on a teacher-constructed classroom map, use the map scale to determine with 100% accuracy the distance between two given points on the map.
        3. After discovering and discussing cardinal and intermediate directions with the class, the students--divided into small groups--will follow specific cardinal and intermediate directions to specific locations with 100% accuracy.
        4. After construction of a large neighborhood map as a class, the students will individually use given directions to trace routes from one location to another on the neighborhood map with 100% accuracy.

     5.   After planning and constructing a new com-
munity as a class, the students will individually make their own maps of the new
community with 100% accuracy.

C.   Specific attitudes
    1.   As a member of a large, task-oriented group for
the construction of a neighborhood map and of the
new community, the students will demonstrate self-
confidence as they offer suggestions to the group.
    2.   After assignment to small task-oriented groups to
play games, the students will demonstrate in their
personal relations with others the attitude of
respect as measured by teacher observation.
    3.   After working as members of large and small
groups for the study of mapping, students will
show their attitudes toward
group cooperation on an
attitude inventory.

III. Content Outline

A.   What is a map?
    1.   How to make a map.
    2.   Uses of maps.
B.   Classroom maps
    1.   Using scales.
    2.   Directions (cardinal and
intermediate).
C.   Neighborhood maps
D.   Planning a new community

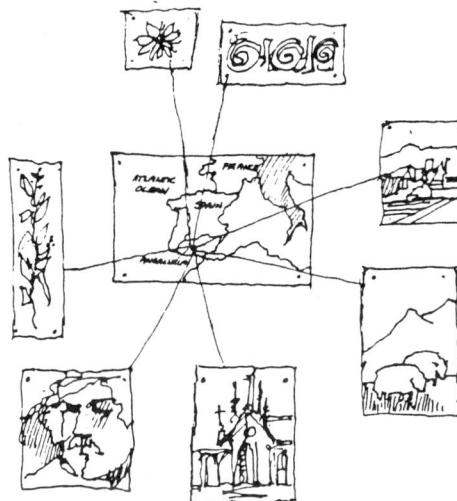

IV. Activities

A.   Initiating activities
    1.   The students will at convergent and evaluative
levels discuss as a class what they think a
map is and what maps can be used for.
    2.   Film "Maps and Their Uses."
    3.   Display and discuss the importance of various
types of maps as well as what things are on a
map. Examples of maps include: road maps, blueprints, weather maps, state maps, airline maps,
and U.S. and world maps.
    4.   Guest speaker - A mail carrier will discuss how
important maps are to mail carriers as they use
a neighborhood map to know where to deliver the
mail.
    5.   This introduction to maps will take 2 class
periods.
B.   Developmental activities
    1.   Mapping our classroom. Have the students pretend
they are viewing the classroom from a perch near
the ceiling. Have them construct a simple map
to show what the classroom would look like from
the perch. The students decide on the symbols

and the teacher should assist in determining a scale. Further discuss symbols and scales.

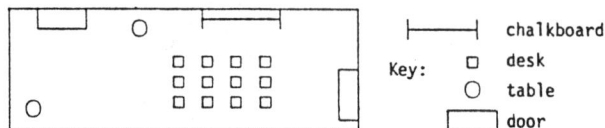

2. Using scales. Provide the students with a teacher-constructed classroom map. Have the students use their rulers and interpret the scale to answer questions such as, "About how far is the table from the bookshelves?"

3. Cardinal directions. Take the students outside on a sunny day. Have the students identify the cardinal directions using the shadows cast by the sun. N, E, S, and W should then be labeled on the classroom walls and on the classroom map. Introduce intermediate directions.

4. Treasure hunt. To practice following cardinal and intermediate directions, play the following game. Divide the students into small groups and give each group a card. The cards will have cardinal and intermediate directions on them that lead to the "treasure" (for example, take 5 steps N). The students can then plan their own treasure hunt directions.

5. The school neighborhood. After becoming acquainted with the parts of a map, scale, and directions, attention can be turned to the school neighborhood. Have the students imagine they are looking down on the school from an airplane. Stimulate imagination by showing aerial photographs. On a large piece of paper a neighborhood map will be made with the teacher's assistance. The streets should be drawn in and the students should construct models of the school, stores, their homes, gas stations, etc., and place them in position on the map.

6. Working with the neighborhood map. The relation between a map and the real world can be established by playing the following game. Divide the class into small groups. On the neighborhood map, the teacher will name two locations and the students are to trace the shortest route between them and give directions as they go. A matchbox car can be used to "drive" to the locations.

7. Additional practice. For additional practice working with the neighborhood map, the following activities can be used:

   a. Have one student describe to another student, with directions, how to get from one place to another.

   b. Have directions written on cards for an individual to "drive" from one location to another.

8. This phase will take 9 class periods.

C. Summarizing activities

1. Planning a new community. As a class, the students must decide what a community needs. Things such as airports, buildings, stores, parks, roads, homes, landforms, and so on should be included. They should then use construction paper and pieces that are three-dimensional, like pieces from a Monopoly set, to lay out what they, as a group, feel would be the best community. Then, individually, each student will make a map of the new community. It should be properly labeled, including directions, and have an appropriate key.

2. This phase will take 2 class periods to complete.

V. Materials and Resources

A. Reading materials, A-V materials, and others

1. Film - "Maps and Their Uses" (Coronet).

2. Maps - Various types of maps can be obtained from places such as the U.S. Weather Bureau, the airport, service stations, city and state Chambers of Commerce. Blueprints can be obtained from a real estate agent.

3. Barth, James, Elementary and Junior High/Middle School Social Studies Curriculum, Activities and Materials (Washington, D.C.: University Press of America, 1983).

4. Weaver, V. Phillips, People and Resources (Silver Burdett Co., 1979).

B. No other outside resources or facilities will be needed. However, if the students want to research for further information, the library will have additional information.

C. For this unit I want to bring in a guest speaker. To do this I will need the permission of the principal.

VI. Evaluation Procedures
   A. The unit begins with an introductory film about the
       uses of maps and is followed by discussions of what
       makes a map. Following the film will be a guest
       speaker who will tell about the importance of maps
       in their work. The evaluation of these activities
       will be done in small group discussions. The teacher
       will observe and participate in each group discussion
       to see how the children interpreted the materials
       presented. From this the teacher will know how much
       to expect from further class discussions and activ-
       ities and will have a better idea of what to cover.
   B. Ways for students to measure their progress -
       1. The games and activities provide immediate
           feedback in most instances.
       2. Through the making of maps and comparing and
           discussing them, the students will realize
           that there are many variations of a single
           map. If the essentials of a map are present,
           no one's map will be wrong.
       3. Students will be working in large and small
           groups whereby they can perceive each other
           and judge for themselves how much they have
           participated and contributed to each activity.
           I will use a simplified (for third graders)
           variation of the forms "Pupil Evaluations of
           Self and Group" and "Student Evaluation of His/
           Her Group Participation" in Elementary and Junior
           High/Middle School Social Studies Curriculum,
           Activities and Materials.
   C. Ways of measuring student growth -
       In this unit I will measure student growth in under-
       standing, skills, and attitudes by examining their
       completed maps which I will ask for and by their par-
       ticipation in the large and small group activities and
       discussions. A simplified version of "Student-Teacher
       Activity Evaluation" in Elementary and Junior High/
       Middle School Social Studies Curriculum, Activities
       and Materials will also be used. Finally the student
       will be asked to identify in a short quiz the six
       uses of maps that we had discussed in class.

Unit Plan Designed for Sixth and Seventh Grades
AFRICA -- THE PEOPLE SOUTH OF THE SAHARA

Heidi Shisler
Seventh Grade
Teacher

I.   Introductory Statement

A.   This unit will be taught to sixth or seventh grade students.
B.   This unit will take 10 days to complete.
C.   This unit is a part of a nine week unit on the Continent of Africa.

ask me

II. Objectives Stated as Performance or Behavioral Objectives

A.   Knowledge
1.   After completing the research and reading on a country in Africa, the students will be able to compare and contrast in a written exercise the ways of life of the people of different countries in Africa.
2.   Having read a folktale from Africa, the students will be able to compare the lifestyle of the Africans in the story with their own lifestyle in a small discussion group.
B.   Specific skills
1.   The students will improve map interpretation skills after having worked with maps of different countries on a written exercise.
2.   The students will demonstrate cooking skills as part of their project by making an African dish.
3.   The students will improve research and reading skills using SQ3R after examining various materials from the library and by writing an in-class paper.
C.   Specific attitudes
1.   Students will demonstrate an attitude of cooperation by working and sharing with others in their groups as observed by the teacher.
2.   The students will demonstrate a positive attitude toward different ways of life which are characteristic of a people in Africa as demonstrated in class discussion, and a pre and post-test attitude survey.

How're you going to do it?

III. Content Outline

    A.   The countries south of the Sahara
         1.   Tanzania
         2.   Ivory Coast
         3.   Nigeria
         4.   Ghana
         5.   Kenya
    B.   The people and their ways of life
         1.   Work
         2.   Customs
         3.   Food

IV. Activities

we have to create

    A.   Initiating activities
         1.   Pretest - students will write a few paragraphs on "What I expect the people of Africa to be like."
         2.   Class discussion on the different views of African life based on the pretest. This will include where the ideas were obtained.
         3.   Film - the film shows a variety of lifestyles of different people of the countries of Sub-Saharan Africa.
         4.   Discussion about the changing views of the African people since seeing the film.
         5.   This portion will take two days to complete.
    B.   Developmental activities
         1.   The students will work in task-oriented small groups of four to study one of six countries in Sub-Saharan Africa.
             a.   Each group will locate a given country on a map or globe and make a map of the country on poster board.
             b.   Each group will use encyclopedias and other references to learn about the work, customs, and lifestyles of the people of the country. The class will review SQ3R reading comprehension strategy.
             c. Each group will read a folktale from their country and use this story to present one of the country's customs.
             d.   Each group will plan and prepare one food dish common to their country.
         2.   This portion of the unit will take five days to complete.
    C.   Summarizing activities
         The last three days will be devoted to group presentations on the six countries: displaying maps, explaining customs, serving food.

V.   Materials and Resources
   A.   Reading materials and A-V materials

Books

      1.   Burnheim, Mark and Evelyne, In Africa (Atheneum, 1973).
      2.   Murphy, E. Jefferson, Understanding Africa (Crowell, 1969).
      3.   Portraits of the Nations (J.B. Lippincott Co.) [Series of books that have most countries in Africa].
      4.   Burnheim, Marc and Evelyne, From Bush to City (Harcourt, Brace & World, Inc. 1966).
      5.   Allen, William D., Africa (The Fideler Company, 1968).
      6.   Gidal, Sonia and Tim, My Village in Ghana (Pantheon, 1969).
      7.   Singer, Edith G., The Ibo of Biafra (Wm. Morrow & Co., 1969).
      8.   Kaula, Edna Mason, African Village Folktales (World Pub. Co., 1968).
      9.   National Geographic magazines.
    10.   World Book Encyclopedia.
    11.   Activity #10, "African Recipes," in Global Studies for Secondary Schools (7-12) by J. Barth.
    12.   Film - African Village - Life Series IFC JSCA.
   B.   The school and public library are the outside resources I would use. For the cooking portion of the unit, I would (with permission of the principal) enlist the help of some of the students' parents by first presenting the idea to the students and sending a memo home with them for feedback.
   C.   With the permission of the principal, I would go to the nearest university to see if any African students would be willing to share their lifestyle with the students.
   D.   To be certain that students could use the libraries effectively, I would review research techniques with them--including using the card catalog and Reader's Guide. I would also inform the librarian of my plans.

VI. Evaluation Procedures
   A.   Procedures for where children are in the beginning.
      1.   Pretest.
      2.   Discussion using the four levels of questions after pretest and after film should show me where the children are.
   B.   Procedures for children measuring own progress.
      1.   The children will be given a task to perform in their groups each day. Their completion of each task in the allotted time will enable them to measure their progress using "Student Evaluation

310

of His/Her Group Participation" on pages 253-254 of <u>Elementary and Junior High/Middle School Social Studies Curriculum, Activities and Materials</u>.

2. After each presentation the other members of the class will give a written critique to the group on the effectiveness of their presentation on "Oral Report Evaluation Form for Students" on page 240 of <u>Elementary and Junior High/Middle School Social Studies Curriculum, Activities and Materials</u>.

3. Each group member's personal self-evaluation of his work should be visible in his enthusiasm on the day of presentation as well as on a "Pupil Evaluation of Self and Group" form on page 175 of <u>Elementary and Junior High/Middle School Social Studies Curriculum, Activities and Materials</u>.

C. Teacher's evaluation
1. A written essay-type test will follow the unit asking the students to compare and contrast two countries of Africa. The test will also include a question asking for some differences between African lifestyles and the child's own life-style. Part of the test will be a take-home paper.

2. The final group map will indicate the progress of the students in map interpretation.

3. The presentations will serve as a medium through which I can evaluate the students' accomplishments in oral presentation skills, research and reading skills, and their attitude about cooperation and sharing.

4. The class discussion using cognitive-memory, convergent, divergent, and evaluative questions will be a means for evaluating students' progress in valuing other cultures.

Below are daily lesson plans for the unit, "Africa - The People South of the Sahara." The first six daily lesson plans are filled in.
Instructions: fill in the remaining four days demonstrating your ability to turn unit plans into daily lesson plans.

First Day –	Second Day –	Third Day –
OBJECTIVE: Students will demonstrate a positive attitude toward different ways of life which are characteristic of the people of Africa as demonstrated in class discussion and a pre- and post-written exercise.	OBJECTIVE: Having viewed film on African lifestyles students will compare and contrast what they saw on film with their views from previous day in a written paragraph, followed by a class discussion on how their views may have changed. Class discussion will verify different perceptions.	OBJECTIVE: The students will improve map interpretation skills after having worked with maps of different countries on a written exercise. Students will demonstrate an attitude of cooperation by working and sharing with others as observed by their teacher.
CONTENT: People south of the Sahara.	CONTENT: People south of the Sahara.	CONTENT: Selected and assigned countries to be studied.
TECHNIQUES & STRATEGIES: Pretest--few paragraphs written on "What I expect the people of Africa to be like." Class discussion, putting main points on board.	TECHNIQUES & STRATEGIES: Film on African lifestyles. Class discussion noting on board the major points of difference.	TECHNIQUES & STRATEGIES: Map study on poster board. Working in small groups.
SUMMARY & ASSIGNMENT: Review main points on board. Prepare students for next day's film on lifestyles of people in different countries.	SUMMARY & ASSIGNMENT: Note points on board. Divide class into five task oriented small groups assigning a country to each group in preparation for third day.	SUMMARY & ASSIGNMENT: Display maps around room. Prepare students for research and library work on fourth day. Review SQ3R to improve comprehension.

Fourth Day –	Fifth Day –	Sixth Day –
OBJECTIVE: After completing research on a country in Africa, students will be able to compare and contrast in a written exercise the ways of life of the people of different countries in Africa. The students will improve research and reading skills having used various materials from library by writing a paper. Students will demonstrate an attitude of cooperation by working and sharing with others in their groups as observed by the teacher.	REPEAT OF FOURTH DAY	OBJECTIVE: Having read a folk-tale from Africa, students will be able to compare lifestyles of the Africans in the story with their own lifestyles in a small task-oriented group. Students will demonstrate an attitude of cooperation by working and sharing with others in their groups as observed by the teacher.
CONTENT: People south of the Sahara and selected countries.		CONTENT: People and countries south of the Sahara.
TECHNIQUES & STRATEGIES: Small group work. Library research.		TECHNIQUES & STRATEGIES: Folk-tale of assigned country. Small group work.
SUMMARY & ASSIGNMENT: Summarize groups' progress. Review library research techniques for fifth day.		SUMMARY & ASSIGNMENT: Summarize what groups' progress should be in preparation for group presentations starting on eighth day.

312

(Fill in last four days using the unit plan.)

Seventh Day –	Eighth Day –	Ninth Day –	Tenth Day –
OBJECTIVE:	OBJECTIVE:	OBJECTIVE:	OBJECTIVE:
CONTENT:	CONTENT:	CONTENT:	CONTENT:
TECHNIQUES & STRATEGIES:	TECHNIQUES & STRATEGIES:	TECHNIQUES & STRATEGIES:	TECHNIQUES & STRATEGIES:
SUMMARY & ASSIGNMENT:	SUMMARY & ASSIGNMENT:	SUMMARY & ASSIGNMENT:	SUMMARY & ASSIGNMENT:

Unit Plan Designed for Eighth and Eleventh Grades
CIVIL WAR

Cindy Sudduth
Junior High
Teacher

I.   Introductory Statement
    A.   The unit is for eighth grade. Could also be used in eleventh grade by changing the readings.
    B.   This unit will take three weeks to complete.
    C.   This unit is the first half of a section on the Civil War, Reconstruction, and the West (Text Unit Six: Division and Reunion 1850-1900). The course is a chronological study of American History.

II. Objectives Stated as Performance Objectives
    A.   Knowledge
        1.   After reading and class discussion on Chapter 16 of the text, the students will recall the meaning of secession and be able to list on paper four of the main events causing conflict between the North and South.
        2.   After task-oriented small group work comparing northern and southern advantages, the students will be able to write a list of several advantages for each side.
        3.   After reading Chapter 17, the students will be able to identify in class discussion the basic northern war strategy.
        4.   After reading and viewing a filmstrip, the students will list the key battles and be able briefly to explain the importance of each in a quiz.
        5.   From reading section 4 in Chapter 17 the students will demonstrate in an essay or role-play (student-choice) key events during the war.
        6.   After viewing a filmstrip, students will be able to recall orally in a class discussion several black contributions to the war effort.
    B.   Skills
        1.   As part of the unit the students will improve map study skills as measured by their oral interpretation of maps on the Confederacy.
        2.   As part of the unit the students will improve essay skills as measured by pre and post-test essays and evaluated by an essay evaluation checklist.
    C.   Attitudes
        1.   The students will demonstrate a positive attitude toward minorities, especially blacks, having read

Chapter 16 and viewed filmstrips, on a post-
attitude inventory.
2. The students will exhibit a more critical
attitude about the complex emotions and issues
involved in the war and national problems
having read Chapter 17, as measured on a pre
and post-test opinion survey.

III. Content
    A. The Slavery Problem
       1. California Statehood
       2. Compromise of 1850
       3. Rising southern defensiveness
    B. Conflict between North and South
       1. Uncle Tom's Cabin and Abolitionists
       2. Kansas-Nebraska Act
       3. Kansas Statehood
       4. Republican Party
       5. Dred Scott Decision
    C. Slavery divides the nation
       1. Lincoln and Douglass
       2. John Brown's raid
    D. War begins
       1. Lincoln's election
       2. Secession
       3. Confederacy established
       4. Fort Sumter
       5. Lincoln's goal - reunion
    E. Northern Plan
       1. The first modern war
       2. Northern and Southern
          advantages
       3. Union and Confederate
          strategies
    F. The War
       1. Blockade
       2. Key battles
       3. Key people
       4. Emancipation Proclamation
       5. Surrender
       6. Lincoln's death
    G. Effects of the war
       1. Losses
       2. Blacks
       3. Union preserved
       4. Attitudes of people

IV. Activities in Which Students Will Engage
    A. Initiating activities
       1. Class discussion using four types of questions:
          What is a civil war? What other countries have
          had them? What causes them? Suppose the Civil
          War had not been fought? How do you feel about
          the Civil War now?

2. Filmstrip - "Causes of the Civil War."
3. Survey and pretest (done as assignment) - this will include a survey of their attitudes toward minorities. The pretest will be short answer questions posed in the unit introduction: Why did the U.S. fight a civil war? What effects has it had?
4. Encourage students to bring in Civil War materials for display.
5. Time: 1 1/2 days.

B. Development activities
1. Read and discuss Chapters 16 and 17. Review SQ3R reading strategy.
2. Reports (written) of 1-2 pages on a person or event discussed in Chapters 16, 17, 18.
3. Map study of Confederate states and war strategy.
4. Class discussion of conflicting values as evidenced in "John Brown's Body," Uncle Tom's Cabin, excerpts from Slavery Defended, Calhoun's speech.
5. Chart completions - Steps Leading to War (Teacher's Manual, p. 175) and Northern-Southern Advantages (Teacher's Manual, p. 182). This includes small group evaluation of the advantages in predicting the war's length.
6. Filmstrip - "Slavery and the War Between the States" and discussion of the part Blacks played in the war. Tie in the results of the minority survey.
7. Film - "America in the First Modern War."
8. Essay or role-play on the effects of the war (student choice).
9. Bulletin board display of Civil War pictures and materials brought by students.
10. Time: 8 days.

C. Summarizing activities
1. Class discussion on "Thinking About History," text, p. 451.
2. As an assignment, write responses to #2, p. 451 (choice of 3 of the 10). This asks students to explain the reaction of a typical Northerner, Southerner, and abolitionist to events leading to war. Opportunity would be given the next day for several to present their responses, using a TV editorial format.
3. The above are for Chapter 16. Time 1 1/2 days.
4. Question and answer review of Chapter 17 using book, pp. 473-474, especially question on values on p. 474.

5.   Essay - 1 1/2 pages, chosen from "Thinking About History," p. 474, #1-5.
6.   The above two are for Chapter 17. Time 1 1/2 days.
7.   Small group discussions analyzing various names given the Civil War and what it shows about the point of view of the user of that title followed by the form "Pupil Evaluation of Self and Group" on p. 175 of Elementary and Junior High/Middle School Social Studies Curriculum, Activities and Materials.
8.   Review for test: study questions and quizdown.
9.   Test over Chapters 16 and 17.
10. Time: 2 1/2 - 3 days.

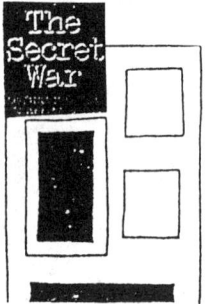

V.   Materials and Resources
   A.   Reading materials, A-V equipment, etc.
      1.   Textbook - America: Its People and Values, pp. 431-474.
      2.   Filmstrips - "Causes of the Civil War" and "Slavery and the War Between the States."
      3.   Film - America in the First Modern War (8mm film and cassette).
      4.   Records - "John Brown's Body" and "Folksongs of the Civil War."
      5.   Picture collection on Civil War (Purdue).
      6.   Jackdaw No. 106 - The Civil War (Purdue).
      7.   Study prints and vertical file (at school).
      8.   Transparency set on U.S. at beginning of war (at school).
      9.   Other books:
         a.   Colt, Margaret L., John C. Calhoun (Boston: Houghton Mifflin Co., 1950).
         b.   Craven, Avery O., Edmund Ruffin, Southerner (Baton Rouge: Louisiana State University Press, 1932).
         c.   Marshall, Richard E. and Waltz, John Edward, Civil War and Reconstruction (Philadelphia: J.B. Lippincott C., 1973).
         d.   Stowe, Harriet Beecher, Uncle Tom's Cabin.
         e.   Slavery Defended.
         f.   Civil War Collectors' Encyclopedia.
         g.   Weapons of the Civil War.
         h.   American Heritage Pictorial History of the Civil War.
         i.   Indiana in the Civil War.
         j.   Barth, James L., Elementary and Junior High/ Middle School Social Studies Curriculum, Activities and Materials (Washington, D.C.: University Press of America, 1983).
      10. Alternate film choices:
         a.   "Webster's Sacrifice to Save the Union"
         b.   "Civil War: Its Background and Causes"

      c.   "History of the American Negro: Civil War and Reconstruction"

      d.   "1861-1877, The Civil War and Reconstruction"

      e.   Set of 71 slides and cassette on the Civil War

B.   Resources outside the classroom

    1.   The Benton Central Library has a fairly good selection of Civil War materials and good biography section. Students will use it as a resource for their reports.

    2.   The library can be reserved for entire class use.

    3.   A collection of books on the topic can be collected by students and held in reserve at the library during the course of the research.

C.   Student contacted resources

    1.   If students are contacting a person, I will suggest the manner in which to make appointments, etc., and make preliminary calls if necessary.

    2.   In securing materials, I want to encourage them to bring in Civil War artifacts, etc. I would remind them to be careful with borrowed materials, to thank lenders, and suggest possible sources such as relatives, historical associations, family friends with such a hobby or interest.

    3.   I would encourage students who have visited battlefields to bring in pictures, slides, postcards, etc.

VI. Evaluation Procedures

    A.   Procedures for pretesting students

        1.   Survey and pre and post-attitude inventory.

        2.   Class discussion on civil wars (four levels of questions).

    B.   Ways for students to measure their progress

        1.   Small group evaluation sheets - individual.

        2.   Performance on daily quick reviews.

        3.   Performance on study questions, essays, and quizdown.

    C.   Ways of measuring student growth

        1.   Teacher observation of performance in group work and class discussion.

        2.   Performance on quizzes, essays, and reports.

        3.   Unit test covering Chapters 16 and 17, including a short essay question to measure growth in that skill.

        4.   To find out how students identify the quality of their work, I will ask them to complete "Student-Teacher Activities Evaluation" on pp. 249-250 of Elementary and Junior High/Middle School Social Studies Curriculum, Activities and Materials.

Unit Plan Designed for Twelfth Grade
MINORITIES

Pam Acheson
Twelfth Grade
Teacher

I.   Introductory Statement
   A.   This unit is to be taught to twelfth grade students, ages 17-19.
   B.   This unit will take six class days to complete.
   C.   This unit on minorities is part of the general survey of the organizations of society. It is the final topic to be covered and is required in the phase-elective program. After completing this required introductory phase, the students will move on to an elective course of study of their choice.

II. Objectives Stated as Performance or Behavioral Objectives
   A.   Knowledge
      1.   After reading the textbook, Chapter 9, the students will be able to accurately define, according to the book, what a minority is (in a classroom discussion and on a written exam).
      2.   After reading the textbook, Chapter 9, and participating in classroom discussion and oral reports, the students will be able to write a list of six different minorities in the American social structure.
      3.   After reading the textbook, Chapter 9, and attending lecture, the students will be able to analyze by comparing and contrasting on a written exam the five behavioral patterns of the dominant members of a society toward its minorities versus the six behavior patterns of minorities toward the dominant category.
   B.   Specific skills
      1.   Students will practice oral report techniques which will be evaluated with an oral report checklist.
      2.   The students will improve their reading comprehension by applying SQ3R to their homework assignments as measured by pre and post-tests.
   C.   Specific attitudes
      1.   During the unit students will demonstrate a positive attitude toward ideas presented by classmates which may be contrary to one's own beliefs as measured by an attitude checklist.
      2.   During the unit students will exhibit an open mind and a feeling of respect toward members of a minority as measured on a pre and post-attitude inventory.

III. Content Outline
    Minorities in the Social Structure -
    A.   What is a minority?
    B.   Who are the minorities in the American
         social structure?
    C.   How do minorities and the dominant members of the
         society relate to each other?

The **American** *Experience*

IV.   Activities
    A.   Initiating activities
        1.   Administer a pretest strength scale inventory
             on students' attitudes and feelings regarding
             minorities.
        2.   Reading assignment - Chapter 9 (textbook).
        3.   Film on blacks in the United States.
        4.   Hand out topics for oral reports; students will
             have their choice.
        5.   Film on American Indians - An "awareness" film.
             The purpose is to help remove stereotypes of
             native American Indians.
        6.   This portion will take two days to complete.
    B.   Developmental activities
        1.   Short lecture and/or explanation of any
             terms or concepts that are
             unclear to students.
        2.   Each student will
             join in a task ori-
             ented small group to
             prepare an oral report
             on the group's topic.
             Small groups based on
             choice of topic to be
             pursued.
        3.   Preparation and pres-
             entation of short five
             to ten minute oral
             reports. These
             reports will cover
             various topics on
             minorities and
             reactions and feelings toward the minority groups.
             These reports will expose attitudes of students,
             parents, community, and society as a whole.
             Discussion of the oral reports will be encouraged
             and evaluated by "Oral Report Checklist" on
             p. 239 of Elementary and Junior High/Middle School
             Social Studies Curriculum, Activities and
             Materials.
        4.   This part of the unit will take three class days
             to complete.

C. Summarizing activities
1. Administer the same strength scale (post-attitude that was given the first day) on students' attitudes and feelings regarding minorities. Discuss possible changes in attitudes and why changes occurred.
2. Test - My test will come directly from my stated behavioral objective. The test will total 100 points.
3. This part of the unit will take one day to complete.

V. Materials and Resources
A. Reading materials, A-V materials, and others
1. The regular class text - Thomas, Laverne W. and Robert J., Sociology: The Study of Human Relationships (New York: Harcourt Brace Jovanovich, Inc., 1972).
2. Film - Black History: Lost, Stolen or Strayed.
3. Film - A Better Life.
4. Barron, Milton L., Minorities in a Changing World (New York: Alfred A. Knopf, 1967).
5. Marden, Charles F. and Meyer, Gladys, Minorities in American Society (New York: Van Nostrand Reinhold Co., 1968).
B. In this unit, outside resources will include school library (or any other library). I will also provide extra textbooks available to students to use during the day or to check out overnight.
C. In some of the oral reports, it will be necessary for students to make contacts outside the classroom. These will mainly involve parents, friends, and the student will have the responsibility of these contacts left up to them. If further contacts are needed, I would aid the student by making suggestions and also by obtaining the resource person's address and phone number, and information about him/her. (I would have this cleared through the principal first.) I would suggest that the student be prepared with questions for the resource person. I would expect the students to make these contacts basically on their own. If students are having trouble, however, I would do what-ever is necessary to help them.

VI. Evaluation Procedures
A. By using the strength scale at the beginning of the unit I will be able to determine the attitudes of the students regarding minorities. The discussions during class time or the films will also help me with this beginning evaluation. I will have a short session at the beginning of the unit asking students what certain terms mean to them (i.e., discrimination, stereotyping,

        segregation, integration, etc.). This will help me
determine what to focus on throughout the unit.

B.   Class discussions and comparisons and contrasts of
the individual's attitudes and beliefs with classmates will assist students in comparing their own
attitudes with others. Immediate feedback from their
oral reports will help students gauge their mastery of
specific skills. The pre and post-strength scale will
hopefully dramatically illustrate to each student the
change of opinions and attitudes.

C.   How to measure students' growth in understanding,
skills, attitudes, etc. throughout the unit - My test
will be an essay test focusing on the textbook
materials and my content knowledge objectives. The
reason why the focus will be on textbook material is
because much of the unit is centered around personal
beliefs and practices and cannot be measured by a clear
right or wrong in a testing situation. By the use of
oral reports I will have the opportunity to evaluate
the students' oral and listening skills. The pre and
post-strength scale will be a determining factor in
deciding if the specific attitude objectives were
achieved.

Topics for Oral Reports
1.   Discuss minorities in the local community and how they are treated.
2.   Interview two members of minority
categories to determine their
attitudes toward the dominant members of society or to find out
about their personal experiences
as members of minority categories.
Discuss this in class.
3.   Do a current event article
dealing with some aspect of
minorities.
4.   Prepare a bulletin board dealing with minorities and
discuss and explain in class.
5.   Are there people in your community who would never
be invited to your home or circle of friends? Why?

Below are daily lesson plans for the unit on "Minorities."
The first three daily lesson plans are filled in.

Instructions: fill in the remaining three days demonstrating
your ability to turn unit plans into daily lesson plans.

First Day –	Second Day –	Third Day –
OBJECTIVE: During the unit students will demonstrate a positive attitude toward ideas presented by classmates which may be contrary to one's own beliefs as measured by an attitude checklist.	OBJECTIVE: After viewing films and reading Chapter 9 in text, students will be able to define minority and identify different minorities in the U.S. The accuracy of definition will be measured by class discussion and on a final written exam. From a selection of topics each student will elect to join in a task-oriented small group to prepare an oral report on the group's topic.	OBJECTIVE: Students will practice oral report techniques which will be evaluated on an oral report checklist.
CONTENT: Definition and identification of different minorities in the U.S.	CONTENT: Define and identify different minorities in the U.S.	CONTENT: Selected topics concerning different minority groups and reactions and feelings toward minority groups.
TECHNIQUES & STRATEGIES: Pretest strength of scale inventory on student's attitudes and feelings regarding minorities. Two films on minorities in America followed by class discussion.	TECHNIQUES & STRATEGIES: Film on American Indians followed by discussion with purpose of establishing definition of minorities and identifying groups that fit that definition.	TECHNIQUES & STRATEGIES: Preparation for two days of oral reports. Groups meet and organize presentation. Part of period may be research in library.
SUMMARY & ASSIGNMENT: Read textbook Chapter 9, review chapter using SQ3R technique to strengthen reading comprehension.	SUMMARY & ASSIGNMENT: Assign topics for oral reports to task-oriented small groups and pass out oral report check-list. Sum up discussion on "What is a minority?" and "Who are minorities in the American social structure?"	SUMMARY & ASSIGNMENT: Prepare for task-oriented small group oral reports.

(Fill in last three days using the unit plan.)

Fourth Day –	Fifth Day –	Sixth Day –
OBJECTIVE:	OBJECTIVE:	OBJECTIVE:
CONTENT:	CONTENT:	CONTENT:
TECHNIQUES & STRATEGIES:	TECHNIQUES & STRATEGIES:	TECHNIQUES & STRATEGIES:
SUMMARY & ASSIGNMENT:	SUMMARY & ASSIGNMENT:	SUMMARY & ASSIGNMENT:

CHAPTER XV

PRACTICE TEACHING:
MICROPEER–TEACHING, FIELD EXPERIENCE, AND STUDENT TEACHING

OBJECTIVE: Having read this chapter, identify how micropeer-teaching and field experience provide practice in questioning and planning in preparation for student teaching.

> Originality and commitment
> are the basis
> of high quality education.

Putting you first

This final chapter concerns practice teaching which includes (1) micropeer-teaching, (2) field experience, and (3) student teaching.

Micropeer-teaching, a form of practice teaching, is "scaled down teaching," and is usually a strategy applied during a methods class. You are given an opportunity to practice briefly a specific teaching skill for five minutes before your peers while being videotaped followed by an evaluation of your performance on the tape. The objective of micropeer-teaching is to gain experience practicing and evaluating teaching skills.

Field experience. Within the last few years, a pre-student teaching field experience has become an important part of most teacher preparation programs. Many states now insist that "early and continuous field experiences" be a part of all teacher certification programs. Students must have continuous contact over a period of years with public schools, teachers, and students--that is experience with the real world of teaching.

Student teaching is usually the final field experience in a teacher certification program. Teaching classes under the supervision of a professional teacher and a university supervisor is intended as a practice teach. Student teaching is practice teaching which means that student teachers are expected to practice the skills identified during the methods course.

MICROPEER–TEACHING

A Short History of Microteaching

Most teacher training has included the practice of peer teaching (practice teaching before classmates) for a very long time, but microteaching was originally developed in 1963. Microteaching grew out of two ideas coming together at the same time. The first idea was that technology such as television could play a significant role in teacher education, and the second notion was that teacher training in certain specific skills should be improved before the student teaching experience. There has always been criticism that teacher training has not been specific enough and, there-fore, such training could not guarantee that teachers had acquired and could practice good teaching skills. Microteaching has from the beginning been thought of as complementary to, but never a replacement for, teaching practice. It has been regarded as a preparatory technique where a student teacher tries to acquire and refine teaching skills before teaching practice.

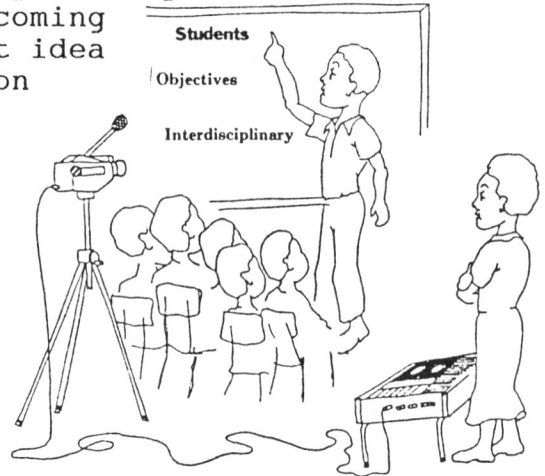

How Effective Is Micropeer-teaching?

The reason for the intense interest in microteaching since 1963 is that this technique has proven to be just slightly less powerful in the percentage of learning and remembering than student teaching. Do you remember Chapter IV on research, where you discovered that students learn and remember 90% of what they attempt to teach others, i.e., practice teaching? Micropeer-teaching ranks in terms of learning and remembering at 80% of what we experience directly or practice. Other advantages of micropeer-teaching are:

1. Micropeer-teachers acquire teaching skills because in micropeer-teaching each teaching skill is isolated and practiced in turn: Introducing a Lesson, Questioning, and Lesson Closure.
2. During micropeer-teaching real teaching takes place although to a limited number of students and within a short period of time.
3. Micropeer-teachers receive feedback on their performance from their supervisors and peer observers. This helps them identify their weaknesses and strengths.

What Is Microteaching?

Microteaching is defined as a scaled down sample of teaching. The term micro not only denotes the reduction in lesson and class size, but also adds the idea of precision in the sense that microteaching serves to make observation more precise. That is, one can focus on specific teacher behavior.

Microteaching is essentially an opportunity to develop and improve teaching skills with a small group of students (5 to 7) by means of a brief (5 minutes) single concept lesson. This lesson is recorded on tape--either audio or video--for the microteacher to review, respond to, refine and if need be, reteach.

The theory is that microteachers will exhibit the same behavior in front of the microclass that they would normally show in a regular class situation. In other words, the problems one might have as a teacher would surface in a microteaching session just as they would in a regular classroom. The microteacher, having completed the microteach lesson, listens to or reviews the taped session with a microsupervisor and in some instances with a microclass for the purpose of critical evaluation.

Microteaching is extremely useful for determining if a microteacher has learned a particular skill. Suppose that the skill the microteacher is to demonstrate is that of asking different levels of questions. Suppose that the microteaching in a five minute microteach lesson demonstrates the asking of only two of the four different levels of questions. The microsupervisor as well as the microclass, who have marked evaluation forms, would suggest the two types of questions that were not asked. The microteacher would then be required to plan for a second microteach (reteach) with emphasis on asking the four different levels of questions once again. The microteacher would continue practicing the lesson until demonstrating competency in performing the skill of asking questions.

The important point is that microteachers either see or hear themselves as they actually perform before a microclass. They can often see for themselves that they are not performing the skill properly and, therefore, are less likely to resist suggestions for change. The microteacher, having replanned the lesson on asking different questions, reteaches the lesson to a different microclass. The session is once again recorded after which the microsupervisor and the microteacher evaluate the teaching performance.

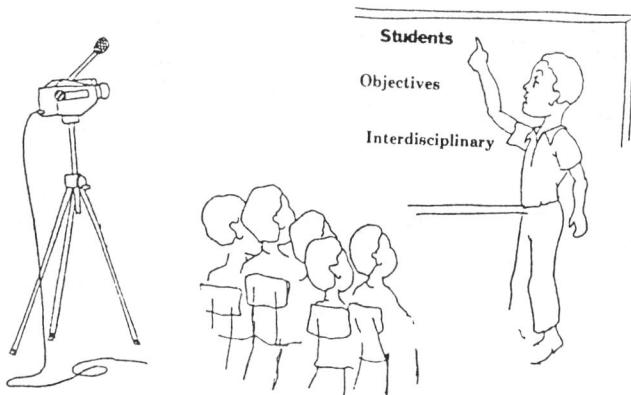

AN EXCITING TEACHING RESOURCE

```
Steps in Microteaching

Step 1. Identify a specific skill that the microteacher
        should demonstrate.

Step 2. The microteacher should plan the five minute
        microlesson.

Step 3. Microteacher presents five minute lesson to the micro-
        class (5 to 7 members).

Step 4. The microsupervisor and microclass fill out evaluation
        forms during microteaching.

Step 5. The microsupervisor and microclass discuss (about five
        minutes) their evaluation of the microlesson with the
        microteacher.

Step 6. If the microteacher has successfully demonstrated the
        skill, then the lesson is over.  If, however, the
        microteacher did not adequately demonstrate the skill,
        then he/she should prepare for a reteach to a different
        microclass at some future date.
```

Though having suggested above that certain procedures for organizing microteaching have evolved over the years, it is still the prerogative of the teacher trainers to establish the length of time, the number of students and the type of supervision and evaluation that are most appropriate for their circumstances. However, in summary, there are some common elements in effective microteaching. Briefly, they are: a microteacher, microclass, a microsupervisor's evaluation instrument, if possible a recording device (either audio or video), a planned microlesson, and finally a teach-reteach.

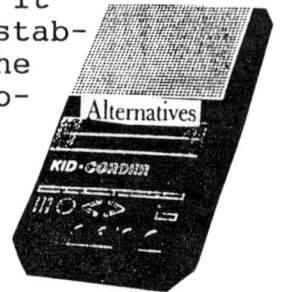

There are three specific skills that we recommend for practice during microteaching: (1) asking the four levels of questions, (2) introducing a lesson, and (3) lesson closure. Of course, there are many other skills that could be practiced, but the three recommended are those that seem to be the most important to the practice of teaching social studies. We will concentrate in this chapter on the three recommended skills. Those three skills can be equally well practiced at inservice workshops or as preservice training. The point is that these fundamental skills need to be continuously practiced and perfected. Information on how to plan and evaluate each of the skills is presented below.

The Skill of Asking Questions

Microteaching can strengthen the practice of asking four levels of questions. At this time would you please turn to the chapter on questioning if you need to review the four levels of questions: cognitive-memory, convergent, divergent, and evaluative. As a microteacher you must demonstrate the skill of asking all four levels during microteaching.

Planning a Microteach on Asking Questions

Recall the term "strategy." A strategy requires the sequencing of techniques to accomplish a specific method. In this microteaching, the method is problem solving with the objective of demonstrating a questioning strategy. Now as a microteacher how do you organize a questioning strategy to stimulate students to solve problems?

Remember the research chapter--"teaching is more effective when the students . . . are actively involved in learning the lesson," and it goes on to say, "Students learn best when teachers use different levels of questions." We have evidence that some patterns of questioning promote problem solving while others discourage it. The pattern that most generates problem solving is one which includes all four levels of questions. The following points and examples illustrate how you might plan a microteaching lesson.

questions yield more questions

Point 1. Select a topic that is most likely to be relevant to the microstudents you are going to teach. Remember you are planning a five minute questioning strategy that will stimulate students to solve problems. Just to get you thinking, the following topic is an example. "What environmental policies should the United States be following by the year 2000?"

Point 2. Sequence the level of questions to fit the students you are teaching and the topic you are presenting.

For example, a sequence might look like this:

1. Cognitive-memory. We all know from personal experience that there are a number of serious environmental problems in the United States. Name the three major environmental problems identified by the President.
2. Convergent. Now that you have named the three problems, would you please explain each one as outlined in the President's speech?
3. Divergent. What do you suppose other environmental problems will be by the year 2000?
4. Evaluative. What is your best guess on which environmental problems will be most important after the year 2000?

Did you identify the questioning strategy? The sequence started with a (1) cognitive-memory question followed by (2) convergent, (3) divergent, and (4) evaluative. This is a traditional questioning strategy. Be sure to identify below other questioning strategies that may be more promising. See another strategy below.

Remember the number and sequence of the different levels of questions asked would depend on the class taught. Sometimes evaluative and divergent questions are followed by cognitive-memory and convergent questions. This strategy allows students to give their opinions (evaluative question) and then asks them questions that focus their thinking on specific evidence (cognitive-memory and convergent) that might support their opinions. As students express their opinions they often voice different points of view. These points of view often provide the teacher with the source of questions for a challenging problem solving discussion.

For example, try this sequencing strategy as a way to stimulate thinking.

1. Evaluative. What would you judge to be the best measures that the government could take to deal with the cycles of drought?
2. Convergent. As you know we have just completed a year cycle of drought. How did the drought affect the country?
3. Cognitive-memory. Name other countries that were also affected by the drought.
4. Divergent. Knowing what you and your family experienced in the past year cycle of drought, predict what the President will recommend to prepare the country for the next cycle.

Did you identify the questioning strategy? The strategy started with (1) an evaluative question followed by (2) convergent, (3) cognitive-memory, and (4) divergent. This sequencing strategy will most likely lead to a lively class discussion over the divergent question which asks the students to predict what the President will recommend. In short, to answer the question, the students will have to think of creative answers which require higher levels of thinking.

You must be aware that the level of questions you ask determines the level at which students think. If you ask cognitive-memory questions, you get nothing but recall. If you ask only convergent questions, you get nothing but a short answer recitation. Teachers often seem not to recognize that most of their questions--and those in textbooks--simply ask students to recall and repeat information. Do you think that education is nothing but recalling what someone else said? If not, then perhaps you think that education, and especially social studies, needs to promote other kinds of thinking. We are not saying that questions that call for a memorized or short answer response are unimportant, we are saying that all levels, both low and high levels, are important for the training of modern citizens assuming they are to participate in determining the quality of their lives.

A suggestion

A very common complaint of teachers is, "I can't get my students to answer questions," or "When I ask a question, they just sit there and refuse to answer." Students refusing to answer is the reason often used to justify teachers doing most of the talking. Students' lack of response represents, in part, a failure of the teacher to think systematically about classroom interactions and about why students do not answer or ask questions. Students have been taught to believe that the only good questions are cognitive-memory and convergent. Teachers do not recognize that if they want students to think at higher levels, they should include a much broader range of questions. Your challenge, then, is to include all four levels of questions in a microteach.

Now plan your five minute microlesson on asking four levels of questions using the points above:

1. Select a topic.

2. **Have a question** Sequence and write out 4 levels of questions:
    (1)

    (2)

    (3)

    (4)

Evaluating Your Microteaching on Asking Questions

The following form will evaluate microteaching practice on the skill of asking questions. Before planning a microlesson, please note the criteria by which your microteach is to be evaluated.

Use This Now

EVALUATION FORM ON THE SKILL OF ASKING QUESTIONS

Microteacher _____

Observer (1) _____

(2) _____

Teach _____ Reteach _____

YOU HAVE

	Very Weak	Fair	Good	Very Good	Superior
1. The teacher's questioning strategy held your attention.	1	2	3	4	5
2. The strategy was designed to relate your experience to the topic.	1	2	3	4	5
3. The strategy stimulated you to want to answer the questions.	1	2	3	4	5
4. The strategy actively involved you in the discussion.	1	2	3	4	5
5. The sequence of questions encouraged you to inquire.	1	2	3	4	5

6. The strategy included all four types of questions. Circle the levels of questions used.

Cognitive-memory   Convergent

Evaluative   Divergent

You are encouraged to make comments on the strong points of this presentation and on areas that need modifications for the reteach.

_____

_____

_____

_____

_____

_____

_____

The Skill of Introducing a Lesson

"In the Beginning"

There are many ways to introduce a lesson. In this case the skill, introducing a lesson, should be designed as a problem-raising exercise to actively involve students. The five minute microlesson is to stimulate interest, to get students' attention and to get them thinking with you about the topic. Set the topic in a problem situation to which your students can respond. Do not give out great quantities of information--that type of introduction does not generally stimulate much other than a passive student response. Think instead of how you might introduce a lesson with an experience upon which the class can reflect. In summary, a problem-raising experience that arouses students' interest is one strategy for introducing a lesson.

Planning a Microteach on Introducing a Lesson

AN EXCITING TEACHING RESOURCE

Point 1. Selection of a delimited topic. For example, some topics might be:
- a. To ensure agricultural independence the United States should increase emphasis on agricultural farms and cattle farms.
- b. Rapid economic development might well destroy valued beliefs.
- c. Should we be concerned with ecology problems?
- d. Should strikes (withholding of services or obligations) be allowed?

Point 2. Finding the problem in the topic. The way one goes about finding a problem is to ask oneself what is there about this topic that (a) is likely to create doubts in the minds of these students, or (b) what is there about this topic which is likely to evoke two or more contradictory values or beliefs.

For instance, consider the topic mentioned above, "Should strikes be allowed?" People believe that the right to strike is part of the heritage of freedom; that is, the withdrawing of one's services in order to obtain higher wages or better working conditions is an aspect of freedom in our society. However, most people believe that there is a class of workers--public workers such as policemen, firemen, students, teachers, and private persons (such as physicians)--whose services are so absolutely essential that they are not entitled to withdraw them for any reason whatsoever. Many people hold both of these conflicting beliefs at the same time. This conflict in beliefs when pointed out may stimulate doubts and create interest.

Point 3. Deciding on the appropriate experience to raise the problem. One must decide on either (a) the right question to ask or the right statement to make, or (b) the right demonstration, picture, television sequence, role-playing, or other experience that will evoke the desired reaction.

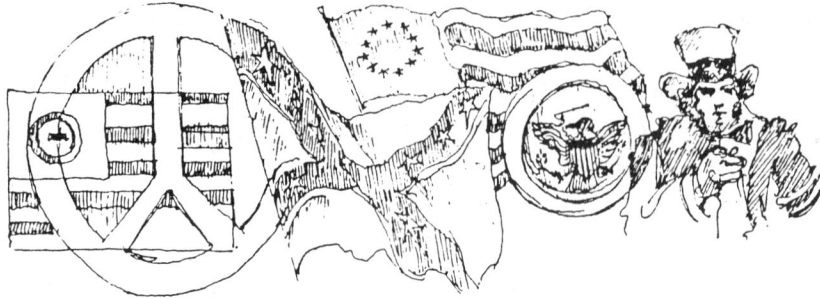

Here is an example of a series of questions to ask:
"Do teachers have the right to strike?"
"Do firefighters have the right to strike?"
"Do students have the right to strike?"
"If you answer two questions yes and one question no, then tell me what principle you are using that allows you to decide who can and cannot withhold their services or obligations?"

(Keep in mind that the goal of this introduction is to get students to reflect and respond--that is, get their attention on the topic.)

"If you do permit all classes of persons to strike, how are you going to provide substitutes for their services, i.e., how will you provide someone to substitute for firemen or teachers? Is there a substitute for students who are on strike?"

Point 4.   Gathering of arguments and data that support both positions or that are designed to refute any argument that might arise.

Before your begin your microlesson, please think through the kinds of arguments or beliefs that students are likely to hold. You might even quiz your friends or family to find out what they believe. Then gather your facts, data, arguments, and positions in a well-organized fashion.

Point 5.   Figuring out a "clincher" or conclusion for your introduction. What would be the best way of concluding the introduction? With a summation? With a student-created statement on the chalkboard? In other words, the introduction should create "high interest" and act very much like a springboard--launching the class into the lesson.

Just a suggestion: when you have the microlesson planned, try it out on a friend, anyone who will give you five minutes. We guarantee this practice will help.

Now plan your five minute presentation on the introduction of a lesson using the five points above.

1. Select a delimited topic.   **WORLD HUNGER**

2. Find the problem in the topic.   **SAVE THE DOLPHINS**

3. Decide on the appropriate experience.   **ZERO POPULATION GROWTH**

4. Gather arguments and data.   **For Earth's sake!**

5. Figure out a conclusion for your introduction.

Evaluating Your Microteaching on Introducing a Lesson

The following form will evaluate your microteaching practice on the skill of introducing a lesson. Before planning a microlesson, please note the criteria by which your microteach is to be evaluated.

Improve your skills

EVALUATION FORM ON THE SKILL OF INTRODUCING A LESSON

Microteacher _____

Observer (1) _____

        (2) _____

Teach _____ Reteach _____

YOU HAVE

	Very Weak	Fair	Good	Very Good	Superior
1. The teacher's technique of introducing the lesson was interesting; that is, it held your attention.	1	2	3	4	5
2. The teacher's technique of introduction attempted to relate your experiences to the topic being introduced.	1	2	3	4	5
3. The teacher's technique of introducing the lesson motivated (which means to stimulate or provoke) you to want to go into the body of the lesson by causing you to question or reflect.	1	2	3	4	5
4. The teacher's technique of introduction got you actively, rather than passively, involved.	1	2	3	4	5
5. The teacher indicated through a statement or summary what would be covered in the body of the lesson.	1	2	3	4	5

You are encouraged to make comments on the strong points of the introduction and on areas that need modification for the reteach.

_____

_____

_____

_____

_____

_____

_____

The Skill of Lesson Closure

Another skill to practice is lesson closure. When you have finished a class period, closure is the procedure you follow to bring that lesson to an effective end. The skill involves summarizing at the end of the period the ideas which the class has covered. The skill of closure, just as the other two microteaching skills (asking questions and introducing a lesson) is an activity which you will perform as a classroom teacher and, therefore, needs to be planned and practiced.

There are three points to developing an effective lesson closure: (1) closure should be a summary in which the teacher briefly reviews any new ideas that have been introduced since the beginning of the class period, (2) those ideas should be illustrated with relevant examples and teaching aids, and (3) the summary of ideas should be extended to include any new ideas that will be presented in the next lesson. Closure should help students identify the relationship between the ideas which have been covered previously and those which are going to be covered in the near future.

Planning a Microteach on Lesson Closure CONCENTRATE

The following is an illustration of how to plan a closure following the three points. The class discussed early explorers in Africa, and it is now the end of the class period and you are bringing the lesson to a close. The following is an illustration of closure.

Point 1.   Review of ideas covered in lesson. **Should**
"The lesson today was on the Portuguese explorers. We discussed dates they landed, the parts of Africa they visited, the materials they traded, and the religion they introduced, and finally we discussed why the Portuguese failed to make permanent settlements in some places where they visited."

Point 2.   Now that the review is complete, suggest how the topic is relevant to the students.
"The principal concept we have been studying is that of discovery. Discovery is not something the Portuguese did or the English or the French or any other country, but it is something we all do in our lives. We discover new things every day and often it is the discovery of new things which interests us to seek even more new discoveries. Just as you have a sense of discovery, so you can begin to understand the Portuguese desire to discover also."

Point 3.   Finally, prepare students with mention of ideas or events that will be covered in the next lesson.
"We have looked at the concept of discovery and how the Portuguese were early discoverers. In our next

lesson we will look at countries in other parts of
the world which were visited by the Portuguese."

Some Final Thoughts on Closure   ## classroom problems

The bell rings, the students quickly leave the room. There
has been no closure, no summary. If students are asked to
describe what they had been doing during that class period, they
say something like, "We just spent our time talking, and as
always Tom and John tried to outshout each other." "Well, what
did you learn?" Student's reply, "I didn't learn anything."
"What do you remember about the lesson?" "I don't remember
anything."

The teacher in that class did have a good discussion going.
True, Tom and John did try to dominate, but nevertheless most of
the points were made. The fact is the class needed a summarizing
closure to put the arguments in perspective. Students are not
going to carry different points of view in their minds. The
teacher's responsibility is to clarify and summarize the points
of view so that the students can identify patterns, in short, can
learn and remember.

Now plan your five minute presentation on lesson closure
using the points above.

1.   Review the ideas covered in the lesson.

2.   Suggest how the topic is relevant to the students.

3.   Prepare students with mention of ideas that will be
     covered in the next lesson.

Closure is the point at which the class should start the
next day. For example, "Do you recall the ideas we talked about
yesterday? Would you find in your notes the summary of those
ideas. Do you remember we talked about Portuguese explorers and
that today we would discuss other parts of the world where the
Portuguese visited? Would you now turn to your atlas and find
the map of the world on page 10?"

Evaluating Your Microteach on Lesson Closure

The following form will evaluate your microteaching practice
on the skill of lesson closure. Before planning a microlesson,
please note the criteria by which your microteach is to be
evaluated.

EVALUATION FORM ON THE SKILL OF LESSON CLOSURE

Microteacher _____

Observer (1) _____

      (2) _____

Teach _____ Reteach _____

YOU HAVE

	Very Weak	Fair	Good	Very Good	Superior
1. The teacher's closing summary of the lesson held your attention.	1	2	3	4	5
2. The closing summary was presented in such a way that it would be useful as a beginning reminder for students at the start of the next day's class.	1	2	3	4	5
3. The closing summary did relate the ideas covered in class to relevant examples and illustrations.	1	2	3	4	5
4. The closing summary did show how the ideas covered in class relate to future lessons.	1	2	3	4	5

You are encouraged to make comments on the strong points of this presentation and on areas that need modification for the reteach.

_____

_____

_____

_____

_____

_____

_____

_____

THE PRE-STUDENT TEACHING FIELD EXPERIENCE

We want you to identify the purpose and function of your pre-student teaching field experience. While it is obvious that you will be evaluated throughout this field experience, you should know that evaluation is not the specific purpose. The purpose is to offer you an opportunity to practice skills and attitudes learned in the methods course. You will be encouraged during the field experience to demonstrate planning skills which include questioning, activities, evaluation, and the use of technology and instructional resources. A secondary purpose is to continue contact with the "real world of the classroom." Working in a social studies class on a regular schedule with teachers, students, and the school administration will help you prepare for the final practice teach, student teaching.

Student Responsibilities in the Field Experience Program

Rationale

is so important

The purpose of the field experience program is to provide an opportunity for you to work with students in a school setting prior to beginning your student teaching. As part of the field experience program you will be placed with a supervising teacher in a junior high/middle school or senior high where, in addition to performing many of the routine tasks all teachers are faced with each day, you will also work with students individually and in groups. Your supervising teacher or teaching team is depending on you so . . .

1. BE THERE! -- at the time and date you and your supervising teacher(s) have agreed to as being most convenient. There is a minimum amount of time you must spend in a school class with a supervisor. If, for some very compelling, persuasive reason you must miss an assignment, notify your cooperating school well in advance. The best way to do this is to call the school secretary (if the school is in session). If school is not in session, call the teacher at home. If, for good reason an assigned observation/ participation is missed, that assigned period must be made up. An incomplete field experience is grounds for failing the course.

2. A field experience participation form is to be filled out for each visit (see following form). The completed forms must be turned in to your methods course instructor no later than the end of each week. This informs your instructor what you are doing and when you are doing it. The instructor and the school supervising teacher will determine with you the type of classroom experiences that will fulfill the field experience program.

Setting standard for success

3. Information about the school, teachers, and students is completely confidential.

4. Teaching doesn't always proceed the way your methods instructors and/or you think it should. You are a guest in the school which means that you should not, must not, be critical while in the school. The proper place for evaluation of what you experience is in the written "Field Experience Participation Report." Please don't get this message wrong. We are merely warning you not to be critical of administrators, teachers, and other school personnel while in their school.

plan
Improve your skills

WHAT WOULD HAVE HAPPENED TO THE COLONIES, WITHOUT
1.
2.
3.
4.

PERFORMANCE

PRIORITY

SUPERVISING TEACHER'S RESPONSIBILITIES
IN THE FIELD EXPERIENCE PROGRAM

(The following is a letter sent to the supervising teacher.)

Dear Teacher:

We appreciate your cooperation in the placement of secondary methods social studies students who will be under your supervision. The students with whom you will be working have had a "Directed Experience in School" course. These students having observed/participated in schools for a semester, and should now be ready for more active participation in your classroom.

In short, we want to build on the earlier "Directed Experience in School" course in preparation for student teaching by requiring the following experiences.

1. Participate in the planning and teaching of a class; this includes teaching in front of the entire class, working with individual students and in small groups.

2. Prepare and present at least several lessons to the entire class
                    (and)
3. Perform some clerical work that is related to teaching, i.e., duplicating handouts, grading tests, taking roll.

This field experience is scheduled to last for approximately one month or the equivalent of five visits of two hours each at a scheduled time. If the students should miss one of the scheduled visits for an excusable reason, they are required to make up the visit. One missed visit is grounds for failure of the course.

Finally, we would like to involve you in the overall evaluation of the students' performance. We will provide you with an evaluation form for each of the students you are supervising.

Sincerely,

FIELD EXPERIENCE OBSERVATION/PARTICIPATION FORM

Student's name_____

School where assigned_____

Supervising Teacher_____

Was this student absent from any scheduled visit without being excused?

_____Yes   _____No

If you believe the student has achieved at an outstanding or exceptional level in any of the nine categories below, that student should receive a rating of 5 (highest) in that category; an average rating would be 3; and 1 is the lowest rating signifying that the student did not achieve in that category.

1. Responsible, completed assigned tasks, arrived on time.   5 4 3 2 1

2. Demonstrated ability and willingness to work cooperatively.   5 4 3 2 1

3. Was enthusiastic about students, learning, and the subject taught.   5 4 3 2 1

4. Accepted criticism gracefully and responded appropriately to suggestions.   5 4 3 2 1

5. Confident, tactful, courteous.   5 4 3 2 1

6. Genuinely cared about students. Listened to them.   5 4 3 2 1

7. Volunteered for work. Participated when given an opportunity.   5 4 3 2 1

8. Used time efficiently.   5 4 3 2 1

9. Had high standards. Capable, competent.   5 4 3 2 1

Total points_____

Comments: Your comments are important and useful. Would you want this person as a student teacher?

_____Yes   _____No

FIELD EXPERIENCE PARTICIPATION FORM[*]

<u>Instructions</u>

One of these forms will be completed for each time period spent in the cooperating school. The completed form must be delivered to your methods course instructor by Friday of each week.

****

Name of Social Studies Methods Instructor Professor Barth

Date_____February 24_____   Cooperating Teacher Mr. James Spencer

Your Name Jerry Smith_____   Cooperating School North Montgomery

Grade Level Am.Hist. 11th Grade Total Time Spent in School 2 hours

Your Assignment for This Day two Am. Hist. classes (9a.m. - 11a.m.)

_____Also visited briefly Mr. Horney in World History class._____

In the space below describe and comment on your activities at the participating school.

This week both my classes had the same activities. Both periods began with a 15-minute discussion of the end of the chapter, followed by an exercise in which the students worked with maps. The idea for the exercise was my own, and the reason for it was that last week I realized that the students knew far less about maps and what they are used for than I previously thought. The first group did very well in locating and listing the physical characteristics of the country they chose. The second group, though, had more problems, requiring me to provide individual help.

Before I started this participation I had no idea what eleventh graders would be like. I had always wanted to work with seniors in high school, but now that I have spent some time with this age level I really like them. I am also thinking about teaching in junior high, perhaps even in upper elementary. Anyway this experience helped me understand that I could work well with a lot of different age students, and I didn't think I could.

The visit to Mr. Horney's class was interesting because his major teaching technique is small groups where the students are actively involved in projects.

[*]Sample

STUDENT TEACHING

The Best, the Brightest

Inventory Checklist on Student Teaching

The following is an inventory checklist on student teaching problems. The checklist will help identify some of the fears and apprehensions which you might have about student teaching. In a sense the checklist is a pretest to this section on student teaching. Please take the time right now to check those statements that best reflect your feelings about student teaching.

PROFESSIONAL FEARS AND APPREHENSIONS **RIGHT NOW**
THAT MAY BE EXPERIENCED BY TEACHERS*

_____ 1. Will I be allowed to use my own initiative?
_____ 2. What should I do if my material has been covered and there is extra time?
_____ 3. What should I do if I make a mistake in a statement or a suggestion?
_____ 4. Can I deviate from the plan of work as outlined?
_____ 5. How should I dress?
_____ 6. Will the grades I will give be accepted?
_____ 7. Will I be required to turn in my lesson plans, and who will evaluate them?
_____ 8. Do I really know my subject matter?
_____ 9. Will the pupils like me and respond to my guidance?
_____ 10. Will I be able to maintain desired standards of behavior?
_____ 11. What will these pupils be like?
_____ 12. What will the students be likely to do "to try me out"?
_____ 13. What will the students do if I make a mistake?
_____ 14. How should I behave if I am unable to answer a student's question?
_____ 15. How informal or formal should I be with students?
_____ 16. Will I be able to do what is expected of me?
_____ 17. Will anything drastic happen if I make a mistake in following school policy?
_____ 18. Will my teaching assignment be too much for me to handle?
_____ 19. How will the faculty and staff accept me?
_____ 20. Who is responsible for evaluating my teaching and giving me a grade?
_____ 21. How will I be evaluated?

*Adapted from Michael L. Thompson. "Identifying Anxieties Experienced by Student Teachers," Journal of Teacher Education, 14 (December 1973), 436.

Now that you have checked those statements that best reflect your feelings, we have a few questions for you. Look back over the statements checked.

more questions

Question: Do you identify any patterns of concern, i.e., discipline, wanting to be liked, planning, etc.?

(Respond here.)

```
┌─────────────────────────────────────────────────────────┐
│                                                         │
│                                                         │
│                                                         │
│                                                         │
│                                                         │
│                                                         │
└─────────────────────────────────────────────────────────┘
```

Question: Which items in the checklist are you most concerned about, what items are you least concerned with?

(Respond here.)

```
┌─────────────────────────────────────────────────────────┐
│  Most concerned:                                        │
│                                                         │
│  Least concerned:                                       │
│                                                         │
│                                                         │
└─────────────────────────────────────────────────────────┘
```

Student Teacher's Legal Rights

Nobody asked me

Regarding the legalities of student teaching, each state has its own laws. The following, an illustration of one state's policy, is from the Indiana State Teachers Association booklet, A Teacher's Legal Rights and Responsibilities.

A 1969 Indiana statute authorizes school corporations to enter into formal agreements with teacher training institutions to provide student teaching experience. A 1973 statute covering teachers and giving them authority to take any action reasonable necessary to carry out or prevent interference with the educational functions of which they have charge also extends that authority to student teachers.

A recent State of Indiana court decision held that student teachers have the same constitutional rights as licensed teachers with regard to freedom of speech.

However, other decisions indicate that the opportunity to do student teaching is not a guaranteed right and a school corporation may refuse to accept a student teacher whose reputation is questionable.

The liability of student teachers in the event of injury or damage to a student in their charge would seem to be quite similar to that of a regular teacher. If a student teacher has acted prudently to protect students, a court would probably not rule negligence. However, a student teacher probably should not attempt to administer corporal punishment.

Requirements for Student Teaching

is so important

There is common agreement among student teachers and their school and university supervisors that one of the most important experiences in the teacher education program is student teaching. In most teacher certification programs, more time and credit are allotted to student teaching than to any other professional course.

While you need no convincing as to the importance of student teaching, you do need to be convinced of the importance of knowing the requirements for successfully completing student teaching. At least two supervisors will be looking over your shoulder with some frequency. This is not necessarily a comforting thought for no one really wants to be evaluated by anyone. However, there is at least one way of mitigating the anxiety: knowledge of the criteria by which your student teaching will be evaluated.

Be Sure to Read These Forms

Coming Events

On the following pages there are five sets of forms that you absolutely must pay attention to for these forms will affect how you student teach. The first form, "Social Studies Student Teaching Requirements," consists of eight points of information which instruct you on social studies student teaching. The second form is a "Student Teaching Schedule" that must be turned in to your university supervisor when you begin student teaching. The third form is a "Weekly Schedule Form" that must be turned in to your university supervisor weekly. The fourth form is a letter from the university supervisor to your school supervising teacher setting forth expectations and criteria for evaluation. The fifth set of forms are mid-term and final evaluation forms that are the specific criteria used when evaluating your performance as a social studies student teacher. **Use This**

SOCIAL STUDIES STUDENT TEACHING REQUIREMENTS

TO: Stan Williams
FROM: University Supervisor   **important**
RE: Requirements and Information

(1) Read carefully and note the requirements listed in the university supervisor's letter to the school supervisor. That letter notes what the university supervisor will expect the student teacher to practice during the ten weeks of student teaching. (See copy of letter in a following section in this chapter.)

(2) The ten weekly schedule forms (see sample following) should be mailed or delivered to your university supervisor on Wednesday preceding the week to which the schedule applies. This is important for without the schedule the university supervisor cannot keep track of what you are planning and will be unable to visit you.

(3) You should begin teaching gradually; don't take over during the first week all three or four classes you are going to teach. Plan to assume responsibility for at least one or two classes by the end of the first week. The number and type of classes you are to teach should be cooperatively determined by you and your university and cooperating school supervisors.

(4) Lesson plans should be made for all teaching. No written plans, no teaching. Daily lesson plans and long-term unit planning is required. Your university supervisor will ask to see your lesson plans for the classes visited.

(5) Your university supervisor will make arrangements to visit you. The visits will normally be made sometime during the first weeks, the middle weeks, and the last weeks of student teaching.

(6) Your university supervisor, during each visit, will observe you teaching classes, examine your lesson plans, and have a conference with you and with your school supervisor.

(7) You should follow the holiday schedule of the supervising teacher in your assigned school.

(8) If an emergency arises causing you to be absent from classes, advance notice should be given to both the principal and your school supervisor. Also, if you are to be absent, the best part of wisdom is to notify your university supervisor so that he/she will not visit your school and find you gone. If you cannot reach your university supervisor at home, leave word with his/her secretary at the university.

(Sample form of class schedule)

STUDENT TEACHING SCHEDULE

Student's name ___ Stan Williams

Address ___ 1536 Stadium Street

Supervising Teacher's full name ___ John Thrall Richards

School ___ Miller High School   Town ___ Miller Township

Principal ___ Alfort Hammer   Superintendent ___ Samuel P. Broad

Period	Time	Class/Subject	Room	Teacher
1	8-9	American Government	14	John T. Richards
2	9-10	American Government	14	"
3	10-11	Observation Period	Resource Room	Obs. teachers throughout building
4	11-12	Lunch/Supervision (11:30-12:00)	Trs'	Lunch room
5	12-1	American History	21	John T. Richards
6	1-2	Preparation	Resource Room	
7	2-3	American History	21	John T. Richards

Other:
Have chosen to work with History Club and assist the Junior Varsity Basketball Coach.

I will supervise a lunch room for three weeks during fourth period, and I have arranged with my supervisor to talk with him every day during 6th period preparation.

348

WEEKLY SCHEDULE FORM

Your University Supervisor should have this form on the Wednesday preceding the week scheduled below.

Name __Stan Williams__   School __Miller High School__   Cooperating Teacher __John Richards__

Week Beginning __December__ __5__
                  (month)   (day)

Period	1	2	3	4	5	6	7
Monday	Am.Govt. Lecture T	Am. Govt. Lecture T	Prep.	Lunch	Am. Hist. Movie T	Visit with Vice-Prin.	Am. Hist. Movie T
Tuesday	Am. Govt. Lecture T	Am. Govt. Lecture T	Prep.	Lunch	Am. Hist. Lecture T	Prep.	Am. Hist. Lecture T
Wednesday	School Assembly	Am. Govt. Movie T	Visit Guidance C.	Lunch	Am. Hist. Test T	Prep.	Am. Hist. Test T
Thursday	Am. Govt. Test Review T	Am. Govt. Test Review T	Prep.	Lunch	Am. Hist. Oral Reports T	Media Center	Am. Hist. Oral Reports T
Friday	Am. Govt. Test T	Am. Govt. Test T	Observe English Tchr. T	Lunch	Am. Hist. Debate T	Prep.	Am. Hist. Debate T

Please use the following code for indicating your activities during each period.

T - Teach

A - Assisting the cooperating teacher

O - Observing: no active participation in classroom

Note: Will be meeting with History Club Th. 3-4.
       Helping coach at Basketball game Friday.

(Letter to school supervising teacher from university supervisor
setting forth expectations and criteria for evaluation.)

Mr. John T. Richards
Social Studies Department
Miller High School
Miller Township, Indiana

Dear Mr. Richards:

We agree with you that Stan Williams ought to have certain basic
training before he begins teaching under your supervision. Stan
should know how to plan, both unit and daily lessons; he should
be familiar with a wide variety of teaching techniques; he should
have developed skills in questioning and test construction; and
finally he should know how to deal effectively with reading,
special students, and discipline. Because we agree with you that
professional attitudes and skills should have been learned, we
want to guarantee that Stan's training at this university did
include all of the above.

In fact, the University School of Education guarantees the
performance of each teacher that graduates from our program. We
are serious about the guarantee because it is our declaration
that University graduates are starting their teaching careers
with excellent professional training. Please join with us to
enforce the practice of those professional attitudes and skills
during student teaching.

The following may help to explain how we together can maximize
Stan's professional development during student teaching.

A.   Planning is an absolute requirement. Stan should not teach
     until there has been careful written planning.

B.   Lesson plans are to be written daily, and after the first
     week a long-range "unit" plan should be developed in
     addition to daily lesson plans. Stan has practiced using
     the following unit plan outline and will be expected to use
     this plan when discussing long-range planning with you.

UNIT PLAN OUTLINE

I. Introductory Statement: how unit fits into long-term planning	IV. Activities: initiating, developing, summarizing
II. Objectives: knowledge skills, attitudes	V. Materials and Resources: teaching aids
III. Content Outline: subject content	VI. Evaluation Procedures

C. Each daily lesson plan should contain as minimum each of the following: specific objective, content, teaching techniques, summary, and assignment.

DAILY LESSON PLANS

First Day	Second Day	Third Day	Fourth Day	Fifth Day
OBJECTIVE: CONTENT: TECHNIQUES & STRATEGIES: SUMMARY & ASSIGNMENT:				

D. Planning must be checked. All lesson plans should be carefully checked by you, the school supervising teacher, before the plans are carried out in the classroom. If Stan does not show you written lesson plans, he should not teach the class. No plans, no teach.

E. Demonstrate competence in questioning. We expect Stan to make a conscious effort to improve his questioning strategies. He has learned to ask cognitive-memory, convergent, divergent, and evaluative levels of questions and, therefore, is expected to demonstrate competence in using all four levels.

F. Active learning is emphasized. Of course, student teaching is practice teaching. We expect Stan to practice a wide variety of classroom techniques including grouping, using audio-visuals/teaching aids, games and simulations, debates, oral reports, panels, quizdowns, lecture and recitation, but the emphasis should be on active learning.

G. Reading comprehension. University students have received training in how to improve students' reading comprehension. Stan should practice the skills he has learned. If he does not practice working on reading comprehension, he will not use those skills in the future. Please encourage his use of this skill.

H. Instructional media. We all know that instructional media is important, particularly when teaching difficult abstract ideas. Stan has received training in the use of media, and he should be encouraged to practice using media as often as possible.

Finally, we would like to review Stan's required responsibilities during his student teaching.

(1)   Stan is to teach at least three or four classes during a major portion of his student teaching.

(2)   Obviously, Stan is not teaching a full day. The two or three periods that remain after teaching three or four classes should not be free time to be used at his discretion. One period should be used for observation, one for supervision other than in the classroom, and one for planning. Some student teachers assume because they are only teaching three or four periods that they have the remainder of the day to plan and grade papers. This is not a good use of their time and gives them a false picture of the actual responsibilities of a teacher. Stan should have a planning period just as teachers do, but the remainder of the time should be devoted to educational experiences beyond classroom teaching.

(3)   Stan should supervise an activity; i.e., study hall, lunch room, hall duty, where he does not know the students. It is one thing to supervise students you know by name in the classroom. It is quite another to supervise students you do not know.

(4)   Stan should make observations not only of other social studies teachers, but should meet guidance counselors, librarians, and school administrators. During the ten weeks of student teaching, he should have no less than thirty to forty observations.

(5)   Stan should attend all school functions that are appropriate. In short, he should expect to participate in a total school program including all faculty meetings.

(6)   Stan should become familiar with and participate in cocurricular activities: coaching, sponsoring or participating in clubs, providing service at athletic and other school events: plays, open houses, special programs.

(7)   The University program requires Stan to meet with you a minimum of one hour each week for a general evaluation of his progress and, of course, meet each school day to review daily lesson plans and discuss problems.

We realize that student teachers have a short ten weeks to practice their teaching. You are the most significant supervisor, for if there are problems it is primarily to you that Stan must turn, and it is with your help that he will develop right skills and attitudes during student teaching. A concise checklist or required activities is attached.

SOCIAL STUDIES STUDENT TEACHER CHECKLIST OF REQUIRED ACTIVITIES

Name_____Date_____School_____

Class Observed_____University Supervisor_____

1. Review of Current Unit Plan
   A. Introductory Statement ....NA   1   2   3   4   5
   B. Objectives ....NA   1   2   3   4   5
   C. Content Outline ....NA   1   2   3   4   5
   D. Activities ....NA   1   2   3   4   5
   E. Materials ....NA   1   2   3   4   5
   F. Evaluation ....NA   1   2   3   4   5
   Comment_____

2. Daily lesson plan
   A. Derived from unit plan ....NA   1   2   3   4   5
   B. Met objective for the day ....NA   1   2   3   4   5
   C. Content ....NA   1   2   3   4   5
   Coment_____

3. Questioning skills
   A. Clear and appropriate ....NA   1   2   3   4   5
   B. Use of all levels ....NA   1   2   3   4   5
   Comment_____

4. Active Learning
   A. Student-centered activities ....NA   1   2   3   4   5
   B. Variety of techniques ....NA   1   2   3   4   5
   Comment_____

5. Reading
   A. Awareness of student's reading levels.NA 1   2   3   4   5
   B. Use of reading comprehension techs....NA 1   2   3   4   5
   Comment_____

6. Media
   A. Variety in media ....NA   1   2   3   4   5
   B. Appropriate use of media ....NA   1   2   3   4   5
   Comment_____

7. Relationship with students ....NA   1   2   3   4   5
   Comment_____

8. Use of outside of classroom ....NA   1   2   3   4   5
   Comment_____
   _____

Spencer 1990

TAKING CONTROL

Coming Events

Mid-Term and Final Evaluation Forms Are Important

Forms such as those you are about to view on the next few pages are important because they provide you with feedback from your school and university supervisors. You may think, "But isn't my school supervisor with me every day, if not in the classroom, at least in the building? Don't I talk with my supervisor every day? We have an ongoing evaluation, but don't talk about it." The answer to these unspoken questions is, frankly, no. You will be lucky if you have a supervisor who will sit down with you each day or even each week and give you critical evaluation of your performance. This evaluation probably should happen, but in some instances does not happen.

The fact is that most student teachers are starved for critical evaluation. It is not at all unusual for school supervising teachers to be hesitant about critically evaluating another teacher, including a student teacher. It is not unusual for a student teacher to go for weeks without any critical comment except, "You're doing fine, kid, keep it up." This is understandably frustrating for student teachers who need specific feedback.

You Have a Right to Know:
Mid-Term and Final Evaluation Forms

Student teachers have a right to know how well they are progressing and they ought to see evaluation in a written form. The following forms were developed by school supervisors and administrators to evaluate the mid-term and final progress of student teachers.

The final evaluation is very important in getting a social studies job. The school supervisor's form and the university supervisor's form will be placed in your credential file, and will be read by any prospective employer. Please read the following evaluation forms so that you will know the criteria used to evaluate student teaching performance. Your grade depends on it.

the Inevitable

MID-TERM EVALUATION

STUDENT TEACHER: ___Stan Williams_____

SCHOOL: _Miller High School_____ SUBJECT: Social Studies_____

Evaluation completed by: __John T. Richards_____ DATE: _November 1_____

Check one: ___X___ Supervising Teacher _____ University Supervisor

- -

	EXCELLENT	VERY GOOD	AVERAGE	BELOW AVERAGE	UNACCEPTABLE	NOT OBSERVED

PROFESSIONAL QUALITIES

	EXCELLENT	VERY GOOD	AVERAGE	BELOW AVERAGE	UNACCEPTABLE	NOT OBSERVED
Clarity: Goals and objectives, explanations, and questions are clear.			✓			
Cooperation: Demonstrates qualities necessary to work cooperatively with colleagues.			✓			
Enthusiasm: Demonstrates enthusiasm for the subject, learning, and students.				✓		
Flexibility: Accepts criticism gracefully and responds appropriately to suggestions.				✓		
Subject Matter: Has command of subject matter; has broad general background with a variety of interests.	✓					

PERSONAL QUALITIES

	EXCELLENT	VERY GOOD	AVERAGE	BELOW AVERAGE	UNACCEPTABLE	NOT OBSERVED
Appearance: Is dressed and groomed appropriately.		✓				
Poise: Is confident, poised, tactful, courteous, and free of distracting mannerisms.			✓			
Sensitivity: Is sensitive to students' needs and interests.				✓		

CLASSROOM MANAGEMENT AND ORGANIZATION

	EXCELLENT	VERY GOOD	AVERAGE	BELOW AVERAGE	UNACCEPTABLE	NOT OBSERVED
Classroom Atmosphere: Creates an atmosphere of openness and acceptance while maintaining control of the classroom situation.				✓		
Planning: Learning activities are sequential and carefully planned. Time is used effectively.				✓		
Variety: Uses an appropriate variety of activities, approaches, methods, and materials.				✓		

SUMMARY EVALUATION

	EXCELLENT	VERY GOOD	AVERAGE	BELOW AVERAGE	UNACCEPTABLE	NOT OBSERVED
Potential: This student's teaching potential is:				✓		

COMMENTS: PLEASE TYPE. CONFINE COMMENTS TO SPACE BELOW.
Please make comments which will be helpful to a potential employer, including strengths and/or weaknesses of the candidate.

Mr. Williams has been student teaching for the past four and one half weeks. When he, the university supervisor, and the school supervisor met for a mid-term evaluation the following points about Stan's strengths and weaknesses were discussed. His strengths are in knowing his content. He has developed a good content outline. The weaknesses, however, are that he is not planning the practice of the different techniques of teaching. He just seems to be lecturing, so he must improve his unit and daily planning to reflect how he is going to work with students in active learning situations. The students are falling asleep in his class. He appears passive, speaks in a monotone, and seems unable to excite learning. Confidence is a problem, and though he accepts criticism, he does not respond to suggestions. Class discipline is becoming a problem. The next four weeks he must work on the weaknesses identified here or he surely will receive an unfavorable student teaching evaluation.

It is suggested that this evaluation be discussed with the student.

STUDENT TEACHING EVALUATION FORM

This document becomes a permanent part of the student's file in the Educational Placement Office. Please complete it carefully.

STUDENT TEACHER: ___Stan Williams___

SCHOOL: ___Miller High School___ SUBJECT: ___Social Studies___

Evaluation completed by: ___John T. Richards___ DATE: ___December 16___

Check one: ___X___ Supervising Teacher _____ University Supervisor

PROFESSIONAL QUALITIES

	EXCELLENT	VERY GOOD	AVERAGE	BELOW AVERAGE	UNACCEPTABLE	NOT OBSERVED
Clarity: Goals and objectives, explanations, and questions are clear.			X			
Cooperation: Demonstrates qualities necessary to work cooperatively with colleagues.				X		
Enthusiasm: Demonstrates enthusiasm for the subject, learning, and students.			X			
Flexibility: Accepts criticism gracefully and responds appropriately to suggestions.				X		
Subject Matter: Has command of subject matter; has broad general background with a variety of interests.	X					

PERSONAL QUALITIES

	EXCELLENT	VERY GOOD	AVERAGE	BELOW AVERAGE	UNACCEPTABLE	NOT OBSERVED
Appearance: Is dressed and groomed appropriately.		X				
Poise: Is confident, poised, tactful, courteous, and free of distracting mannerisms.			X			
Sensitivity: Is sensitive to students' needs and interests.				X		

CLASSROOM MANAGEMENT AND ORGANIZATION

	EXCELLENT	VERY GOOD	AVERAGE	BELOW AVERAGE	UNACCEPTABLE	NOT OBSERVED
Classroom Atmosphere: Creates an atmosphere of openness and acceptance while maintaining control of the classroom situation.				X		
Planning: Learning activities are sequential and carefully planned. Time is used effectively.			X			
Variety: Uses an appropriate variety of activities, approaches, methods, and materials.			X			

SUMMARY EVALUATION

	EXCELLENT	VERY GOOD	AVERAGE	BELOW AVERAGE	UNACCEPTABLE	NOT OBSERVED
Potential: This student's teaching potential is:				X		

COMMENTS: PLEASE TYPE. CONFINE COMMENTS TO SPACE BELOW.
Please make comments which will be helpful to a potential employer, including strengths and/or weaknesses of the candidate.

Stan received a C- for student teaching. He taught 2 classes of Government and 2 classes of American History during his 10-weeks assignment at Miller. His attendance was regular and punctual; his daily preparations were incomplete; his attention to routine classroom operations was satisfactory. There was little question that Stan was well-equipped academically in the areas of government and history. Stan's greatest difficulty was in communicating with students or the school faculty. He seldom discussed or sought advice about his assignment. He incorporated few suggestions offered on teaching and made little progress toward "humanizing" his teaching. To become an effective teacher, I believe Stan would need to demonstrate a willingness to improve his classroom techniques and personal involvement with the students. Unless this is done, I doubt his future success as an educator.

It is suggested that this evaluation be discussed with the student.

_____
Supervisor Signature

Classroom Students' Evaluation of Student Teacher

The Mid-Term Evaluation form and the final Student Teaching Evaluation form are used by university and school supervisors to evaluate your progress. But what about your progress with your students? We have provided another form that you may use to "collect responses" from your students. But before you decide to use the form, you should think about the following.

Some Thoughts Before Deciding to Use Student Evaluation

Even though student responses would be useful to you and even though it takes courage to ask students for their responses, it does not follow that if you are reluctant to do so you are less than courageous or do not care what your students think of you. Some teachers and administrators argue that student evaluations are unfair and have no place in the classroom. With some justification, they maintain that students should not be encouraged to think that their judgments of a teacher's performance could be used to reward or punish that teacher. The reasoning goes like this. Students have little choice but to be in a public school classroom. There are teachers who, in order to gain good evaluations, cater to their students' baser feelings, i.e., they lighten up on homework and practice grade inflation. It stands that a hard-nosed teacher who demands a good deal--but is equally hard working and conscientious--may not, at the moment, be appreciated by students. Given the above reservations by some teachers and administrators, you should make some effort to find out how the students perceive your teaching. If you intend to use the following student evaluation, be sure to obtain permission from your school supervisor.

How're you going to do it?

STUDENT EVALUATION OF TEACHER FORM

TEACHING SKILLS: Consider how much you have learned in this class. Do you have a feeling of accomplishment? Does the teacher make you think? Are there different things to do, or is every class period just like all the others? Do you think your teacher knows the subject?

A. I have learned: problems

 _____
    A great deal   Some   Very little   Almost nothing

B. I have enjoyed this subject:

 _____
    Always   Most of the time   Some of the time   Never

C. We have interesting problems to solve:

 _____
    Always   Most of the time   Some of the time   Never

D. Daily class activities are different:

 _____
    Always   Most of the time   Some of the time   Never

E. Our teacher knows the subject:

 _____
    Very well   Average   Fair   Very poorly

F. Our teacher encourages us to work:

 _____
    Very hard   Some   Very little   Never

G. We know what we are trying to accomplish:

 _____
    Always   Most of the time   Some of the time   Never

H. Our class periods seem organized, regulated:

 _____
    Always   Most of the time   Some of the time   Never

I. Our teacher maintains order in the classroom:

 _____
    Always   Most of the time   Some of the time   Never

J. Our teacher's tests:

 _____
    Make us use as   Make us remember   Are fair, but   Are too easy
    well as remember   mostly facts   too difficult
    facts

PERSONALITY: Consider how your teacher seems as a person to you. Is the teacher fair to everyone in the class? Does the teacher have a good sense of humor? Does the teacher have a lot of enthusiasm? Is the teacher helpful to those who have problems? Is the teacher ever sarcastic? Does the teacher lose his/her temper too easily?

A. Our teacher has the kind of personality:

wrong image

_____
I like very much   I like somewhat   I like little   I dislike much

B. Our teacher is fair to us:

_____
Always   Most of the time   Some of the time   Never

C. Our teacher's sense of humor is:

_____
Very good   Average   Fair   Very poor

D. Our teacher's enthusiasm for teaching is:

_____
Very high   Average   Fair   Very low

E. Our teacher's appearance is:

_____
Pleasant   Average   Fair   Unpleasant

F. Our teacher is sarcastic and makes fun of some of us:

_____
Never   Some of the time   Most of the time   Always

G. Our teacher loses his/her temper:

_____
Rarely   Sometimes   Often   Very often

H. Our teacher is sympathetic to our problems:

_____
Always   Most of the time   Some of the time   Never

I. Our teacher seems:

_____
*Always relaxed and   Mostly relaxed and   Sometimes tense   Very tense
comfortable   comfortable   and nervous   and nervous*

J. Our teacher's voice is:

_____
Pleasant   Average   Fair   Unpleasant

EXPLANATION OF YOUR RATINGS: Include any other items not covered in the above. If you desire, include specific events that happened in the classroom to illustrate why you gave a certain rating.

POSTSCRIPT

> It has always seemed odd that formal education
> has become "learning" responses to rather
> meaningless questions asked by others in a
> society that requires self-realization and
> creativity.

You have received occasional warnings in the Preface,
Chapter I, and elsewhere throughout the other chapters, that this
text has a point of view, a message: teachers teach students not
content. This is my way of saying, given the way schools are
organized and the attitudes of students, teachers are often
obligated to convince students that their courses are worth time
and effort. All of the chapters in this text on methods and
techniques, reading, discipline, coping skills with special and
disadvantaged students are recognition that the interests and
problems of students are a major concern for effective teachers.
An anonymous experienced teacher from Idaho put the message this
way:

> More and more children in our community are being
> raised by grandparents. We are seeing more children
> who are emotionally disturbed and mentally impaired,
> the result of their parents' drinking and drug abuse.
> Some children come to school unwashed and worse,
> unhugged and unloved. We clean them up, hug them
> and try to make up for what is missing in their
> lives.
>   I'm not complaining. Teaching is the most
> rewarding and important career in the world, but I
> hope in my lifetime that the teaching profession will
> be elevated to the respectable position now given
> medicine and law. Believe it or not, every doctor
> and lawyer was once a second-grader.

In short, if you propose to teach school, you may have no
choice but to first cope with the concerns that students and
teachers spoke about in Chapter I. Do you remember the students'
and teachers' responses in Chapter I? They talked about
motivation, interest, empathy, boredom, misunderstanding, and
discipline, but almost never about content, other than to suggest
that their perception of social studies was that its content
remained irrelevant and depressing. Given the students'
responses, can you now relate to why social studies was intended
to reform citizenship education at the turn of the century?

The critics were right when they looked into the future of
the twentieth century. They saw rapid change, fractured
families, loss of a sense of community, rootless, wandering
technocrats who they feared would fail to maintain the values and
beliefs upon which the country was founded. The school became,

in the midst of rapid change, the community; classroom and cafeteria and athletic fields became the home; and the teachers became the parents. What was social studies to be?

Social studies was assigned the mission of citizenship education. That mission included the study of personal/social problems in an interdisciplinary integrated school curriculum that would emphasize the practice of decision making. The skills that one would need to be an effective citizen were: to gain knowledge, process information, identify and examine values and beliefs, and finally learn how to participate in decisions about the social concerns of the community. The social studies reforms have never quite been realized. Classrooms remain for most students gaining knowledge through the study of linear, chronological, structure function, in short, the memorization of facts, events, and the organization of social institutions. The skills of processing, valuing, and participation, which relate most closely to the students' needs and interests, remain essentially unpracticed.

What can be said for the future? For the moment there can be no reason to assume change will not be more rapid as modern society becomes technology society. The citizen in the twenty-first century may well have more choice, more opportunity, and less stability than those in the twentieth century. As access to information becomes generally available to all, perhaps the emphasis on consuming content will become less important, and more importance will be assigned to the practice of processing, valuing, and participation. If that were to be the future, then the social studies reform will find a prominent place in the future education of citizens.

Social Studies
The American Experience

NOTES

Chapter I

1.   The dialogue found in this chapter is based on written responses from approximately fifteen hundred students and several hundred teachers. Each student or teacher statement represents a concern that was often mentioned in the written responses. The dialogue, in most cases, is taken directly from the students' and teachers' written responses.

Chapter II

1.   <u>Social Studies Guidelines</u> (Washington, D.C.: National Council for the Social Studies, 1970). For a fuller treatment of the practical application of the four objectives, see the Social Studies Curriculum Series, two books which are organized at each grade level, K-12, according to the four objectives. J.L. Barth. <u>Elementary and Junior High/Middle School Social Studies Curriculum, Activities and Materials</u> (Second edition) (Washington, D.C.: University Press of America, 1983) and J.L. Barth. <u>Secondary Social Studies Curriculum, Activities and Materials</u> (Washington, D.C..: University Press of America, 1984).

2.   For a clear and concise development of the Three Traditions Approach see: Barr, Barth, and Shermis. <u>The Nature of the Social Studies</u> (Palm Springs, CA: ETC Publications, 1978); also Barr, Barth, and Shermis. <u>Defining the Social Studies</u>, Bulletin 51 (Washington, D.C.: National Council for the Social Studies, 1977).

3.   The original chart, "The Three Social Studies Traditions," was published in Barr, Barth, and Shermis, <u>Defining the Social Studies</u>, p. 67, and has been modified for purposes of this text.

Chapter III.

1.   John Jarolimek. "Conceptual Approaches: Their Meaning for Elementary Social Studies," <u>An Anthology of Readings in Elementary Social Studies</u>, Huburt M. Walsh, Ed. (Washington, D.C.: National Council for the Social Studies, 1971),124.

2.   Alma Shufflerbarger and Wilma Shafer. "Indiana K-12 Social Studies Curriculum," <u>Teaching Social Studies in Indiana</u> (Bloomington, IN: Indiana Council for the Social Studies, 1985), 12.

3.   Jacquelin Stitt and Perry Marker. "Definitions and Examples of Facts, Concepts, and Generalizations," <u>Principles of Social Studies: The Why, What, and How of Social Studies Instruction, Second Edition</u>, (J.L. Barth, ed.). (Washington, D.C.: University Press of America, 1984), 17-21.

4.   Ibid., 20.

Chapter IV.

1.   "The Use of Direct Observation to Study Teaching," in R. Travers (Ed.), <u>Second Handbook of Research on Teaching</u> (Chicago: Rand McNally, 1973).

Chapter V.

1.   For many other applications of techniques and strategies we recommend the Social Studies Curriculum Series: Barth, <u>Elementary and Junior High/Middle School Social Studies Curriculum, Activities and Materials</u> and <u>Secondary Social Studies Curriculum, Activities and Materials</u>.

Chapter VI.

1.   Deborah B. Strother. "Developing Thinking Skills Through Questioning," Phi Delta Kappan (December 1989), 325-326.
2.   Benjamin S. Bloom (Ed.), <u>Taxonomy of Educational Objectives: The Classification of Educational Goals. Handbook I: Cognitive Domain</u> (New York: David McKay, 1956).

Chapter VII

1.   M. Laughlin, A. Hartoonian, N. Sanders. "Commentary," <u>Social Education</u>, 53, 7 (December 1989), 449.

2.   Larry Cuban. "School Reform by Remote Control: S.B. 813 in California," <u>Phi Delta Kappa</u> (November 1984), 214.

3.   "The Symposium on Information Literacy and Education for the 21st Century: Toward an Agenda for Action," Report of the American Library Association Presidential Committee on Information Literacy. April 14-19, 1989, Leesburg, VA.

4.   This cone is an adaptation of the original cone of experience developed by Edgar Dale. <u>Audio-Visual Methods in Teaching</u> (New York: Holt, Rinehart and Winston, 1969), 108.

5.   The categories suggested here were developed in cooperation with the Instructional Media Research Unit, Libraries and Audio-Visual Center, Purdue University, 1973.

6.   D.S. Kendall and H. Budin.   "Computers in Social Studies," <u>Social Education</u>, 51, 1 (January 1987) 32.

7.   B. Hunter.   "Knowledge-Creative Learning with Data Bases," <u>Social Education</u>, 51, 1 (January 1987) 38.

8.   Ibid., 41.

9.   Gene E. Rooze and Terry Northup.   <u>Using Computers to Teach Social Studies</u> (Littleton, CO: Libraries Unlimited, 1986), 1.

10.   Ibid., 2.

11.   J. Lengel.   "Emerging Technologies: Multimedia," <u>SIG-CASE</u> (October 1989) 3.

Chapter VIII.

1.   This strategy is recommended in <u>Reading Effectiveness Program/Middle, Junior and Secondary School Guide</u> (Indianapolis: Indiana Department of Public Instruction, 1975), 55.

2.   Francis P. Robinson.   <u>Effective Reading</u> (New York: Harper and Bros., 1962), 31-32.

3.   <u>Reading Effectiveness Program</u>, 62-63.

Chapter IX

1.   The case study on Cindy first appeared in S.S. Shermis and J.L. Barth.   <u>Cultural Foundations of Modern American Education</u> (Lexington, MA: Ginn and Co., 1981), 10, and has been revised for inclusion in this text.

2.   Ibid., 110.

Chapter X.

1.   J.L. Barth and S.S. Shermis.   <u>Teaching Social Studies to the Gifted and Talented</u> (Indianapolis: Department of Public Instruction, 1981).

2.   O. Backman.   <u>The Visually-Impaired Child</u> (Gaborone, Botswana: Ministry of Education, 1986). 22-36.

3.   J. Corlett.   <u>The Hearing-Impaired Child</u> (Gaborone, Botswana: Ministry of Education, 1985). 16-34.

4.   J. Haseley. The Mentally-Handicapped Child (Gaborone, Botswana: Ministry of Education, 1987). 10-36.

Chapter XI.

1.   Daniel Selakovich. Social Studies for the Disadvantaged (New York: Holt, Rinehart and Winston, 1970). 25-26.

2.   Ibid., 26.

3.   "Identifying Your Values," "The Cultural Chasm," and "Test Your Understanding" are all from Shermis and Barth. Cultural Foundations of Modern American Education. 77-79.

4.   This chart was originally developed by Ralph Segalman, Professor Sociology at Texas Western College. He presented this chart at the Rocky Mountain Social Science Association Conference (Spring 1965) with the intent of helping professional educators, social workers, and others identify differences between socioeconomic classes. It should be noted that distinctions between middle and lower classes as simplified in the chart are perhaps not as clear as they were prior to 1965. However, values have not so altered since then as to make the chart invalid.

Chapter XII

1.   The three criteria were originally developed by Robert F. Megar in his now classic Preparing Instructional Objectives (Palo Alto, CA: Fearon Publishers, Inc., 1962), 12.

GLOSSARY

The following is a list of words from this text. The definitions reflect how the words are used in the text and are not intended as dictionary definitions.

Use This

Affective Domain - One of the classifications of educational objectives. The objectives in this classification describe changes in interests, attitudes and values, and the development of appreciations and adequate adjustment.

Anthropology - The social science discipline that is built around a cultural approach in studying various groups of people.

Attitudes - Patterns of thinking that influence the way people react to their natural or cultural environment. Attitudes may be based on emotions or on reasons or both.

Basic Needs - What is important for survival; food, clothing, shelter.

Behavioral Objectives - Instructional objectives prepared in terms that clearly identify the changes desired in the student as an outcome of the instruction.

Beliefs - An acceptance of the truth of something without positive proof.

Change [cultural] - Basic alterations in a society's general attitudes or ways of life.

Change [social] - Alterations in people's day-to-day patterns of living in groups or communities.

Chaos - A condition of confusion or total disorder.

Chasm - A deep crack or break emphasizing differences in interests or opinions.

Chronology - The sequence or arrangement of events in time.

Citizenship - Membership in a nation, with attendant rights and responsibilities.

Civilization - The total cultural or social organization of a specific group of people.

Cognitive Domain - One of the classifications of educational objectives. The objectives in this classification range from those which emphasize simple recall to actually combining, synthesizing, and developing intellectual abilities.

Community - A social group of any size, whose members live in the same place, and who share governmental, cultural or historical heritage.

Concept - An idea or notion represented by a word or term standing for a class or group of things, which may range from simple ideas to complex abstractions.

Concept Wheel - A visual diagram or illustration of the relationship of facts, concepts, and generalizations.

Conflict - Opposition of individuals and groups, or opposition of emotions within an individual.

Consensus - A group arriving at a collective agreement.

Cooperation - Activity shared for mutual benefit.

Critical Thinking - A careful, persistent, and active consideration of any belief, value system or formation of knowledge. It is a process of validation where truth is determined in light of the evidence that supports it and in terms of the conclusions that can be generated from it.

Culture - The learned behavior of a group or people.

Custom - Usual and accepted behavior or practice among a group of people.

Decision Making - The dynamic process of interaction among all participants who determine a particular policy choice. Decision making studies focus on all factors relevant to policy choice.

Deductive Reasoning - A problem solving method which moves from the general to the specific, breaking down a generalization into separate concepts and then to established facts.

Democracy - A system of government in which the people rule.

Discipline - A recognized body of knowledge with its own method of inquiry, method of proof and unique structure.

Discovery Method - A problem solving method that involves students in the process of thinking things through and determining for themselves.

Ecology - The total pattern of relationships between living things and their environment.

Economics - The social science discipline that concerns itself with the study of production, distribution, and consumption of goods and services.

Environment - All the conditions and events that surround and influence living things.

Expanding Horizons or Widening Horizons of Expanding Environment - Educational theory of learning that assumes students move from the known to the unknown through developmental steps.

Fact - A concrete symbol, something that exists, can be verified, or is known as clearly established.

Family - A group consisting of one or more adults and one or more children, the adults being responsible for the maintenance and care of the children.

Freedom - Possessing civil rights and liberty from arbitrary authority.

Generalization - A statement or theory which describes some relationship among concepts. It involves a statement or some principle that has wide application.

Geography - The social science discipline concerned with the study of the interrelationship of man and his physical environment.

Group - A number of people who interact, communicate, and share common interests and goals.

History - The social science discipline concerned with the study, recording, and examination of man's activities in the past.

Hypothesis - A testable assertion, statement or proposition about the relationships between two or more phenomena in the field of inquiry. It can be proved or disproved through supportive data.

Identity - Awareness of one's own values, attitudes, and capabilities; self-knowledge, individuality.

Individuality - The sum of a person's characteristics and qualities.

Inductive Reasoning - A problem solving method which moves from the specific to the general, starting with facts which combine to make concepts which combine to form a generalization.

Industrialization - Introduction of a system of production based on large-scale use of nonmanually powered machinery; the accompanying economic, social, and cultural change.

368

Inquiry - A problem solving method which encourages students to manipulate data, raise questions, seek solutions and thereby determine answers for themselves.

Integration - To unify all parts into a single whole.

Interdependence - Reliance upon the exchange of goods and services among nations or among several members of a group.

Interdisciplinary Approach - A teaching approach which builds a social studies program, course, or learning opportunity by drawing upon the facts, concepts, and generalizations of more than one and often all of the social science disciplines (history, geography, sociology, economics, anthropology, political science, and psychology).

Jeffersonian - The small rural, farming community was the Jeffersonian ideal that would preserve democracy. In a Jeffersonian ideal the community taught the right values and beliefs.

Justice - The ideal of fair treatment for all.

Linear - Something one dimensional, straight and narrow.

Location - The position of an individual or a place.

Maps and Globes - Representations of reality; the earth, universe, or parts of them. Can be used to locate peoples, places, landforms, and other features.

Method - The way teachers generally intend to approach their teaching, as in transmission method or problem solving method.

Motivation - That which inspires or impels someone to do something.

Organization - A group of people committed to accomplishing some goal or work. The arrangement of things, events, or information in an orderly manner according to some guidelines.

Political Science - The social science discipline concerned with the question of how people govern themselves and their interaction with their political environment.

Problem Solving Method - A teaching method which uses a mode of inquiry allowing students opportunities for finding answers to questions or solutions to problems. Problem solving includes both inquiry and discovery.

Psychology - The social science discipline concerned with the study of behavior or behavioral change.

Region [geographical] - A part of the world that has at least one feature common throughout the area.

Resource Unit - Is usually planning for one term or an entire year that pulls together all the resources that might be available to teach a particular subject or topic; includes content, resources, methods, techniques, strategies, appropriate technology, and bibliography.

Resources [human] - People and the skills they have acquired.

Resources [natural] - Things in nature for which man has found a use.

Responsibilities - Obligations accompanying membership in a group.

Rights - Prerogatives to which a person is entitled.

Role - The part played by someone in a particular event; patterns of behavior adopted by individuals in carrying out specialized functions of a group.

Role-Playing - A teaching technique that provides a group problem solving situation in which students explore the problem, alternatives available to them and the personal and social consequences of the proposals.

Rule - A guideline for behavior.

Scope - The development of a theme and depth of study undertaken on a theme at a particular grade level.

Self-Esteem - The respect one has for oneself.

Sequence - The progression from themes that are near at hand, concrete experiences, to those that are abstract experiences for the purpose of expanding the environment.

Simulation - A teaching technique in which a simplified model of a social situation is established so that students may work through a specifically devised problem, having at hand materials and equipment needed.

Skills - Organized ways of dealing effectively with materials, problems, or situations.

Social Participation - Involvement or interaction with others. This requires many skills such as communication and working with others. This is one of the broad goals of social studies and includes both the quality and quantity of the interaction.

Socialization - The process by which social attitudes and roles are taught and learned.

Society - A group of people having some common interests, beliefs and attitudes.

Sociology - The social science discipline that concerns itself with the nature, conditions, and consequences of group interactions.

Specialization - The development of a variety of jobs or roles, each designed to meet specific wants or needs of the community.

Spiral - Themes coiling upward through the curriculum from kindergarten to twelfth grade.

Strategy - A particular way of sequencing or organizing a given selection of techniques, i.e., during one class period the strategy was to use the following techniques: lecture, discussion, and workbook.

Structure of the Discipline - The organization of the cognitive composition of a field of knowledge. Usually it is in terms of the concepts, generalizations, theories, laws, and models that define a subject area. Structure also can relate to the processes used by the practitioners of the various disciplines in forming hypotheses and gathering proof for validating the hypotheses.

Taxonomy - The classification or process of classifying something. Bloom's Taxonomy is a classification that describes how a group of educators believe mankind uses knowledge.

Technique - The teacher's specific choice of means to achieve the general method, i.e., lecturing, grouping, role-playing, debate, or panel discussion.

Technology - The system through which people supply their needs and wants. The teaching aids, materials, and media used to enhance teaching.

Traditions - Handing down of beliefs, legends, and customs from generation to generation.

Transmission Method - Hand down or impart content, skills, and attitudes directly to students. To give the information to students as in lecturing or recitation.

Unit Plan - Usually covers one topic, extending from several days to several weeks; contains statement of specific objectives, content outline, activities, materials and resources, and evaluation procedures.

Values - The results of judgments made by an individual or the society as a whole which determine the relative importance or worth of a thing, idea, practice, or belief.

Values Clarification Approach - A teaching strategy which is used to focus on the process of valuing rather than the content of values. It attempts to help students answer questions about how values are formed and to develop their own value system.

Value Judgment - A judgment which rates things with respect to their worth. This may be a positive, negative, or prescriptive evaluation.

Verification - Teaching strategies that require the students to test their knowledge through such processes as seeking and solving problems, making and applying generalizations, and model building and prediction.

I know you
BELIEVE
you understand what you
THINK
I said,
But I am NOT sure,
you realize that what you
HEARD is NOT what I MEANT!